Team 19 in Vietnam

Foreign Military Studies

History is replete with examples of notable military campaigns and exceptional military leaders and theorists. Military professionals and students of the art and science of war cannot afford to ignore these sources of knowledge or limit their studies to the history of the U.S. armed forces. This series features original works, translations, and reprints of classics outside the American canon that promote a deeper understanding of international military theory and practice.

Series editor: Roger Cirillo

An AUSA Book

TEAM 19 IN VIETNAM

An Australian Soldier at War

DAVID MILLIE

Foreword by
General Gordon R. Sullivan, USA (Ret.)

UNIVERSITY PRESS OF KENTUCKY

Scholarly publisher for the Commonwealth,
serving Bellarmine University, Berea College, Centre College of Kentucky, Eastern Kentucky University, The Filson Historical Society, Georgetown College, Kentucky Historical Society, Kentucky State University, Morehead State University, Murray State University, Northern Kentucky University, Transylvania University, University of Kentucky, University of Louisville, and Western Kentucky University.

Editorial and Sales Offices: The University Press of Kentucky
663 South Limestone Street, Lexington, Kentucky 40508-4008
www.kentuckypress.com

17 16 15 14 13   5 4 3 2 1

Library of Congress Cataloging-in-Publication Data

Millie, David.
Team 19 in Vietnam : an Australian soldier at war / David Millie.
pages cm
Includes bibliographical references and index.
ISBN 978-0-8131-4326-2 (hardcover : alk. paper) —
ISBN 978-0-8131-4327-9 (epub) — ISBN 978-0-8131-4328-6 (pdf)
1. Millie, David. 2. Vietnam War, 1961-1975—Personal narratives, Australian. 3. Vietnam War, 1961-1975—Participation, Australian. 4. Vietnam War, 1961-1975—Regimental histories. 5. Vietnam War, 1961-1975—Vietnam—Quang Tri (Province) 6. Australia. Australian Army Training Team, Vietnam. I. Title.
DS558.6.A8M55 2013
959.704'3092—dc23   2013022784

This book is printed on acid-free paper meeting the requirements of the American National Standard for Permanence in Paper for Printed Library Materials.
♾

Manufactured in the United States of America.

Member of the Association of American University Presses

Dedicated to those who served
and to their families.

Contents

Illustrations

Maps

Tables

Photographs

Map 1. Military regions of South Vietnam.

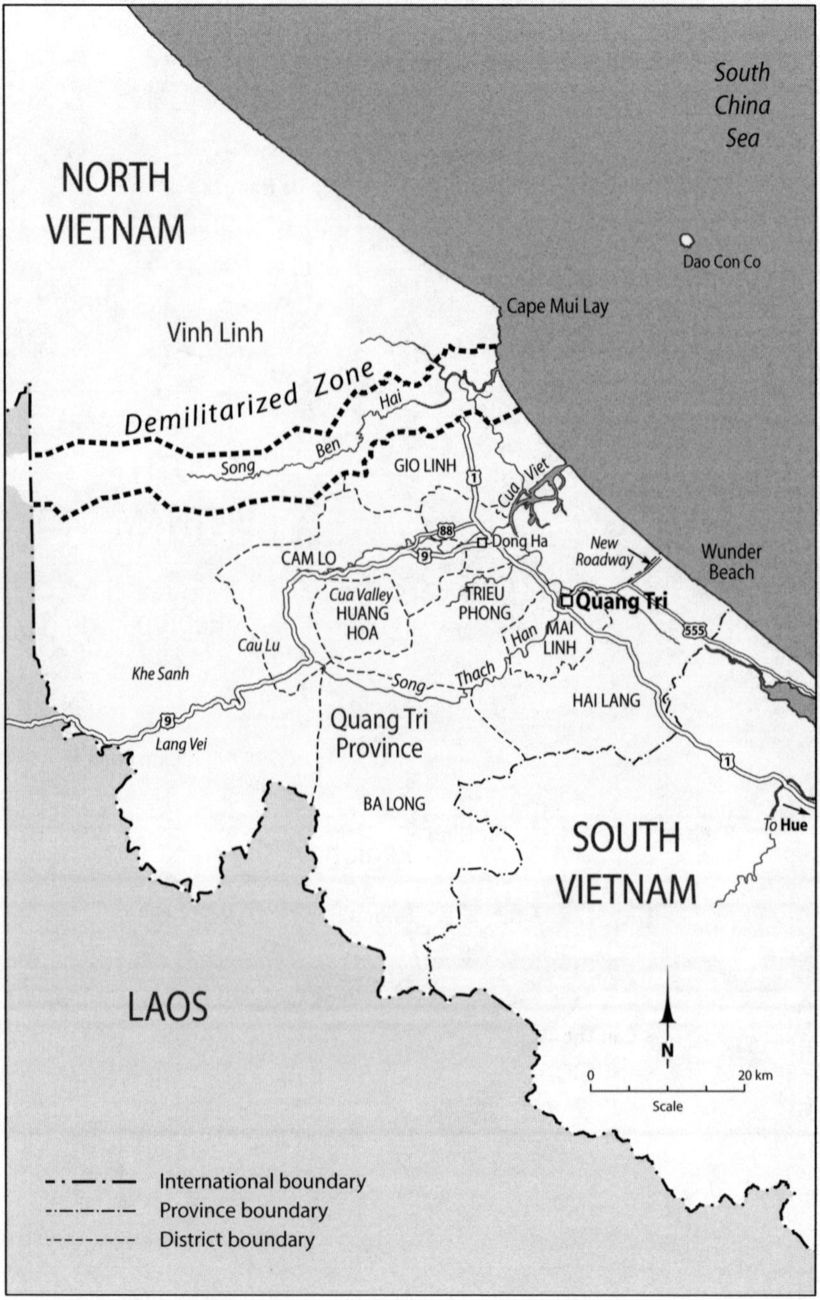

Map 2. Quang Tri Province, 1968.

Foreword

The western democracies began to use military advisors to impede the militant spread of communism shortly after World War II ended. It wasn't long after the French departed from Indochina that the effort began in South Vietnam. The United States took the lead, but the Australian Army started to send advisors in the earliest days and was steadfast in its support of the advisory effort throughout the period of deployments by their units that paralleled the buildup of American units. From the outset, Australian officers and warrant officers were welcome in advisory teams at every level. Many had experience in Malaya or New Guinea, and all were outstanding professionals with excellent tactical acumen.

This memoir by then-Major David Millie presents the complexity of the advisory effort as it had evolved by 1968. I was an advisor in 1963, serving initially in a small team advising at the district level—the same sort of job Major Millie had when he arrived five years later. I served much farther south—he was in the northern reaches of South Vietnam—but there were plenty of similarities between our experiences. He captures the importance of establishing sound relations with counterparts, seriously studying the potential for difficulties before a crisis arrives, and the need for high standards of performance at every level in an organization—enduring challenges in any advisory effort that will be familiar to soldiers engaged in similar work today. But there are important differences. Because he was near the demilitarized zone, he worked in an operational area where the U.S. Marine Corps, the U.S. Army, and the Army of South Vietnam were all engaged in conventional operations. At the same time the marines were embedding small teams of infantry with the local defense forces that Major Millie advised. Most advisors did not encounter so much complexity, but Millie's account analyzes advantages and challenges associated with the reality he faced.

Only a few names in this story will resonate with today's readers—not because they don't know very many Australians, but because most soldiers live, fight, and die in obscurity—whether Vietnamese, American, or Australian. This memoir helps rescue the work of a vast number of dedicated soldiers from that obscurity while reminding us that these events happened long ago: one name familiar to most of us is Major John Shalikashvili, who later served as the chairman of the Joint Chiefs of Staff. The stories of these men and their work have an enduring appeal, and they are well told in this account.

This memoir resonates with me because it reinforces my strongly held view that soldiers in a democracy find the payoff of their hard—often dangerous—service in knowing that what they do has been done to the best of their ability. They can find fulfillment in that knowledge, no matter what may occur at levels far above their arena of action.

General Gordon R. Sullivan, USA (Ret.)

Preface

The diary of my military service experience in Vietnam laid in my desk for about thirty-five years. As the pages were filled with cryptic entries of a controversial conflict, I realized I had a duty arising from my involvement there. This was to present the events in a readable form for my family and for people who might have an interest. While seeking and sorting the source material, a thematic structure of the manuscript slowly evolved. Fortunately, letters sent to my family had been saved and were an invaluable memory jogger. Other sources, such as scrapbook items and research of written histories of the war, added to the body of the work. I sincerely hope I have done justice to the people who participated in the epic events in which we were involved.

Gradually, as the significance of the content of my story became clearer to me, I realized that career military staff officers are seldom seen and rarely heard. Commanders, formations, and units rely on them for the efficient and effective planning and conduct of operations. Bookshelves are crowded with worthy Vietnam War histories written by historians, biographers, and others, as in the sample listing in the bibliography, but few operational staff officers have written of their experiences. As an Australian Army officer in U.S. Army Advisory Team 19, I had a privileged insider role to play in a multilayered and multicultural setting.

I cannot claim to have a complete grasp of all the influences at play in my remote province of South Vietnam, but I have judged that what I did experience was worth noting then, and worth writing about now. Snapshots of some of the small, medium, and big cogs in a giant military system may be of interest. Each cog needed oil, and the axles needed to be greased. In some instances there was a need for glue—for instance, to help keep an operation going. It was an effort at times to overcome negative feelings of frustration, futility, sadness, and concern.

I expect my story, set in Quang Tri Province, will be of interest to American and Australian military, past and present, to students of the military art, historians, researchers, politicians, and people who have a desire to learn about the conflict in a fascinating part of central Vietnam. I hope readers enjoy this rare exposition.

1

Leaving Home for War

May 1968

"I shall not seek, and I will not accept, the nomination of my party for another term as your President."[1] When I heard the commander in chief of the United States of America, Lyndon B. Johnson, make this announcement on 31 March 1968 I thought: "This is not a good omen." As history has shown, my concern was to be confirmed.

My departure day for Vietnam was approaching. I had been posted to operational service in South Vietnam by the Australian Army. It was not a surprise that a family farewell of some magnitude was upon me. The time away was expected to be twelve months. In the early 1960s the Australian government judged it to be in the best interests of our nation to make a further military response to the threat posed by aggressive communism.[2] A military force from Australia was already engaged in Malaysia. In 1962 advisors were committed to South Vietnam. In 1965 Australian combat units were deployed.

I was to join the Australian Army Training Team Vietnam (AATTV), known as the "Team," a unit that had established a fine record of service in South Vietnam.[3] Individual members were allocated for duty to U.S. Army advisory teams. I considered the posting to be a professional honor. Preparation for service in Vietnam was thorough and rigorous. The Australian Army had inculcated the habit of maintaining a high level of professional skill and fitness. For the past two years I had been a pilot—fixed and rotary wing—and then adjutant in the Aviation Regiment at the Royal Australian Air Force base at Amberley, Queensland. As a family we lived in a married quarter in Ipswich, a nearby city.

Special training was undertaken at the Jungle Training Centre, Canungra, in southeast Queensland. Thirty warrant officers and captains selected for AATTV service were put through rigorous activities for three weeks. Our instructors were men who had served in Vietnam with the Team and who had recently returned home. They were excellent trainers. The training was thorough. Then there was an intensive period of briefings at the Army Intelligence Centre, Woodside, South Australia. As well as being briefed on U.S. Army, Army of the Republic of Vietnam (ARVN), and Regional Force/Popular Force organization and methods of operation, we were made familiar with Viet Cong (VC) and North Vietnamese Army organization, methods of operation, and weapons. A Vietnamese colloquial language component was included in the course.

As future Team members we had to be prepared for anything, and I felt as though we had been trained in everything. We were well prepared to cope with any eventuality. You are ready, said the Army. I was ready to make my contribution and was looking forward to being involved in Vietnam.

Eva and I were married in December 1965. Before we became engaged I had informed my darling wife-to-be that war service was a likely obligation on me that we would have to face in the not too distant future. I felt that the grace and serenity that Eva showed with that prospect was full of dignity. Two of her aunts had faced similar experiences when their husbands went off to the fighting in World War II. Furthermore, her parents were pioneers on the land and had faced hardship. It was now her turn—my observation, not Eva's.

With a few days to go before my deployment, Eva had assumed full responsibility for all the household and family tasks that had to be undertaken and faced on the home front for the next twelve months. She did it with aplomb. There was an underlying resignation that she might have to face her future life without me. The thought was sobering for each of us. Family, friends, and neighbors were supportive. The army culture of supporting our own was well established. Assistance was only a telephone call away. A former schoolmate and his wife lived in Brisbane and were prepared to assist when needed, which they did. Eva and I were both very grateful for the deep friendship and understanding that we developed with them.

Before departure I spent a special day away from home. My faith was firm and sure. Some things had to be given deep reflection though. Although I had undertaken the four-year course at the

Royal Military College, Duntroon, in Canberra, and had become an infantry officer and an army aviator over the next eight years, I was to face combat for the first time. The prospect of killing, wounding, and being involved with carnage needed to be thought through. Survival was high on my personal agenda as well. So I had a day at a monastery at Marburg where I was able to reflect on these things, and put myself in God's hands. The contradictions in my mind had been reconciled. My personal motto was settled: persevere (the motto of the Team); patience, prayer, and security would see me through. I was now ready to go.

Departure day, 8 May 1968, was a gut-wrenching experience. Eva had gathered our sons with me in the family room for the final farewell. Julian, at five months, was asleep in a bouncer net. Daniel at sixteen months was standing quietly next to his mother. Eva was calm and outwardly placid. On reflection we had prepared well; we each had our respective roles to carry through. As I walked to the staff car my heart was heavy and my mind numb, leaving home for war.

Keeping in touch with family and friends was a big factor in keeping my morale up while in Vietnam. In 1968–1969 the main medium of communication was the personal letter, being in the era before the communications revolution. Some extracts from those letters will appear in this story. I wrote about two or three letters each week. Some tape-recorded messages were also exchanged with my family. My thanks and deep appreciation go to the family members and friends who wrote to me. I tried to reply to each letter received. My time in South Vietnam confirmed that a sense of duty for a cause can be more compelling than marital love. A safe return and a rebalancing of priorities made the sacrifice all the more rewarding.

Morale was not only a matter for me and my family at home, but for many people in South Vietnam, the United States, and Australia. I was drawn to create a brief chronology of 1968 and 1969 while preparing the narrative. It appears here as appendix C. Some entries reflect negative impact markers on morale, like death, injury, or assassinations in the United States. However, two entries, the first for 1968 and the last for 1969, are like pillar bookends in my story. They represent presidential pronouncements that were of the highest strategic significance in the war over this period, having particular impact on President Thieu and his people in South Vietnam.

President Johnson had given notice and opened the door to peace talks. Then in June 1969 the new commander in chief, President Richard Nixon, formally gave President Thieu notice of the planned withdrawal of U.S. forces from South Vietnam. These two events were not only of political importance but impacted on morale in both negative and positive ways, depending on points of view, and location. I leave it to others to examine the spectrum of these matters in detail.

In the field of operations, leadership played a steadying and influential role in the maintenance of morale. I was in a position in Quang Tri Province where I had a close working relationship with many senior U.S. and Vietnamese commanders and senior staff officers. In many cases I have not included what conversations took place, as I was but an observer or listener. I have judged it worthwhile to include their frequent presence in Quang Tri, away from their respective headquarters, to illustrate how they went about exercising their responsibilities. The leadership maxim could be summarized as "to see, to listen, and to be seen," some of the ingredients in the equation of the maintenance of morale. The names and appointments of leaders and others are shown in "Appendix A: Some of the Characters, 1968–1969," at the back end of the book. The way Australian leaders carried out their responsibilities is described in chapter 17.

I hold that the narration to follow is not only my story, but the story of many other characters that may not be heard, or even known. The list in Appendix A is my way of acknowledging and saluting the people—Vietnamese, Americans, and Australians, military and civilian—who were deeply involved in the conflict in Quang Tri Province. In particular, the list recognizes our Vietnamese counterparts-in-arms in the conflict. I trust this technique of presenting the personalities will assist the reader in following the story.

I present the daily routines, excitements, disappointments, moods, and reflections of a field staff officer working with his American allies in support of the Territorial Forces and the people of South Vietnam, in Quang Tri Province. Flexibility and tact were required, despite testing situations. Activities included involvement in the planning of joint military operations against a determined enemy—the North Vietnamese Army (NVA) and communist supporters in the South, called the Viet Cong (VC)—as well as planning pacification campaigns, refugee resettlement projects, and civil affairs. As the story unfolds, the tragedy experienced by many of the participants is revealed.

The chapter structure of this narrative is based on some bedrock themes, reflected in the titles assigned to each chapter, and presented in a sequence that made sense to me and hopefully will for the reader as well. Levels of authority and activity in a multilayered and multinational setting allow me to explain the structure of a complex story in this way:

Chapters 2, 10, 16, and 18	Higher level influences
Chapters 8, 11, 14, and 19	Province/Sector level operations
Chapters 5 and 6	District/Sub-sector level operations
Chapters 3 and 12	Supporting activities
Chapters 9 and 13	Staff work and associated activities
Chapters 7 and 15	Host country insights
Chapters 4 and 17	Australians
Chapters 1 and 20	Stand-alone themes

The principles of war are a fundamental of the military art. I include the ten principles for the convenience of readers: the selection and maintenance of the aim, maintenance of morale, offensive action, security, surprise, concentration of forces, economy of effort, flexibility, cooperation, and administration. There is a school of thought that public opinion should be included in the principles of war. Throughout the narrative a reader should be able to discern whether strategies, operations, tactics, and allocations of resources satisfied the listed principles, and to what extent. My story hopefully provides an opportunity for researchers and other readers to assess these matters in greater detail, Vietnam-wide and for over a longer period of the war.

Abbreviations and acronyms have a place in the language of the military, and in other professions. Some used in the narrative are listed in "Appendix D: Abbreviations and Terms." I have a view that there is an interesting evolution going on in the world of human communication. The military made use of abbreviations earlier for the purposes of simplicity, brevity, and clarity in writing operational instructions, operational and administrative orders, and signal messaging. Now texting has taken shortcuts in communicating to a new level. In Vietnam acronyms were part of the military linguistic evolution, with an acronym occasionally developing into a word. For example:

Regional Forces/Popular Forces	RF/PF	ruff puff
Army of the Republic of Vietnam	ARVN	arr vin
Civil Operations and Rural Development Support	CORDS	cords
Naval Construction Battalions	CBs	Seabees
Military Assistance Command Vietnam	MACV	mac vee
Hercules aircraft	C-130	Herc
utility helicopter	UH-1	Huey
Tactical Air Support Squadron, USAF	TASS	tass

In defending the case for the U.S. Army and the Australian Army in the use of acronyms I wish to add that there was a contribution by the U.S. Marines and the U.S. Air Force to the tally. Acronyms are a mixed blessing. I have made an effort in the narrative to minimize the use of abbreviations and acronyms for the benefit of the readers, but at the cost of more words. I hope the above explanations about the chronology, the list of characters, themes, the principles of war, and acronyms assist the reader in comprehending my story.

I was assigned for duty with Military Assistance Command Vietnam (MACV) Advisory Team 19, which was deployed in Quang Tri Province on the demilitarized zone (DMZ). The first four months were spent as a district senior advisor, and for the next eight months I worked as a planning and operations staff officer at the province level. I soon discovered that being with the Americans was like being with brothers-in-arms on a common mission. I was also the senior Australian Army officer for up to fourteen other AATTV members in the province, most being with U.S. Army advisory teams linked to combat units of the Army of the Republic of Vietnam.

In the next chapter I set the scene, the big picture, to allow for a better understanding of the organizational complexity surrounding the conflict in Vietnam.

2

The Big Picture

1950–1968

Resistance to foreign occupation in Vietnam had been growing steadily since well before World War II. Aspirations for self-determination for countries under colonial rule had been pursued and rebuffed after World War I. Vietnamese resistance during the Japanese occupation had been supported by China and the United States. A nationalistic alliance within Vietnam evolved after 1945 with an emphasis on anti-imperialism and land reform. When the war against the French concluded in 1954, representatives of the Vietminh and the French signed a cease-fire agreement in July.[1] Thereafter the Democratic Republic of Vietnam (North Vietnam) gradually developed policies to unite the two Vietnams. The political vehicle of communism was adopted by the Northern leadership (and some Southerners) to achieve a grand strategy of undermining the weakening central government in South Vietnam and bringing about reunification.

Strategically, a succession of events in the 1940s and 1950s brought about a U.S. commitment in South Vietnam. In July 1950 the United States began sharing the financial burden with the French in the conflict against the Vietminh. The next month a U.S. Military Assistance Advisory Group of thirty-five men arrived in Vietnam. The advisory organization was to grow in numbers and scope over the next two decades. Vietnam was provisionally partitioned at the 17th parallel into North and South Vietnam. The demilitarized zone (DMZ) was created. Gradually the North moved toward a war of national liberation against the South, with guerrilla warfare escalating to wider warfare in South Vietnam by 1965.

A limited ground war within the boundaries of South Vietnam gave the VC and the North Vietnamese Army (NVA) flexibility in the prosecution of their war effort in the South. This boundary limitation was adopted by the United States for sound policy reasons. The prospect of having other nations join forces with the North Vietnamese government was of major concern to the United States. Warfare over a land area beyond South Vietnam could have led to foreign ground forces supplementing the NVA in an expanded conflict. This restraint on the U.S. ground forces to remain within land boundaries could arguably be likened to self-imposed leg chains.

The relative strengths of the belligerents can give one a sense of the size and scale of the military activity in this theater of war. The population of South Vietnam was about 16 million. In 1968 the Army of the Republic of Vietnam (ARVN) was composed of ten infantry divisions, two independent regiments, and Ranger and Airborne units.[2] In addition, each of the forty-four provinces of South Vietnam had Territorial Forces under the control of the province chief.

By early 1969 the U.S. Army in South Vietnam comprised the equivalent of three corps headquarters, seven divisions, four independent brigades, and advisory groups in each of the four regions of South Vietnam. Additional combat support and logistic services provided for the force needs. The U.S. Marines Corps' contribution was made up of the Third Marine Amphibious Force (III MAF), comprised of a headquarters, two infantry divisions, an air wing, and two regimental landing teams afloat. Marine landing force elements afloat were deployed as required. The marines were deployed in Region 1, the northern of the four regions of South Vietnam. In addition, the United States had out-of-country military support from the U.S. Navy, the Strategic Air Command, the U.S. Merchant Marine, the Strategic Air Transport, and the Studies and Observation Group.

The Republic of Korea provided a field force of forty-eight thousand men. Thailand provided a force of up to twelve thousand. Australia, with New Zealand support, provided a task force of eight thousand men. The Philippines was a significant support base for the United States. The American, Korean, and Australian forces in South Vietnam at the end of 1968 are shown in table 2.1.

In 1968 and 1969 the main force ARVN, U.S. Army, USMC, and allied formations (divisions, brigades, and regiments) were provid-

Table 2.1. Allied Forces in Vietnam, 1968.

MACV	1st Air Cavalry Division (ACD)
USARV	1st Infantry Division
1 FFV	4th Infantry Division
2 FFV	9th Infantry Division
XXIV Corps	25th Infantry Division
I Corps Advisory	101st Airborne Division (Air Mobile)
II Corps Advisory	23rd (Americal) Infantry Division
III Corps Advisory	1st Aviation Brigade
IV Corps Advisory	173rd Airborne Brigade
	196th Light Infantry Brigade
III MAF	1st Brigade, 5th Mechanized Infantry Division
1st Division USMC	3rd Brigade, 82nd Airborne Division
2nd Division USMC	
1st Marine Air Wing	ROK FFV
	1st Australian Task Force

ing a security shield to the populated areas of South Vietnam while waging a limited war of attrition against the VC and the NVA main forces. Simultaneously, other U.S. military elements (including advisors) were involved with Republic of Vietnam agencies and people in counterinsurgency and pacification.

The enemy military forces included approximately fifty VC battalions and up to sixteen NVA divisions, some of which were located in North Vietnam. In 1968 and 1969 the USMC in Quang Tri Province had engaged with five identified NVA divisions. Other NVA divisions were further south. With relatively safe havens in North Vietnam and Laos, the enemy had an advantage when in those areas. The war had reached a point where some attrition battles in South Vietnam could have been characterized as conventional warfare, involving battlefield maneuver and extensive firepower.

The population in North Vietnam was estimated at about 17 million. The Northerners, supported by the Soviet Union and China, made good use of imported technologies. They had a very small navy. Their air force was not seen in South Vietnam, but they did have early warning and antiaircraft systems, which were effective against U.S. aircraft. An underdeveloped industrial base and limited rail and road systems placed challenging logistic limitations on the NVA. On top of this situation, North Vietnam and its supply routes were subjected to heavy bombing from time to time.

The NVA operating in South Vietnam was an infantry army equipped with heavy weapons. Its troops were determined and tenacious. Despite having long lines of communication via Laos and Cambodia, which were frequently subject to interdiction by the USAF, the forward divisions received their provisions. The enemy deployed forces had limited combat support, with medical services and amenities quite inferior to that of the U.S. and allied forces. Due to their technical inferiority in weaponry and communications, the NVA units were generally tactically inflexible. On any measure, the Free World Forces were superior to the enemy forces in combat power, naval and air power, battlefield mobility, and logistics. Overall, it was an amazing feat of arms that the NVA persisted to the extent that it did.

The countrywide enemy Tet offensive in early 1968 was on a broad front, but shallow in depth. The offensive was not a military success for the NVA or for the VC, but politically and psychologically it was a strategic turning point with respect to the settlement of the conflict. Decisions announced by President Johnson in 1968 and President Nixon in 1969, referred to in the first chapter, made it clear that the United States was to phase out of Vietnam. The Northerners had time on their side.

The headquarters of the Military Assistance Command Vietnam (MACV) directed the war effort for the United States in South Vietnam. The United States Army of South Vietnam (USARV) was commanded by General William Westmoreland. He also commanded MACV. In 1967 the U.S. authorities from the president down placed the responsibility for pacification within a reconstructed organization named Civil Operations and Revolutionary Development Support (CORDS). The new system placed the military in charge of pacification. Civilians were embedded within a wartime command. The MACV headquarters was based in Saigon, and worked with and supported South Vietnamese government and military authorities and agencies.

Between Saigon and the provinces were several levels of command and control. In the case of the northern provinces, we were in GVN Military Region 1, also referred to as I Corps, pronounced

"Eye" Corps. Two U.S. corps equivalent headquarters were in Region 1: III MAF (USMC) and XXIV Corps (U.S. Army), with III MAF having operational control. Province advisory teams in the corps area of responsibility reported directly to the regional deputy of CORDS. These advisory teams helped province chiefs deliver the security and pacification programs.

The enemy infrastructure within provinces was a prime target for the counterinsurgency and pacification campaigns in 1968 and 1969. The Viet Cong Infrastructure handbook, published in December 1968, was one of the source documents available to advisors. I found the handbook to be a very useful reference, as it described the organization of the Vietnamese communist political infrastructure for South Vietnam. The introduction in the handbook stated that it was not an exhaustive account of all the many subsidiary agencies affiliated with the People's Revolutionary Party (PRP) and the National Liberation Front (NLF). The document went on to say: "The primary agency which directs the Viet Cong insurgency in South Vietnam is the People's Revolutionary Party (PRP) whose existence was officially acknowledged in 1962. The PRP is the southern branch of North Vietnam's Communist Labor Party and ultimately receives direction from Hanoi through the Central Office for South Vietnam (COSVN). Branching out horizontally from the PRP are its Front organisation (the National Front for the Liberation of South Vietnam) and the Liberation Army. Both the NLF and the VC military units are directed and controlled by the PRP."[3]

The two northern provinces of South Vietnam, Thua Thien and Quang Tri, did not come under COSVN. The North Vietnamese desired to annex these two provinces. The Quang Tri NLF, located in Area 101 in the mountains to the west, answered directly to Hanoi.

The allies recognized that the sovereign power rested with the South Vietnamese. President Thieu of South Vietnam came into the head of state role in 1967. The U.S. president and commander in chief, Lyndon Johnson, was elected president in his own right in November 1964. In practice the U.S. effort carried South Vietnam through to the early 1970s.

President Thieu's policy had a significant influence on the Paris Peace Talks, which commenced in 1968. Thieu's basic policy was that of the Four Nos:

No recognition of the enemy.
No neutralization of South Vietnam.
No coalition government, and
No surrender of territory to the enemy.[4]

These four points were the core of the political contest in Paris and in South Vietnam. The military effort was supportive of the political objectives. The North Vietnamese elected to have a protracted political and military campaign to achieve their goals.

On the ground in South Vietnam in 1968 it was clear the ARVN and the Territorial Forces, with the U.S. Army, faced two kinds of enemy threats. The first was the long-running threat from the VC military and the VC infrastructure (VCI), referred to as the insurgency, which was guided and supported by North Vietnam. This conflict was arguably a widespread insurrection of civil war proportions. The allied response to the insurgency was the counterinsurgency, and a nation-building and internal security effort, described as pacification. The counterinsurgency and pacification campaigns were a political and cultural problem of the most challenging magnitude. There were divisions of opinion in the South that were detrimental to the achievement of a unity of purpose. The divisions ranged from those within a central government (GVN) that was expected to do better, to those of a politicized military, to those of a suffering and fragmented population. Associated with the political problem was the provision of security by the police and military, and a weakened economy undermined by corruption. The use of force within the populated areas in response to the enemy threat needed to be measured.

The second enemy threat was the armed aggression by the North Vietnamese Army, a tenacious enemy. This part of the conflict required a response on a limited war scale, where maneuver and firepower were dominant, usually away from the populated areas. The two threats were operating in Quang Tri Province in 1968 and 1969. The allied forces in the province (the U.S. Marine Corps, U.S. Army, and ARVN) demonstrated flexibility in adjusting to the various activity levels of the enemy. There were significant tactical responses by the belligerents after the enemy offensive of Tet 1968, which are described later in this narrative.

The command and control arrangements of the allied forces within Region 1 flowed down through a minimum of three levels to Quang Tri Province. These military levels were linked by at least four formal channels of communication: ARVN, USMC, U.S. Army, and U.S. Army Advisory. In addition, other agencies had their respective levels and channels. Geographic areas of operation for allied formations and units were determined by staff consideration and liaison through the command and control levels. These areas of responsibility were varied to meet the ebb and flow of operational needs, in some cases taking into consideration political (province) boundaries. The USMC and U.S. Army formations and units in Quang Tri Province were under the operational control of the commander of XXIV Corps. The province of Quang Tri was the tactical area of responsibility for the 3rd Marine Division.

The entry of the 1st Brigade, 5th Infantry Division, into Quang Tri in July 1968 and the departure in November 1968 of the 1st Air Cavalry Division added further to the variability of geographic and combat tasking. The 3rd Marine Division, very flexible in the grouping of units for tasks, had to adapt within its area of responsibility to meet the changing circumstances, in liaison with the 1st and 2nd ARVN Regiments. As a province (sector) advisory unit, Team 19 did not have an allocated area of operations. U.S. Army advisory teams operated in the areas of operation of the Vietnamese divisions and sectors (provinces) to which they were linked. For security reasons, maps showing areas of operation were not displayed in our team tactical operations center.

"Counterpart" was a term applied equally to advisors and Vietnamese colleagues, very similar to a buddy system. I observed throughout my year in South Vietnam that this partnership model was applied from the top down, where senior leaders, American and Vietnamese, were closely aligned to each other in a complementary way. In Region 1, the commander of I Corps (ARVN) was the responsible Vietnamese military authority for Region 1's five provinces. III MAF's area of responsibility was superimposed on the I Corps area, with the marine commander being the counterpart to the I Corps commander. Officials of CORDS played a like role in the execution of their responsibilities. In the two northern provinces of Region 1, Thua Thien and Quang Tri, the commander of the 1st ARVN Division was the responsible Vietnamese military authority, and the commander of the XXIV Corps was his counterpart. At the province level the province chief had the province senior advisor as his counterpart. The relationship at the district level was similar, district chief and district advisor.

One lesson I learned from my Vietnam experience was the need to be careful as to where you placed yourself in a potential or actual conflict situation. Due care applies equally at the level of presidents and governments, as well as to individuals. Wisdom dictates that there needs to be an awareness of a safe way out, in the event of a change of circumstances. Intervention, unless seriously studied and thought through, can become a disastrous misadventure. Perhaps this lesson could be described as a dictum. War is clearly one of the worst ways to sort out a dispute about ideas, as was the case in Vietnam.

I was to hold two positions in a counterinsurgency setting within a limited war. The positions were full of complexities, being primarily military but in an environment where security, cultural, political, religious, and economic issues were intertwined. In the counteroffensive to the enemy 1968 Tet offensive, the GVN and U.S. pacification campaigns dominated. Planning and operational matters dealt with were wide ranging and central to the survival of the nation-state of South Vietnam. North Vietnam was determined to reunite the two Vietnams by any means.

The next chapter relates to my settling into South Vietnam, which was spread over eleven days in May 1968.

3

Travel to Quang Tri and Orientation

14–24 May 1968

I spent the weekend prior to my departure for Vietnam in Sydney with Captain Adrian Nesbitt, a classmate in our times together at the Royal Military College, Duntroon, Canberra. He had served with the Team from July 1965 to November 1966 in IV Corps. Chatting with him helped me make the mental transition from peace and harmony to conflict and discord. His sister and her husband were at Sydney Airport to bid me farewell on the evening of 13 May, a very kind gesture and much appreciated.[1] Later in the evening the advance party for the 4th Battalion Royal Australian Regiment (4 RAR) boarded the charter aircraft at Brisbane. The flight route was over Darwin, then south of the island of Borneo to Singapore. I felt the relief with the other 160 passengers as we stretched our legs at the Singapore airport terminal on 14 May 1968. Civilian shirt was the dress of the day. The warm, humid conditions of the tropics were a precursor of what was to come in Vietnam.

The route after Singapore was across the South China Sea, and then parallel to the flat coastal area of the Mekong River delta to Saigon. From the air the city looked like a jumble of matchboxes thrown from a height into an area that could not accommodate them. I was viewing Vietnam for the first time, with my mind wondering what was to unfold. The airport had drabness about it. Aircraft activity was intensive. Mortar and rocket damage could be seen on buildings and infrastructure. I thought, "Welcome to South Vietnam."

I was met at the airport by Ned, a Vietnamese employed as the Team headquarters driver. He had been with the Team since 1962. A former soldier, he was still eligible for call up. He had a wife and five children. What became of him after the war is unknown. I lunched with some Australians at the Buis Hotel and spent the night at the

Embassy Hotel. A 7 P.M. to 7 A.M. curfew was in force. The streets were completely free of traffic. The common view was that the effectiveness of the curfew was due to trigger-happy ARVN and "White Mice" (a nickname for the National Police). This put a new meaning to keeping people at home and off the streets.

Crump, crump sounds of artillery were heard day and night in Saigon. Views from the Embassy Hotel were thought provoking. Flares glowed in the night around the city. Military aircraft patrolled overhead. There was no blackout, as there was no enemy air threat. A further failed communist offensive, designated the "mini-Tet," was winding down in Saigon. This enemy offensive, which ran for about a week, commenced on 4 May. The enemy intention was to help influence the mood at the peace talks then being convened in Paris.

In the enemy Tet offensive of February 1968 a small area of Saigon city was subject to severe fighting, including air strikes. A half-square-mile area was bulldozed during the mop-up. Many buildings, including the U.S. embassy and the Korean embassy, showed pockmarks of small arms fire. As I stood at the curbside the next morning waiting for a vehicle, I mused about the peaceful and placid setting, typical of many places on earth. War and peace, hand in hand, an incredible paradox. The days of Saigon being the "Paris of the East" were but a romantic memory now, despite the best endeavors of the Saigon tea bar girls.

The road traffic appeared to be chaotic. Cars, trucks, taxis, motorbikes, and rickshaws were going in all directions. Drivers seemed to make their way without accident, and pedestrians calmly crossed the roads safely. Refuse was everywhere. Garbage disposal arrangements were not evident. Trash was simply dumped in the streets. Apparently there was a cleanup every so often, with a front-end loader device needed to handle the mass of mess. A refugee center was being constructed in Saigon city. Row after row of timber and galvanized iron structures were being built next to a tented refugee camp. Basic public hygiene standards were barely being met.

The evening breeze was pleasant at the restaurant and bar on the hotel rooftop. It was probably the pick of the places in Saigon for relaxing. The presidential palace was one hundred meters down this road in the most attractive setting of the city. Two television channels funded by the United States provided news, current affairs, and entertainment. From the rooftop I watched the heat lightning and the night lights of the city, which could be seen all around. The humidity and temperature were like Brisbane in the summer. The monsoon season was not far off. In the north of South Vietnam the dry season was just commencing.

All the necessary administrative matters had been carried out expeditiously during the day. Weapons—a rifle and a .45 pistol—ammunition, clothing, equipment, and a metal trunk were collected from Australian and U.S. storehouses. A U.S. Army driver's license was issued to me at the motor pool. The commanding officer of the AATTV, Lieutenant Colonel Ray Burnard, was away from Saigon visiting Team members. I was to meet up with him later in the field. Time was available to visit Cholon Post Exchange (PX), a supermarket bigger than a Big W of today. This PX was one of the many ways that the needs, and wants, of the troops were being met. It was noticeable that the Koreans were buying up refrigerators and other goods for resale in their own market.

I now set out on what was to become a nine-day travel and orientation journey, from Saigon to Da Nang to Quang Tri to Hue, and then returning to Quang Tri. On 16 May I flew the first leg in a USAF C-130 Hercules transport aircraft. We traveled at thirteen thousand feet, well above any artillery or naval gunfire trajectories. People of many nationalities were on board. I wondered whether they were visitors, contractors, or residents. As the weeks passed I realized that people of many nationalities were working in Vietnam.

Da Nang was a quieter, cleaner place than the capital, and less frenetic. The military organizations in Region 1 required massive complexes to support them, as was the case in the southern regions. Da Nang was a significant center for the effort in the northern region of South Vietnam. I was pleased to discover that military telephone communication links worked from Da Nang to Saigon, and to Quang Tri.

Warrant Officer Ron O'Brien, with the 2/5 ARVN at Quang Ngai, met me at the airport. We went to Australia House in Da Nang. This was a special day for the Team, as the Commander Australian Force Vietnam (COMAFV), Major General A. L. MacDonald, and the Army chief of personnel were on a familiarization tour to Region 1. Little did I realize then that hosting visitors, and senior commanders and staff, was to be a part of my life for the next year. It was here that I met Lieutenant Colonel Ray Burnard. He confirmed that I was to replace Major Michael Casey in the role of district senior advisor (DSA) in the advisory team at Mai Linh District in Quang Tri Province. At a barbecue happy exchanges were made with new and old faces. Australia House was to be like a home away from home over the coming year.

In the afternoon I was introduced to the art of scrounging, a way of obtaining things by begging or bartering. From time to time it was necessary to gain a military item from others informally, rather than being subject to the perhaps never-never of the formal process of requisition. This kind of action was not for personal gain but for the collective good. I accompanied Major Graham "Curly" Templeton to the Deep Water Disposal Vehicle Park to scrounge wireless parts for the 4th Cavalry, ARVN. A deal was clinched with a bottle of spirits and a promise of two AK-47 rifles. Next was a visit to the 5th Special Forces Mike Force at Marble Mountain for a live shoot into a sand dune firing range. I was given a refresher on my personal weapon, a pistol. I was determined to retain my basic military skills, as one day my life might well depend on it.

Later that day Major Ian Porteous (AATTV) briefed me on the situation in Region 1, with an emphasis on the Quang Tri area. He highlighted that the mountain regions of South Vietnam were now in enemy hands. Base Area 114 to the west supported NVA operations against Hue. Further north, Base Area 101 supported NVA operations in Quang Tri. There was a gradual NVA movement toward the coast. The security of Da Nang was a key to the stability in the northern provinces; it was essential to keep the NVA forces off balance. The U.S. logistic effort in the Da Nang area seemed enormous. Large volumes of material were being shipped in. I wondered as to where the items were going, and who had ready access to them. Distribution depots were operated by the USMC, the U.S. Army, and USAF and CORDS contractors, with several of their depots being in sand dune areas.

Not far from Australia House was the MACV club. There were slot machines in the club, reminders of home. I enjoyed an evening meal with fellow Australian officers, and an early night was in order as a curfew applied in Da Nang from 9:30 P.M. to 7 A.M. I noted that close friendships with local females was a matter of fact for some uniformed people. I was surprised to hear a degree of cynicism from some U.S. service people of the conduct of the war in South Vietnam. Comments ranged from the extent of aerial bombing in the Khe Sanh area to the limited capabilities of some of the ARVN combat units to the level of corruption within South Vietnam. I was to learn that individual professional actions and personal views could be contrary. The responsibility of duty was clearly stronger than personal views.

Early morning travel on 18 May from Da Nang to Quang Tri was by a HH-3E Jolly Green Giant helicopter from a search and rescue (SAR) squadron. The pilots on this trip were from the U.S. Coast Guard, doing duty in Vietnam. The flight was at one thousand feet over the South China Sea. The helicopter flew over the hospital ship USS *Repose* and the LPH *Princeton* as we proceeded north. Over the land I viewed my patch for the coming year: sand dunes, hamlets, paddies, rivers, and roads. Inland were the foothills and forested mountains, which included the battle areas of Khe Sanh and the head of the Ashau Valley. The chopper crew was not as relaxed now as when we were over the sea. The helicopter was at thirty-five hundred feet. The Ben Hai River, in the demilitarized zone (DMZ), was visible. We held at that level for about ten minutes, as faint beeps were being received. SAR tasking involved being on standby for the rescue of downed U.S. pilots in Laos, North Vietnam, in country, and at sea. The helicopter had in-flight refueling capability. This time we landed at Quang Tri for refueling and the drop off of a relieved passenger.

On reflection, this mode of entry to Quang Tri was novel as well as a very interesting introduction to part of the air war in Vietnam. The search and rescue detachment at Quang Tri was composed of three helicopters: one airborne at ten thousand feet at full alert for a rescue mission, one on the ground waiting, and the third as backup as soon as another was committed. The scene around me was of sand, pierced steel plank matting, tents, and temporary buildings. The air was hot, dry, and dusty. The landing point was about ten kilometers north of Quang Tri City, my destination.

I discovered the road to Quang Tri City was temporarily closed due to enemy action. In light of this situation I decided to travel to the Citadel by helicopter. I went to the nearest USMC helicopter unit, a general support squadron equipped with UH-1, CH-34, CH-36, and CH-47 aircraft. I was wearing a slouch hat, making me noticeable in the company of U.S. troops and providing a guaranteed conversation point. Later I sensed that some Americans liked to hear the Australian accent. Major Rusty Hansen, USMC, came to my assistance. He arranged for one of his crews to fly me to the Citadel pad in a UH-1B helicopter on the way to another task. From there I hitched a ride in a jeep to the MACV compound eight hundred meters away. Here I met Major Mike Casey, Lieutenant Colonel Thresher, the U.S. Army assistant province senior advisor, and six Australian warrant officers.

The province senior advisor (PSA), Mr. Bob Brewer, a World War II veteran, welcomed me to Quang Tri and to the MACV Team and said: "Some of our folks in the south think this is an out-of-the-way place." He went on to say: "You watch the eyes of people when you let them know you are serving in Quang Tri; they light up. When that happens it gives me a great feeling." I was already feeling that way myself from the events of just my first day. Brewer displayed outstanding leadership in successful defensive actions in January and February during the enemy Tet offensive.

I flew south to Hue the next day in a USAF single engine L-19, also known as a Cessna O-1 Bird Dog. Major Robert Ball, USAF, a forward air controller (FAC), flew the aircraft. I think Mike Casey set me up for that one. The flight was low level, and with the rice harvest under way the countryside was picturesque. The railway was out of action, and the highway appeared to have been blown up in some places. The airfield in Hue was severely damaged during Tet and the remains of many destroyed light aircraft were on the side of the strip. Sadly, Major Ball was killed in Quang Tri a few weeks later while on airborne FAC duty.

A jeep ride took me to the MACV compound in Hue. There I met Warrant Officer Ben Rule, with the Reconnaissance Company of the 1st ARVN Division. Ben was a helpful guide in a city that had reached its heights in earlier days. The room allocated to me at the compound was drab, and had many bullet holes in the wall, a reminder of the battle for Hue in February. I pondered the contrast of the present disorder and the imagined order of the past.

Hue was still a beautiful city, but knocked about during the Tet battles. I was impressed by the huge, long city wall. The old central area, including the former Imperial Palace, was surrounded by the wall and many waterways. Some of these features had been developed as Hue evolved as the imperial capital. The bridges were European in style and the roads, not made for vehicle traffic, were full

The damaged Imperial Palace at Hue, Tet 1968.

of ruts and very dusty. The Perfume River was about seventy meters wide, with grassy banks that were not cared for.

I was in Hue to be briefed by the leadership of Advisory Team 4 at the headquarters of the 1st ARVN Division. On my way to the advisors' morning briefing I met the divisional commander, Brigadier General Ngo Quang Truong. He had just attended a routine Monday parade of his headquarters staff. The brigadier, later to be promoted, was full of energy and engaged me in conversation. I was to see him on many occasions in Quang Tri.

Twenty-three officers were in attendance at the daily Advisory Team 4 meeting.[2] I was surprised to hear the senior advisor (a lieutenant colonel) tell his intelligence officer that there was a need to capture at least one member of the Viet Cong Infrastructure (VCI).[3] He went on to say that the ARVN had not been able to capture a single enemy in recent months. He made the point that the VC knew all about the Central Intelligence Agency (CIA) organization in Hue prior to the enemy Tet offensive. All CIA agents had been killed during the offensive. There was a need to capture a VCI member now, as the division commander wanted to gain information from a firsthand source. VCI members guided NVA and guerilla infiltrators across the DMZ, and from the west. There were insufficient U.S.

and ARVN troops available to stop infiltration, even though it was known that the usual routes were along the axis of the railway line and creek beds.

On reflection, the situation could have been that the enemy was so disrupted as a result of the allied counteroffensive in Hue during February and March, and elsewhere, that surviving VC had gone underground, or to the mountains, as had the battered NVA units. A sustained allied counteroffensive against the enemy throughout 1968 came to transform the morale of the South Vietnamese, as will be evidenced in later chapters.

I was then introduced to a number of U.S. Army staff officer advisors. Training in Australia helped prepare me for the scenario that followed. The "spaghetti like" entanglements of the multitude of national, military, paramilitary, police, and civilian organizations were explained. The reasons for this description may become clearer as this story unfolds. I learned also of the significant U.S. civil agencies operating in South Vietnam. The significance of the "body count" was outlined, of both the enemy and our own troops. It was the current way of measuring progress in the attrition phase of the war. The emphasis on attrition was to change after General Creighton W. Abrams assumed command of MACV in June 1968. The Americans I met were all very pleasant fellows, and I found them very welcoming. They offered me assistance, were cooperative, and the prospects looked fine on the fraternal front.

I was aware of explosions around the city during my two nights in Hue. I felt shockwaves throughout the night. It must have been very unpleasant to be on the receiving end. I was informed in Hue that operations in the area were being directed toward protecting the rice harvest and keeping the VC and the NVA from food sources. Rice supply denied locally to the enemy meant the NVA had to transport rice from North Vietnam. NVA logistic supply was mainly along the Ho Chi Minh trail in Laos and Cambodia into the mountains of South Vietnam, a manpower-intensive activity. I returned to Quang Tri by helicopter, flying at very low level.

Orientation in Quang Tri started with a briefing by the MACV Team 19 operations (S3)[4] and intelligence (S2) staffs at the advisors' headquarters. Mike Casey then took me by road to meet contacts. At Dong Ha we called on Major Leon Constantan, U.S. senior advisor to the 2nd ARVN Regiment. A Huey (UH-1 Iroquois) helicopter took us on an air reconnaissance of Leatherneck Square, which ran

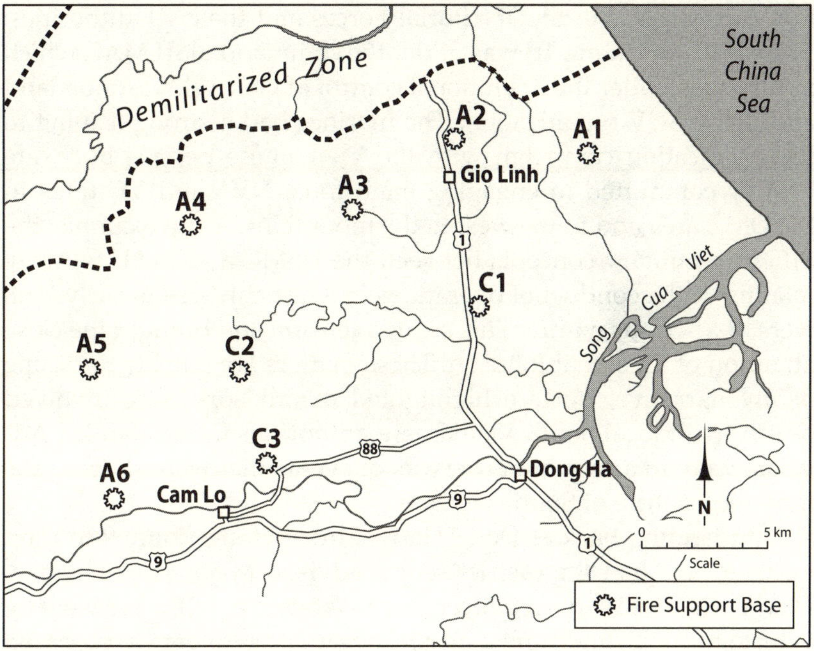

Map 3. Fire support bases.

below the DMZ from Gio Linh in the east to the north of Cam Lo in the west. Leon pointed out fire support bases (FSBs) C1, C2, C3, A1, A2, and A3. The fire support bases, shown on map 3, were fortified and protected defensive positions. These positions were manpower intensive, a situation that was soon to change. I observed several hamlets north of Dong Ha that had been reduced to rubble during earlier battles against the NVA forces. People had left their homes and had become refugees. To the south of Route 9 toward Cam Lo was Camp J. J. Carroll, a major USMC and U.S. Army fire base. From the southern edge of the DMZ we could see the Ben Hai River and "Freedom Bridge." The flag of North Vietnam was flying on the northern end of the bridge, and the flag of South Vietnam was flying on the southern end.

Reference to maps 2 and 3 provides a convenient and perhaps simplistic way for me to highlight some of the fundamental ideas about the conduct of the war that were discussed between USMC, ARVN, and U.S. Army senior leaders in 1966 and 1967. The ARVN was closer to the populated areas and hence engaged in the pacification campaign with the Territorial Forces and the civil authorities. The USMC in Quang Tri was under the command of III MAF, which in turn was under the operational control of General Westmoreland and the MACV organization. The marines had a strong leaning to the pacification campaign with the Vietnamese people, but were heavily committed in engaging main force NVA and VC units in the DMZ area and to the west in the mountains. As an example, the differing military concepts between the USMC and the U.S. Army relating to the conduct of operations in Khe Sanh area in early 1968 were of a serious nature. This created tension and brought the close attention of President Johnson. These matters are outside the scope of my narrative, but are highlighted as advisors were involved closely with local South Vietnamese authorities in the conflict. Advisors were in a way but observers of events that were shaping the long-term future of South Vietnam.

On landing back at Dong Ha we drove along Route 9 to Cam Lo. Here we met the district senior advisor, Major John Hannan, U.S. Army, and Warrant Officer Peter Wooden, AATTV. We went by vehicle to a FSB, and from a marine observation tower we observed an NVA bunker north of the DMZ, used for directing artillery fire into Quang Tri.

A large refugee camp had recently been established at Cam Lo to provide for displaced people from the Khe Sanh and Lang Vei area, in the mountains toward the Laotian border and the DMZ area. The NVA incursion earlier in the year had brought about their evacuation. To compare the campsite to the Australian climate and geography, it would be like placing the people in the remote Bourke area of western New South Wales, or at Alice Springs in the center of the Australian continent. There were about twenty-four thousand people in the camp. The refugees appeared to be in a passive and gloomy mood, understandable in their circumstances. Their basic needs were being met through a lot of U.S. support. At the reception area to the camp we met Father Co, who had left North Vietnam in 1954 and traveled south with his parishioners. He asked the advisors for a bottle of whisky or gin and for some magazines for his M-16. I thought "here is a man that has been hardened by his past experiences."

Back home in Australia a nongovernment organization, Austcare, was leading an initiative to raise funds for refugees in Vietnam. Eva was in a group in our local neighborhood who decided to do some fund-raising for this cause. After my visit to Cam Lo, I wrote the following to her in early June:

> I am proud of you Eva for being so generous with your time and effort to help the Austcare fund. However I've seen the camps that were the prime source of the information for the articles in the newspapers. I have met the US officers and officials who are working the areas involved. Everything possible is being done for the refugees. There is adequate food, clothing and building materials for them. There is an organization in place to administer this assistance to the refugees. The only way it would not get down to the people who are in need would be if greedy and corrupt local people divert the goods to other areas. The $1,000,000 raised in Australia would be a drop in the ocean by the time the goods are delivered here. The fund raising and the donation is sufficient for Vietnam in my opinion. I would much prefer to see us increase our weekly giving to our parish than to see the money come up here. Our family effort, with me up here, is I believe sufficient sacrifice on our part for the Vietnamese people. A few prayers of course may help.

We made a brief visit to the 3rd Marine Division headquarters at Ai Tu to the south of Dong Ha on the return trip to Quang Tri City. We were informed that one of the battalions of the division was at headquarters III MAF at Phu Bai, where they were acting as "Palace Guard." I was to do a lot of work with marines in the coming year. To round off my orientation, short visits were made by road to Trieu Phong District (Warrant Officer Doug French) and to the nearby ARVN Casualty Clearing Station (Warrant Officer Gordon Fitzgibbon) in Quang Tri City. In a letter to Eva after being in country for a week or so I wrote: "I feel that the years of training study and work are fitting into place. The transition is not difficult. The key word to describe where the challenges are may be summed up as 'the environment' in which I am to work."

Before describing my experiences in Mai Linh District, an overview of Quang Tri Province is now presented to provide the broader setting. A physical description of the province and a brief historical outline follows. I am indebted to my fellow staff officers in Team 19 who helped produce the source document in late 1968.[5]

Quang Tri was the northernmost province in South Vietnam. It was bordered on the east by the South China Sea, on the south by Thua Thien Province, on the west by Laos, and to the north by the Ben Hai River. The province covered about forty-six hundred square kilometers of land, less than half of which was inhabited. About 270,000 people lived in the province.

Geographically, the province could be divided into four regions: the mountains, the foothills, the low paddy land, and the sandy coastal region. The mountains, which covered the western half of the province, were mostly uninhabited, except for some ten thousand Montagnard, mostly of the Bru tribe. The natural resources of the mountains were timber, minerals, and water for power, though yet to be exploited. Route 9, the only all-weather road running into the Truong Son Mountains, went from Dong Ha through Khe Sanh into Laos. The mountains were known as the Annamites during the French period.

The foothills, or plateau region, consisted of red soil that was mostly fertile and was suitable for a wide range of fruits and vegetables. Several roads led into the foothills and, although not of hard surfaces, were easily maintained because of ready sources of laterite. This area was sparsely populated and was not under government influence.

The low delta or paddy land was the productive rice-growing zone. Although the riceland was relatively infertile, it could be improved with fertilizer and better agricultural practices. The arable land was used for one rice crop each year, although some areas could support two crops with improvement. This region was the more densely populated of the province, containing three-fourths of the population on one-fourth of the total land area.

The coastal region was composed of white sandy plains and beaches that were salty and unproductive. This region was sparsely populated and supported only fishing villages along the beaches. The shifting of the sands by wind and water was causing this area to expand inshore onto the bordering paddy land.

Weather has a profound influence in this province since the seasons are intense. Quang Tri has the hottest and the coldest temperature extremes in South Vietnam. In January and February the temperature sometimes drops as low as 40°F. The rainy and dry seasons are almost exactly the reverse of the seasons in Saigon. These meteorological phenomena had to be kept in mind in planning programs for the province. Agriculture was almost nonexistent in the hottest months of the dry season. The season from March through to September often had a very steady, hot, dry wind out of Laos, called the "Cheo Lao." The heavy rains beginning in September or October usually resulted in floods during October and November. The intensity of the rainy season permitted major construction only during the dry season. As will be described later, this characteristic was discounted for one memorable project. Field trips by wheeled vehicles during the heavy part of the rainy season were at times impossible since only Routes 1 and 9 were all-weather, hard surface, and sealed roads.

Quang Tri's recorded history begins in about the fourteenth century, when the Vietnamese, pushing down from the north, began to drive out or subdue the indigenous Cham people, who had long resided in the area. After many years of civil war between north and south, the Emperor Gia-Long in 1802 unified the country, founded an imperial capital at Hue, and established the Nguyen dynasty, which endured until Bao Dai's abdication in 1954. Since that time Quang Tri and its people have had close ties to Hue. The imperial city represented the seat of government, culture, and learning. In 1968 most of Quang Tri's leaders had strong connections with Hue, through family, property, and religious superiors. Moreover, the people of Quang Tri had a strong regional pride which typified central Vietnam, centered on Hue.

From the early 1800s the Quang Tri Citadel was a political, military, and economic center for Quang Tri Province. The Nguyen dynasty rebuilt the Citadel in brick about 1837, strengthening a military stronghold and the northern approach to Hue. The structure was imposing, with a perimeter of two kilometers comprised of high and thick walls. Protection of the Citadel was enhanced by a surrounding moat.

Toward the end of the nineteenth century, while the French were still consolidating their hold on An Nam (central Vietnam), the resisting royal court, having been driven from Hue, maintained for a time a capital in the jungles of the western part of the province. Quang Tri continued to be a center of anti-French resistance throughout the Vietminh period. "The Street Without Joy," which runs along the coastal area of Trieu Phong and Hai Lang Districts into Thua Thien Province, was the locale of unsuccessful French operations that provided the title for Bernard Fall's famous book.

Quang Tri Citadel and Thach Han River, with MACV compound in the top right-hand corner, 1968.

Ironically, Fall was killed in Hue in 1967. Until 1954 Quang Tri Province included an area that extended about fifteen kilometers north of the Ben Hai River. This area was part of North Vietnam's Quang Binh Province.

My familiarization was complete. I noted my mood at this point with a reflection. "I was trained to be a warrior, then an advisor. My immediate future requires me to become a mentor to Vietnamese, Americans and Australians." The next chapter is devoted to the AATTV members who served in Quang Tri during my year there. They were a group of individuals with whom I developed a special professional and personal relationship.

4

Australian Army Advisors in the Province

May 1968–April 1969

On arrival in Vietnam each member of the Australian Force Vietnam (AFV) received a small card titled "NINE RULES." The preamble said:

> We as a military force and as individuals are in this country to help the Vietnamese Government and People to win their long and courageous fight against the Communists. The product of victory is a democratic State with stable government and contented people. The Communists will use any weapon to discredit the Government and countries, like ours, in the eyes of the Vietnamese people. Don't let your behaviour be a propaganda weapon which helps in any way to destroy Vietnam. Here are nine simple rules for conduct whilst in Vietnam:
>
> 1. Remember we are here only to help; we make no demands and seek no special treatment.
> 2. Try to understand the people, their way of life; customs and laws.
> 3. Learn the simple greetings of the Vietnamese language and use them frequently.
> 4. Treat friendly people, particularly women with respect and courtesy.
> 5. Don't attract attention by rude behaviour or larrickinism.[1]
> 6. Avoid separating us from the Vietnamese by a display of great wealth or privilege.
> 7. Make friends among the soldiers and people of Vietnam.

8. Remember decency and honesty are the signs of a man and a soldier; bad manners are the sign of a fool.
9. Above all remember you are an Australian, by your actions our country is judged. Set an example of sincerity and fair play in all your dealings with Vietnamese and with other people who are assisting them.

The Australian Army Training Team Vietnam (AATTV) component in Quang Tri Province in 1968 typically numbered about fourteen members, an officer and thirteen warrant officers. Individuals were allotted to a U.S. Army advisory team. For the Australian Army there had been a learning experience on how best to utilize the advisory effort from the time of arrival in August 1962. By 1965 the deployment of Team members had settled and a pattern developed, which was well established by 1968. Within the expanded U.S. Army presence in South Vietnam, positions were made available for Australians to be combat advisors with units of the ARVN and the Territorial Forces, and as leaders in Special Forces units. In Quang Tri Province in 1968–1969, AATTV members were deployed with ARVN and Territorial Forces advisory teams.

Almost all of the battalions of the two ARVN divisions in I Corps had an Australian in their advisory team. Each team was comprised of four members: a U.S. Army captain, an Australian warrant officer, and two U.S. Army specialists in weapons and communication. The 1st ARVN Division had the divisional headquarters in Hue to the south of Quang Tri, and two regiments in Quang Tri Province. Australians were with the four battalions of the 1st Regiment and with the five battalions of the 2nd Regiment.

Warrant officers were also allotted to divisional and corps troops advisory teams, including the 11th Artillery Battalion and the 7th and 11th Cavalry Regiments. The cavalry units, and subunits, were mobile and deployed as required into Quang Tri Province as well as to the adjoining province of Thua Thien to the south. A warrant officer of the medical corps was advisor to an ARVN Casualty Clearing Station located in Quang Tri City.

To complete the deployment picture in the province, warrant officers were also allocated to sub-sector advisory teams in two districts: Trieu Phong to the north of Quang Tri City, and Cam Lo to the northwest, abutting the demilitarized zone (DMZ). My allotment as an advisor was with a district advisory team initially, and then with the province advisory team, which I will expand upon later in the narrative.

I was very impressed with the service given by the Australian warrant officers, and with their attitude. Not only did they have to adapt to working with the U.S. advisory system but they faced a greater cultural challenge in the need to adapt to working mainly with the Vietnamese military. With sound predeparture preparation and in-country orientation, they rose to the occasion. They were truly tested and found not to be wanting. The operational life and experiences of the warrant officers and others in Vietnam have been described elsewhere by Ian McNeill (*The Team*), Bruce Davies and Gary McKay (*The Men Who Persevered*), and Barry Petersen (*Tiger Men*).

There was a need to maintain a command structure within the deployed Team for administrative purposes so that an officer could ensure the warrant officers in their area were properly looked after and employed. As the senior Australian Army officer in Quang Tri Province, I was a point of contact for my fellow Team members in the area. My link to the commanding officer AATTV was through Da Nang, to the south, where we had a major in a staff officer advisory role at the headquarters of I Corps. Major Ian Porteous was in place on my arrival, and in February 1969 Major Frank Johnston was Ian's successor. They and the commanding officer AATTV were frequent visitors to Quang Tri, and they cared for my interests and that of other Team members in much the same way as I did for the warrant officers.

A general employment policy of the AATTV was that during a twelve-month tour of duty a member would have two placements, desirably each of six months. *The Men Who Persevered* includes a nominal roll of men posted to the Team and includes areas and advisory teams in which members served during their time in Vietnam. This excellent tabulation has helped me to better understand the difficult job successive commanding officers had in managing and allocating troops to their tasks. Also, the tabulation enabled me to have a clearer picture of my diary entries on the comings and goings of the warrant officers in Quang Tri Province.

During my year I was associated with thirty-four warrant officers who served in fourteen U.S. Army advisory teams with the ARVN and the Regional Forces (RF) and Popular Forces (PF) in Quang Tri. Table 4.1 shows the names of the Australian Army advi-

Table 4.1. Australian Advisors in Quang Tri Province, 1968–1969.

ARVN Units	
1/1/1	A. Robinson, J. Bourke, H. Patch, R. Purton, H. Beesley
2/1/1	R. Oliver, K. Gabriel (WIA)
3/1/1	R. Purton (WIA), E. Snelling
4/1/1	R. King, W. Tillet
1/2/1	J. Geedrick (WIA), J. Barker
2/2/1	D. Phillips, R. Carter (WIA), J. Geedrick, F. Bell
3/2/1	D. Hill, V. Stack
4/2/1	L. Kapp, R. Robinson
5/2/1	P. Wilkes, J. Barker
11th Arty	B. Emberson, D. Hill, L. Gorman
7th Cav	A. Hunter, H. Stuttard (WIA), J. Bond (KIA)
11th Cav	H. Stuttard (WIA)
CCS	N. Fitzgibbon (now G. Grant), W. Deanshaw
Sector Advisory Team 19	
HQ	D. Millie, H. Bell
Cam Lo	P. Wooden (WIA), K. Chester, J. O'Donnell[a]
Mai Linh	M. Casey, D. Millie
Trieu Phong	A. French, R. Purton, H. Patch, J. Garrigan (drowned), B. Saxby, R. O'Brien

[a] AATTV War Diary, AWM 95, 1/2/70, dated October 1969. "Major Harry Bell reported that Warrant Officer O'Donnell attained a degree of trust with the RF command unequaled by any advisor in MACV Team 19. Until the arrival of a new DSA O'Donnell was the one person that kept the Cam Lo team running."

sors and their Vietnamese unit advisory teams. The average time spent in the province by these members was seven months. Ten of the thirty-four spent from nine to thirteen months in Quang Tri, with some moving from one advisory team to another within the province.

Some individual Team members had more than one tour of duty in Vietnam. Of the thirty-four warrant officers mentioned above, seven had two tours, four had three tours, and Warrant Officer Kevin Gabriel had five. Some of those members with multiple tours had postings with other Australian Army units which operated in Phuoc Tuy Province, either before or after their AATTV posting. More details on multitour soldiers can be found in *The Men Who Persevered*.[2]

Foreign and Australian awards were granted to thirty-one of the thirty-seven AATTV members shown in table 4.1, recognition of the outstanding service performed by these men. I have relied upon the award lists in the books by McNeill and Davies and McKay to compile this summary: U.S. military awards, twenty-four; Republic of Vietnam Armed Forces awards, thirty-five; Australian military awards, seven, making a total of sixty-six awards. I was privileged to serve with this fine group of Australian soldiers.

There were three instances where personal incompatibilities caused warrant officers to be reassigned. Two cases were resolved within the province. In the other case the warrant officer was reallocated outside the province. The three cases arose from personality clashes within the U.S. advisory teams, not with the Vietnamese. In each case the commanding officer AATTV accepted the recommendations, which were based on what was in the best interests of the member and his advisory team. The warrant officers benefitted by these experiences and went on to give good service to the Team.

The impact of casualties also caused turmoil, not only to families at home but also to advisory teams. Warrant Officer John Garrigan (Trieu Phong sub-sector) tragically died by drowning after being with us for just over a month. Warrant Officer Peter Wooden (Cam Lo sub-sector) was wounded in action after being in the province for less than three months, having previously served at Hoa Vang sub-sector, Quang Nam Province, for four months. Seven other warrant officers sustained wounds while in action in Quang Tri. Cases of sickness, like dysentery and suspected hernia, also arose.

Garrigan drowned on 27 December. He was on a Regional Force company combined operation with elements of the 1/5 Infantry Brigade, undertaking a river crossing on an APC. The carrier struck an underwater obstruction, and the troops on board dropped off into about ten feet of water. John could not be reached by other troops in the immediate area. He did not respond to resuscitation. He was given the last rites at a medical battalion. This was terribly sad for his wife and children. A memorial service was conducted for John in Da Nang the following Sunday morning. All ranks of the U.S. brigade contributed money to be given to Mrs. Garrigan, John's widow. Arrangements were made for their officer, while in Australia on R&R, to be escorted to Wagga Wagga, New South Wales, to present the gift.

Wooden was a casualty from a booby trap incident at the water project at the Cam Lo refugee village on 12 June. A Special Forces sergeant pulled an anti-U.S. sign from the ground, and a M26 grenade at the bottom of the stake exploded. The sergeant was killed and three others were wounded, Wooden being one of them. The sign (translated) read:

> Our people should not cooperate with Americans and followers.
> Keep away from Americans and followers.
> Regional and Popular Forces! You should go back to the people.
> Do not sacrifice your own life for Americans in this place.
> Liberation Force's artillery has already been prepared.
> Down American-Thieu-Ky, and all the team who betray the country.[3]

Warrant Officer Fitzgibbon and I flew in a Chinook from Marine Air Group 39 to visit Wooden on the hospital ship USS *Repose* on 16 June. The helicopter trip took us via the hospital ship USS *Sanctuary.* Wooden was being given expert medical attention. Our return trip to Quang Tri was an indirect one. We took a Huey to the 1st Marine Division airfield at Phu Bai, to the southeast of Hue, and then proceeded further south to Da Nang in a USAF C-123. There were no further flights north from Da Nang that day. We returned to Quang Tri the next day by C-123. Although we experienced an interesting air journey, we were very satisfied in being able to visit Peter Wooden. We hoped our visit helped him in his recovery. Other Australians were able to visit him on the ship. A few days after Wooden was wounded his district senior advisor, Major John Hannon of Cam Lo sub-sector, visited me. He was very concerned about the incident, and expressed his best wishes for Peter and that he would have a quick recovery. Hannon treated Wooden as one of his own, a brother-in-arms.

From time to time my leadership nous was tested by some of the warrant officers in Quang Tri. I was thirty years of age, with nine years of commissioned service. The average age of the warrant officers was thirty-six. Their ages ranged from the late twenties to mid-forties. They were all experienced soldiers, with some being veterans of the Korea, Malaya, or Borneo campaigns. Three soldier management cases in particular were in the category of tough love. I judge them to be worthy of explanation and commentary.

The first concerned a warrant officer with an ARVN infantry battalion advisory team. He had arrived about two months before me and was located with his battalion in one of the fire support bases near the DMZ. Shortly after my arrival in the province his team leader, a captain, expressed his concern to me about the warrant officer. On 1 June 1968, I met with the captain, his next senior, a major, and their commanding officer, Lieutenant Colonel Parsons. Two points concerned the captain about the warrant officer: his actions under fire and his taking command when the captain was away. As I was a listener in this discussion, without firsthand knowledge, I relied on the colonel to provide guidance to the captain. Parsons told the captain to go back and train the warrant officer, an approach I supported. I judged that it was up to the captain to develop the relationship, at the same time hoping that the warrant officer kept calm and would do his best.

The warrant officer visited me the next day and asked to be relieved from his team. The captain had not yet talked to him about the meeting of the previous day. After hearing reasons for his request, it was my turn to advise the warrant officer. I suggested he have a talk with his captain at an appropriate time about his concerns. If a working relationship was not possible, then he should seek an interview with the captain's senior advisor. I also suggested to him that if his position was untenable, then he was to bring his gear out if he was not prepared to stay.

My entry of that day stated: "Kept him with his team to see if personality clash can be resolved; and also am not prepared to recommend an inter-battalion swap of advisors within the regiment due to the short time of other Australians in their jobs, and the subsequent talk that could possibly have followed the conversation with Parsons."

On 12 June an Australian warrant officer in another advisory team within the same regiment gave me some of his views about the concerns of the warrant officer. I was pleased to hear that there had been a chance for the two men to talk about the situation. The warrant officer gave me his view that his fellow Team member should be relieved from his team as soon as it could be managed. I agreed generally with his opinion. The captain had lost two of his team members through wounds in action a few days before. The warrant officer said he would not like to be in the captain's team. The situation was not looking good. Also on this day Peter Wooden sustained his serious injury at Cam Lo.

The warrant officer in question had a short break at Da Nang later in June. He continued with his team and with the captain into July, when his planned rotation came due. The warrant officer then moved into another military region, to a more demanding appointment, in which he conducted himself well. To his credit, I thought he came through a very difficult and worrying experience in exemplary fashion, and showed depth of character in doing so. He truly lived up to the Team motto: Persevere.

The second case related to a warrant officer who was in his first tour. This was his second placement in South Vietnam. His first three months had been spent in another province with an advisory team whose role was similar. Before taking up his duty he had his due R&R break. Within three weeks of his arrival in Quang Tri, I was so concerned about his attitude to his work that I discussed the warrant officer with our Team chaplain, Kevin Hoffman, on his routine visit in mid-July. It struck me that the mind of the warrant officer seemed to dwell in other places. His behavior demonstrated a predominant self-centeredness that was not conducive to his being a good team member. I explained to Chaplain Hoffman that I was very uncomfortable with the warrant officer's attitude. We concluded that a wait-and-see approach should be taken.

During September, when the routine Army procedure for considering soldiers for officer training was being undertaken, I advised our Team commanding officer that I would not recommend the warrant officer for advancement at the present time. As a consequence, he did not proceed on an in-country education course to help him meet the education standard for officer qualification. Naturally the warrant officer was disappointed when I informed him of this development. My advice to him was to apply himself diligently to his work to prove his worth to his advisory team, to the Team, and to the Australian Army.

In October the warrant officer in question managed to be on a report for an incident with the military police. By this time Major Ian Porteous was taking an interest in the warrant officer, which was of some relief to me. In fairness to the warrant officer, this enabled the AATTV's commanding officer to receive a second opinion. Porteous advised the warrant officer to get on with the job in his team. This was sound advice that he had heard before. Porteous and I agreed that he was presently immature, and perhaps impetuous. The warrant officer was advised he could possibly take up an education course by correspondence by the end of 1968.

For the remainder of his tour in Quang Tri the warrant officer applied himself well to his allotted tasks. He was probably full of relief to hand over the assignment to his Australian successor. He took a little longer than most to understand his role in the art of perseverance. Subsequent to our time together in Vietnam I have met him at a number of Team reunions. He is proud of his place in the camaraderie of the Team.

The third case was an exceptional one filled with relief, disappointment, and reward. A warrant officer arrived in Quang Tri to take up his initial advisory team posting seven days after arriving in Vietnam. One month later he was on an aircraft to Da Nang. He had failed himself and all who worked with him. His American advisory team leader, Major John Shalikashvili, at Trieu Phong subsector, was a man of enormous drive and ability. Australians found him uncomfortable to work with. However, the major was firm and fair as a professional soldier. Those in his team who took him lightly soon realized that, like him, they had to seize the day, each and every day. Alcohol at the sub-sector was not allowed, a rule known to all.

Within ten days of the warrant officer's arrival in Quang Tri, I had reason to speak to him to clarify some matters. I considered that he might have misread some of the interpersonal relationships at play at his location. Based on some lessons learned from the case described earlier, I was able to more clearly state what was expected of him in the particular role he had in his team. I had discussed and agreed on these matters with Major Shalikashvili before he arrived. The warrant officer had the talent, skills, and ability to perform his function well. I emphasized to him that he needed to exercise sound judgment and maturity in all that he did.

In what was shaping up to be a possibly fateful day, it was reported to me that the warrant officer had not returned to his advisory team the evening before. It was known that he had been on a liaison visit to the adjacent Marine Air Group base. Questions came into my mind: What has he done? What could have been done to him? What resources can be used to find him? What will be the aftermath? His well-being was paramount. Fortunately, Warrant Officer Bill Deanshaw was nearby. I called him in to assist me with this problem. Kidnapping and abductions were not uncommon, and as the warrant officer was unaccompanied that possibility could not be ruled out. Bill Deanshaw rallied available warrant officers and allocated follow-up tasks to help find our missing teammate. I reported the incident to my province senior advisor, Colonel Harley Mooney, outlining the problem and actions now being taken, with which he agreed. He asked to be kept informed. I then had to advise Ian Porteous at Da Nang. It was midmorning now. My report to Ian was succinct: "One of our members is reported as missing." He agreed that local U.S. marine and army formation headquarters should be advised, as well as the Vietnamese authorities, military and civilian.

The warrant officer walked into the MACV compound in Quang Tri City at 2.15 P.M. while Bill Deanshaw and I were discussing the very situation. With great relief we welcomed him. For us this was a "prodigal son" moment. He was very sheepish and showing signs of suffering a hangover. Immediate action was taken to advise those contacted that our warrant officer was no longer missing. He informed us that his vehicle had broken down and that he had spent the night at 4th Marines. He apologized for failing to inform anyone of his predicament. He could not give me, at that time, a reason for his behavior. It was disappointing, I reflected, after the clear warning given to him three weeks earlier.

Colonel Mooney was advised of the return of our colleague. He and I discussed the circumstances, and he agreed with my recommendation that I was to pass to Ian Porteous, that the warrant officer be relieved of his position in the local advisory team and be relocated to Da Nang forthwith. This would allow sober reflection by the individual, and for our command chain to coolly reflect on consequential actions. The warrant officer was advised of his pending relocation, and I judged that he was relieved to hear of that decision. Accompanied by another warrant officer, he returned to the location of his advisory team, packed up his belongings, and made his farewells there. Three of the Team were at the local light aircraft strip to bid him farewell. He was transported by an Air America Porter aircraft to Da Nang.

The next day Major Frank Johnston, on changeover with Major Ian Porteous, came from Da Nang to discuss the facts of the case. We agreed that the warrant officer should remain with the Team, but that the commanding officer AATTV should give him a formal warning and appoint him to another area in Vietnam. The province senior advisor supported this approach and thought that the outcome was appropriate. I thought the replacement warrant officer would have to be a mature, experienced fellow who would be able to handle the situation at Trieu Phong.

Years later I met up with the warrant officer. He expressed his appreciation for the way his indiscretion was handled in Quang Tri, at Da Nang, and by the Team. He explained that his following ten months in Vietnam were most satisfying, and that his career in the army thereafter was rewarding for him. This was another case of perseverance prevailing.

By their nature, Australian warrant officers assimilated easily and worked well with the Vietnamese, despite some language problems. In my experience in Quang Tri there was not a single case of a warrant officer not getting on with the Vietnamese that they were working with. On reflection, the cultural differences were significant. However, a buffer to the Vietnamese seems to have been provided by the advisory team, where the Australians worked closely with their U.S. team members. It was within this team that differences could arise.

Within the U.S. advisory teams the Australian warrant officer was usually looked upon as the father figure of the group. On average, he was about ten years older and had usually served in some other campaign. In combat situations the Australians' opinions were often sought. Our warrant officers were well regarded in their teams, and were highly respected by the Vietnamese officers and soldiers with whom they served.

Several warrant officers expressed a common view to me that ARVN soldiers had a favorable disposition toward NVA soldiers. They fought them as hard as they possibly could and treated prisoners of war well. On the other hand, if VC were captured by the ARVN, they received no mercy at all. The warrant officers also had the view that ARVN junior leaders needed to perform better than at present.

In a reflective moment in November 1968 I wrote a personal view, one that other Australian advisors may also have reached:

> As an Australian and as a military advisor I am in an unusual situation. In Vietnam I am working with and for the US Forces, and at the same time acting as an advisor to the local

> Vietnamese authorities. The Australian in the US advisory team can have a dual role being an advisor to the Americans and to the Vietnamese. Thankfully most of the US advisors are very easy to get on with, but I feel sub-consciously that it does add an increment to the burden of service in Vietnam with the Team. Needless to say it is easier for the Australian to be of one mind with his fellow American team members than it is to be of one mind with the Vietnamese, who have their own cultural, political and religious views to deal with, which we foreigners barely understand.

Underlying and within many Vietnamese were their major historic beliefs: Confucianism, Taoism, Buddhism, and Christianity. Our predeployment training in Australia prepared us for the circumstances we found ourselves in, but the reality was thought provoking.

The MACV compound in Quang Tri City was close to the south wall of the Citadel. It provided all the administrative services an advisor would need on a daily basis: accommodation, catering, and club facilities. Some of the ARVN regimental advisory teams had accommodation in large residential buildings in the town. The facilities in the compound provided a meeting place for many advisors, military and civilian, and our warrant officers gathered there on occasions when off duty from their operational teams and out of the line. I enjoyed their company when they were in. Our medical warrant officers were the main administrative point of contact for our fellows in Quang Tri, and they kept me informed on who was coming and going.

Another testing leadership case arose in August. An Australian Army captain arrived in Quang Tri in mid-June to take up an ARVN battalion senior advisor position. He had had an earlier tour in Vietnam with an infantry battalion and was highly regarded. His senior advisor was favorably impressed by him. But he had to be relocated south after two months. What happened?

Within two weeks I noticed that when out of the line he had a swagger about him that caused me to note that he was not setting a good example to our warrant officers. For the next few weeks the captain was doing all that was expected of him. With the benefit of hindsight the Australian warrant officer in his team, who arrived a month later on his third tour, was as unsettled as the captain.

At about the two-month point, while we were relaxing together in the club, the captain became upset—and nearly became aggressive—when a Korean, a former marine, was hit on the head with a beer can held by a Filipino. One side of the Korean's face was covered in blood. The captain was under the impression that the military police in attendance could not handle the situation. When he realized that other officers were watching, and not acting, he got up and without much thought intended to become involved. Fortunately, I was able to guide him out of the club to my room. He was clearly upset over the incident. I was of the opinion that he may have overindulged in beer that day, and was finding that the advisory role was not to his liking. In our discussion then I suggested he not get involved with civilians while in Quang Tri.

Later that night I was telephoned by the compound commander. He advised me of an incident involving the captain and of a possible shot having been fired in a barrack room. No one had been injured. As I was involved in an RF operation early the next morning in a local village, my follow-up would be delayed. This case was becoming an embarrassment for the Australians, and the Americans. After completing my duties with the RF operation, I met with the captain. He told me he had been drunk and that when he could not find a can opener he decided to fire his pistol to open a can of beer. It was not difficult to decide he needed a break from Quang Tri and should go to Da Nang. The chain of command agreed.

The captain was a troubled person. I had to prepare a formal charge statement, which I handed to him at the airfield as he headed south. The adjutant compiled a summary of evidence. He was brought before the commander of the Australian Force Vietnam and given a reprimand. He remained in country to complete his twelve-month tour. My view then was that he was not fit for operational service. I do not know if he was subjected to a medical assessment.

Some years later we met up, and he informed me that a root cause of his past difficulties was alcoholism, an addiction he was later able to control. The captain successfully completed a long army career. Later he did epic things. He persevered with his life in a splendid way.

In early July an idea had evolved among the warrant officers that it was time for the Australians in Quang Tri to offer hospitality and some entertainment to our Vietnamese hosts, the Americans, and others. A project team was formed and an event was arranged at the MACV compound. The timing for the event was based on the availability of an Australian concert group that was touring the northern provinces on a U.S. contract. So, on or about 12 July 1968 invitations went out for a concert and party commencing at 3 P.M., Saturday, 20 July 1968.

The manager/producer/promoter of the Swinging Kangaroos was Bill Revell, a Britisher. He provided some technical guidance for the setting up of a stage, sound system, and parachutes as shade cloths. Gordon Fitzgibbon had made the contact with Bill in Da Nang, and Arthur Robinson had arranged matters with their treasurer. The compère of the show was Alan Carb, who was supported by three musicians, three dancers, and a singer. The show ran for an hour, beginning at 3:20 P.M., with entertainment that appealed to most of the audience. The compère presented a female statuette to a warrant officer for being recognized as lover of the year. In response, he sang some words from: "I Want to Go Home" and "I Want to Stay Here." The concert was a complimentary one for the Australians.

The province chief and all his military and civil staff attended. Our fellow MACCORDS people assisted in the hosting, and the compound staff provided the catering and bar facilities. The informal setting provided opportunities for a lot of business to be carried out. It was an opportunity for friendship building, which was my main motivation for strongly supporting the event. Bob Brewer and a few other key staff were able to offer side rooms with their counterparts during the afternoon for informal gatherings. Ian Porteous traveled up from Da Nang to join us. Following afternoon tea and other refreshments, the band of the 3rd Marine Division entertained the crowd, which by this time greatly exceeded our expectations, with hundreds in the audience.

The compère and Bill Revell entered into the spirit of the day for the Australians. They called us up onto the stage for a chorus item. I was able to give thanks to all who had made a contribution to the happy and enjoyable party, with a special acknowledgment being given to the province chief and Lieutenant Colonel Nhan for their attendance. The band departed at 6 P.M. by Chinook helicopter for Phu Bai, having completed their northern engagements. They had two more shows to perform that night. The group had a demanding life on the road in Vietnam. Occasions like the concert afternoon were rare and greatly appreciated. Fun was had by all. Morale was given a boost. It was a welcome break from the daunting realities that faced one and all each day.

The mail delivery service was satisfactory, with our postal address being: Australian Army Advisor, Advisory Team No Quang Tri, APO 96269, San Francisco, USA. It was recommended that "Australian serviceman on duty with US Forces in Vietnam" be added in the left-hand bottom corner. Receiving mail from home usually was good for morale, but unpleasant news sometimes came in letters. Some team members confided to me of their concerns, usually when the news aroused feelings of helplessness. This trust placed in me by the warrant officers was treated with strict confidentiality. Some news was delayed. A Team member returned to Australia found that a "roger-the-lodger" was in his home while he was in Vietnam. This could be heartbreaking news. Another expressed his concern over a lack of mail, as he had not heard from his wife in two months. He did not go home for R&R, despite being advised to do so. Instead he sent purchases home from Hong Kong.

I admired the character of our soldiers, my fellow Team members, who displayed the highest levels of professionalism, even when they may have been torn inside emotionally by personal disappointment, doubt, and sadness. Our men were involved in intensive combat operations in Quang Tri Province. The level of military activity was of conventional war proportions: extensive use of firepower and maneuver against a determined and capable enemy, the NVA and the VC. This northern area of South Vietnam was a hotspot. That the tenure in Quang Tri averaged seven months speaks volumes for the Team members doing arduous duty there. The AATTV patron, the late Lieutenant General Sir Thomas Daly, Chief of the General Staff from 1966 to 1971, recognized these qualities, referring to the Team as "a band of gallant Australians."[4]

The next chapter covers the period of my first assignment with MACV, as a district senior advisor at Mai Linh District, in Quang Tri Province. I was to be involved in counterinsurgency, a generic term given to the type of conflict being waged. The local Territorial Forces and the police provided security in the populated areas to allow the government of South Vietnam to meet the needs of its people and to allow them to live in freedom. The advisors were present to assist and to help facilitate support from their allies.

5

Counterinsurgency in Mai Linh Sub-Sector

May–August 1968

To assist in countering local insurgency, each province chief had his own military headquarters, known as sector headquarters, to command and control the Territorial Forces in the province. The Territorial Forces were composed of Regional Force (RF) companies and Popular Force (PF) platoons. Regional Force troops were recruited by the province chief from within the province and organized into companies, each about one hundred in strength. In 1968, Quang Tri Province had nineteen RF companies. Their role was to provide security to the lines of communications and key installations within the province and to provide a reaction force for the province chief. The six companies allocated to Mai Linh District were deployed within the city of Quang Tri. Some RF companies were grouped together to form an embryonic RF battalion.

To help RF companies in their skills development, the U.S. Army provided mobile advisory teams (MATs). The MAT role was to assist in training and advising RF companies for three to four months before moving on to the next unit. The emphasis was on improving individual military skills and the minor tactics of a company. Eight MATs were allocated to Quang Tri sector.

Under the sector headquarters were district chiefs, who each had a sub-sector headquarters to control allocated troops. I was the senior advisor to the Mai Linh district chief. Chiefs, province and district, were appointed, not elected. Popular Force troops were recruited by the district chief from within the district and organized into platoons. Mai Linh District had seventeen PF platoons. Their role was to provide security for the hamlets and villages, like a local militia. Enlistment terms and conditions of service limited the PF to employment within their district. The Vietnamese individuals with whom I worked in Quang Tri Province are listed at the back end of the book in "Appendix A: Some of the Characters."

In the northern provinces advisors with sector and sub-sector advisory teams worked closely with the USMC-sponsored Combined Action Program. The overall marine concept was for USMC and ARVN formations to act as an outer shield to provide a screen behind which the Territorial Forces could conduct counterinsurgency, assisted by Combined Action Companies, in the populated areas. The companies were grouped into Combined Action Groups. In 1965 General Lewis W. Walt, the Marine Corps commander in Vietnam, keen to free his units from the task of defending the populated areas, instituted the program. Under this concept the PF platoons deployed for the defense of villages and hamlets were reinforced by squads of marines to form Combined Action Platoons (CAPs). This was a village security approach to help facilitate pacification, with an emphasis on population control. The task of the marines was to bolster the fighting capability of the PF platoons as well as to train and advise them. In Mai Linh sub-sector marine squads were under the command of a USMC officer located at the sub-sector headquarters. Major Jim Brown was the Mai Linh officer, with four CAPs under his control. The marines thought this program worked well, thus justifying the drain of manpower from marine infantry units.[1]

My district chief was Captain Ton That Phong, an officer of the Army of the Republic of Vietnam. He was well educated and able to converse in English and French, a bonus for me. He was competent, a capable administrator, and experienced as an army officer. Phong was from Hue. His house there had been destroyed during the enemy Tet offensive. Having an Australian advisor was not a new experience for Phong. Major Michael Casey (Infantry), who I was replacing, had been at Mai Linh since December 1967. He was preceded by Major Neville Wilson (Infantry), who was in the position from September to December 1967. The Australian major in Quang Tri Province prior to Wilson was Major John Hughes, district senior advisor at Trieu Phong District, who was wounded in action at Trieu Phong in August 1967. That position was allocated back to the U.S. Army, as it was a sensitive district senior advisory position, and had to be filled promptly by the then U.S. Army district senior advisor at Mai Linh District.

Casey had a schedule of work organized for me and without fuss he set about introducing me to the place that was to be my patch for the next few months. On our first vehicle tour we passed by the local railway station. It was noticeable that some of the rails had been removed, there was an absence of rolling stock, and all of the railway buildings were locked up. The railway system was not operating. In a droll way Casey said: "Seems to be a prolonged strike over something or other."

Not far from the district headquarters was the ARVN Casualty Clearing Station where Warrant Officer Gordon Fitzgibbon (Medical) was the advisor. Doctor Hong was the officer in charge and gave me a short tour of the facility. The building was of a permanent nature. Used as a hospital, it was rather primitive to my eye, and reminded me of a typical outback hospital in Australia. One patient was a wounded NVA prisoner, looking sad and lost, and wisely without any apparent malice. Fitzgibbon was happy in his work there. He had a good rapport with all at the facility, including the prisoners. During the year Doctor Hong shared and enjoyed social occasions with the advisors. Fitzgibbon (now Gordon Grant) later told a story of taking Vietnamese into the base area of the 3rd Marine Division, fully aware that Vietnamese were not allowed entry. Fitz required them as a loading detail. Eventually he and his work party were permitted entry for a short time. Fitz did not tell the marines that some in the work party were NVA prisoners undergoing rehabilitation while recovering from wounds.

Later that day I met Staff Sergeant Ramos, U.S. Army, the only member present of my advisory team at the sub-sector of Mai Linh. He had many military specialist qualifications and was to prove to be good company. He tended to be preoccupied about the best career stream that he should follow to give him the highest pay. Ramos was from the Commonwealth of Puerto Rico. Puerto Ricans were U.S. citizens. When living on the island of Puerto Rico they could not vote in presidential elections, but they also did not pay federal income taxes. Ramos was happy to be in Vietnam, part of the gravy train of life, from his point of view. My assistant in the advisory team, Captain Bill Coviello, was away from Quang Tri on rest and recuperation leave and was to return soon. I met Binh, my interpreter.

Mai Linh District covered a populated area, including Quang Tri City and the villages to the south. The people in the district numbered about sixty-two thousand, living in seven villages and thirty-six hamlets. A number of hamlets in a cluster formed a village. About twenty-six hundred refugees lived in the district. From a security aspect, four hamlets had been abandoned, three were assessed as being controlled by the Viet Cong, and six were contested. Of the twenty-three hamlets under government control it was judged that fourteen were under day-only control. This security situation influenced the way the district chief went about his job, and the manner in which we would travel around the district. The insurgents and their subversive activities were foremost in his mind.

Bill Coviello introduced me to the Hamlet and Village Evaluation Report, shortened to Hamlet Evaluation System (HES). The report was a statistical assessment of rural security and development at the hamlet level in South Vietnam. He led me through a list of 240 questions in the report that had to be answered for each monthly return. The HES reported the hamlet's security classification on a six-point scale: A, B, C, D, E, or VC. The first three categories indicated the extent of being relatively secure. D and E indicated contested, and a VC classification indicated "under VC control." The returned data were processed by computer in Saigon and then analyzed. One had to hope that this system of reporting was but one of many sources of information in the decision-making process of MACV and the GVN, and then up the chain to Washington.

My first thought about the HES report was that if this was what the counterinsurgency and pacification effort had come to, then it might be time for the allies to leave the country. Despite being guests here, we, meaning the U.S. and its allies, could remind the Vietnamese that there was a strong case in the HES reports for the GVN to improve performance by increased effort. As the assessment process was about the security of hamlets and villages, I pondered the merits of the report's being filled out by the Vietnamese rather than the advisors. The requirement to complete a monthly HES report was clearly necessary, and onerous. My initial reservations had to be set aside so as to not fight the problem. A positive approach was required to meet higher level needs.

Within a month I reached a preliminary conclusion that the need for advisory effort within Mai Linh had probably peaked, as I found that the Vietnamese officers at my district level did not need much advice. The assistance given at the local level could arguably have

Table 5.1. CORDS Organization in Quang Tri.

Director	
Deputy Director for New Life Development	Deputy Director for Civil Operations
RD Team Leader	Psychological Operations
Static Census Grievance	Special Police
Highlander Affairs	Vietnamese Information Service
Agriculture	Chieu Hoi (APTs)
Education	PRU
Public Works	MILPHAP (Navy)
Youth Affairs	General Services Office
Social Welfare	Logistics
Refugee Affairs	Administration

Source: MACV Team 19 Brochure, Quang Tri Province, 1968.

been considered as token. However, the reporting system and the contents of the reports called upon personal judgments and opinions to be recorded. Once into the military and civilian bureaucracy the data could take on a persona, giving the summaries a rosy outlook, or some other slant. On the other hand, there might have been a political element within the results to help build up a case that the GVN could be moving toward some sort of self-sufficiency. My general conclusion, my hope, was that the HES could be a useful management tool.

Advisors in sub-sector teams and at the sector level were part of the countrywide advisory organization known as MACCORDS: Military Assistance Command Civil Operations and Revolutionary Development Support. CORDS advisors included both civilians and military. In the case of the Mai Linh District, CORDS advisors were not allocated, as their province-level people were able to meet local needs and were practically co-located with the Mai Linh sub-sector. This arrangement was beneficial for Mai Linh District, as the district chief and I had direct access to the province-level CORDS staff. Table 5.1 shows an outline of the organization in Quang Tri.

There was a lot to do in the military counterinsurgency role. The formal duties were:

1. Advise and assist the district chief and staff in all matters pertaining to pacification and nation building.
2. Assist local and transient RVNAF and US and FWMAF to accomplish their missions.
3. Provide liaison between US and FWMAF units and the district chief and his staff.
4. Command the District Advisory Team including assigned MAT teams.
5. Advise and assist in the development of district forces into an effective fighting organization. This includes the responsibility to:—
   - Monitor training, evaluate performance, recommend improvements, and provide any other assistance leading to improved effectiveness of RF and PF stationed in the district.
   - Accompany units in the conduct of operations as necessary to evaluate the effectiveness, and make recommendations to improve capabilities.
   - Make recommendations and provide assistance, to improve troop leadership, discipline, motivation, and morale.
6. Make recommendations and provide assistance to strengthen tactical and logistical support for district forces.
7. Assist in the integration of district forces and ARVN and FWMAF in the planning of RD within the District.
8. Maintain communication and liaison with US Forces stationed or deployed in the district.
9. Assist in the implementation and supervision of the US civil assistance programme.

I judged that the first duty had the highest priority, namely to assist the district chief of Mai Linh District. His highest priority was the security of the population. My work in the wider pacification program in Mai Linh is described in the next chapter.

The first night at the Mai Linh compound gave me an opportunity to have a "getting to know you" discussion with Major Jim Brown, USMC, the resident Combined Action Program commander of the 4th Combined Action Group. Jim had spent the first half of his tour as a company commander in a marine infantry battalion. He had been assigned to his present post in January 1968. I gathered he was happy to be at Mai Linh. We were quickly able to agree on how we would work together. The cooperative nature of the arrangements was very pleasing. He was solely responsible for his CAPs, and my role was with the district chief, in the broad range of other matters. He controlled his CAPs from a command post in a bunker where he spent the night hours.

My first formal experience at the district headquarters was to attend an awards parade where presentations were made to worthy RF and PF soldiers by the assistant district chief, Lieutenant Sang. This ceremony, as is the case in many armies, was well attended by comrades, families, and officials. There were celebrations for the remainder of the day, an opportunity to set aside the worries of living in a very unstable part of the world for a few hours.

Familiarization rounds with Mike Casey continued, with a visit to the main MACV advisory compound in Quang Tri City, named Kilroy Compound.[2] Accommodation and catering and other amenities were provided there. Amenities included laundry and room cleaning services, provided by maids, usually widows of deceased members of the military and police. I shared Ba (Mrs.) Le with a number of other officers. The work done by Ba Le was much appreciated, relieving each officer of routine housekeeping tasks. I was particularly interested in the security measures that were in place, as the compound and its occupants would have been an installation of interest to the enemy. On two sides there was urban occupation and on the other sides agriculture, grazing, and paddy. Casey was a bit hazy on who was responsible for the defenses within the compound. This was more than a surprise to me, as I thought we would have had a role in a response to any enemy threat. My view was that there was a need for degrees of alertness throughout each and every day. I observed that there was an absence of medium to heavy weapons in the compound.

There was no organized mutual support or coordination with other defensive localities in the adjacent area. It crossed my mind that the U.S. military seemed to take security seriously, yet here in the compound tactical or security basics were not obvious. There were plenty of indicators within the compound that during the enemy Tet offensive small arms fire hit the area. But penetration by enemy forces was not achieved. That was reassuring. The permanent compound security guard, under compound commander Major Bob Phillips, had some of the characteristics of a foreign legion. The guard was composed of three Vietnamese, one Nung, two marines, and two soldiers. The Nung were of an ethnic minority group who were a source of men for security work.

Humor was prevalent among the men within the compound. A garden hose was running water onto a concrete base at the foot of the flagpole. A marine remarked: "Whoever put it there was thinking like those running the war. Is it the intention to make the pole grow, or the concrete green, or both? I just cannot see the point of it." This comment is a fair analogy of the bewilderment that existed in some minds about the conflict.

The month of May was rice harvest time. As rice was a staple food for all of the Vietnamese people, the military forces had the responsibility to make sure the rice harvest was secured in safe areas. The VC and the NVA had to be denied food replenishment from the growers, or the merchants, under the National Rice Denial Program. The district chief had a local responsibility to deny the enemy rice and did so to the best of his ability.

I accompanied the district chief on a rice denial operation, a one-day daylight patrol. The main military elements were composed of three RF companies, grouped as a battalion. Our area of operation was to the south of the city, about four kilometers distant, on the east bank of the Thach Han River. Hamlets here were judged to be in a contested area, VC by night, GVN by day, as evidenced by our presence. The PF did not have a permanent presence here. I observed bunkers dug inside each house, a necessity for safety and survival. Later in the morning a young boy was introduced to us. He had suffered gunpowder burns to his face, chest, and legs. He was transported to the city hospital by canoe, one of about twenty that carried the recently harvested rice to the city center for secure storage.

As the patrol advanced farther south we came across a former French fort, a triangle in shape, on the riverbank. It was in a beautiful but dangerous area. Folklore was that a PF platoon located there was attacked in 1963. The area had been destroyed. Schools in adjacent hamlets in the area were not operating, as teachers were not available. At Tri Buu hamlet a suspected VC was being held by the RF company. Ramos thought the captive should be taken to the district headquarters, but the district chief decided to leave him with the company. I wondered what the suspect would be in for. The remainder of the day was uneventful.

The evening was a typical one for the ARVN artillery. Harassment and interdiction artillery was fired at intervals from the 11th

Artillery, as directed by the 2nd Regiment at Dong Ha, toward the DMZ. To the best of my knowledge there was no battle damage assessment to follow up such action.

The north-south highway and railway crossed over the Thach Han River in the southwest sector of the city. In times of peace the two links were vital to the transportation system in this part of Vietnam. The Highway 1 road bridge was named Nung Bridge and the railway bridge was known as the Ga Bridge. The Ga Bridge had been permanently out of service due to a collapsed span. The assistant province chief had informed me that it was the responsibility of the district chief to have the railway bridge brought back into service. I concluded that nothing was to be done to reopen the bridge, as it was beyond the government's ability to provide security for an operating railway, let alone find the resources to fix the system, which had not been operating for some years. The district chief knew the score. The status quo was to prevail for the broken-down bridge.

Two RF companies, No. 124 and No. 126, provided security for the two bridges, with the main effort being on the road bridge. The Nung was a vital link on a main supply route for the American forces in the province and for the ARVN. Commanders of U.S. and ARVN forces in the province were aware of the importance of the Nung Bridge. U.S. Navy dive teams were deployed frequently, adding to the protective defense measures already permanently in place.

The hamlet of Tich Tuong, four kilometers south of the district headquarters, was assaulted by an NVA platoon about 2:00 A.M. on 31 May. This kind of attack usually took defenders by surprise and was very effective, militarily and politically. The resident PF platoon offered assistance, unfortunately suffering eight soldiers killed. The attackers lost two killed. In the after action review it was thought by the sub-sector staff that the target could well have been the RD team located in the hamlet. Another view was that as the provincial reconnaissance unit had a contact that night on the western side of the river, there was an enemy interest in getting to know the approaches to the bridges. Confusion can easily be created, and anxiety levels can arise from minor incidents. Subsequently, the two NVA bodies were left where they lay for a few days. I noted that the bodies were thin and small in stature. They were dressed in shirt and trousers only, without footwear. They had been carrying satchel charges. The bodies were a sobering reminder to each side, and neutrals, that stakes were high in the war.

Map 4. Mai Linh District and surrounds, 1968.

Early in June word came down that the province chief had been promoted to colonel. The view of the advisory team was that this was partly earned as a reward, as the city of Quang Tri did not fall to the enemy during the Tet offensive earlier in the year. His profile in 1968 read as follows:

> Colonel Nguyen Am has a distinguished record of military service. He was born on 1st July, 1924 at Quang Xa, Quang Binh Province, a northern province of Central Vietnam now in North Vietnam. He completed high school in Hue in 1940. His military service started when he joined the French Colonial Army and served under the French until 1945. In 1947

he joined the ARVN. He had been trained in the National Military Academy at Hue in 1950, and attended the Command School at Dalat in 1954.

The colonel holds the fourth highest decoration of the Government of Vietnam. His other decorations include the Combat Infantryman's Badge, the Purple Heart, and two campaign decorations. He has received Army honours on seven occasions, Corps honours on three occasions, and Division honours on three occasions.

The Colonel has held command positions since 1943, and has been a regimental commander since 1957. In addition to his duties as commander of the 1st Regiment, 1st Division of ARVN, he assumed the position of Province Chief on 15th June, 1966. The previous province chief, Mr Nguyen Trung Thoai, resigned after six months in office. Although this is Colonel Am's first experience in civil administration he is rapidly becoming aware of the problems and responsibilities of provincial administration.

The colonel is married to Nguyen Thi Nhung, and is the father of twelve children. He is every inch the military man. His manner is pleasant and he enjoys the respect of the people of the province. He speaks fluent French and has a clear but limited English vocabulary.

My next operation was with 911 RF Company on 6 June. The company was to establish a blocking position at the hamlet of Van Van, to the east. An RF battalion was carrying out a patrolling sweep from the north. In company with the district chief, the advisors moved by vehicle to the locality of the operation. The hamlets in this area were very attractive. Water was plentiful, growth and greenery were prolific, the land flat. The district chief said that the PF platoons in the village of Hai Quy were good. The people in the hamlets were assessed as being 95 percent anti-VC. I hoped that they were 95 percent pro-government.

A peaceful night was spent in the hamlet of Van Van. There was no contact with the enemy. On day two the troops were in a happy frame of mind and very relaxed, too carefree for my liking. After this experience I concluded that the operation had a significant "showing the flag" component within it. The troops' presence confirmed that the government was in control. The local people accepted the presence and seemed relaxed and very healthy in their particular paradise. My acclimatization continued.

News of the death of Senator Robert Kennedy on 6 June was a shock. My American friends could only shake their heads, being at a complete loss of words over the death. I made this note two days later: "The services provided by all Americans, whether civil or military, are very good. Their generosity and desire to give is impressive and possibly a 'fault,' as the standards set will be very difficult for the Vietnamese to achieve, and to maintain, unassisted."

On the night of 8 June a CAP at Ai Tu, to the north of the Nung Bridge, had a contact with the enemy and killed one VC. The next day the body was placed in the sitting position on a chair on the roadside of Highway 1. There was an empty beer can in one hand and a cigarette in the other. A hat was placed on the head of the body and a disabled weapon was across his knees. This was a thoughtless action, and a poor show. I had a word with the district chief. Responsible action to remove the body was soon taken, and the body given proper respect.

Major Ball, senior forward air control pilot for the province, was killed at 6.45 A.M. on 10 June. I had flown with him to Hue in May. I wrote in my diary that evening:

> God may his soul rest in peace.
> A good man, his loss will be felt by many.
> But little changes,
> Life and war go on.
> A family without a father.
> A soul to rest in peace.
> A man has fulfilled his mission.

The tragic and the unexpected often occurred. After lunch one day I was having a quiet time standing on the north side of the compound close to the Citadel, watching some children at play on the road. Away from this scene a loud explosion was heard, coming from near to the Citadel, in the area of the surrounding minefield. It was reported that an RF soldier, on duty as an observer on the top of the wall, had fallen from the wall onto a mine. The explosion killed him instantly. There were no other casualties.

A couple of days later Ramos, Binh, and I joined up with RF company No. 121 at the Ga and Nung bridges for the night. A company relief-in-place was under way. I wanted to become more familiar with the protection and defensive measures in place and to assess their effectiveness in the event of any enemy action. It was clear to me that this was a critical point, being the main arterial road to the northern part of the province. Other friendly forces had a similar view. The nearby air cavalry brigade had an artillery forward observer (FO) located on the bridge, with two dismounted infantry squads (sections) in support. The FO was on the other end of the bridge from the RF company commander. An interpreter had not been provided, nor was there any formal communication means between the FO and the officer commanding the RF company. This deployment solution had some fundamental problems: poor internal communication (both radio and language) and inadequate liaison, making cooperation difficult. The layout was putting at risk a prompt and secure response to any enemy action against the bridge. I initiated corrective action early the next day with the respective superior headquarters.

The troops of the RF company were in high spirits and were delighted that the sub-sector advisory team was with them for the night. Below the bridge, based on one bank, was a USMC scuba team. They threw fragmentation grenades into the water at irregular intervals, as a deterrent to any VC underwater saboteurs. An old span from the rail bridge sat in the water from the Japanese days in the early 1940s. As the marines had a rubber boat on the water, they gladly gave me a run along the Thach Han River to a platoon outpost on the west bank to the south of the bridge. Their siting was sound, but their protective measures were minimal—one strand of concertina wire—and there was a lack of communication to the company headquarters on the bridge.

A curfew was in force from 7:00 P.M. to 7:00 A.M. and was rigidly controlled by the U.S. and Vietnamese military. That was a pleasant surprise. The night sky was clear of cloud, the moon shone, and a warm, gentle breeze made it a beautiful setting. Fishermen were out on the river before dawn. Binh mentioned that children could swim in the river in more peaceful times but not now. During my time in the province the bridge was not attacked. Perhaps the enemy wanted to keep the bridge intact for their later use.

There were many examples of dedication to duty by my fellow district advisors. One of note was Major Simpson when he came out of Gio Linh, homeward bound. He had served his twelve months there, broken by two months on a hospital ship recovering from hepatitis. He had not taken R&R leave during his year. I admired his endurance, a credit to the man.

I took an opportunity helicopter flight in a Huey to the Cua Viet with the naval liaison officer on 21 June. The police advisor accompanied us. The purpose was to have initial discussion about deploying NPFF members on naval boats undertaking ship-to-shore resupply to the Dong Ha ramp. The police had an interest in the local fishing fleet. The knowledge gained on this visit proved to be useful a few months later during Operation Fisher. The Cua Viet waterway was a supply route for the allies into Quang Tri. Huge tonnages came in by barge to the Dong Ha ramp, fourteen kilometers inland. The throughput was running at fifteen hundred tonnes per day. The capacity at Dong Ha was higher than Wunder Beach in Hai Lang District.

That night at 10:30 P.M. a practice stand-to alert was exercised at the MACV compound. This was the first turn-out since my arrival in Quang Tri. In my view the alert highlighted shortcomings in what should have been a straightforward procedural drill. There was scope also for improved sighting of machine guns, the main defensive weapons at our disposal. The compound had another turn-out on the night of 17 August upon receiving an alert from Hue. To complicate the routine, a commanding officer's directive had been misunderstood by the compound commander. It was not the intention to go to a 50 percent alert immediately. The officer in charge looked and behaved like Ensign Parker in *McHale's Navy.* In essence, professionals were acting like amateurs, but it was a useful learning experience for all involved.

My reflection in the diary entry written late that night was: "Some people say this war is a crusade. Who is the infidel? Where is our charity, understanding and wisdom, gained from history and experience? It is time for me to remember and not forget the elephant in the room: armed aggressive communism."

On another round of inspections with the district chief I observed a PF platoon and two RD teams endeavoring to provide security for a civilian work party. It was evident that they were undertrained. They did not appear to have any semblance of effectiveness. I thought that a major resource allocation would be required to lift their skills. The obligations of PF and RD people in regard to their employment was so limiting with respect to location and flexibility of deployment that on-the-job training would be the best way to lift their performance. Talented leadership was a core need for improvement, but sadly was lacking.

The I Corps senior RF/PF advisor, Lieutenant Colonel Rice, came up from Da Nang for a familiarization and assessment visit on 24 June. He was well prepared, as his knowledge of the Territorial Forces was comprehensive. It was obvious he had undertaken a thorough map analysis in his office. The sector RF/PF advisor, Major Brad Oliver, U.S. Army, was the nominated local escort officer. Mai Linh was the last sub-sector to be visited. Ramos, two interpreters, and I were the guides for the Mai Linh part of the visit. Three key bridge sites were visited, as they each had an RF company located on them to provide protection. Two villages to the east of the district, Hai Quy and Hai Troung, were also visited. In these we observed PF platoons at the hamlets of Thuong Xa and Van Van. It was arranged with the village chief of Hai Quy that the visiting party would stay overnight in his locality.

We were content to fit into the usual night defensive routine for the local hamlet. However, other plans were set in motion. The village chief was making sure that the visitors were well protected, and that we were not to be put at risk in his village. Our presence there gave rise to the amending of defensive plans that had already been agreed to some days before. By 5:00 P.M. changes were passed down the line and adjustments commenced. The result was the redeployment of three PF platoons and two RD teams. A marine CAP squad had to conform to the new defensive layout. As their plans had already been approved, they were obliged to seek authorization to redeploy themselves, to conform to the PF relocation. To his credit the CAP commander handled the situation well, exercising his responsibilities in an exemplary manner.

It was a balmy night. Our hosts in the village made sure each of the visitors had a bunker or weapon pit close at hand should enemy action take place. During the early hours a few shots were heard on the south side of the creek, which caused an alert. Families scrambled into their own bunkers. Activity quieted down, and no further action was required. The sentries continued with their watching and listening. The villagers slept.

There was relief all around at dawn as the night had been uneventful. After going through the courtesies with our hosts, the PFs and the CAP squad moved out. Rice was satisfied with his visit. He had been seen. He had seen and he had listened to us and the

Vietnamese. The visit was one of those more pleasant experiences that gave satisfaction. I had wondered, of course, while so deployed how we would have performed if the enemy had committed themselves to an impromptu attack. In the circumstances a response was most unlikely, as enemy action was normally preceded by thorough, time-consuming reconnaissance. That night the odds were well in our favor.

A few days later sub-sector staff and advisors attended a sector-sponsored armed forces display of our own and enemy equipment. This was a propaganda event and went off well. To add entertainment value to the day a USMC L-19 aircraft dropped leaflets into the arena. In conversation with a USAF FAC pilot at the display I discovered that the pilot was in a whimsical frame of mind that day: "The U.S. had occupied the wrong country after the Gulf of Tonkin incident. We should have gone into North Vietnam, as the South had done little wrong."

An Air America helicopter was made available to my team for reconnaissance purposes on a Friday afternoon in mid-June. Bids for this kind of support were sometimes called for by sector. As a staff officer, infantryman, and aviator, it was too good an opportunity to ignore. For a second time I headed for the Cua Viet delta area to our north, seven kilometers from the DMZ boundary. A number of waterways found their way out to sea through this area, including the Cam Lo River from the west and the Thach Han from the southwest. My particular interest was on the nature of the terrain and the influence it would have on mechanized operations, both our own and the NVA's. The major obstacle was the waterway.

The next morning I drove south and then east into Hai Lang District, with a view to become familiar with a recently established beachhead named Wunder Beach. The distance from Quang Tri City was twenty-two kilometers. Just seven kilometers short of the coast, I crossed Route 555, one of the local "Streets without Joy." The hamlet of My Thuy was relocated to make way for the Wunder Beach complex. I attended the 57th Transport Battalion weekly briefing as a guest of the commanding officer, Lieutenant Colonel Deagle. This unit had an important but narrow role, moving combat necessities like ammunition, wire, sandbags, and rations to the forward maintenance bases in the Dong Ha area. They were busy and seemed to be outside the information loop of MACCORDS. I was pleased to make an advisor contribution to their knowledge when asked to speak. They were not aware that there was a district senior advisor at Hai Lang sub-sector. I wondered what the DSA at Hai Lang was doing. Deagle and his team helped my district advisory team in that they made available to us building materials no longer required by them, including lumber, cement, and corrugated iron sheeting for civil affairs projects.

An arbitration situation arose on 28 June. I was to discover that the advisor had a role to play in friendly disputes, and on occasions the outcome was resolved by convincing the parties that they had to live and work with the situation at hand. Open communication, cooperation, and sound coordination were the main ingredients. Interpreters were always useful in such a situation. Command perceptions were sometimes an underlying issue, and could not be avoided and had to be understood. "My turf" and "your turf" mentalities added to the mix.

The first case involved the RF company and an Air Cavalry Division (ACD) squad at the Nung Bridge. They had a disagreement over a grassfire in a minefield. This led me to liaise with the operations officer (S3) at the 1st Air Cavalry Brigade headquarters and the S3 at sector level. Clearly the parties were having difficulty in working together, and each had a separate chain of command. As the fire ran itself out so did the dispute. Time healed this conflict.

The next advisor call-out at the bridge was to avoid a possible dispute. A company from a battalion of the ACD was in a defensive locality at the bridge. This company had a secondary role, which was to respond to a recall to the local ACD fire base. Advisors were required to act as liaison should a recall of the company occur. The artillery FO and accompanying squads, as earlier mentioned, were to remain in place. There appeared to be a degree of nervousness within the ACD, which had to be respected. A relief arrangement for the advisors was created, and the necessary preparations made. A recall did not arise, so the arrangements were not tested.

Binh, my interpreter, was a source of interesting information. After about two months of our working together he had these two pearls for me. First, for those PF soldiers who were not available for duty, but were working elsewhere, the personnel officer would retain their pay for his own use. The quandary for me as an advisor was what to do with that kind of information? Could it be rumor or fact? Either way, I decided to not take the information any further.

I also judged the next matter to be beyond the scope of my responsibilities. There was a national draft system for young men to give service in the ARVN. Further, all people had to carry an identity card. If a person was a member of the RD, police field force, PRU, RF, or PF and the like, that information was shown on the identity card. So as to avoid the national draft, a young man could enlist in one of the local organizations, military or paramilitary, and his identity card would show such employment. Binh explained that a bribe could be made to an issuing officer for an identity card that showed membership in one of these organizations without having to show evidence of such membership. As sharp practice throughout Vietnam was not an exclusive activity of only high-level officials, one could only make note and get on with the job at hand.

A celebratory event was organized by the province military staff for recently promoted officers on 6 July. Major Nhan was being promoted, to lieutenant colonel, along with two junior officers. It was a pleasant social occasion, with entertainment being provided to help lift the spirits. I was to work closely with Nhan in the coming months. His interests outside the military, however, were to be his undoing in 1969.

Bill Coviello and I hosted our counterparts and the police chief to the club for a social get-together on 8 July. We worked closely with these men, and on most days our security and safety was in their hands. So, expressing our appreciation of them this way showed them that friendship was part of the relationship. We took them seriously and respected the responsibilities that they carried in their communities.

As a follow-up to the earlier visit of Lieutenant Colonel Rice, the principal ARVN staff officer for the RF/PF in I Corps, Colonel Vinh visited the sector headquarters. He wanted to hear from the local commanders involved with the Territorial Forces in Quang Tri Province. The meeting was advertised as a training conference. At a large gathering of district chiefs, and all available RF/PF commanders, Colonel Vinh let them have their say. Some advisors were present. It was a very useful open forum and pleasing to see junior leaders and to hear their concerns. The stand-out problem from the floor was a general concern about a shortage of barrier materials—sandbags and wire and iron pickets, described otherwise as defense stores. It was stated that the 1st ARVN Division headquarters had control of these materials. Stocks were available, but they were not getting through to Quang Tri. Perhaps there was a lack of understanding of staff responsibilities in these matters. A logistic problem was creating an operational problem. The need for ARVN and Territorial Forces integration was highlighted. This failure to have unity of command in such a vulnerable area on the DMZ was not in the national interest. The officers from Da Nang followed up on all matters raised.

The accumulation of new experiences over the past two months and their impact on me led to another reflective moment on 14 July: "Sometimes I feel I have lost some of my exuberance, due maybe to the responsibilities of my profession and my family. Perhaps this is a natural and good thing, as with the gaining of experience and responsibility the perspective on life matures the getting of wisdom."

A CAP patrol at Thuong Xa, acting on information from sector, killed an enemy soldier named Bui Tu on 16 July. He was a senior VC in this area, wore an NVA uniform, and carried an AK-47. He also carried a lot of information by way of documents. This was a big intelligence breakthrough by the local forces. Bui Tu carried a "Hammer and Sickle" flag in his pack, the flag of the U.S.S.R. Photographs of police and other minor officials were also in his pack, as well as layouts of all vital places in Quang Tri City, including the police station and CORDS houses.

Further information trickled out about Bui Tu. His appointed office was that of a VC district chief with the rank of captain. Lieutenant Colonel John Bibb of CORDS was very pleased on hearing of the death of Bui Tu, as he had been after him for two years. John claimed that he was the province senior advisor equivalent for the VC in the province. Bui Tu was clearly a key organizer and administrator for the VC, and arguably could have been an organizer of guides for NVA units coming in from across the DMZ. My counterpart, Captain Ton That Phong, expressed the view that the loss to the VC would be equivalent to a GVN loss of a province chief. As a follow-up, the sector authorities arrested two VC males, one being an interpreter working with a nearby unit. Morale lifted with these results. Retaliation by the enemy's 10th Sapper Battalion to the death of Bui Tu was expected by the PF and CAP at Thuong Xa. Fortunately this did not come to pass. A month later awards were presented to ten PF soldiers for the Thuong Xa action. Lieutenant Colonel Nhan conducted the ceremony.

A counterintelligence team (CIT) was allocated to Mai Linh on 19 July. The team specialized in security and intelligence matters.

Lieutenant Colonel Ngo Thanh Nhan and Captain Ton That Phong, July 1968.

It was very pleasing to have a local CIT, as the team allowed for a quick response to any information that needed to be acted upon. More pleasing organizational news was to follow on 27 July.

On the night of 20 July the local police, assisted by PF platoons, carried out a sweep through buildings and houses around the Mai

Linh District headquarters compound. The advisors were not informed of this operation, but were pleased to hear of it the next day. Our attention was drawn to the activity by the continuous barking of dogs. Suspects were rounded up. Suspects were those not in possession of identity cards, draft dodgers, deserters, or strangers to the area. Activities similar to this were routine, and their merits were debatable, but on balance, in the prevailing conditions, they were necessary. During my time in Quang Tri Province the Mai Linh compound was not attacked. This was a reflection of the level of security that had been achieved since Tet. The local VC organization was probably in a demoralized state.

During the second half of July three incidents highlighted the fact that vigilance at the Nung Bridge area and on the west side of Thach Han River had to be maintained. The RF company had a contact on 15 July, resulting in seven enemy killed and no friendly casualties. Lieutenant Colonel Nhan was prompt in recognizing this result by presenting four awards in a ceremony on the bridge the following afternoon. One week later an RF battalion conducted an operation on the west side of the river, moving from south to north. Unfortunately, a booby trap mine exploded, killing four RF soldiers and wounding four others. There were no enemy casualties. The RF company at the bridge had an incident with a squad of the ACD located there on 24 July. The cavalry troops had been drinking beer, and the young officer present was not in full control of himself or his troops. Despite a report being provided, the officer was not relocated. This area was to have our attention over the coming months.

U.S. Air Force FACs had a team located in our compound. They were designated as a detachment of the 20th Tactical Air Support Squadron. We were pleased to host them, as they were a fundamental link for close air support operations. As part of their aerial function they performed reconnaissance, acting as airborne observers of events, actions, or movements on the ground. The FACs flew their aircraft from a landing ground at La Vang.

Our co-located USAF FAC pilots took me for reconnaissance flights in a Cessna O-1 over areas adjacent to the DMZ on four days late in July. By this time in my career I had flown over 1600 hours in my Australian Army aviation appointments. The FAC overview of the battle areas complemented ground coverage by the troops and other sensor devices deployed. The relatively remote Balong area to the southwest was also covered on two occasions. When flying in a light aircraft over possibly hostile territory, I did not allow my mind to be distracted by imaginings of the likelihood of enemy ground fire being directed at the aircraft. There were no positive sightings made on these missions. The most exciting moment of each sortie was the landing, with a twenty-knot crosswind.

I learned a number of in-flight techniques used by the FAC pilots on their single-pilot visual reconnaissance missions. One concerned the locating of possible infiltration routes used by the NVA in grassland country. Flares, or white phosphorus grenades, would be dropped into dry grasses to burn off the growth. The next day they would return to that area to discover if any trails had been revealed. Someone else had to discriminate the animal trails. Reports to intelligence staffs were then submitted. Another technique required the use of binoculars. The Cessna O-1 had a stick control, which the pilot could hold between his knees to retain stability, allowing two hands to be applied to the binoculars. This aircraft had advantages over the Australian Army Cessna 180, which had a wheel-type control column, requiring the pilot to have at least one hand on the control column most of the time.

On the morning of 27 July the Mai Linh sub-sector headquarters conducted a meeting under the chairmanship of the executive officer with a view to organizing a District Intelligence and Operations Coordination Center (DIOCC). After much discussion, the chairman made the decision to get things started in three days' time. As soon as I was satisfied that the center was to commence operations, contact was made with the S2 of the 1st Brigade, ACD, and the assistant G2 of the 3rd Marine Division. They were invited to become familiar with the Mai Linh center. Their interest was in the enemy order of battle and what was known of enemy intentions. Any information of the enemy was useful to their analysts. By early August the center was judged to be effective, and was deemed a source body on enemy information for the district and province authorities, and for the police and military staffs. As the DIOCC evolved it became evident that photographs and fingerprinting were essential tools for interrogation teams. These province-level teams needed to be mobile and had to work closely with each center. Joint interrogations with center representatives were judged to be necessary to ensure optimum intelligence outcomes.

As discussion on the enemy organization developed, the knowledge base on the sensor devices below the DMZ increased. The

USAF dropped sensor devices in certain outer areas of the province and over the border in Laos. A picture could be built up on what the enemy movements might be in those areas, but there was conjecture about enemy intentions. Response to elements of information could not be acted upon immediately. Trends had to evolve. The outer security shield could then be tasked later with certain objectives.

I found myself conducting orientation visits for newcomers to the province by the end of July. The advisory elements at the sector level encouraged such activity, as familiarization for new arrivals was essential, and at the same time it was a "showing of the flag" to local people. On this occasion the party included Major David Dahl, USAF, one of the FAC team, Sergeant Bob Hogg, and two members of a counterintelligence team. We visited hamlets in Hai Quy village, the Choi Hoi hamlet, and the Trieu Phong District headquarters. The journey was uneventful, but I thought the passengers were a bit on edge, a natural sensation for those new to the province.

Some days had a garrison community aspect about them. Socializing was maintained, judged as important, despite being in a theater of war. At the local helicopter pad Warrant Officer Bill Deanshaw and I met four Australian warrant officers on a visit to Quang Tri from Hue. Bill took them in hand. At lunch that same day I was a guest of the commander of the 1st Brigade, ACD, Colonel John F. Stannard. The principal guest was his division commander, Major General Richard L. Irby. Other guests included Lieutenant Colonel Hanh, commanding officer of the 1st ARVN Regiment, Major Ferguson, his senior advisor, and officers of the staff of the ACD. Later that day I attended a reception held by the province chief. In a private conversation he was lamenting about things in general, and expressed his feelings of inadequacy in his job. With an "all care and no responsibility" attitude of mind I expressed my view, one of encouragement along the lines that he should have confidence in himself as he continues in the job and needs to be seen to be leading. I reminded him that the difficulties during the Tet offensive were in the past, that the enemy had been dealt with, and that he had been promoted.

I summed up the situation on 1 August with these words: "Things very quiet, and right now the VC and the NVA have retired hurt. We are on the alert, planning to seek out and to close with the enemy." The NVA and VC main force units had withdrawn to their base areas to the west, in the forested mountains abutting their supply route in Laos. They had left the battlefield for the time being. Senior U.S. commanders were sorting out a strategy, with the GVN, for the future. The Paris Peace Talks were getting under way. The U.S. MACV commander, General Westmoreland, had handed over his responsibilities to his deputy, General Creighton W. Abrams, on 12 June 1968. I wondered if our respective home fronts were being informed of the plight of the enemy and the dominance of the allies on the battlefield.

I visited the ACD at LZ Sharon on 3 August, where a battalion of the recently arrived 1/5 Infantry Brigade was lodged. The terrain was open here. There was a heavy troop concentration. The troops had dug in with overhead protection, to provide defensive precautions against mortar and rocket attack. I noted that wire obstacles, a protective measure against enemy ground attack, were not well developed.

Diary entries in early August further reflected happenings of a garrison duty nature: "The District Chief informed me that a PF platoon in a La Vang hamlet reported that US troops from the neighbouring Cavalry Brigade were in the settlement seeking female company. It was fortunate that the troopers were not shot. Next day I accompanied the district chief to the headquarters of 1st Brigade, ACD, so that he could formally lodge his concerns. It was clearly time for the Cavalry to move on."

Then there were foolish accidents. A report came in of two mortar rounds landing in La Vang hamlet. On investigation the next morning it was found that a PF soldier on sentry duty had held grenades in both his hands, with the safety pin removed from each. It began to rain so he took action to put on his raincoat, setting the grenades on the ground, forgetting that he had removed the safety pins. One soldier was killed and another was seriously wounded.

Later in the day I accompanied the district chief to visit the family of the dead solider in their home. The body was laid out on a bed, wrapped in a white sheet. Candles burned with a crucifix and holy pictures set on a bedside table. There was a profound sadness within his family over their tragic loss. This scene would be a typical and a frequent occurrence throughout Vietnam, North and South. Vietnamese people were bleeding and weeping, for what? Forty-one years later, Eva and I were able to better appreciate the heartache of a parent at the loss of child, when our beloved youngest son died.[3]

The next night was disturbed on two occasions by civilians firing their weapons over the district headquarters compound. All ranks were on alert. The question each time was: "What next?" The district chief was practical, with the down-to-earth cryptic comment: "civilian forces." We stood down, continuing normal night routines.

On 6 August we were back at La Vang Trung hamlet. A police operation was under way. A warrant authorizing a search had been issued by a province judge following the arrest of a male person selling opium eighteen days before. Those involved in the search included the police, PF troops, and hamlet officials. The house subject to the search was occupied by a fifty-nine-year-old grandmother and her pregnant daughter, aged thirty-three years, who was the mother of nine children. The search was orderly, with reports written on the spot recording the result. Nine people signed the documents. Civil order did prevail it seemed, despite the warfare.

Major David Dahl, Bill Deanshaw, and I traveled along Highway 1 to Dong Ha and the headquarters of the 2nd ARVN Regiment the next day. There was a very big traffic jam at the Nung Bridge, due to the deployment of the newly arrived 1/5 Infantry Brigade. The convoy spread over miles. This was the first occasion that David, the FAC pilot, had traveled this far north on the ground. To add interest to the visit, incoming enemy artillery rounds were landing in the Dong Ha area but not near the 2nd Regiment headquarters.

We attended a regimental orders group for Operation Lamson 250. This operation involved the construction of a road and a bridge from the Gio Linh headquarters west to fire support base A1. The road was designed to assist in the interdiction of NVA infiltrator routes, the latter being creek beds and the railway. An ARVN engineer officer conducted the orders, which were long and verbose. The supporting plans presented were well thought out, covering artillery, air, the enemy, and areas of operation.

The engineer commander had a sense of humor. When asked how long the operation would take, he patiently replied, "Probably fifteen days then back for a drink, but if NVA artillery targeted the operation, then perhaps three months." Later this area was to be included in a joint land clearing operation that concluded in February 1969. At the end of the proceedings the three of us drove back to the city. There was a rare incident two days later. While airborne, Dahl's aircraft had an engine failure. He skillfully landed the single-engine aircraft on Highway 1, to the north of Dong Ha. The aircraft was recovered the next day by a CH-47 Chinook helicopter and returned to the home airfield at La Vang.

Sector advised the sub-sectors of an intelligence summary that indicated a VC offensive against Quang Tri City. The time frame was 10–20 August, with the most likely time to be 18–20 August. This was passed down the line, giving the RF and PF reason to sharpen up. An offensive did not occur, but it was a timely reminder to be alert.

The USMC's Combined Action Program occasionally involved advisors when CAP relocation was to impact upon PF activities and dispositions. The district chief requested that I accompany him and the CAP commander to the hamlets of Dai Nai and An Thai. It was a reconnaissance. They selected the site for the deployment, near Highway 1, and then asked me for my views. Using the standard problem-solving logic of the military appreciation method, I was able to quickly gather my thoughts and spoke about the essentials: the task, the enemy situation, our troops, the terrain, and the civilian population. In the context of the defense of Quang Tri City and PF skills improvements, I thought it was a soundly based plan of action. So I was able to reassure the officers when I supported their scheme of things. There were smiles all around, and life proceeded.

The presence of CAPs provided scope for discussing the merits or otherwise of the allocation of areas of operation for their activities. The commanding officer of the 4th Combined Action Group, Lieutenant Colonel John Greenwood, had a strong preference for areas of operation for his CAPs. I supported the view of my district chief. He said that as the CAPs were working with the PF, it was the PF who had the responsibility of reporting their activities. He insisted planned patrols and ambushes be submitted to the headquarters of the delegated officer responsible for the area of operations each day, namely the district chief. I judged that the usefulness of frequent discussion on such a matter was counterproductive, especially when the local Vietnamese leader had the final say. Other marine channels at the province level may have been at work to ensure that the Combined Action Group view prevailed. By September the deputy province senior advisor agreed with the Vietnamese point of view on the issue, but cautioned against further discussion until October. This was a political move, as a PSA change-over was due at the end of September.

In early September the 4th Combined Action Group introduced a mobile training team into the district to work with the PFs. The marines to be involved in this initiative were experienced combat soldiers who to this point had no experience in working with the Vietnamese. I pondered on the economy and practicability of such an initiative, as the U.S. Army had similar MAT teams working with the RF.

The raising of a new RF company for Mai Linh District was announced on 9 August. The ceremony for this event was followed by a social to celebrate the occasion. The meal was very good, although I was not keen on eating initially due to an upset stomach. That evening an RF battalion operation was postponed. The headquarters of the 1st Brigade, ACD, was not prepared to agree to the proposed joint operation.

Documentation checks of Vietnamese people by the police were continuous. In a 20 July operation about one hundred people were required to further explain their circumstances. Explanations were normally required when shortcomings were discovered in personal documentation. A further police operation was conducted in the Quang Tri City area (part of Mai Linh district) on the night of 9 August. The district chief and I joined the police at dawn. The fieldwork was finalized by 9:00 A.M. Nine people without identity cards were escorted to the district headquarters for further investigation. I noted that the police appeared to be very casual in going about their tasks. I judged there was no point in sharing a personal view over the operational laxity, as it was clearly a district chief matter, one for him to ponder.

The next day I accompanied the district chief on a liaison visit to the headquarters of 1st Brigade, ACD, to organize a RF battalion operation in the La Vang hamlet area. The district chief was to control the operation. Other local forces to be involved were two PF platoons and thirty men of the district police. Troops from the ACD were not directly involved. Start time for the operation was 6:30 A.M. on 12 August. The start line was in the area of the basilica at La Vang, with a line of advance to the east as far as the railway, about two and a half kilometers. Progress was then north heading toward the city, terminating at the Chieu Hoi village, on the edge of the built-up area. The frontage for the operation was two companies forward, with the balance of the troops following.

There was a blast on the right, on the southern flank, soon after setting out. A mine had exploded, activated by a booby trap. Three PF soldiers and five RF soldiers were wounded. A medical evacuation helicopter was called in and collected the wounded in two lifts. This was a prompt response. With the casualty clearing station within six kilometers, the casualties were out of the operational area in minutes, less than half an hour after the incident.

About six hamlets in a rural setting were investigated during the morning. Suspects were rounded up as we progressed, gathered in the rear under control of the troops and police. In all, seven VC organizers, ten VC suspects, and seventeen other Vietnamese civilians, about half being female, were arrested. Most of the suspects held identity cards, but as they were in VC-controlled villages they were to be interrogated. The police carried out the interrogations in the field, or in housing out of sight. The VC organizers were encouraged to talk under the coercion of water treatment. This was torture, painful, but not to the point of death. As an Australian military professional, I was educated in the protocols that were in place about torture. To me what was happening was unacceptable, and thought provoking. There and then, but privately, I passed on these thoughts on torture to Captain Phong. The results of such interview techniques, or of the operation overall, were not passed to the advisors participating in the operation. The troops returned to barracks at 1:00 P.M. that day.

The people at the receiving end of this treatment, or who were inconvenienced by the operation, did not appear to be particularly upset outwardly. Since 1942 they had been in turmoil under one form of control or another; they were accustomed to suffering. On the face of it they appeared to be stoic, accepting the unacceptable as part of a way of life which they had little control over. What they were thinking was another matter. How was one to judge where their allegiances lay?

A week later the district chief and I were back at the ACD for a business lunch. A further operation planned for the next day was to be discussed to ensure the various friendly military units in the area clearly understood the plan of action. This operation was to be on the west side of the Thach Hanh River, to the southwest of Quang Tri City. This was in the area of the abandoned hamlets, centered on Nhan Bieu Two hamlet. Troops involved included an RF company, two PF platoons, and police, in all numbering about 140. The targets were forty-six blacklisted VC organizers.

We rose well before dawn on 19 August, finalized details, and left the district compound at 5:45 A.M. Some troops were moved in trucks and had a bandit appearance about them. Morale was high, the troops showing a lively spirit. Security and noise control were very poor at the start. Once in position the troops settled down. An advance to the south was on two axes. Six enemy suspects were seen in the distance. They were running to the southwest. Artillery fire support was brought down on them without any obvious success. They had gone to ground. A follow-up commenced.

In the meantime some information came to us from females working in a dry paddy. They led a PF platoon to a VC bunker, which was promptly attacked. Four soldiers were wounded in the assault and three VC were killed. One was Phan Thi, on the top ten wanted list for the province. Materials captured included an AK-47, one 9 mm pistol, binoculars, papers, and clothing, all useful for the intelligence people. Again the wounded were lifted out by a medevac helicopter.

With the excitement of the successful operation, the district chief called off the follow-up on the earlier sightings. On the way back to the start point, the main body with which I was moving was fired upon, small arms only. The district chief moved north with his team, out of the area of action, leaving the skirmishing to be organized by the RF company commander. The advisors remained with the troops. The RF company held its composure, deployed, and returned fire into the general area of the enemy. The firing of the small arms on each side was generally ineffective, with one PF soldier being slightly wounded. It seemed the troops on each side decided that enough had been done for this day, and methodically disengaged. As the troops moved north we regrouped with the district chief. He and the troops were very pleased with their efforts on this day and rightly so. The province chief and the PSA were advised of the death of Phan Thi.

Late that afternoon sector directed me to undertake an aerial visual reconnaissance in the Nhu Le area, and then further along the Thach Hanh River to the southwest. A light helicopter duly arrived to take me on board. The task originated from an ACD report of suspected enemy troop movement in the area. The district staff thought civilians working in the area might have been sighted. No unusual sightings were observed, so there was nothing of substance to report. So much for that, but alertness was required.

Widespread but limited enemy mortar activity occurred on the night of 22 August. Over fifty rounds were fired into Hai Lang, Ai Tu, and La Vang and into the Citadel. The MACV compound was on alert for ninety minutes. There was no follow-up by either side.

In the second half of August 1968 two reports highlighted the uncertainty that existed in the populated areas. First, a police report claimed that a regiment-sized NVA force was eight kilometers to the east, in an area on the edge of the arable land, abutting the sandy coastal fringe. The city was placed on alert and a curfew was applied from noon. All ranks were required to test-fire weapons. Opinion was that enemy action could take place at night. The report had sharpened alertness. There was no contact with the enemy. Second, on the same day VC dressed as soldiers of the ARVN infiltrated into the Ai Tu marine airport terminal area and exploded a claymore mine hidden in a bag. Some U.S. casualties resulted.

Later in August the work of local intelligence gatherers within the district led to a noteworthy action, and a good outcome. Information came in that VC propagandists were to work in the hamlet of Thuong Xa that night. They were mobile visitors, not local villagers. The military plan was to deploy three PF platoons on their likely withdrawal and departure routes from Thuong Xa. The result was seven VC killed that night. Of particular interest was that marine CAP elements had not been assigned to the three PF platoons. The district chief was pleased with the results of this operation. A further positive outcome was that the district chief announced that he was now in favor of sharing command post facilities with the advisors at the sub-sector headquarters.

Up to this time military advisors had not been closely integrated with their counterparts within the district headquarters. There was more to co-location than being in the same compound as those whom we were assisting. Physical separation up to then could have been as a result of a combination of factors: cultural, language, security, separation of lines of command and control, and perhaps a lack of mutual trust.

Sharing command post facilities was an operational necessity in my view. To some it may have been treated as an experiment. Although we had to hasten with caution, my approach was very positive as I was already convinced that as advisors it was imperative that we be as close to our counterparts as possible. There were long-term consequences here. We were in the business of saving South Vietnam. We had to be fully immersed in thinking, preparing,

Happy soldiers after finding a package of VC TNT, August 1968.

planning, and executing military operations with the South Vietnamese against the NVA and VC forces. In the short term there were advantages in helping each other be better informed on all issues. These were life and death matters for all of us.

A recent intelligence report indicated that the VC were being supplemented by three-man teams of NVA soldiers. It could be that the North was operating with advisors along the MACV model. If true, this further reflected the poor state of VC units in South Vietnam.

A steady stream of commanders and staff officers of the many U.S. units and headquarters made contact with advisors of Team 19 during the month of August. This highlighted that the counteroffensive was under way. In hindsight, these interactions were preparing me for my later employment at the sector level with Team 19.

Two days later we were back in the Nhan Bieu Two area. Captain Sang had operational control of two RF companies and two PF platoons. It was a follow-up to what was now being referred to as the earlier "Phan Thi operation." Although control of the sub-units left a lot to be desired, their search discovered the former position of an 82 mm mortar base plate, two mortar rounds, forty-eight pieces of C4 explosive, and a four-gallon drum of explosives. This operation was well resourced. An observation helicopter was in support, with the district chief and Captain Coviello being able to scout aloft. We were better prepared on this operation for any follow-up should any suspects decide to withdraw to the southwest as the troops advanced. There were no sightings.

The sub-sector was involved in a sector operation in the area of An Thai, to the southwest abutting Highway 1, on 4 September. The dominant factor of the day was heavy rain. The RF battalion, operating to the east, suffered four wounded from a grenade booby trap. The pouring rain prevailed, with the operation declared at an end at 10:30 A.M. Short-term field operations, some less than half a day, and often driven by conditions of employment rather than operational needs, did not reflect well on the Regional Forces. Their lack of capability for sustained operations in the field, regardless of weather conditions, was detrimental to effectiveness, and a frustration for advisors. These negative signs did not argue well for the future.

The VC provided a response to our activities on the other side of the river. That night the Quang Tri Citadel was mortared at 10:10 P.M. from an area to the southwest around Nhan Bieu Two. Five mortar rounds fell near the tactical operations center. There were no casualties. The next morning the Mai Linh S3 and I went on a ground reconnaissance to the Nhan Bieu Two area on a follow-up to the action of the previous evening. It was a washout, with the pouring rain washing away any evidence. Procedural processes set in train in response to the mortaring highlighted the need for co-location of command posts and TOCs at each level. Reduction in time delays in decision making was necessary, such as a response to a mortar attack.

In early September I accompanied a battalion commander of the 1st Brigade, ACD, on an aerial reconnaissance of the Nhan Bieu Two area to indicate possible locations of the mortar base plate sites from which the city had been mortared. This close cooperation at the unit command level reflected well on the effectiveness of the policy directions coming from the GVN and MACV levels. I was then involved with the S5 of the 1st Brigade, ACD, in an early morning investigation of an accidental discharge of an M79 grenade launcher. This incident caused two deaths and injured eight civilians. This was in the La Vang village area close to the ACD location. We were unable to assist and left the inquiry to the local and military police to sort out.

In a few days' time I was to leave my position in Mai Linh and move to a sector operational staff officer appointment. Before covering that part of my story I would like to describe my involvement as an advisor in the civil sphere of Mai Linh District. Pacification was the term used to describe the nonmilitary activities undertaken within a combined set of GVN and U.S. aid programs in South Vietnam.[4] They were intertwined with the counterinsurgency activities outlined in this chapter.

6

Pacification in Mai Linh District

May–August 1968

The responsibility for the policy and organization of pacification programs and material support rested mainly on a number of U.S. civil agencies, including the U.S. Agency for International Development (USAID), the Central Intelligence Agency (CIA), the U.S. Information Service, the U.S. Department of State, and the USAF Logistic Support Group. In the field, CORDS with military support delivered the programs. The funded programs provided the long-term building blocks for economic, social, and political development that would be influential in partially determining, with the military effort, the sustainability of the sovereign state of South Vietnam. By these means we were determined to win the hearts and minds of the people. Here is a snapshot of my part and that of others in this enormous joint enterprise. The preparation and implementation of two later national pacification campaigns is described in chapter 10, "Pacification Campaigns, Strengthening the Spine."

An early rural experience in the district was educational for me. Prompted by U.S. civilian advisors and a local Revolutionary Development (RD) team, the district chief arranged a demonstration of rice threshing at a local rural village. The demonstration was the basis of a comparative efficiency test between a buffalo and a purpose-built machine. This device relied on pedal power to rotate it for rice threshing. The existing rice threshing system traditionally involved two buffaloes and a boy. Rice stalks were stacked in a circle about four meters in diameter, and the buffaloes walked around the circle for about two hours. The stalks were then turned over, and the two-hour process was repeated. (Those of us observing did not have to sit through a full four-hour demonstration.)

We then watched a brief demonstration of the machine with

farmers and village officials. After twenty minutes of observation the group then adjourned for a cup of tea. A long discussion ensued. I am unable to say what was finally decided. It was an interesting experience. This demonstration of mechanization illustrated the extent of the U.S. presence, and the attempted cultural penetration into the established rural way of life of the South Vietnamese. From the Vietnamese point of view there was a lot to be said for the buffalo. The usefulness and contribution of this event to the war effort was questionable.[1] One of the buffalo used in the rice threshing demonstration was killed that night by troops of the nearby Air Cavalry Brigade. This unfortunate occurrence took some of the gloss off the goodwill that may have been gained during the demonstration the day before.

Within a few days of my settling into Mai Linh, in May 1968, there was a sharp explosion outside the district compound. Two young boys had been playing with a hand grenade and in the process accidentally killed themselves. I recorded that "there must be extensive sadness in many families here, but it is not obvious."

The district chief, Captain Coviello, and I visited the CORDS warehouse on 26 May to get the facts on a report of a suspected theft. It appeared that troops of the 1/4 ARVN Regiment were threatening the civilian staff and local security forces at the warehouse site. The soldiers, about to depart south to the National Training Center for retraining, were seeking certain provisions. Having listened to the various points of view, the district chief gave his ruling and settled the dispute.

My early days were spent accompanying the district chief around the district inspecting and checking on village defenses and a garbage dump being used by the 1st Brigade, Air Cavalry Division. The dump was creating some difficulties. Described as a "garbage dump" by me, the United States used the term "sanitary fill," the need for which arose as a direct consequence of a large military concentration in a populated area. A local contractor had been organized by the brigade to provide a garbage removal service. This story highlights a wartime occupational health and safety issue in a friendly foreign country that would not have been tolerated in our parent countries.

After extensive prior consultations between brigade staff and local civil agencies, the sanitary fill was to have been operational within a few days. We were advised that some of the proceeds of any sale of recyclable materials would be allocated to local self-help organizations. Commitments were made by Vietnamese officials that security and protection would be in place the day before opening. However, a security detail was not provided, much to the frustration of the brigade staff. There were a number of security and public health issues to be resolved promptly. Major McDowell, the representative of the brigade, and I had no idea how this deal was going to work out.

Local people were scattered across the site, seeking food and salvage items. Children were being injured. It was a very depressing and sad situation. I returned to the district headquarters and convinced the district chief that he should have an on-site inspection. Despite his claim of being busy, he reluctantly agreed to my request. He knew the brigade staffs were concerned about the sanitary fill. I was able to tell the district chief that Major McDowell was clearly frustrated and felt let down. The PF security detail had not been allocated. The chief explained that he could not employ troops for this kind of work unless agreed to by the province chief. The district chief felt that if the people saw PFs recycling rubbish they could conclude that the returns would be going to him, and not the needy. We were back to basics when the district chief had fifty children on the site arrested on the afternoon of 31 May. They were confined for the night. It was alleged that they had been pilfering materials from the sanitary fill, and had been climbing onto passing trucks. The chief spoke to them firmly the next morning, laid down guidelines, and stated that their parents were to collect them. Those children remaining were to stay in confinement until collected by their parents.

Once the issues were resolved, it was not long before deals within deals became evident. Our advisory team was now referring to the sanitary fill as the district chief's garbage dump. The contractor had workers on the dump site collecting recyclable materials. He had two vehicles on the task. The materials were being sold on to the local market. Major McDowell then advised me he had to get legal clearance before he could sign a contract. By 11 July signatures had not been secured from the district chief or the contractor. My own frustrations about this experience had to be held in check, as was the case for McDowell. I judged that neither of us had imagined we would be involved as military officers in such a shamble as this particular sanitary fill. We just had to put up with it and do our best. To help lift our spirits McDowell and I tried to time his business visits to the district headquarters so that we could lunch together. This gave him a welcome change of diet.[2] He was very pleased to speak to me about his family and other personal events, and I was able to reciprocate with my family tales.

Eventually the province chief gave clearance for the district chief to task local police and the military to provide for security and safety on the site. Scavengers were to be excluded. The contractor thence had free rein to do his job, probably conditional on the province chief and the district chief receiving a percentage of the proceeds of sales. In early August I inspected the sanitary fill following a request from the brigade executive officer to keep people away from the trash dump. The local police and military detail were not on site, despite more recent assurances from the district chief that he and the police chief were providing the necessary men, mainly to meet the fair U.S. requirements from a public safety point of view.

The district chief was more concerned about the interests of the contractor and the recovery of good material than the health and well being of the people. He stated that there were only two hundred police, and that they were all committed to other tasks. Standing with him at the sanitary fill and after hearing his views, the main thought I felt like expressing to him was, "You are talking garbage, chief." I refrained. There were more dramas over money, and offerings were made to McDowell and me by minor officials that could be considered bribes. We told the various players that we were not interested in what we considered to be possible corrupt practices. We tried our best to keep it solely a Vietnamese project. Tolerance was the order of the day for us, each day. The brigade left the area some weeks later, as did the problem of the sanitary fill.

A young Australian tourist arrived in the city on 5 July 1968, unannounced. He soon found the local Australians, Gordon Fitzgibbon and myself. John Everingham was from Queensland. After completing his schooling at eighteen years of age, he set out to see Asia. He had spent one year in Papua New Guinea, and then moved on to Thailand and Cambodia. He came into Vietnam from Laos on a one-month visa. That was his story. He spent the night with us at the MACV compound. The next day he flew out on travel orders with Fitzgibbon, to Phu Bai. We wished him safe traveling and a happy return home.

The district chief and I inspected the church/school/dispensary in the hamlet of Quy Thien, to the northeast of the Citadel, just beyond Tri Buu, on 30 May. The purpose of the visit was to hear a report from the Hai Tai village chief on the rice harvest. This was a beautiful village, traditional in form and culture, with lush vegetation and well-nurtured paddies. Under sound village and hamlet leadership, all was going well. The district chief was full of praise, and obviously would be wishing that other villages in the district would be of a like standard.

On return to the sub-sector headquarters we found the PSA, Mr. Brewer, present. He pressed upon us the need for the distribution of cement and corrugated galvanized iron sheeting so as to keep up monthly quotas. He pointed out that nothing had been carried out since Tet. The evidence indicated that there was an invisible barrier to be crossed between the saying and the doing. Captain Phong was able to remind the PSA that as district chief he planned for a district warehouse to be constructed. The district chief was firm as to what he wanted to do. He was not going to be diverted.

About two weeks later Brewer sent his local CORDS troubleshooter, John Cleary, on a courtesy call to see the district chief. The intent of the call was to discuss the material requirements to rebuild a local elementary school. The district chief thanked the advisors for calling on him and reminded the advisors that the matter was a GVN responsibility. He went on to explain that the school was not in the self-help category. There was no point in our pressing this matter further.

At the invitation of the district chief we then proceeded to the nearby refugee village at Tach Mon. In a regrettable incident, recent friendly artillery fire had destroyed a twenty-five-meter line of houses, home to some thirty families. The extent of casualties was not discussed. The district chief requested food and materials to help alleviate the distress being experienced by the refugees. There was clearly an opportunity for CORDS to carry out relief here. John Cleary informed the district chief that he would take the task on as a project. This was pacification at work.

At the end of May I noted that each day had been busy, and that time had seemed to pass quickly. I thought I was developing a good working relationship with the district chief, and I was generally happy with pacification progress in the prevailing circumstances. The record said: "It is hard to pinpoint just what has been achieved, and even if it has been minimal, we have been very busy doing it." I perceived the role of advisor could be a misnomer, as often my function was a matter of me being with the chief, when he invited me to join him, rather than me giving him a running commentary on whatever he was doing or planning to do. As a mentor I was there to assist him in his work, when requested.

I had been reflecting on and recording "impressions so far." The month had been a transforming one for me. The personal part of me asked these questions: "Is the morality of this war right?" and "Is the discord and the other side effects of war making the prosecution of the war worthwhile?" The professional part of me provided a reminder that "armed aggressive communism, with a rotten ideology and reliance on terrorism, wants to take over South Vietnam. I have to keep a focus on the task at hand. I am here to assist the people of South Vietnam to live in freedom."

In between the various field activities I had been undertaking with the district chief, time was being devoted to building contacts with the civic action officers in the various U.S. units in the province. Over several days I had discussions with Lieutenant Colonel Thompson, a G5 staff officer of the 3rd Marine Division. The marines indicated that they were committed to civic aid to the Vietnamese. The other significant U.S. military formation in the province, the ACD, was engaged in fighting in the west against the NVA, leaving little capacity for civic action at the present time.

On 31 May, Thompson held a meeting to consider a civic action program in the city. It struck me that more time might be spent on reports than on projects. However, the intentions were admirable. Likely projects were identified, ranging from medical aid posts to a dental team to work in Xuan An. It was noted at this meeting that the 41st Civic Action Unit was working with refugees in Quang Tri. Consultations then followed over the coming weeks with the district chief to set up a schedule of works for the district. By the end of June, I was in a position to provide a priority list to the civic action officers of the U.S. units. By mid-July positive responses came from the units. Funds were allocated for a number of district projects, including a generous amount for the purchase of desks and benches for schools in need. These commitments were welcomed by all parties involved in the initiatives.

Ramos was on an "ask no questions, boss" job and radioed in for assistance. He had a load of toys on his vehicle, which had broken down on Highway 1, and needed a lift. A light vehicle was borrowed so I could go out to help him. We transferred the packages, and as Ramos's vehicle was inoperable, we had to push it to the side of the road for later recovery. Despite indicating to a group of local police and Vietnamese military standing by that we needed help to push the vehicle to the side of the road, there were no volunteers. This was a disappointment, and noted as another frustration.

As a hobby, the district chief had some fish ponds near his residence. He cultivated carp. Two fish I saw taken from the water weighed about one and a half kilograms each. I did not really feel like sampling the product, as I knew what sort of water that the carp had grown in. The district chief was proud of his freshwater fish, but "fresh water" was as far from the fact as one could possibly get.

The morning of 18 June 1968 saw all of the staff of the district headquarters on their toes, as well as staff from the province level. Some very senior visitors were to come in to receive firsthand reports on local matters. The regional commander, I Corps' Lieutenant General Hoang Xuan Lam, from Da Nang, and the commanding general of III Marine Amphibious Force, Lieutenant General Robert E. Cushman, accompanied by their staff officers, made up a very impressive group on arrival at the humble district headquarters of Captain Phong. It was to be a three-hour visit.

It was an occasion for the advisors to be seen and not heard. Local Vietnamese leaders filled about half of the time briefing the visitors, and the remainder was spent on a guided tour to a village in the district. I felt right out of things, as there were too many cooks in this kitchen. Also, it was enlightening to see the confident manner in which the local officials, military and civil, went about their duties. What I learned then as an advisor was that if you feel you could be going around in circles, or marking time, it was best to keep out, especially if you felt redundant for the time being. Visits of this nature were confidence builders for all who shared the experience. It was becoming clear that the VC were generally demoralized. It was significant that the people in Quang Tri had not rallied to the communists during Tet 1968. This was so over most of South Vietnam.

One of the first projects that I initiated in the district came to fruition within one month. On one of my early orientation trips in the Dong Ha area I observed a section of a Bailey bridge abandoned in a field, and of course out of place. A few days later when accompanying the district chief on an inspection to the south of the district headquarters we came to the end of the roadway, at a creek running into the Thach Han River. Looking to the other bank, it was clear that a bridge had spanned the gap in the past. As we continued south on foot, I discussed the idea of providing a bridge to make it easier for the people and light vehicles to move around the area. The district chief was amenable to the idea, adding that it was planned for the bridge to be replaced but that from a government funding aspect it had a very low priority.

It was the kind of civil affairs pacification project that U.S. military units were keen on undertaking. It came to pass that a CH-54 Skycrane helicopter from the 1st Air Cavalry Division was available to carry the piece of bridging to near the site. A detachment of Seabees, navy construction engineers, prepared the site and fitted the bridge into place. On 23 June 1968, at a small ceremony, the district chief and the hamlet chief drove across the bridge. There were many smiling faces that day.

I gave a progress report to Mr. Brewer. Earlier he had given me clear guidance on a number of matters when I assumed my role in his team. I was more than satisfied to advise him of the outcome of the bridge initiative. At this discussion he was able to provide some further clarification about the Revolutionary Development (RD) team role. My observations on the RD contribution to pacification are to come later in this chapter.

Up to ten thousand graves were relocated by one thousand Vietnamese people in early 1968 to make way for the expansion of the 3rd Marine Division maintenance base at Ai Tu, five kilometers west of Quang Tri City. The marines handed over money for the project to the district chief. Only four hundred people were paid. It was asserted that the remainder of the funds went into the pocket of the district chief. The district chief claimed that the marines had yet to finalize the payment for labor as agreed earlier. Consequently, the people of Nhan Bieu had drafted a protest to General Lam at I Corps. On 17 August, I visited the G5 of the 3rd Marine Division and negotiated an agreement for the payment of the laborers from Nhan Bieu for the work done to remove the graves. When I advised the district chief of this development he said, "Thank you," without further comment.

The next major project was to be the construction of the district warehouse. GVN funds were not readily available. The district chief was keen to build a warehouse, so we worked up a project plan together, with design assistance from Lieutenant Grey of the 41st Civic Action Unit. As district senior advisor, I was responsible for an AIK (assistance in kind) revolving fund. Some of these funds were to be used to provide gravel and timber for the warehouse. My team had to scrounge bagged cement. The 3rd Marine Division Transport Battalion was to provide reinforcing iron and corrugated galvanized iron sheeting. The district chief was to organize sand and labor, possibly from the local civil prison. The design plan was presented to the district chief on 29 June. The chief approved the plan and authorized work to commence. On 4 July Lieutenant Grey marked out the site for the project.

I had a conversation with the RD advisor about his budget, and about the assistance available for the construction of a warehouse. The two of us later met with the district chief, enabling us to achieve an understanding of roles and contributions. A better working relationship was established. By mid-July the warehouse was about 50 percent complete. All the necessary materials were on site. Doors made up at a local joinery were delivered on time. The building was at lock-up stage in early August, and completed in September. The district chief was pleased with the outcome, as was our advisory team. During the warehouse project one was able to see snapshots of commercial reality in the business life of the local people in Quang Tri. Graft and corruption were part of the way of life for the Vietnamese, and as advisors we could not intervene, but just had to go along with it. One authoritative fellow told me that about 80 percent of money and resources toward particular projects could be expected to be lost on account of handouts, underhanded methods, pilfering, and theft.

In early July my advisory team experienced a brazen theft. Accommodation at the Mai Linh District headquarters was not provided for the advisors. Lieutenant Colonel Thrasher, assistant sector advisor for Team 19, had been urging my team to move out of the MACV compound in Quang Tri City and go to Mai Linh. I agreed in principle to that proposition, but until adequate accommodation became available it was not achievable, particularly as our rationing and amenities were at the nearby compound. All operational requirements were being met under the existing arrangements, so there was a bit of a stalemate. Additionally, I insisted that as the senior Australian in the province I was entitled to a room in the compound to help meet AATTV local needs.

It was prudent for me to keep my U.S. senior happy, so I kept him informed of my plans to build accommodation at Mai Linh for the district advisory team. At the time we were three in number and had an authorization of five. Essentially, we had to scrounge materials for the building. The Wunder Beach complex was a useful source for some basic materials. Tentage was not offered as a solution, and was not asked for. The district chief had already allocated a site to meet our needs. Materials for the construction of our building were stockpiled in the Mai Linh compound.

On the night of 6–7 July the materials disappeared. We suspected theft. Also missing was a variety of defense stores gathered to improve the perimeter defense for the compound. This theft was a disappointment. A trust had been broken. A few days earlier I had asked my interpreter to warn off a number of soldiers who had showed more than a cursory interest in the materials. When requested to recover the items, the district headquarters' First Sergeant Phuc informed my interpreter that the matter was for the district chief to resolve.

After considering possible actions, and consequences, I decided to insist that the items be returned within a day. This was a challenge to the district chief, and to make it clear about how seriously I considered the matter I informed him that should the items not be returned then any further direct material support from his district advisory team would be at risk. Material support for projects would continue, with direct delivery to the relevant sites. The thieves could do their stealing elsewhere, but not in our backyard.

Later that day I heard that the district chief had called his staff together after our chat and given certain instructions. Early the next morning I paid a courtesy call on the district chief and received a frosty reception. He discussed the pilfering problem, as we each realized it was necessary to keep on good terms, based on personal as well as sound professional relationships. As the district chief expected, the materials found their way back during the day, and the status quo was restored. Resulting from this relatively minor happening I think we came to understand each other a lot better. My initial irritation passed quietly, and although it would have been naive to think that there would not be any further difficulties, we had a firm base to work on. The district chief and I cemented our relationship with a cold drink that evening in the club.

A new district of Dong Ha was created on 10 July 1968. Invited guests from all districts in Quang Tri gathered at the township of Dong Ha, under province arrangements. The district chiefs of Cam

Lo and Trieu Phong signed the formal papers to transfer the land and hamlets to the new administrative entity. It all made sense, as there was a lot of activity in this area by allies, VC/NVA, and refugees. Advisors were impressed with the government's undertaking such a step when under serious stress.

Interpreter Binh had traveled to Dong Ha with me. He was not only a good friend by now but a teacher. Our conversations helped keep my morale up. While in a convoy of jeeps proceeding to the Dong Ha ceremony he informed me of some Vietnamese customs that had been written into a poem: "If invited to a party get to the food first," and "If you have to cross a river go last." We then discussed the Vietnamese flags, described by Binh as:

> The flag of South Vietnam: the background of yellow for skin (or race), and the three red stripes for the blood of the South, Central and North parts of Vietnam.
>
> The flag of North Vietnam: Red for the blood that must flow for the country and the yellow star for race.

On the way back to the city from Dong Ha we called on the U.S. Army's 18th Surgical Hospital to talk to a blind Vietnamese girl and her mother. They were going out to the hospital ship for treatment. Binh was able to ease some of the anxiety the pair were suffering. On the way out of the base Binh was able to collect some scrap wood for his house. People like Binh, then and now, were constantly on the alert for material that was treasure for them, but perhaps treated as trash by others.

The outgoing commanding general of the 1st ACD, Major General John J. Tolson, visited Mai Linh on 11 July to say farewell to the district chief. Captain Phong was not present. The chief had knowledge of the visit but elected to attend a meeting elsewhere. This was a disappointment. I was unable to fathom the reasoning of the district chief for this behavior, but I did not wish this particular event to lead to any general conclusion about allied relationships. That same day an advance party of the 1/5 Infantry Brigade was briefed for two and a half hours by sector staff. This was a timely dialogue for all parties; the dividends of the briefing were to be seen in the coming months. The pacification plans and needs were highlighted. The main body of this fresh formation was to arrive in the province toward the end of July.

Two days later the district police chief had me and Binh as guests at his home for a social occasion at 4 P.M. He and his wife had six children. His good friend was there, the local chief of the National Police Field Force. He was the father of nine children. They were both Catholic. They talked of local problems, giving me insights that I would not normally be privy to. Their view was that the VC controlled the countryside, where the people were poor. They thought that the VC were influential among the refugees. At this time there were about forty thousand refugees in Quang Tri. Both agreed that the war could go on for a long time, and that should a truce be struck, and the U.S. and the NVA leave South Vietnam, then a civil war would ensue. As the future was to reveal, they were about half right, in that the U.S. combat units were out of South Vietnam by 1972, but not the NVA.

A few days later I drove with the police security chief at his invitation to the Y junction on Highway 1 to inspect a wrecked police post there. The district chief would not accept a requisition for the purchase of materials to repair the post, as he held the view that it was a government asset, and thus did not fall into the RD/Self-Help category for funding. After discussion at the site, the policeman decided to deem the post as a meeting place with a psychological warfare role. A new requisition was lodged the next day, and duly approved.

The district chief, acting under direction of the province chief, requested that I purchase medals to be awarded to two U.S. Marines and three Popular Force (PF) soldiers. This was a surprise. I had to politely inform him that I was not in a position to do such a thing. It did not show much national pride in the GVN military awards system. On reflection I thought that the question may have been put to test me.

In mid-July Sergeant Bob Hogg, a U.S. Army medical corpsman and the fourth member of my district advisory team, arrived for duty. I gave him eight areas of responsibility. He noted these and created a job for himself. He was good with tools and decided to fix our accommodation problem at Mai Linh District headquarters before he did anything else. He handled the electricity and refrigeration trades as well. My diary entry at that time said: "Things have been humming along lately, and I'm getting plenty of satisfaction in my work." On reflection, having a competent advisory team made for a more effective contribution by the advisors, as is the case in most enterprises. Also, to be covered later, more military staffs were coming into the area as a consequence of the Tet counteroffensive. Just to spoil a nice run, our team vehicle was on its last legs.

Then a more mundane thing occurred. Sergeant Hogg's effort included provision of some office space for the team. One morning there were signs of entry into the office, via the roof, and defecation from above onto a chair. The district chief gave the view that it was one of the marines living in a roof bunker who was the culprit, being upset that the advisory team had an office to work from. The district chief had the last word. "Move on" I said to myself. Once our building was completed we found we had company—rats. Despite precautions, rats continued to run around our bunker and accommodation at Mai Linh.

My writings and letters to home during the last week of July included the following:

> Work still enjoyable and I am beginning to sense that the Vietnamese officers on the District Chief staff now do more work, and the advisors a little less. Confidence within the Vietnamese may have been returning following the negative effects of the earlier enemy Tet offensive. The apparent positive recovery is creating optimism in the soldiers.
>
> Over the past week I have been getting a little impatient with the Vietnamese. Their attitude is just not conducive to them winning the war. If the people who are anti-VC could employ the same methods against the VC as the VC employs against them then the end would be a lot nearer. With their present way they are absolutely reliant, and dependent, upon the USA. Just how the US can break out of their obligation I do not know, and I feel at the present time that our government in Australia should not commit itself so wholeheartedly with the US and the GVN.
>
> It's amazing that one can be acclimatized, as I hardly notice the heat these days. In fact it is only at the end of the day that I feel I am becoming tired, and then it strikes me that it has been a hot one.

The assistant divisional commander of the 1st Air Cavalry Division visited the district headquarters to see the district chief on 29 July. He was accompanied by the local brigade commander, Colonel

Stannard. The district chief asked me to do the briefing, which came as a surprise to me. The areas of interest were outlined. Stannard let me know he was disappointed with the effort put into the visit. A fair comment, a lesson learned. The advisor was expected to be more than a mentor. Who was running the show, the Vietnamese or the advisors?

The day prior to a Team gathering in Da Nang to celebrate the AATTV unit birthday the district chief approached me with a request. He asked me to purchase a refrigerator for himself and his family while I was in Da Nang. I agreed to do so, and he gave me cash. I discovered that demand for refrigerators was high. At the fourth PX visited, the Air Force PX, I managed a purchase. The refrigerator was freighted to Quang Tri in a cargo aircraft, escorted by some other Australians. The district chief collected the item at the local airfield and was given back some change from the purchase. He got a good deal.

The district chief was thrilled, and when I saw him an evening later he had a very cold can of beer to present to me. It was given to me as only a very appreciative man could give a gift to a friend. Breadfruit pieces were offered and were as pleasant to taste and eat as mango, delicious. I thought that the effort to obtain the refrigerator for the district chief was well worthwhile. His family was obviously going to benefit. Being an advisor required flexibility.

Three children at the Chieu Hoi Center were killed by a grenade explosion.[3] This center was at a hamlet set aside for former communist Vietnamese who now gave allegiance to the GVN. This was a tragedy for the families and their community. The province chief had located the hamlet in an area as attractive as a desert: very sandy, treeless, without water, and hot in summer. Staff had noted that the Chieu Hoi rate, that is the number of returnees, was declining. A possible explanation for this was linked to the prospect of a peace settlement. Wavering VC were unlikely to come back to the GVN and be marked if they did return. It was probably advantageous for a VC person to carry on until the future was clearer.

A unique U.S. program was titled "Kit Carson Scouts." The scouts were returnees employed by the marines. The monthly payment to the Kit Carson Scouts was higher than that paid to the Territorial Force soldiers. This caused some ill feeling within the ranks of the latter. There was some irony in this USMC push for Kit Carson Scouts, as the U.S. forces would not enlist former criminals into their services.

Social gatherings were held from time to time. Being hospitable was a trait in all of the folk with whom I was working. The social intercourse reminded me of the civilities of the peacetime setting, and the informality helped to build friendship and understanding. Typical was a lunch with the district chief, his assistant, my assistant, Captain Bill Coviello, Major Jim Brown, and my interpreter, Binh. A shared meal seemed to be a worldwide pleasure. I recall also that the midday siesta was part of the culture in Vietnam, especially during the hot season. A core reason for sharing in hospitality was that it fell under the umbrella of "winning the hearts and minds."

PSA Brewer and a couple of other civilian advisors gave a party for the Vietnamese officials and their advisors. I was invited. The occasion was a type of house warming for a guest house established for VIP visitors. Mr. Brewer gave a surprise gift to each Vietnamese official. It was hilarious and very clever, as each gift had some link to the job the Vietnamese carried out. My district chief was given a fishing rod, linked to the fish pond at the district headquarters. Spot on.

At dusk on this party occasion there was a great noise outside, and of all things the local people had organized rickshaw races. The local version of the vehicle was of three wheels, with a man on a bicycle seat riding behind the carriage. Each vehicle carried one passenger. The race was around the city blocks. A police vehicle and a military police vehicle cleared the roads for the races, and behind them came the supporters, on motor bikes of all descriptions and bicycles. It was all very exciting, and a good sign to see the people enthusiastic enough to take on such an event.

I discovered that the need for extra-regimental appointments went on in operational areas. Major Brad Oliver and I had been elected to the board of management of the club at the compound in June. New equipment was needed to improve the amenity of the club. Brad received the support of the board and the endorsement of the supervising officer, Lieutenant Colonel Thrasher, to proceed to Okinawa to purchase equipment: an ice maker, a beer cooler, and six air conditioners. Club funds up to $4,000 were authorized for the purchases. The goods were purchased and delivered within a week.

I shared these thoughts in a letter home to Eva:

> The local inhabitants have really been a trial over the past few days but I have adjusted myself and am now content.
>
> We have not been pushing things with work over the last week or so. The District staff has been left to their own devices for a while. They can ask for assistance of me, without me taking the initiative. I'm happy with this way and so are the other fellows in the team. If we make ourselves completely available to them then we are just not going to be able to get out of Vietnam as soon as we would like.

When I met the bandmaster of the 3rd Marine Division Band, he asked if I could get him the words to: "Tie Me Kangaroo Down Sport." This request went home to my wife. The musicians apparently liked the tune and wanted to get to know the words. Sheet music with words duly arrived from home and was presented to the band.

In another letter to Eva I wrote: "The weather is very mild now due to an occasional heavy shower each day. We were out in the countryside on an operation for the first half of the day and it was just an ideal day for moving outdoors. We started off at 5:00am and finished at 2:30pm. There were no angry contacts. On return I slept for three hours."

I found that small but important achievements were noteworthy. By 8 August the cleanup of scattered ammunition and claymore mines at the Mai Linh District compound was completed. This was a safety issue. I had identified the task when I first arrived in May.

The relationship with the district chief could not be better at this stage, I noted. "I have learned to ignore the things that may have irritated me earlier in our relationship. Some may say I am now a master of compromise. It could well be that my diplomatic skills are improving." The warrant officers made up a sign which was placed over my doorway at the MACV compound: "Australian Consulate–Quang Tri." I was heartened by the gesture. It was an Australian way of showing the flag.

Captain Sang, the district executive officer, gave a promotion and house warming party on 10 August. In my work with him I found Sang to be a very good officer. The atmosphere was one of optimism. There was a banquet of six tables, with most of the Mai Linh staff present as guests. The family prepared the food and drinks. The guests presented Sang with a grandfather clock to mark the occasion.

Staff Sergeant David Cairo, the musical arranger for the III MAF Drum and Bugle Corps, with Warrant Officer Thomas Dolan (right), ANZAC Day 1969, at Danang. (Original image provided by Australian Department of Defence, Copyright Australian War Memorial, AWM LES/69/0255/VN.)

Early in August, the district chief was given leave of absence for a few days by the province chief to go to Hue to organize materials to repair his house, damaged during Tet. He deserved the break. Later in the month he had a festival occasion to celebrate: the first month since the birth of his latest child. Then in mid-August I received an extract from a confidential CORDS letter titled: "Corrupt and/or Inefficient GVN Officials." My counterpart Captain Phong was reported as "not a strong leader and hid in Hue during Tet and did not recover psychologically." My district chief did not see this letter and I did not discuss its contents with him. A view was expressed to me that the listed names were on General Lam's I Corps blacklist of officers and officials. Phong, like many others, was on holiday at Tet 1968. I had not noticed any psychological shortcomings with his behavior. Captain Coviello, at Mai Linh during Tet 1969, provided this report to me:

> During Tet we were worried for Phong because the VC and the NVA controlled almost all of Hue for a short time, and were executing anyone who had anything to do with the South Vietnamese Government. Phong was trapped inside his parents' house and hid in the rafters to escape detection. He may not have been able to leave Hue once his area was secure. The fight for Hue took almost a month. When it was over Phong returned to Quang Tri. I'm sure the safety of his family was his main concern. Prior to the Tet offensive all of the local search and destroy missions had a "search and avoid" flavor. There was no such thing as noise and light discipline by the troops in any of our sweeps. I commented to Phong on my first operation when a PF soldier threw a hand grenade into the river not far from where I was standing. Phong said that the soldier was fishing, and wanted some fish to go with his rice. That same day there was gunfire; I thought we were making contact. Again I went to Phong and he was laughing. He said the soldiers were shooting at birds for food to add to their rice. I realized that they were not serious in fighting this war. They were letting the VC know that we were coming. This was a "you leave me alone and I will leave you alone" approach to the conflict.

Bill Coviello continued:

> This all changed when Phong returned to Mai Linh after Tet. I could see in his face and certainly saw it on the first operation that we went on. We were now operating with strict light and noise discipline. He was a person looking for some

> payback. We made contact and took five prisoners along with their weapons. This was the first time I saw maltreatment of prisoners, but he got the information he wanted. The stage was set. The boxing gloves were off. Thereafter all the operations were conducted properly, resulting in numerous contacts, elimination of the VC and making it difficult for them to operate. Phong had metamorphosed after Tet to be an efficient field soldier.

My response was to write a long letter in support of my district chief. This was passed to the PSA, Mr. Brewer, who assured me later that the letter had been sent to CORDS in Da Nang. What happened after that was beyond my control. My hope was that his name would be removed from such a list. He continued in his job. One pondered on the penetration of U.S. officials into GVN/ARVN affairs.

The CORDS part in the advisory organization had elements of an enigma about it. Other writers may have a more positive approach to the organization, but here are some comments of how CORDS impacted on me:

> CORDS organization is a lot of huff and puff. Some CORDS people are not motivated and are vague. Requests to Da Nang seem to have rarely been met, especially big ones: e.g. tin, cement and air support. The local airfield had been cleared for operations, yet the pilot refused to land the contracted aircraft. The PSA was upset as this was the day some Buddhist monks were to view the province from the air.
>
> Da Nang CORDS staff is not very effective. It seems the senior military staff there is not prepared to put issues to Mr. Cross.
>
> Young men working for CORDS could be "boys on a man's job." I pondered on how effective they were in their RD jobs. A CORDS man was heard to say: "Today was a good day as I did not lose any ground."

Perhaps the civilian members of CORDS had similar views about military people. To give due credit, the CORDS organization held the flag high in the refugee program and in Operation Fisher, to be described in chapter 11.

Road security was composed of many elements. Two enemy threats were of common knowledge: ambush and mines. Highway 1 had the verges swept by engineers at dawn each day to help find any mines laid on the road edges overnight. The sealed part of the road was visually checked also for any signs of interference. Ambush was a tactic used by the VC, usually after thorough planning and reconnaissance. I became concerned about a possible ambush site being presented in the district on Highway 1 to the south of the city. U.S. Army and USMC trucks were lining up each day after the lifting of the curfew but before the road mine clearance sweep had been completed.

In early August I started noticing long lines of road traffic gathering after dawn, and being held up beyond the place locally referred to as the "Y junction" on Highway 1.This traffic originated from the Quang Tri maintenance bases at Ai Tu and was heading southeast to collect supplies from Wunder Beach in Hai Lang District. The short arm of the Y was the turn off from the highway to Quang Tri City. For security and safety reasons, I considered that a better system of vehicle movement needed to be examined at a high staff level. I was convinced that a long column of unprotected stationary vehicles was a possible VC target. Facts needed to be produced. For a week my advisory team members conducted a survey of the vehicles lining up. The early morning traffic was recorded by date and time, vehicle registration, and unit identification sign without bothering the drivers, who were just doing their jobs.

A covering memo with the documented evidence attached was passed to the DPSA, Lieutenant Colonel Mooney. He was due to attend a provost marshal meeting in early September. At the meeting he tabled the report, which was duly referred to the chief of staff at 3rd Marine Division headquarters for consideration. Later, vehicle assembly procedures changed, with vehicles remaining in unit lines until daily road clearance had been completed. My team was more than satisfied with that outcome.

On district rounds I noticed how the road maintenance team went about one of its routine tasks. Where a temporary road repair was necessary a bag of cement would be broken open on the damaged spot, then spread by raking and watered. This was judged locally as a quick way to provide an instant road repair. The repair would have a very short useful life, and struck me as a metaphor for

MACV compound flood, September 1968.

the future of South Vietnam, where the existing security uncertainties clouded prospects of a sound and safe future.

Despite the security situation, some progress was being made in the agriculture area. The district chief and I visited an experimental rice plot at Long Hung hamlet, near the Y junction, on 17 August. IR8 was promoted as high-yield rice and resistant to local diseases. Three crops per year were possible, with an expected 120 days from planting to harvest. On a quality test the rice was said to be superior to the rice types in current use. We were informed the research work had been carried out in the Philippines.

It was very wet on 4 and 5 September. The enthusiasm of the Vietnamese and the Americans was at a low point. Typhoon Bessie was upon us, and by 6 September the rain was still pouring down. I tried to exercise the minds of the team members by discussing planned works for the compound for the next dry period, particularly the need for a combined operations center. The typhoon was stationary. The rivers and creeks burst their banks; the city and surrounds were inundated. Many houses were more than half under water. The political reasons for keeping apartments opposite our compound vacant were overturned, and some homeless villagers were provided access. Our compound was under a foot of water and all rooms were flooded. Even the district chief's fish pond was flooded.

Helicopters and boats were the only usable means of transport. We were concerned about the children, babies, and elderly people. Surprisingly, the Vietnamese took all of this in stride. They moved to high ground areas without fuss. What to me seemed like a forty- or one hundred–year flood was to the local people probably an annual occurrence, to be put up with and then gotten over. There were lessons here for us foreigners. The province chief showed good leadership by visiting the district headquarters and the surrounds. This was rather an exception for him and was probably an indication of the seriousness of the flood. It was his first visit to Mai Linh since my arrival in May. The rice harvest, which was to commence later in the month, would now not take place as the crop was ruined. The U.S. would soon overcome this problem by importing rice to make up any shortfall. This kind of action was generosity beyond fault.

It was thought that the VC would probably be in trouble now, as all of their underground bunkers, tunnels, caches, and hospitals would be flooded and possibly destroyed. On top of that, some of their rice would be ruined. With no harvest coming up, the VC would have a massive logistics problem in keeping comrades supplied. In fact, the flood could well influence the capacity of the VC to carry out activities in the short term. There were no obvious local contingency plans in place to respond to such a flood, but clearly people knew what to do. More surprising was that the U.S. advisory machine was not called upon to assist the people affected by the flooding. The Vietnamese people demonstrated stoic behavior over these days, the flood being another incident in a noble and tragic history.

After four months of working in Quang Tri, I had seen and heard a lot about the RD program, a GVN program coming under the CORDS umbrella. It had a high profile, a large budget, and was an agency that had a key role in pacification. In the field I had noticed that the RD workers had long fingernails, and I wondered if that manicured state was conducive to encouraging—or doing—hard work. Teams of fifty-nine men worked in hamlets and villages assisting people with their farming, wells, irrigation, and the like. The program could be compared to a large-scale national peace corps. Mai Linh District had an allocation of nine RD teams. To help

A Revolutionary Development Team.

me better understand the RD ethos, Mr. Brewer kindly nominated me to attend a short course at Vung Tau.

In late August I attended the two-day orientation course at the Vietnamese National Revolutionary Development Training Center at Vung Tau. In a professional development sense, attendance at this course ticked the last box in my eligibility to be a sector operations staff officer in a MACCORDS advisory team. Travel to Saigon was by an Air America Beech (Volpar) aircraft. The seminar group then flew to Vung Tau, and immediately after arrival toured the training center. The center was run along military lines, with nine battalion training areas, each of six companies in two groups. Recruits were trained over a thirteen-week course. Demonstrations of training activities were presented. The youth in training were encouraged to demonstrate their leadership skills. Leaders had to be identified early, as RD team leaders were in demand with the expanding program.

The badge of the RD organization depicted the entirety of Vietnam, highlighting the aim of the movement to reunite the nation. The black uniform of the RD was a sign of affiliation with the people, whose preferred color of clothing was also black. Lieutenant Colonel Be was the NTC commandant. He had pioneered the RD idea in his home province in 1965. That program became a national one in 1966. Be was a man of intense enthusiasm, an idealist, a nationalist, and a revolutionary, hence the name RD. He likened communism to a disease.

Some of the U.S. course members expressed their anxiety about the enormous amount of U.S. taxpayer money being spent on programs being undertaken by the RD teams throughout South Vietnam. I could empathize with them. My own views had been shaped by occasional contact with RD teams in Mai Linh, which had led me to note the following:

> RD visitors in Mai Linh district for the day and did not make a courtesy call or report to the district HQ.
>
> I visited the RD team at Nhan Bieu One with the DC. He gave them a pep talk on defensive matters, and their role and working relationship with the PF.
>
> Through carelessness, an RD person was injured by an accidental grenade blast in the house of a PF soldier.
>
> I went to an afternoon RD hamlet meeting conducted by the younger generation, where an old farmer sat through it without adding anything, except his presence. I concluded then that the RD was undertaking tasks that could be done by the RF/PF.

The next day in discussion Colonel Be was questioned about President Thieu's nonrecognition of the NLF at the Paris Peace Talks, and the effect that position might have on his vision. His response included the observation that the Chieu Hoi program was an attempt to get NLF people back into the fold. The question was well answered, but had Be thinking. This question had come up in the context of a presentation on political training of recruits. The quiet, sinister shadow of the Paris Peace Talks was cast across our gathering.

Attendees were informed that the Mekong delta area had a rice surplus arising from higher yields from the new IR8 strain of rice. Transportation and security were a big problem in the countrywide distribution of rice, as was market manipulation. Presenters highlighted that the French did not establish or train a credible Vietnamese civil service, and that this was a weakness that the South Vietnamese government administration was then experiencing.

The presenters asserted that RD people were revolting against corruption, hatred, and the VC. They wanted to improve standards of living, and to bring a new life to the people. A new umbrella name to cover a number of GVN programs was therefore introduced: New Life Development. CORDS introduced the term into its structure. That vision was the ideal, but it fell short in practice, unfortunately. The course gave me a better perspective of the U.S. mission in South Vietnam. Later the name Rural Development replaced the term Revolutionary Development. The program was disbanded in 1971.

The foregoing has provided the pacification setting in which I found myself as a military advisor. The four months at Mai Linh District proved to be an invaluable preparation for me, leading into the planning and operational staff work I was to undertake at the province (sector) level. That part of my story will be taken up in chapter 8.

Part of my time in Vietnam was relatively close to the people, especially in the first four months. Some of my experiences with the Vietnamese people in Quang Tri Province follow.

7

With the Vietnamese People in Quang Tri

May 1968–April 1969

I have elected to place this chapter of the story here, as the security of the people of South Vietnam was at the core of the conflict. They were a central element of my experience while in the country, and I judged that the people aspect be presented now, rather than later. Our advisory team role was to do our best to help provide the people of Quang Tri with opportunities for a better life.

My first encounter with a large number of Vietnamese people was at a Sunday morning Mass in Quang Tri City. A children's dialogue Mass was being celebrated, with the boys sitting in the right-hand pews and the girls on the other side. It was pleasant to listen to sung responses by the youngsters, all in the Vietnamese language. As an observer, I felt there must have been a lot of sadness within families, but it was not obvious. The children appeared to be like those of their own age the world over. The people on the whole were well dressed and there was no shortage of food, thanks to the generous supplementation by the U.S. agencies, USAID, and Caritas.

My recorded impressions of the local people in the first month in Quang Tri reflected the impact on me of the local culture and customs. Clearly life for a mother and wife was tough. The women had big families and their work was hard. I saw women carrying heavy loads of rice and water for kilometers. Some women in the rural areas had black teeth. I was to learn later that their teeth were made dark from a three-day process of "nhom rang."[1] A lunch meal in a hamlet was a new experience. The hospitality was welcoming. Chicken, pork, rice, red peppers, corn, and salad were served, with tea at the end. Chopsticks were no problem when used the Vietnamese way, as a type of spoon with the bowl resting against the chin.

I had a very pleasing morning in a village named Van Van to the east of the city. The farming land was rich and fertile. This village was a very attractive place, with bamboo avenues and plenty of trees. The people were strongly anti-VC, and their local security force, a platoon of PF, were good fighters and had had many clashes with the VC. I sat through the lunch, not eating, as I was unwell. All the food presented was from the locality, except for the spaghetti. Food served from the house included fish, meat, vegetables, rice, peppers, and dressings.

Family life was very important to the Vietnamese. In fact, their main concerns were for the safety of the family. Each dwelling had a bunker, a necessity for protection from bullets and mortar fragments. One had to admire their attitude toward family planning; large families could be explained as a guarantee that the parents would be cared for in their old age. A person's age commenced at the date of conception. Why is it westerners do not look upon the life of a person in this way? I discovered friendship could be manifested in many ways when I saw three women hunkered in a row taking lice from each other's hair, in turn.

The industrious types carried on with light industry enterprises in their homes and backyards. With scraps of timber, tin, ammunition casings, and the like they patiently made beds, containers, cabinets, and pots. The low-skilled workers employed in the MACV compound smuggled remainders out by placing them in CORDS vehicles and collecting the items later when the vehicles were parked at the various villas in Quang Tri City. Then there were the struggling rice growers, without buffalo, who placed their harvested rice stalks on footpaths so that pedestrians passing by did their part of the threshing job for them.

While the conflict continued, so did the education of the youth. I was invited to the local elementary school prize giving. The province chief was the guest of honor. There were fifteen hundred students at the school. I had the privilege of giving out two of the fifty prizes. I felt as though I had been embraced by the school, such was the friendliness.

Some of my American colleagues had a view that the Vietnamese in the South may have been short of talent. There was one school of thought in Quang Tri that former Northerners had influence within the GVN. One wondered about the extent of support the NLF had in the South, with the HES reporting being a guide, probably as accurate as any other form of assessment at the time. The operating pattern of VC political activists was such that any assessment of strengths or of support for the enemy was difficult to deduce. The short-term nature of Regional Force operations gave the VC the opportunity for concealment while government troops and police were about. Evasion and escape to a VC-controlled area was another option if GVN security measures became threatening. National police agencies built up blacklists. Population control measures, such as identity and spot checks, helped the GVN to reduce or neutralize VC infrastructure and sympathizers.

Innate suspicions arose on meeting a Vietnamese stranger for the first time. One was challenged to give trust on face value. What lies in the mind behind each face? I was reminded of how at home one could not always know the political preference of a person, or even if he or she had one. I wondered how the VC tax man could achieve results. However, I thought the majority of people wanted to live in peace.

The downside of life in Quang Tri, like illicit trading, corruption, and other negative side effects of the war, caused me to think about the continuing merits of prosecuting the war. The dilemma created in my mind was to be a constant one for the future. Professional and personal instincts were being pressed and tested, not only in my case, but for many other people, military and civilian.

A CORDS worker asked the U.S. senior military advisor on 12 June about Mrs. Nhan's using U.S. aircraft for flights to and from Da Nang, and questioned how it could be tolerated. It seemed that the then Major Nhan must have had some leverage. He was the senior officer responsible for the Territorial Forces, reporting to the province chief. About seven months later it all fell apart for Nhan and his wife, as will be discussed later.

I traveled to Hai Lang District with Binh, my interpreter, on 30 June. Earlier I had been approached by a Vietnamese man for assistance. For this narrative I have given him the name of Viet. He wanted to make contact with his family. Viet had lived in a coastal hamlet that no longer existed, as the area was now a logistic beachhead called Wunder Beach that was used to support U.S. forces in Quang Tri Province.

Viet's family had moved five kilometers to the southeast along the beach to a refugee village considered to be VC controlled. Viet had been working with Father Ai (more about him later) in Quang Tri and had not seen his family for three months. Viet had at some previous time been captured by the VC. The story was that he had been buried alive, but that he managed to survive after a day under the earth. This was hard to believe, but being buried alive was known to happen.

Viet wanted to see his family. He had not been able to get them to Quang Tri City, as he was unable to arrange accommodation. We went to a U.S. tank battalion at Wunder Beach. After relating why we were there, the unit agreed to give assistance. As the area was not considered to be safe outside the Army complex, four tanks were provided to take Viet and Binh to the refugee village. I remained at the logistic complex doing other things, as cover for this humanitarian rescue job.

The tanks halted on the outskirts of the village. Viet was not prepared to walk into the village to meet up with his family, as the village chief had been assassinated by the VC two days before, in daylight. So Binh walked ahead and the tanks followed. They stayed there for about thirty minutes while Viet met with his family. Three of his five children came out with him. His wife and two other children were to remain until he could find accommodation for them.

The children were filthy in appearance, covered in sores, the dirtiest I had seen. Their ride in the tank and then back to Quang Tri in my jeep was their first experience in a vehicle of any kind. So, it was a big day for them. They had been living about five hundred meters from the beach yet did not appear to have been anywhere near water for some time. They were to stay in an orphanage in Quang Tri until Viet could sort things out for his family.

About two weeks later I took Viet back to his village. In the meantime he had been appointed village chief, to replace the fellow who was assassinated. A difficult decision had to be made by Viet. Advisors were of the view that the village would be assessed as a contested village, with the VC in control at night and the GVN by day. I had a sense that life was being squeezed out of the courageous Viet while he still lived.

At the end of July I heard that Viet and his family had moved to the district center of Hai Lang. A friend of his, who was to move out of the village with him, had been assassinated by the Viet Cong. These hamlet-level assassinations reminded me again that evil existed. Clearly there was an imperative for the agents of evil, the VC, to be contained and dealt with.

Other recorded observations of the people into July and August reflected my fascination with the environment in which I was working. As mentioned elsewhere in the narrative, there was an absence of males at the home front. The losses by the VC were probably high during the failed Tet offensive. Local fashion was of interest. "A significant difference between the ladies here and at home is in their taste of hats. All here wear the straw hat, conical in shape, as protection against the sun and rain. Fashion is a distant second, functionality first."

In a letter to Eva I wrote:

> For the ladies their Sunday best is white, from neck to ankle, with shirts over trousers, with flaps front and back. It is a pretty view to watch them walking along the street in their white outfits. When white is worn, hats are not worn. Their hair is usually long and combed beautifully until it glistens. That is enough of trends and observations for now.
>
> At present it is very safe in Quang Tri city. All the fighting seems to be up near the DMZ and in the mountains to the west. The people do not seem to realise that they have little to fear just now from the NVA. The military defeats suffered by the VC and NVA in the Tet offensive and the May offensive have left the enemy in a state that has put them in disarray and in recovery mode. With their present attitude the Vietnamese are reluctant to rebuild and to get works underway. This is a big problem for the Americans now and for me also as I have to help them to pursue their policies.
>
> A number of out of country contractors provide services to US agencies. I met a Canadian who has worked in Quang Tri for the past two years. While in Vietnam he had fathered two daughters by different Vietnamese mothers. This obviously posed a problem for the mothers, the children and the father.
>
> The behaviour of foreigners in a host country can be ill-considered. A civilian advisor invited me and a warrant officer to a policeman's home to enjoy "entertainment"

> from Saigon. He seemed to be disappointed that we declined the invitation.
>
> Children deserve comment. I have observed lately that a significant number are not well cared for by their mothers. The main observation is of sores on the face and the head. They probably start with measles that are scratched and then they become infected. The flies are attracted, leading to bigger sores. With more careful personal hygiene I'm sure much infection would be avoided. A particular case arose when Binh told me of his concern for his son. I took them to the Province Hospital to have his boy treated for sores on his head, knowing that a MILPHAP[2] team was in place there. Binh was happy with the treatment given to his son.
>
> A VC was killed at Thuong Xa [southeast of the city] last night. Early next morning when on Highway 1 I saw that the body had been placed on a chair with a drink can in one hand. Later in the day the body was identified and claimed by the father, who had another son in the ARVN. He had two other sons who were killed by the Viet Cong. The recently deceased son had gone into North Vietnam in 1964 and had returned to this area.[3]

Lieutenant Jerry Bell, U.S. Navy, was an administration officer within a MILPHAP team at the local public hospital. His work caused him to be depressed from time to time. On a visit to the hospital with Fitzgibbon I could understand why he felt that way. I was shocked to see the injuries that had been suffered by civilians due to the war. It shook up my thoughts and reorientated my thinking about war, politics, and people. I noted: "Is the evil that is being perpetrated now greater or less than the evil which the country was threatened with before the war? People could arguably still have free will under communism. The exercise of that will is restricted in such a society, but peace could bring about a Buddhist and Christian accommodation to foster nationalism."

After my tour of the hospital with Bell, I followed up on some matters which I judged needed special attention. They were arguably outside my area of responsibility, but there was a humanitarian need here. The standards at the local hospital were inferior to that to which I was accustomed and expected. The local people were tolerant to the extreme. I thought they deserved a better deal. I made a visit to the U.S. Civil Affairs Unit.

Upon relating the story to the Civil Affairs staff, action was to be taken on two matters. It was agreed to supply and fit fly wire screens to the windows of the province hospital, and it was also agreed that a pigpen would be built on the hospital grounds to help keep pigs out of the kitchen. My hope was that the services of the Civil Affairs Unit would free up the MILPHAP team to better attend other needs in the hospital, particularly in the wards.

In a letter to Eva after a further visit to the refugee camp at Cam Lo, I wrote: "Today I was a guest at the official opening of a water project for the refugee village at Cam Lo. This was the area of the feature article in the Australian newspaper for the Aust Care Fund. My invitation arose because of the work done by AATTV member Warrant Officer Peter Wooden who was wounded during the construction."

Thousands of people were in attendance, mainly refugees. There was a certain amount of stage management for the occasion, unavoidable in the prevailing circumstances of the conflict. I thought the opening ceremony was a kind of "place of parade" for the crowd. Local allied leaders were in attendance, including Mr. Cross of CORDS Da Nang. Several speeches were given, with the locals giving rousing cheers to the visitors in a not-very-spontaneous manner. I heard while at Cam Lo that the local bakery was not operating, as the business people did not want to run a cooperative for such a purpose.

Ramos, Binh, and I had an evening family meal at the home of the local laundry operator on 14 July. The dining started with soup, bamboo shoots, and crab, followed by fish with tomato and onion sauce. Then chicken and mushrooms were served, followed by steak and potato chips with vegetables. Whisky and beer were served during the meal. Rice was available throughout with tea and biscuits at the end. This was a culinary delight. With many troops in the area, there was profit in a laundry business.

As the guest of honor, I was to eat the head and tail of the chicken. I had been warned of this custom by Ramos; he was gleeful that this was my task. You can imagine what that was like, especially the juicy brain. However, I smiled and with a blank mind chewed and swallowed the fare. All went down without any unpleasant consequences. The wife sat down with the men. Normally such dinners were for men only. The ambience of the evening was French and Vietnamese, a memorable experience.

Binh was to leave the PF soon, to complete his medical training in Saigon. He had three years to go on a scholarship from the government. He had been a good companion to me in our time together, displaying a maturity beyond his years. I could only wish him well. From early September Sergeant Long became my interpreter. I had enriching experiences with my interpreters. They helped me better understand Vietnamese customs, and I was able to help them by explaining western ways. Long told me in mid-November that he was to marry in January. Knowing I was married with children gave him confidence to discuss some private matters that were of concern to him.

Long was a soldier of the Territorial Forces, a Buddhist, and twenty-four years of age. He was to marry a young woman aged eighteen years who lived in Hue. The marriage was arranged by the families, "as was the custom," said Long. He was not particularly keen to marry, yet his family members wanted the bride-to-be to look after them in their later years. In a small way I assisted him in his preparations for the marriage celebrations by purchasing cigarettes and beer. I was given an invitation to the wedding as a courtesy but was unable to attend. We also spent time on discussing the human ovulation process, as he did not seem to desire children at that time. Our friendship was sealed when he gave me two conical hats as a gift. The hats now are displayed in a veterans' museum in Geelong, Victoria.

Later I was to meet an English-speaking Vietnamese soldier who had a sound grasp of Australian slang, perfect in manner and tone. In conversation "mate" was no problem for this character. He had worked as an interpreter with U.S. and Australian advisors for some years.

Another time, two men came to the district compound to dig a well. A circular concrete cast section was placed on the selected site, and the men commenced digging, throwing the sandy soil out of their encasement. Slowly the concrete case settled into the hole. A second section was placed on the first, and the process continued with the aid of a ladder, bucket, and rope. The dig was completed in three days, and water appeared. Wells were in common use, particularly in hamlets and villages, where they were used as family washing places. On many occasions I saw children being soaped up and splashed to freshen up at a well.

Our advisory team employed a young lady, Co (Miss) Bay, to be a maid. She was definitely bone idle, and after a number of warnings about her performance she found her services terminated. Ramos organized a replacement. The former employee, despite being sacked and paid off, continued to be present each day. I pondered on how long she would hang around. I concluded she may have been presenting herself with a view to establishing a personal arrangement with one of the advisors. This was not tested to the best of my knowledge.

The replacement maid did not hold her job for more than a few days. Ramos observed the new maid stealing two cans of soda from the bunker. So there was one more person out of a job, and one more to be found by the team. The word went around about the vacant position at Mai Linh. A young Vietnamese lady came in asking for a job. She was very young and giggly. Her English was sound. She said the priest at the church had given her an introduction to me after she had seen me in the church. Binh said she used to be his student and that she had worked for a number of organizations in the district. The young lady was a cousin to many and not short of referee friends. Her motivation was to earn money so that she could purchase books before going to Hue University. She won the job.

I was one of many invited guests to a social gathering at the home of the province chief on 10 August. The main guests were Lieutenant Colonel Thrasher and three other advisors who were to be bade farewell. The occasion took the form of a buffet tea. The I Corps band was in attendance. The gathering was also entertained by a group of five Vietnamese girls who sang and danced. Awards were also presented. It was a very happy affair.

The early September flood outlined in the previous chapter illustrated that the Vietnamese still had the capacity to manage their affairs in certain areas in a capable manner despite the conditions. They followed well-established custom to move to higher ground, and to shelter, above the flood level. The major concern arising was about health. There was a possibility that the water supply could have been contaminated, as many rats were drowned. Inoculations against plague and typhoid were commenced as a precaution. The water supply was treated. Advisors had been inoculated against this sort of disease threat before leaving home for Vietnam.

The Vietnamese reaction to the flood was not in any way due to advisor influence. In the Vietnamese philosophy of life, natural calamities are accepted as a matter of fact. Their concern for their own situation and that of others was really a disinterested one, in all a routine occurrence. Later in the month eight inches of rain fell overnight, leading to another flood, but not as severe as the earlier one. However, a number of houses were under water again. Advisors commenced work on a monsoon plan in case further rains led to chaos.

In mid-October a sea of water inundated the countryside on the coastal plain. The towns on high ground were drying out. The Vietnamese did not appear to be concerned, showing a remarkable disposition in adversity. Despite the conditions the annual Le Loi Festival was held on 13 October, to celebrate the patron saint of the RF and PF. Medals were presented to many Vietnamese, and some U.S. people were presented with awards.

Contact with local people lessened on moving up to province level work. However, some interaction continued, and I observed that all seemed to be going well for the people and that they seemed to be prospering. The shops were carrying more lines, and the people appeared to be better dressed. I pondered how the appearance of the Vietnamese seemed to become more Caucasian to my eyes as each day passed. Are we more friend than foreigner?

The Military Payment Certificate (MPC) changeover happened on 21 October, known as C-Day. This system was devised by the United States to reduce profiteering from currency arbitrage. The theory was to eliminate U.S. dollars from local economies. MPCs were paper money and were illegal for unauthorized personnel to carry. Many Vietnamese businesspeople were caught with MPCs in their possession, particularly Lieutenant Colonel Nhan. His bonhomie manner and his obvious business interests with his wife seemed to allow him free rein. I was approached by some Vietnamese to convert funds for them, but refused on the basis of its being illegal.

At some point I was informed that the number 117 by tradition was an auspicious number for the Vietnamese, which led to the number of clauses in the Constitution, the number of words in the opening preamble, the number of members in the parliament, and the number of days of sittings. However, those 117 days of sittings were perhaps not the most productive. The politicians and their parties were not particularly action oriented. Rumors were that the politicians were usually busy denouncing the government and each other, in preference to dealing with policy matters.

Flooded hamlets, September 1968.

In a letter home on 1 November I expressed a view:

> Some of the Vietnamese do not seem to be too concerned about their future. They do not have the sense of urgency we have, and I'm of the opinion that any cease fire will only last long enough for the US to get out, and this includes Australians, I hope. History will repeat itself for certain, both in the short and long term, as this country has had one conflict after another. It is futile really to think that the US and Australian presence will bring about peace and freedom for the people. However that's our mission so we have to keep at it whilst we are here.

The first day of November was a local holiday for the Vietnamese, with three events to celebrate: National Day, celebrating the Revolution; Armed Forces Day, promotions and the like; and All Saints' Day, a holy day for Christians. Work continued for the advisors without any celebration. That afternoon at 4 P.M. the province chief had a reception at his home to mark National Day. All of the men present were dressed in their best outfits. The ladies were not to be seen. This was the day when we heard that the NLF, not recognized by the GVN, would be sitting at the Paris Peace Talks from 6 November. What a trying period we were in. My diary entry was: "What is the GVN going to do about that?"

Nationalistic fervor was included in a letter I wrote to Eva that evening: "Vietnamese nationalists in the south have no time for the VC and are not prepared to compromise because in peace they will probably be targeted by them. This attitude is strongest among the leadership both civilian and military who have aligned themselves firmly with the GVN. Also, the nationalists have little empathy with those who have turned back, such as returnees working in the Chieu Hoi program or Armed Propaganda Teams. The ARVN military are determined to kill VC."

In a Dong Ha hamlet a Vietnamese woman took a wounded USMC soldier into her home for care and security following a night contact. This Good Samaritan act was a first to my knowledge in Quang Tri. Humanitarian action was not isolated. The U.S. Army's Sergeant Perry, a combat medical advisor, demonstrated a high level of commitment to the people of Vietnam. I met him in October at the MACV compound when he had an overnight stay. By this time he had served in the province for nineteen months. He had been at Khe Shan village earlier in the year when the NVA had overrun the district administration center of Huong Hoa and the advisory team. He was now with the reestablished Huong Hoa administration in the Cua Valley, which allowed him to continue in his work as a medical assistant. He loved his job and the people he worked with, the Bru tribe people. Some of his fascinating insights were worth recording. He related that one of the challenges in his role was accepting some of the taboos held by the people. Pregnant women were deemed to be "contaminated" for four weeks prior to birth and for two weeks after. They went to a separate house for confinement. The Bru women chose not to have medical assistance during a birth. Further, the Bru people had a preference for the blood of a chicken, pig, or buffalo as remedies before calling for medical support.

Using the sector direct support helicopter, I accompanied the province chief on a brief visit to two hamlets in the rice-growing area of Hai Lang District. At Thon Van Quy the elders assembled with the village officials. There was an absence of women in the assembly. The province chief spoke for about twenty minutes without any interruption. Questions and debate came eventually, and all seemed to be happy. The planned visit to the second place, Thong Phuoc Dien, was cancelled as a communication breakdown resulted in no one being there to meet Colonel Am. The acting Hai Lang district chief who accompanied the province chief was very embarrassed. Hai Lang was usually assessed as not being in good shape, and this visit probably confirmed that view.

I was on an operation where a mobile command post was set up in the grounds of a primary school. It coincided with the start of the school day. All students and staff gathered in the assembly area, where a flag-raising ceremony was held followed by the singing of the national song. The experience for me was encouraging in this Vietnamese setting, but full of sadness when compared with a like setting at home. The school was composed of six classrooms, one without roofing, and overall was generally in need of a complete refurbishment. The school was short of one teacher. Despite the setting, the children were benefitting through education.

Generals Richard G. Stilwell and Ngo Quang Truong called upon a grieving family at La Vang on 16 November. The father of the family had been killed at My Chan. Poverty and squalor were dominant. It was a very sad situation. The visit by these two fine leaders was moving and memorable.

Just before Christmas I purchased gifts for Ba (Mrs.) Le, my housemaid, and for my interpreter, my driver, and my counterpart, Captain Cuu. I had great pleasure in preparing the box for Ba Le, who had six children. Her husband had been killed by the VC some years earlier. The package included a thermos flask, a tennis ball, cigarettes, cards, plastic bags and tins of fruit, lollies, chewing gum, and spare batteries for the radio. These were small things, but I was sure that they would have been very useful to her. I wrote home to say that the Christmas spirit was with us in Vietnam. The Vietnamese held much the same celebrations as at home: children's parties, greeting cards, prayers, and the exchange of presents.

On a visit to Da Nang on 30 December I observed there was a slightly different class of people compared to Quang Tri. The people of Quang Tri were more rural types, with the majority being peasants. Da Nang was populated by urban city dwellers, and was the second largest city in South Vietnam, after Saigon. The people in Da Nang appeared to be healthier and more prosperous. The local priest was French, his church modern and bright.

A message came to advisors on 31 December from the hospital ship USS *Sanctuary* requesting parental approval for surgery on a boy who was a patient on the ship. When the district chief of Hai Lang was requested to assist, he did not want to play any part in contacting the parents. Others followed up on the request. One wondered about the mental state of the district chief at Hai Lang. A section of another hospital ship, the USS *Repose,* was devoted to the care of Vietnamese women and children. On a visit to the ship I was informed that several cases were burns and that one fifteen-month-old child was "bi-sexual." This child was to be operated on by doctors on board. An interpreter was available in this ward.

While in the operations center one evening I joined the Vietnamese duty officers in a card game of pontoon for half an hour. It was fun, with a modest loss. They were delighted that I knew how to play the game. In a chat with my counterpart, Captain Cuu, he informed me that there were 129 prisoners of war in the local jail. They had to be transported to Da Nang. The Vietnamese did not have the airlift capacity to do the relocation, and U.S. resources had not been offered to assist. Clearly transportation by road was an option for the local military. Here was food for thought with this relatively simple logistic problem. On wider issues, how could the Vietnamese agencies cope with a more significant logistic problem if one arose?

An exceptional public Vietnamese exercise of military authority happened on 29 January 1969 in Quang Tri City. The I Corps commander, Lieutenant General Lam, arrived by helicopter at 5:30 P.M. and told the advisors that the purpose of his visit was to relieve the second senior Vietnamese officer, Lieutenant Colonel Nhan, deputy to the province chief, as he was guilty of corrupt practices. It seemed that Nhan was of a political party that (although anti-VC) was not that of the power group and that the corruption story was the lever. Corruption was a fact of life for most Vietnamese, and in his case had been used as reason for dismissal from a very important post. It was obvious that the South Vietnamese Army was not a fully professional one, but had a political inclination, and that the corps commander was really the local warlord. The role of Mrs. Nhan in this case was not mentioned by the general. The dismissed officer had in my view given very loyal and faithful service to his country. It was unfortunate that he was not aligned with the right group. Such was life in South Vietnam.

There were no incidents of note in Quang Tri during Tet in mid-February 1969, unlike the previous year. After a peaceful first evening of Tet the Vietnamese people turned out in their very best clothing, strolling through the streets, greeting friends, and having a very enjoyable time. The province chief visited twelve People's Self-Defense Force posts during the evening of Tet, giving out gifts at each place. The next morning he went to Hue to visit outposts with the commander of the 1st ARVN Division, Major General Truong.

On an evening during Tet celebrations I attended a barbecue as a guest of a neighboring unit and met an ARVN major who spoke excellent English. He was an impressive character. He boosted my morale in that a little glimmer of hope came back to me for the people of Vietnam. I thought that with more of his kind the prospects of the South surviving would be more favorable.

In the second half of February the GVN elections were upon us. An irony of the process was that opponents of the GVN within the country were outlawed and it was illegal for their members to stand for election; so much for the democratic process. There were security precautions in place to protect the people and the officials during the voting process. It was pleasing and puzzling to see a struggling administration endeavoring to organize such a widespread election.

To offset this, I had the view that South Vietnam was still ruled by warlords, whose affiliations with each other tied the country together. The official structure of government was not anywhere near democratic. One had only to examine the various chains of command and the way they worked to see this. On the other hand, the people in the rural villages appeared to be content with their lot in life, mainly food production. There did not seem to be any prospect for their approach to life to move toward urbanization or that of the westerner.

The continuing hazards of life in Quang Tri are highlighted by these observations recorded in the early months of 1969. On the night of 24 February, five boys, aged fourteen to fifteen years, were kidnapped by about twenty VC. The age-old system of the press gang continued to be fashionable, much to the detriment of these youngsters.

In addition, a report came into the sector that children at Cam Lo, who pointed out land mines to mine-clearing sweep teams, were being rewarded for their efforts by payments. This work by children was dangerous. The only metallic part in the current batch of mines in use was the firing mechanism; hence damage was caused mainly by blast effect. We did not receive any reports of injury to children by mines, but concern was expressed about incentives being provided for children to do this kind of work.

There was a humorous moment at a sector level advisory meeting on 29 March, provided by my successor at Mai Linh, Captain Huntly. He reported that the people of the village of Nhu Le were happy, but it puzzled him as to why. He went on to say it could have been because of the GVN presence and efforts to improve things, or because of the VC presence from time to time.

On a patrol through the city on the night of 6 April, I went into the Tri Buu church, where Mass was being said. The church was packed, flares were fired at the offertory, and bells were rung. One hoped their prayers and aspirations were going to be met. I recalled the story of the faithful being blown up by the VC in a crowded church some years before. A shrine had been created on the site to commemorate that tragedy.

After a sector reconnaissance a few days before leaving Quang Tri I wrote the following to Eva: "Things are quiet here and it gives me an opportunity to travel around the province by road with my driver and interpreter. The rice is developing in the fields and for miles one can see the rich green rice crops flourishing in the sun. The scene is not unlike wheat fields. When one imagines that all of the crops were planted by hand, then you can have some idea of the infinite patience of the Vietnamese people. The harvest commences in May and lasts for about a month."

The onset of the rice harvest marked the anniversary of my arrival in the province. During a visit to Quang Tri Province in late May 2012, with my son Peter, I was privileged to see these same traditional agricultural practices being undertaken.

On the day of my departure from Quang Tri I made a home visit to Ba Le, who had provided the maid service in my section of the compound. Her hamlet was typically rural. On the pathway to her home I was impressed by the very typical signs of family life in a compact community. There were cows, chickens, and pigs in the area and rice stalks were laid out to dry. Children were being washed before the midday rest. Her home was very well presented. I was received in the main room, with table and chairs as a centerpiece, set in the customary manner. Family photographs and holy pictures were around the room.

Ba Le was disappointed over my departure, and I felt a heart tug, as we respected each other's role in life and we were friends. I had purchased a transistor radio for her during the previous August while on a visit to Nui Dat. She treasured the radio.

The goodbye was a poignant moment in my mind, as I imagined her to be representative of the South Vietnamese people. She knew of my family from our discussions over the year, and she had experienced the sadness of losing her husband in the internal conflict that was going on. She had her job to continue with in the compound, and her family to look after in Quang Tri, as did I at home in Australia.

The next chapter bridges the activities carried out during my transition from sub-sector advisory work to the sector level, as a planning and operations staff officer.

8

Transition from District to Province

September 1968

During our handover discussions in May, Major Michael Casey (AATTV) indicated that the Mai Linh advisory position for an Australian Army major was not very challenging. His debriefing with the commanding officer AATTV in Saigon included the recommendation that the sector operations officer position would be a more appropriate position. On 20 June 1968 my Australian commanding officer informed me that I was to stay in Mai Linh. This was not of concern to me at the time, as I was still becoming familiar with the general operating environment. Working with the U.S. Army in a foreign country in a war situation was enough to handle in any position.

In hindsight, the first four months was a period of further development for me. I wrote home about the confidence that was growing in me as a military professional. There were frequent dealings with senior officers. The subjects covered in these discussions were associated with counterinsurgency and pacification. It seemed that the point of view of the local Australian was worth hearing. Occasionally differences of opinion existed, but they helped to develop sound professional and personal relationships. I was able to argue my point of view succinctly, without putting in doubt my loyalty and respect to whomever I was addressing, whether a junior, a peer, or a senior.

To Eva I wrote: "I feel it is a culmination of my home life, my schooling and military education, your influence, and my Australian nature that makes me who I am." On 8 July I wrote: "My job goes on from day to day, and my thought each day is that what I am doing is part of our contribution to the people of Vietnam."

A later letter from Eva elicited this mid-July response: "No one will be allowed to take me for granted, have no fear of that. I will work for the Vietnamese as long as they are in need, but they will not be using me, I can assure you. So far I've had to assert myself on two occasions in that direction."

In early September 1968 the weather was dry and mild, and very pleasant for all to work in. In a reflective mood I noted that military operational work with the Territorial Forces was more like a "day time walk in the bush, once or twice a week." We were constantly on the alert when deployed, and prepared for immediate action at any instant. Contacts with the enemy were frequent, but the district chief made sure we were not too close to the action. Such was the security situation at the time. Further, it was not the usual thing for the district chief to be out and about at nighttime. If I had chosen to be on night deployments with a PF platoon or an RF company, I would have become a security problem for the district chief and his staff. He was very protective of each of his advisors, so it was judged to be prudent to work within the boundaries he subtly indicated. This was rather humbling, as the Australian way of operating was to not give the enemy the advantage of the cover of the night.

A clear majority of the Vietnamese people in Quang Tri City and adjacent hamlets and villages were supportive of the GVN. This area was in the coastal plains of the province. It was a relatively secure area, thanks to the allied main force formations that were further out, in the mountains to the west and near the DMZ.

In Australian military doctrine the enemy involved in revolutionary warfare could be carrying out actions in the political and military spheres over several phases: Passive Phase, Active Phase, and Counter-Offensive Phase.[1] The phases overlapped, as was the case in Quang Tri Province, with regression and progression from one phase to another happening concurrently. This situation continuously exercised the minds of commanders at all levels in Vietnam. Many of the post–Vietnam War writings highlight the ebb and flow experienced in the conflict in South Vietnam during this protracted war.

On 8 September my local commanding officer, Lieutenant Colonel Harley Mooney, recommended me for the S3 (operations officer) advisory position in Team 19. The earlier period in the province was an ideal preparation for such a role, and I was ready for more challenging work in Quang Tri. The circumstances behind the recommendation have recently been provided to me by Mooney.[2] The next day the commanding officer AATTV approved my taking up the position. A vacancy had arisen following the appointment of the incumbent, Major John Hannon, U.S. Army (Infantry), to the national MATs Training Team for In-Country Indoctrination. I judged that John was relieved to be moving on, as it was clear that he had not clicked with Mooney.

I felt it was a distinct honor that the position had been offered. I was well prepared for the role. The military environment in the province was unique. I was looking forward to working with Lieutenant Colonel Mooney and the other staff officers in a very stimulating sector of South Vietnam. I wrote home, telling Eva that "it will be a safer job than the present one, but much more challenging and more work of course." On reflection, that was a hollow reassurance to Eva, as risks were taken on a daily basis on the ground and in the air and you knew not when the enemy would strike or a mishap might occur. There was plenty of evidence to support this view.

The duties that went with the sector operations officer (S3) position included:

1. Advise the Vietnamese S3 and assist him as required.
2. Act as the operations staff officer to the province senior advisor.
3. Supervise the Tactical Operations Center (TOC) and Fire Support Coordination Center (FSCC).
4. Liaise with the headquarters of brigades, regiments, and divisions in the area.
5. Monitor pacification (security aspects).
6. Be the training supervisor for MACV Team 19.
7. Process herbicide operational requests for the province senior advisor.

Some details of my settling in as an operational staff officer follow. I had concluded that my appointment to the position arose because my two commanding officers, Ray Burnard (AATTV) and Harley Mooney (Team 19), judged that I was qualified for the job, and that I had the talents to do it.

Before John Hannon departed, I accompanied him to a province chief briefing on a possible refugee resettlement operation. The PSA, Bob Brewer, and the DPSA, Lieutenant Colonel Mooney, were at the briefing. That meeting was a very useful experience as I was able to assess the relationships between the characters present and see how each man carried out his role. After the early formalities, John briefed us on the general concept that was being applied to the major operation being planned, Operation Fisher (which will be covered later). As additional resources to be employed for the operation were to come mainly from U.S. agencies, the province chief gave support with frequent nods of his head while calmly smoking his cigarette. Brewer and Mooney had earlier accepted the concept, and so had little to say. My role at this briefing was a listening and learning one. With agreement achieved and handshakes all around, the visitors were bade farewell by the chief. Smiling, and with some relief, John handed the papers and maps to me, wishing me well. It was clear that planning was to be a big part of my new job. I looked forward to the challenge.

Included in the role of a staff officer is the responsibility to provide assistance to commanders and staff in solving problems. I adopted the military appreciation method for problem solving. Thinking deeply about the problem, identifying the facts, and assessing resources required in a multinational setting rested with me. Taking ownership of a problem was a way to immerse myself in the issues to be considered, enabling the way ahead to be sorted out. I was confident that with the methodology I was to use a soundly based plan would evolve. Fortunately, at the time, the likelihood of enemy interference was at the lower end of the scale.

Our sector Tactical Operations Center (TOC) was the hub for Team 19, and was the center of the communications setup for our sub-sector advisory elements in each of the seven districts in the province. I was not comfortable with the layout of the TOC, and after discussion with the soldiers who did duty there, and some of the other staff officers, I directed some changes be undertaken. Two days later the changes had been achieved, and received nods of satisfaction from those who worked in the center. There was one major shortcoming: the TOC was not a combined one with our Vietnamese counterparts. At the Mai Linh sub-sector headquarters a combined operations center had been established, and that gave me confidence to work quietly toward achieving a similar arrangement at the sector level. A few weeks later the Territorial Forces sector commander, Lieutenant Colonel Nhan, agreed to a combined TOC at the sector level.

Anniversary days and festival occasions were celebrated when possible. On 13 September the 1st Air Cavalry Division celebrated the birthday of the division. The host was the commander, Major General Irby, the oldest member of the division and on his third tour with the unit. Our sector was represented by the province chief, Nhan, Brewer, Mooney, and me. It was a large gathering. Our transport to Thua Thien Province that day was by Air America helicopter. The birthday was a very pleasant occasion, and provided an opportunity to build up the professional friendship network.

My first night roster duty in the operations center came up on 20 September 1968. It was a quiet night. The operators on duty knew their stuff and did a good job. Over the next few days it was evident that there was a calmer atmosphere in the center. Clearly the new arrangements were effective, with less crisis management surrounding routine daily tasks.

In most military units all ranks know that if they keep the commanding officer happy, then their lot in life will be a happier one. After a little more than a month in his job as deputy province senior advisor, Mooney had let it be known in clear terms what he required from his team and its members. He was full of life, and very refreshing. Some staff had unforgettable moments through incurring his wrath. Others also learned from that kind of short, sharp experience and performed better. Clearly not all people were working to their capacity, some discovering that when motivated they achieved beyond their own expectations. For trained soldiers and officers the key was to be self-motivated, and to show initiative when required.

By the end of my first week as the S3, Mooney had briefed me on each of the plans that he had in mind for me to develop. The major one was Operation Fisher, followed by security for the rice harvest. Another was to study the alternatives for the relocation of refugees from poor soil-type areas to more productive areas. Other possibilities were foreshadowed as well as other operational matters to do with the sub-sectors and the many units and formations in the province: ARVN, U.S. Army, and U.S. Marines. The major formations in the province at this time were the 3rd Marine Division; 1st Brigade, ACD; 1st Brigade, 5th Infantry Division (Mechanized); and two regiments of the 1st ARVN Division. I needed to work closely with my counterpart and many others to achieve the goals set.

After ten days as S3 I was thoroughly enjoying my new job. Although the work was demanding, one felt exhilarated each step of the way, each day. New experiences arose daily, and Mooney was putting in a fine performance keeping morale up. He was able to project his very engaging personality effectively. Team 19 was lifting its game, and all ranks were very pleased to hear in the second half of September that Mooney would be the province senior advisor from 1 October 1968. I was delighted, as our working relationship was sound and growing. Mooney was to have a civilian officer as his deputy, who would be taking up the reins on most of the civil operations. I could see myself being involved in a wider range of tasks until the day the new deputy arrived.

Mooney required a training directive to be drafted by me and my staff in late September. My earlier months in Mai Linh District had given me a good insight into the competencies of the military people in our Team 19. One would expect and hope that soldiers posted to a war zone would be qualified and competent in their rank/trade/military skills. So it turned out to be. Maintenance of skills was essential. Also, provisions needed to be in place to help prepare members for the next step in their careers. The paper produced was succinct. It covered the essentials required by Mooney and was accepted by him. It was most satisfying as an Australian Army staff officer to be able to adapt to the needs of a friendly foreign army and produce the goods, in the context of supporting South Vietnam.

Colonel Roy Land visited our headquarters on 24 September accompanied by a major of his staff. The colonel was from headquarters XXIV Corps and headed the psychological operations staff branch, G5. The corps commander, Lieutenant General Stilwell, would have sent him out on this mission. It was puzzling. He was after information, asking questions, with us providing the answers. The subject matter was already available to him in his own headquarters. Were we being examined and assessed? Behind this fact-finding visit there appeared to be some military politics at work. Only time would tell.

In several ways the first day of October was a memorable one, the day Lieutenant Colonel Mooney assumed the position of province senior advisor (PSA). The evening before, the senior intelligence officer of the 3rd Marine Division requested that the PSA and I attend a special briefing the next morning at the divisional headquarters at Ai Tu. The briefing commenced at 8 A.M. We were informed of a regimental operation that was to commence the next day in the Cua Valley to the west, in the foothills, in the area of

Colonel Harley Mooney (right) and Major David Millie. (Original image provided by Australian Department of Defence, Copyright Australian War Memorial, AWM CRO/68/0962/VN.)

our sub-sector at Huong Hoa. The intelligence targets were enemy caches, VC military and civilians, and vehicles.

At 9:00 A.M. we moved further west by helicopter to LZ Stud at Vandegrift Combat Base, near Ca Lu, where the headquarters of Task Force (TF) Hotel was located, commanded by Brigadier Frank

Garretson. The operations briefing commenced at 10:00 A.M. I will refer to the operation as "TF Hotel." At this briefing we and many others, mainly USMC officers, were informed that the 31st Local Force Battalion, a VC main force unit, was reported as being in the area. The 9th Marine Regiment was tasked for the operation. The infantry units to be involved were presently deployed and operating elsewhere, and had to concentrate for this impending operation. I thought that the nominated battalions might be working to their limit. The 3/9 Marines were to be flown in by helicopter. Two battalions, the 2/9 and 2/3 Marines, were to march in from Camp J. J. Carroll, southwest of Cam Lo on the high ground. In this location were a number of heavy-caliber artillery units providing support to units on the ground many kilometers out. The 3/4 Marines were designated as the reserve.

In this limited war and counterinsurgency environment reserves were designated from deployed units or subunits not otherwise engaged with the enemy. Divisional commanders with helicopter lift capabilities available were able to redeploy troops from one area to another within a few hours to respond to changing tactical situations. Commanders kept themselves up to date with the deployment of their troops in their areas of operation by knowing where every company or squadron was located. Planning staff and operations staff had to be constantly alert as to dispositions of troops, particularly those in contact with the enemy. The divisional and brigade commanders could be helicopter-borne for hours each day visiting, observing, and being seen by their troops. A good dialogue was required between commanders and staff to ensure locations and troop movements were accurately known and plotted.

I soon discovered there was a need for me to keep close to Mooney, as he was in conversation with an array of commanders and staff officers during these briefings.[3] We realized that Vietnamese authorities had yet to be informed of the intentions for the next day. This was a wise approach to take from a security point of view, but created some challenges for the advisors, who in this case were being relied upon to make the overall operation work. The notion of advisors being the oil and the glue with our counterparts became very clear to me in this operation.

The intentions were to conduct a relatively large combined cordon and search operation, with the cordon being provided by the U.S. forces. The search inside the cordon was to be undertaken by

Vietnamese forces, accompanied by intelligence staff, including a cell from the marines. One of the possible outcomes was to help bring back GVN control to thirteen hamlets in the district. This was a large-scale precursor to a clear and hold operation, giving pacification a flying start in the Cua Valley.

My role now was like that of a whisperer, giving some of my thoughts to Mooney if he was not engaged with others. We each knew that a number of actions had to be initiated by us quickly. As was the case from my first day in Quang Tri, I carried maps and a manpack radio with me. In addition, signal operating instructions were carried that provided the frequencies and call signs for a number of military communication networks in our sector. As a fallback, we could have asked the marines for the use of their communication facilities, but a streak of independence prevailed, plus an amount of professional pride. We were able to get our messages through without marine assistance. We had the resources to do what we had to do. Furthermore, we had the use of our direct support helicopter for the day. Bob Brewer was unintentionally inconvenienced by our use of the helicopter on this day. Some more about this will be given later.

Some background to the events of this day needs to be outlined before continuing with the story of the planning for the operation. Up until early 1968 the district of Huong Hoa covered the land area of Quang Tri Province from about where we were at Vandegrift to the Laotian border, about thirty kilometers to the west. During the time of the battles around Khe Sanh, NVA assaults caused the abandonment of the Special Forces forward operating base at Lang Vei, as well as the advisory team compound at Huong Hoa. The Vietnamese administration at the district headquarters also abandoned its compound. The Vietnamese officials were evacuated to Cam Lo and the advisors to the MACV compound in Quang Tri City. A refugee flow to Cam Lo also resulted.

The GVN, to minimize the propaganda value that North Vietnam could claim from overrunning the district of Huong Hoa, excised a land area from Cam Lo District and reestablished Huong Hoa District in the wide and beautiful Cua Valley to the south of Cam Lo village. The Territorial Forces were reconstituted there, as was the Special Forces forward operating base and some other minor military and civilian elements. Major Jim Hill, U.S. Army, was the district senior advisor for this new arrangement.

Later in the morning at Vandegrift a verbal warning order was passed to Jim Hill for him to gather leaders of the various elements in his location for a briefing at his headquarters. At 1:00 P.M. Mooney briefed the group on what was to happen, and their respective roles in the operation. Those in attendance included the commander of the forward operating base, Major Clive St. Cyre (also a Special Forces A-Team commander), and Bob Handy, a Montagnard Affairs worker located at Huong Hoa. The district advisory team was to provide a liaison officer to the 9th Marines light command post. Our Vietnamese counterparts were not yet in the loop. This was to be done back in Quang Tri City, where Mooney, as the province senior advisor, would inform the province chief of the operation. Liaison arrangements were discussed.

Mooney and I, accompanied by the liaison officer, then attended a regimental briefing at the 9th Marines at 2:00 P.M. As soon as we could break away, we helicoptered to our advisor on the ground at Ca Lu, Australian warrant officer Ken Chester of the Cam Lo District advisory team. He was with the local PF platoon there. MAT leader Captain Baldwin was allocated as liaison officer to the 9th Marines fire support coordination center (FSCC). We then made our way back to our sector headquarters at Quang Tri City, arriving there at 4:00 P.M.

Arrangements were made with Lieutenant Colonel Nhan. He was to provide an intelligence platoon, two National Police Field Force platoons, an armed propaganda team, some members of the Police Special Branch, and a Phoenix and psychological operations team to supplement an RF company, two PF platoons, and local police. Additional RF companies were to be airlifted out to the operation.

Then at 6:00 P.M. Nhan, his S3, and I helicoptered out to the Cua Valley to assist the Vietnamese in their coordination and tasking arrangements. Nhan and Captain Cuu did an excellent job in making a quick plan and organizing resources for the operation. It was an exceptional day for me and for the PSA on his first day in that role. Involvement in the planning of this marine operation took me into another role, literally overnight. It demanded flexibility and good communication skills. The advisors had been tested and were found to be up to it.

While we were to the west, the remaining advisory staff at sector headquarters that day made the necessary coordination arrangements for a separate sector operation in Hai Lang District, to the southeast of Quang Tri City. These two operations were a big test for Team 19. Our advisory resources were now fully committed for the next few days, as were our communications. We were confident that our contributions were measured, and would meet high expectations.

Later in the evening our sector staff was advised that one of the marine battalions nominated for the operation at the Cua Valley was still north near the DMZ. To add further to the puzzle, a battalion of the 2nd ARVN Regiment was to fly into the abandoned Khe Sanh plateau in the early hours of the morning. These matters were beyond our control. For an operation of this scale, several levels of command in the ARVN, U.S. Marines, and U.S. Army were involved: headquarters I Corps and headquarters 1st ARVN Division, 3rd Marine Division and headquarters III MAF, and headquarters XXIV Corps.

On 2 October Army Chinook helicopters arrived at the large sector LZ at Nhan Bieu One to lift the Vietnamese sector elements to Huong Hoa District. My counterpart, Captain Cuu, and I deployed with the troops. The marine cordon battalions had successfully deployed during the night. There was no contact with the enemy. We were informed that plenty of illumination of the operational area was provided by the friendly artillery during the night hours. The security of the operation could have been compromised by such action. Once the cordon was in place it provided an opportunity for the hard-worked marines to have some rest—and to dry out, as further west in the mountains there was plenty of moisture from either perspiration or rain.

Screening was the term used to describe the interview and interrogation process undertaken within the cordon by the Vietnamese military and police. Sixteen VCI persons and twenty-four VCSs were taken into custody. A top VCI person from the local village was included in the roundup. He was elderly, but I was assured by the Vietnamese that he was a killer. It was revealed that young girls in the village had been taught VC songs, which they had to sing to the village people. As a counter, the police told the girls to learn and sing GVN songs before they could be released. Photographs taken of these girls told a story: they were sullen and resentful, an understandable disposition in their circumstances. During the afternoon on 2 October I was recalled to sector headquarters by the province

Ladies of the choir, Cam Lo.

senior advisor to brief Mr. Cross of CORDS Da Nang. He came in by surprise, seeking a briefing on the pacification plan for the counteroffensive.[4] A later chapter is devoted to the national pacification campaigns of 1968 and 1969.

It was noticeable during the first week of October that the civil and military advisory efforts were coming closer together within the province. Better outcomes by way of advice, and support, to the Vietnamese agencies were apparent. Mooney had been well prepared for the PSA role: "the new broom sweeps clean." Preparations for Operation Fisher were under way. Professional links grew quickly for me within our CORDS team, particularly through social contacts. Sometimes the extra personal effort required to be patient, and to be courteous to others, paid dividends.

By mid-October the staff coordination role was a busy one, not only within the sector advisory team but to headquarters of military formations within the sector. Requests for air support from advisors were frequent, either for reconnaissance or liaison work, troop lift by helicopter, medical evacuation, or close air support. Major Brad Oliver, the Territorial Forces advisor, was easy to work with. He was not hesitant in having a quiet word with me about matters which, on reflection, could be referred to as military culture—with me being the one out of tune. In some cases the matters were hard to fathom, and I realized he was a kind of spokesman for his peer group, using me as a go-between to the province senior advisor.

As the workload was increasing on me, the PSA directed that I not be included in the duty officer roster. Officers of the advisory team staff took turns of duty at night in the operations center. It was not arduous, but nor was it restful. I was off the roster from late September. After a Brad Oliver "chat" I asked the PSA if he could review his earlier decision and allow me to be put back on the roster. The response was a negative, no change to the earlier direction. Mooney, sensing the pressure from my peers, said to me that the job I had was up for any takers and if I received any complaints to refer the officer to him. That settled the issue. I judged my transition from the district to be over then.

The AATTV decision to keep me in Quang Tri for my one-year tour of duty certainly worked in a positive way for me. I was happy to continue in the province, appreciating the challenges ahead in a higher level appointment. Within Team 19, I was required to be responsive to the PSA and to work cooperatively and productively with fellow staff officers and district senior advisors. Empathy was required with colleagues and counterparts.

The next chapter describes my further experiences in operational staff work in Quang Tri sector. With counterparts the "oil and glue" role provided a discovery experience requiring flexibility, patience, perseverance, and constantly being mindful that I was a guest in South Vietnam. As an advisor I was also a mentor, friend, listener, and facilitator to my counterpart and his colleagues, be they military, police, or government officials. More broadly, relationship building with allied divisions, brigades, and regiments in the province was a constant liaison task. My role was not limited to the Territorial Forces, but extended to the ARVN, U.S. Army, USMC, U.S. Navy, USAF, and the Special Forces. Visitors had to be given full attention.

9

Sector Staff Work

The Oil and the Glue

September–December 1968

The previous chapter outlined events associated with my transition to the sector operations advisor position. This chapter describes my day-to-day routine experiences as the Team 19 planning and operations officer up to the end of 1968. Significant projects are narrated in later chapters.

Planning had been under way for a few days for a Territorial Forces sector operation on 16 September. A helicopter assault was to be launched from an airfield to the northwest of the Ga Bridge using Mai Linh forces. The pickup point was between Highway 1 and the Thach Han River to the immediate north of the bridge. There were to be five Huey's and two gunships initially. Then two Chinooks with three sorties each were to follow. The operation was a follow-up to the Mai Linh contacts with the VC in August around the abandoned village of Nhan Bieu Two. The assault landing zone was to the southwest.

The airlift was delayed for two reasons. First, the target landing zone had been moved farther south, with the aim of blocking any VC from withdrawing into the hinterland. Second, we were advised that an information leak at sector level the day before may have compromised the plan. This change led to adjustments in the artillery fire plan. The Team 19 assistant sector advisor, Lieutenant Colonel Karl Schelhammer, U.S. Army, accompanied 911 RF Company. He and the aviators were frustrated by the delays incurred. The operation continued and sweeps by the troops were uneventful. No contact was made with the enemy.

A joint command post had been set up at Nhan Bieu One near a primary school. The children in their breaks gathered around us, being inquisitive. Some interesting side observations were made at the airfield. The command post included a Vietnamese junior officer, Second Lieutenant Phuc, who had the title of communications officer. Phuc was a nephew of the province chief. He acted as though the world owed him a living, and in the vernacular would probably be classed as a brat. My counterpart, Captain Cuu, had to direct Phuc to erect a 292 aerial for our communications. With a "Who, me?" expression on his face Phuc reluctantly got on with the job. Fortunately, we did not have to work with him again. In a personal review of the operation I thought the allocation of U.S. Army helicopters was of training value only to the Territorial Forces, and of little benefit to the operation. The troops came out of the area by foot. They could have approached on foot quietly to gain surprise, rather than by aircraft with the unavoidable noise.

The advisory team at the Gio Linh District sub-sector headquarters was located less than three kilometers from the southern boundary of the demilitarized zone, well within the range of a quick NVA assault. Quang Tri City was twenty kilometers to the south via Highway 1. Lieutenant Colonel Mooney had an aspiration for the Gio Linh sub-sector to be relocated to a relatively safer place. He asked me to speak to the senior district advisor there, Major Chuck Slaby, and to write an appreciation on the problem. Mooney confided to me "each time I see Chuck off to Gio Linh I feel it will be the last time that I will see him." Such was his concern.

A liaison officer from 1/8 Cavalry, ACD, came to the sector headquarters to discuss details of an operation scheduled for the following day at the village of Thuong Xa, six kilometers to the southeast. Two companies were to operate there for the night by forming a cordon around the village. By mid-morning, 18 September, there had been no enemy contact at Thuong Xa. The U.S. troops had been in the cordon all night. Local forces conducted the village search in the daylight hours. Some of the detainees held were under the control of the Vietnamese military and police forces. The cavalry officer in charge requested that the detainees be handed over to them at the conclusion of the search. This request was declined by the local Vietnamese officer in command. The U.S. troops did not argue, probably happy to take back the statistics to headquarters rather than face the administrative problems of managing the detainees. Any intelligence arising would be passed back to the ACD. I hoped there would be a follow-up from the liaison officer on lessons learned from this short operation. There was no joint evaluation.

Again a command post for an operation was close to a school. Children began to arrive at 7:30 A.M. At assembly they held a flag-raising and sang the national song. Concurrently rifle fire and air-to-ground fighter strikes were going on to the west. Leaflets were falling from aircraft overhead, and rotary wing aircraft were flying low in the area. Peacetime activity and war were going on together. The children and the teachers continued with their normal routines. What resilience by the people.

Following information from Saigon, via the usual chain of command channels, preparations commenced to ensure security for a visit to the province by the GVN Minister for Montagnard Affairs. Montagnard was the term given to the people of the mountain tribes of Indochina. They were composed of a number of ethnic groups and were not ethnic Vietnamese. In Quang Tri the Montagnard tribe referred to in this narrative was the Bru.

In the relocated district of Huong Hoa to the south of Cam Lo in the Cua Valley a Bru village had been established in the first half of 1968, after the Tet offensive. A short flight in a light helicopter allowed me to do some preliminary coordination with the local district chief and the district senior advisor, Major Jim Hill. The province chief and the PSA, Bob Brewer, then arrived to finalize details. Discussion followed and agreements were made on matters of concern: locations, timings, speeches, presentations, and hospitality and security arrangements. The sector Vietnamese executive officer and his assistant operations officer then flew with me to Cam Lo sub-sector headquarters for discussions with the local district chief. As an aside, the executive officer suggested to the district chief that he clear up his area. This was tidy towns stuff, an unusual display of civic pride. With Brewer and Mooney we visited the Combined Operations Center at the headquarters of the 3rd Marine Division to coordinate support for the ministerial visit to Huong Hoa. We then went to Gio Linh to discuss pacification plans with Major Slaby. The issues surrounding a possible relocation of the sub-sector headquarters were canvassed.

The visit by the Minister for Montagnard Affairs on 20 September was a big event. The province chief was the local host and carried out his responsibilities with aplomb. The people of the Bru village turned out in their traditional dress. It was a very colorful occasion. In my opinion there is a similarity in stature and appearance between the Bru people and the highlanders of Papua New Guinea. It was an excellent day all around. The buffalo ceremony was one of the highlights. The occasion was celebrated with a feast, a sacrificial buffalo being a focal point. Drummers circled the tethered buffalo, with swordsmen dancing to the rhythm of the drums. The animal was killed by constant knifing. The blood flowing from the animal was collected and mixed with rice wine. Other blood collected from a piglet and chickens were added to the brew. The carcasses were cooked over an open flame. Fortunately, I had not been invited to the feast.

Later that day I had a conversation with Major Slaby about the Gio Linh headquarters and the proposed relocation. Chuck was ambivalent, as was Schelhammer. They were probably representing a Vietnamese position, no change, and may have had difficulty dealing with the Mooney view that there may have been safer options.

That night I was duty officer in the advisors tactical operations center in the Citadel. It was clear that the operators were proficient and enjoyed carrying out their responsibilities. It was a quiet night. After a discussion with our intelligence advisor, Major Paul Laski, I wrote up my contribution to the province monthly report. Concise statements on security and the friendly situation were composed and submitted.

An interesting personality case was running as an issue in the province during the September/October period. The central figure was a CORDS officer located in one of the districts. I met him for the first time on 12 September. He was a civilian advisor employed in refugee support. I will call him Ted Law. Two weeks later it became clear he was becoming involved in military activity. He was enthusiastic and just could not be kept down. From a military point of view Ted was getting out of his depth, not having been trained for what he was trying to do. A judgement call had to be made by the PSA. Ted was advised to give more attention and time to his prime responsibilities.

I had suggested to the PSA in early October that Ted might be more gainfully employed in Revolutionary Development (RD). Advisors were of the opinion that he was a CIA man. Now that Mr. Brewer had left the province we thought that Ted may have lost a patron. A week later he accompanied a senior local CORDS officer to Da Nang. We hoped this would clear the air about this fellow. The district senior advisor, who was well aware of Ted's behavior, was relieved that he was out of his territory. On 21 October reports came in that Ted had returned to his district. He had flown in direct from Da Nang with medical supplies for a certain military agency operating there. This was a surprise to the district advisor and Team 19. The district senior advisor was of the opinion that the program Ted had prime responsibility for in the district had lost momentum with him as leader. Ted was called into Quang Tri City to have interviews with local senior advisors. He left Quang Tri the next day for the south. Ted returned his radio to the district senior advisor a week later. He was not seen in Quang Tri again.

On 21 September my counterpart, Captain Cuu, and I discussed the coordinating details for a sector operation a few days hence. This required a visit to the headquarters of the two local air cavalry brigades and 3/5 Cavalry. Details of these operations were not recorded in my diary, nor were copies of written orders retained. I judged it to be inappropriate to make personal files on these matters, primarily for security reasons.

A further visit to the headquarters of the 1st Air Cavalry Brigade was required early the next morning in order to clarify some issues for a sector orders group at 9 A.M. The meeting went well. Of interest to me was a suggestion that the sector forward command post operate in a mobile role. Lieutenant Colonel Nhan accepted the suggestion. In my first few months in Quang Tri I had observed that the normal procedure was to set up a static forward command post. My view was that this approach was not always an appropriate one as it lacked flexibility and the command post could become separated from the operating elements in the area of action.

Then heavy rain fell. The compound and barracks were flooded. Late in the evening I drove with Lieutenant Ed Logan to the sector operations center to check if the joint operation was still on. Our counterparts assured us that the operation would proceed if the supporting helicopters could come in for pickup. This was positive, as we had formed a view that with the amount of water about, enemy soldiers concealed in bunker systems might have been flooded out and forced to the surface.

Very early the next morning we received advice that the operation was cancelled, due to the rain. When the advisors arrived at the operations center we discovered that our Vietnamese counterparts were in bed. This was disappointing. This lack of adaptability was of concern to me, and I expressed my view to Captain Cuu when he appeared. He in turn passed this exchange to Lieutenant Colonel Nhan, who was very upset to hear of my point of view. It was one of those situations where opinions differed. The rain continued. For the twenty-four-hour period eight inches of rain fell. The VC may have had the same view about the rain as Nhan; don't fight with nature. So that day I spent the bonus time writing up the training directive for Team 19.

Later that day an ARVN artillery logistics lieutenant drove into the Citadel seeking advisor assistance. He was officer-in-charge for a resupply convoy delivering ammunition to fire support base C1, north of Dong Ha. His convoy could not get clearance to proceed along Highway 1. A marine check point at Ai Tu, close to a significant Marine Corps maintenance area, controlled traffic on the highway. Colonel Mooney directed me to immediately attend to the problem. A light helicopter was tasked to fly this mission. The lieutenant and I flew a road reconnaissance, observing the road to be awash in some places. At these sites, scraper machinery had been placed across the highway as traffic blocks. The lieutenant was prepared to take the convoy up the highway despite the conditions.

The lieutenant was anxious to deliver the ammunition. So I decided to go to the top, to the chief of staff at 3rd Marine Division headquarters. He was located near LZ Kiwi landing pad. Fortunately he was available, listened to the problem I outlined to him and to the request for the ammunition convoy, as a special case, to be cleared to proceed, with the lieutenant accepting the risks on the damaged highway. He agreed and then directed his G4 (logistics staff) to give directions to allow the convoy to proceed.

I flew as a convoy escort up the highway, landing at a number of roadblocks. The marine communications worked, and the convoy passed through to Dong Ha. To add further frustration, a jeep had fouled a bridge when crossing in haste and had to be lifted out to clear the passage. This convoy event had a happy outcome for all involved.

Highly regarded Australian journalist Creighton Burns visited Quang Tri on 25 September. He was given briefings by Brewer, Mooney, and Bibb. Then he joined up with General Clifford B. Drake, deputy commander of XXIV Corps, for visits to Huong Hoa, Cam Lo, and Gio Linh. In a letter home that evening I wrote: "We had an Australian journalist up here for the past thirty six hours,

Creighton Burns. He is from The Age Melbourne editorial staff, the political and defense writer. He is a very interesting fellow. The advisory team gave him a good run round the province. I think he would have left here with as much information as was possible to get in the time."

A few weeks later Eva sent to me two articles written by Burns. His reporting about the situation in Quang Tri was very accurate. I gave the cuttings to Mooney. After reading them and acting very surprised, he exclaimed with a smile: "Bob Brewer certainly spoke out."

Another joint operation was being developed. Captain Cuu and I made a liaison visit to the 3rd Marine Division headquarters' operations staff. We then moved on to Cam Lo District headquarters to check in on a small operation there. The light observation helicopter was a wonderful support vehicle for this kind of work. From Cam Lo, we proceeded to Ca Lu, our main destination, it being the location of the 4th Marine Regiment headquarters, commanded by Colonel Sexton. Journalist Burns accompanied us on this mission.

The marines were keen to have the people in three hamlets of Ba Long District screened by the Vietnamese authorities. The hamlets were in the valley of the Thach Han River, on an underdeveloped part of road 556, inland to the southwest of the city. This was in "out of sight, out of mind" country, very isolated. As the marines had the capacity to cordon the area and wanted to undertake the operation, the Territorial Forces and other province resources had to be allocated to make it all happen. Cuu visited Cam Lo on our return to sector headquarters to give warning to his local people of what was coming up.

Later that day, 26 September, I flew out to Huong Hoa to visit Major Jim Hill, DSA. He escorted me around the various military elements in the district, including the Special Forces forward operating base, and a company of the Civil Irregular Defense Group (CIDG).[1] There were engineers in the area on other tasks for external agencies. In the evening I worked on the Ba Long operation, on a document about Huong Hoa District, and prepared a Quang Tri sector brief for the new commander of the 1st Brigade, ACD, Colonel Bair.

On the evening of 27 September the assistant sector advisor, Lieutenant Colonel Schelhammer, Jim Hill, and Paul Laski joined me for a planning session on the Cua Valley, the new home of the displaced Huong Hoa District. Some of the interesting considerations were about CIA-sponsored elements that we knew little about. These were:

- A provincial reconnaissance unit (PRU). A role of this covert civilian-based intelligence gathering organization was to destroy the VCI.[2]
- A forward operating base (FOB). This was a base for Special Forces out-of-country and in-country operations. CIDG elements were involved here.
- A cell of the Vietnamese Information Service (VIS), to take photos and build up files. Data gathered were added to the local census book.

Our Team 19 people on the ground at Huong Hoa were not fully informed on several issues. We had been discussing what we were seeing, but had no involvement in the activities of the three organizations. The then PSA, Bob Brewer, had not briefed Mooney on all that he knew. My notes at this point recorded: "Spooks fooling themselves." The simple conclusion of our deliberations at this point was that we should mind our own business. The planners for the Ba Long operation, both the marines and the Vietnamese, were gathering resources together. The advisors were facilitators in a way; once we had introduced the main participants to each other (marines and sector) our role was to respond to requests, to help achieve the objectives.

On 27 September, Captain Cuu, with me in tow, visited Cam Lo and then the 4th Marine Regiment headquarters at Ca Lu to firm up details for the conduct of the joint operation. Cuu was on top of the details, and impressed his audiences when describing the resources allocated by the sector headquarters to the operation: an armed propaganda team; representatives of the Census Grievance Organization; mobile advisory teams; an intelligence platoon; Police Special Branch and National Police Field Force elements; representatives of the District Intelligence and Operations Control Center; the No. 15 Counter Intelligence Team; sub-sector RF/PF elements; air, artillery, and communication assets; logistic elements; and even toys for distribution to children.

The following day as a follow-up to the previous day's visit to Cam Lo and Ca Lu, Major Bernie Meisel (Logistics) and Captain

Alfred Ellis (Personnel) accompanied me to Cam Lo for further liaison on the operation. This final coordination was necessary as some contingency issues raised at the Team 19 evening meeting had to be addressed.

The same day Mooney, Hill, and I visited the G2 (Intelligence) at the headquarters of the 3rd Marine Division to discuss concerns in the Cua Valley. The advisors thought that the military situation there was poor. The fighting effectiveness of the military elements present was suspect, and possible avenues of approach by the enemy from the south were not adequately covered. Further, Hill thought that the CIDG would be wound up via command channels, through III MAF, with the CIA behind the initiative. Hill expressed the view that the CIDG area would be occupied by the district headquarters to save on government expenditure. These uncertainties were left with the marines, as they were becoming the dominant security force in the province. Team 19 was taking all reasonable steps to protect our own, bearing in mind that Huong Hoa District had relocated from the Khe Sanh area earlier in the year, pressed by overwhelming NVA action.

Later in the day I made a final trip to Ca Lu to arrange for two advisors from Cam Lo sub-sector to be located at the Fire Support Coordination Center at the 4th Marine Regiment headquarters. This was an important safety measure in order to look after the interests of all the Vietnamese elements in the operation. It was a Team 19 responsibility to keep the marines fully informed as to where the various sector elements were located. We did not want friendly fire, artillery, or air strikes being brought down on our own troops.

On the way back from Ca Lu, I dropped into Huong Hoa to pick up a medical case, a Bru parent and son who needed treatment at the province hospital. That evening one of the advisors from Cam Lo at Ca Lu was counseled by Mooney on his attitude toward the marines. Team 19 was anxious for the success of the Ba Long operation, as it was our first major operation since being excised from Team 4. Further joint operations of a similar nature were on the horizon. The key was the performance of the Territorial Force troops involved, and the effectiveness of the oil and glue provided by the advisors.

Early on the morning of 29 September, Mooney, Cuu, and I helicoptered to Ca Lu to view the Ba Long operation. The 3/4 Marines provided the cordon. We heard from the marine viewpoint that the operation, so far, was very successful. The marines were pleased, so we were pleased. A satisfying outcome was likely to be very helpful to Team 19 in the long-term. However, another advisor stepped way out of line when he left the Ca Lu area without his counterpart. He had fussed over a transport matter, on incorrect assumptions. He was paraded to Lieutenant Colonel Mooney on 30 September to explain his case.

That same day a critique was held on the Ca Lu/Ba Long operation. Good points were highlighted, particularly the close cooperation with civil authorities and the civilian population. A minor point was that toys and candy for the children should be distributed by the elders of the community or village officials rather than the Vietnamese military or police.

The marines demonstrated their increasing confidence in the sector by initiating a more ambitious joint operation in the Cua Valley. The planning and implementation of this operation was described in chapter 8. Team 19 involvement in the planning commenced on 1 October, with execution on 2 October. This operation, like that in Ba Long, was testing and exciting.

The first three days of October were characterized by intense command and staff activity. On top of what has already been described, planning for Operation Fisher was building momentum. A high point arose when the PSA and I were required to helicopter south to Phu Bai late in the day on 2 October to attend discussions with Colonel Land at XXIV Corps headquarters.

These talks were vital in helping to shape the combat and logistic support required for the refugee relocation, Operation Fisher. After the talks with Colonel Land were completed I then had to arrange helicopter resources to support the Cua Valley operation. From about 11 P.M. I attempted to confirm helicopter transport to deploy an RF battalion from Quang Tri City to Huong Hoa for the next day. The operations staff at the corps headquarters and at headquarters 3rd Marine Division could not help me achieve the support needed. This was a puzzle to me, as we were doing our best to meet the needs of a USMC operation, which had been agreed to on 1 October. The PSA and I spent the night at Phu Bai, returning to Quang Tri early the next morning.

While these operations were going on, two "must attend to" visitors came into Quang Tri Province, requiring my full attention. The first was Mr. Cross on 2 October, as mentioned in chapter 8. Then on 3 October a very welcome visitor was Colonel David Thompson, the Australian Army's Director of Infantry. He knew me well, as I had been a cadet at the Royal Military College, Duntroon, Canberra, when he was there as an instructor in tactics. He had a full day interviewing Australians, calling on commanders, and lunching with Colonel Mooney.

There was a hiatus on 3 October, with a number of commanders becoming involved in what was the air transport "stuff up." As described earlier, helicopter lift was not available that day to deploy an RF battalion into Huong Hoa District for the joint operation. U.S. Army, USMC, and ARVN brigade, division, and corps commanders all had "more than a finger in a small pie." Six seniors were listed in my diary. Mooney was very upset about becoming involved in a resource matter over which he had no control. The solution was that the RF battalion was trucked into Huong Hoa on 4 October. They were extracted by truck on completion of the operation. I thought a long march out might have been of benefit to the Territorials.

To help bridge communication and perception gaps, Mooney, Nhan, and I met with the commander of the 2nd ARVN Regiment, Lieutenant Colonel Vu Van Giai; the commander of TF Hotel, Brigadier Garretson, USMC; and the commander of the 3rd Marine Division, Major General R. G. Davis, in various locations during the day. Telephone calls were also made to other seniors. Lieutenant Colonel Nhan was upset that the commander of the 2nd ARVN Regiment was involved in the issue, judging that it was none of his business. Garretson and Giai were on very good professional and personal terms. Nhan may have missed that aspect. We all lived to fight the enemy on another day, and were a little bit wiser for the experience.

There was excitement two days later at our local helicopter landing ground, known as the Stadium, when our direct support OH-6A helicopter experienced a flameout, an engine failure, fifty feet above the ground on an approach to landing. The aircraft dropped to the ground, experienced more than a heavy landing, and fell apart. Fortunately there were no injuries. The mangled chopper was salvaged the next day. A replacement helicopter continued to support Team 19.

A sector operation was undertaken on the Hai Lang District coast on 7 October. The 3/5 Cavalry made up the cordon, with five RF companies working within the cordon. The Vietnamese people within three hamlets were the cordoned group that day. It seemed such a contradiction that GVN forces and U.S. forces were conducting an operation against the people of South Vietnam. The targets were VC and VCI within the cordoned hamlets. In my view the people were living a life of peasantry. The day was perfect weatherwise, the beach area placid; the hamlets were well developed. The firing of weapons was not required. I did not record the outcome of the operation.

General Drake, deputy commander of XXIV Corps, visited on 12 October. He was brought up to date on our pacification planning, and the advisors associated with the Phoenix Program gave their spiel. I recorded that the CIA seemed to be involved in too many activities: spying as well as advising and leading RD, Police, PRU, CIDG, and Special Forces. The obvious question was: Who was assessing their effectiveness?

Other activities in mid-October highlighted the kinds of things that went on around me that I could only ponder one at a time. The first provided an opportunity for cautious advisor guidance. It was apparent within the sector headquarters that the Vietnamese military staff did not get into the planning of an operation early enough. This was especially so if they were going to call upon the U.S. Army or U.S. Marines for combat or helicopter support. Short warning times were common—for example, a late afternoon bid for helicopter uplift early the next morning. It begged the question: "After a U.S. departure from South Vietnam, how could the GVN forces cope?"

The second concerned my evening visit on 20 October to our operations center to help organize support for an RF battalion operation for early the next day. The poor preparations came to naught, as our counterparts informed us that it was too wet to undertake the operation. There had not been a reconnaissance for the proposed action, which was probably planned on the basis of local knowledge. In this case detailed planning by counterparts was not evident to me, so the wet weather saved the day for some. The attitude displayed on this occasion was similar to my observation about the same battalion a month earlier, described in chapter 5.

Significant changes were upon us. The over-the-beach supply base at Wunder Beach in Hai Lang was to be vacated by the U.S. Army. This would have been a strategic decision at the highest level. The need in Quang Tri for such a facility had clearly decreased, especially as the ACD was to be redeployed from the region later in the month.

I visited the 3rd Marine Division headquarters the next day for discussions on a "Monsoon Plan" for the Cua Valley and Cam Lo. Participants included the G2 (Intelligence), G3 (Operations), and G3 (Plans). Giving a seasonal name to the plan reflected the nature of Marine Corps operations at the time. The NVA was regrouping and the emphasis was on counterinsurgency. Marine combat units were not under as much pressure now as they were earlier in the year. Intelligence was of the view that the Cam Lo area had been infiltrated by the VC. Undercover action was being taken to help in the assessment of the threat. As an interim measure, a marine rifle company was to be allocated to each of the Cam Lo and Houng Hoa sub-sectors with the mission to conduct night operations. Patrolling made good sense, as the battlefield needed to be better controlled, preferably dominated.

The magnitude of events elsewhere in South Vietnam came upon us in late October. On a routine staff visit to the 1st Air Cavalry Brigade headquarters I learned that the ACD was to relocate to the Tay Ninh area in the south of the country. The 1st Brigade was to commence its move on 3 November, with the other brigades of the division moving earlier. This was a strategic relocation. At a personal level, a number of sound professional relationships had developed with the staff officers and commanders of the ACD. They would be missed.

Reports had indicated that four NVA divisions had been located in Cambodia, in areas to the west of Tay Ninh Province. The ACD was needed there. The 3rd Marine Division, well established in Quang Tri Province, was to be given a broader area of operations within our province, bolstered by the 1/5 Infantry Brigade. This major decision by the commander of MACV would also provide a challenge to the 1st ARVN Division and the Territorial Forces (RF/PF). The Vietnamese throughout the province would have been in a reflective mood on receipt of this news.

As pacification planning stepped up throughout South Vietnam, more units and formations were reaching out to our advisors for information. Following on from discussions with the marines, the 1/5 Infantry Brigade took up the opportunities we provided. The S5 (psychological operations) of the brigade paid us a visit. He was fully briefed on all relevant sector assets and objectives. As a follow-up, I visited the brigade headquarters, now located at Dong Ha, and had discussions there with the commander and his operations officer. Colonel Mooney had already agreed that advisors were to suggest to the U.S. Marines and U.S. Army in our area that units be encouraged to make affiliations with district officials and build relationships for security operations or civil action activities. Commanders and staff warmed to that concept.

Early on 30 October General Stilwell visited the Citadel. He informed sector staff of an operation that was to commence on 1 November. It was to be a joint effort over three days and was to be with ACD involvement, prior to their redeployment south. The location was to be in the area of My Chan, twenty kilometers to the southeast of Quang Tri City, close to the boundary of Thua Thien Province. The extent of resources to be employed indicated that plans had been agreed to at a high level for this operation to be undertaken. USMC assets were not involved. The general was testing concepts and capabilities in a major counterinsurgency operation. At the same time the operation could perhaps provide some deception while the ACD was preparing to move south. The forces warned to be involved in the operation at My Chan included:

Three battalions of the 2nd Brigade, ACD
One battalion of the 101st Air Mobile Division
One battalion of the 1/5 Infantry Brigade
Three battalions of the 1st ARVN Regiment
One battalion of the Regional Forces.

Our advisory staff and available counterparts headed for the 1st ARVN Regiment post-haste. The group who went to La Vang included the S2 for Team 19, Major Paul Laski, Phoenix coordinator Riddell, and the district senior advisor to Hai Lang, Major Paul Fitzpatrick. We agreed that the commander of the 1st ARVN Regiment had to make some resource decisions before detailed tasking could commence. What we learned on arrival at the headquarters was that planning, implementation tasking, and organization was well advanced. Some of the elements to be regrouped into working teams had been identified and included:

a Combined Intelligence Exploitation Center (CIEC)
a detainee compound (Vietnamese responsibility)
an interrogation group comprising teams from:
  1st ARVN Regiment

Province, District, and Special Police
two PW teams
two counterintelligence teams
an Intelligence Group:
Representatives of all units
Representatives of: PRU, Police Special Branch, NPFF, CG, and APT, and
an exploitation group: S2s and S3s of participating units.

Nearly all of the intelligence agencies of the province were represented in this operation.

I accompanied Lieutenant Colonel Nhan and his key staff to LZ Nancy the next day for further briefings. We met the S3 of the 2nd Brigade, ACD, there. He did not know of the operation. The battalions finally tasked were three units of the U.S. Army to perform the cordon and block, and another three units of the 1st ARVN Regiment to perform the search and hold.

I made a brief visit to the operation with Paul Fitzpatrick on 2 November. We found that our Vietnamese counterparts had established an ideal CIEC. Detailed hamlet blacklists were available. The Quang Tri Province list totaled eight hundred names. During the operation suspects were flown by helicopter to the interrogation center. Later in the day my counterpart, Captain Cuu, and I went to LZ Nancy and obtained an overlay of an operation for the next day, also in the My Chan area. The general idea of this supplementary operation was to attempt to apprehend a number of VC who had slipped out of the My Chan cordon.

The next day a visit to the exploitation center revealed that progress was slower than expected, but otherwise the operation was going well. The battalions had been exploiting tactically and achieving results. An enemy breakout had been attempted during the night hours. It had been contained, with twenty enemies being killed in action. The operation concluded on 4 November. Despite the operation's being smaller than intended, the Vietnamese forces involved were able to exercise all their intelligence assets effectively. This was reassuring for the future.

Representatives from the 212th Combat Aviation Battalion visited our sector headquarters on 30 October. They had no doubt been encouraged to do so by staff at the XXIV Corps headquarters. The 282nd Aviation Company at Da Nang had been tasked to support

Team 19. The brief was to provide a helicopter in direct support on a daily basis. This was a timely allocation for us. With Operation Fisher under way we needed this level of guaranteed daily support. For commanders and staff the helicopter had a positive multiplier effect in operations. As a resource-poor advisory team, we were now better able to carry out our role efficiently and with greater effect. Our counterparts would benefit also. Crews were to be accommodated at the MACV compound in Quang Tri beginning 23 November.

Later that day, with one of our operations center staff, we visited the 1st Brigade, ACD, headquarters. They were packing up, preparing for their relocation. We were scrounging up useful materials for our operations center, our S2, and our counterparts. I had a brief conversation with Major Robert Canady, the brigade S3. He was exhausted, nearly asleep on his feet. I wished him well on behalf of all in Quang Tri. We were losing a good friend, as the ACD in Quang Tri was highly regarded.

To end the working day a staff officer of the 3rd Marine Division, accompanied by the S5 of the 1/5 Infantry Brigade, visited sector headquarters. They were concerned about the procedural aspects of clearing artillery fire missions directed near or into populated areas. This was a sensitive and serious subject. None of us wanted to bring friendly fire upon civilians or our own troops. A fire support coordination center had the final say in fire clearances ranging from artillery to naval gunfire to B-52 strikes. So, the fundamentals for "clearance to fire" were outlined, agreed upon, and implemented. Due to the relative inactivity of enemy forces in the populated areas of the province, I was not aware of any significant incidents relating to friendly fire during my time there.

The first day of November marked the commencement of Blackcat support. Mooney took the first arrival, a UH-1H helicopter. The Inspector General of the Army accompanied us on this trip to Cam Lo, Huong Hoa, and Gio Linh. The marines had embraced the concept of affiliations with districts at Cam Lo. Advanced elements of the 2/3 Marines headquarters were present. It was made clear to us that this was not the battalion headquarters of 2/3 Marines, as there were strong political reasons for the headquarters to be located at fire support base J. J. Carroll.

At Huong Hoa District, Jim Hill was pleased to inform us that the mess hall of the 1st Brigade, Air Cavalry Division, headquarters was to be relocated into his area on departure of the ACD. The building would be used as offices for the district chief and his team. A marine company was now operating in this sub-sector. It was noted, for the benefit of the Inspector General, that the GVN had not committed any major funding for this district. The situation seemed to fit the axiom: "The further you are away from the center, the less will be the interest." It seemed Huong Hoa would continue to be the "Siberia" of South Vietnam.

We then flew to Gio Linh, another candidate for the "Siberia" tag. Chuck Slaby told us it was a fairly normal day for his post, with 130 mm artillery rounds coming in from north of the DMZ. No casualties were reported. Chuck flew out with us to Quang Tri City, as he was going farther south to Da Nang for his first break since arrival. It was a well-deserved rest for him.

That night at 12:15 A.M. the VC in Quang Tri sent three rounds of mortar fire into the sector headquarters area. One round landed on the ammunition dump in the Citadel. An estimated 800 tonnes of ordinance was caught up in the resulting big bang: 105 mm, 81 mm, 155 mm, and small arms ammunition. Sadly, it was a great fireworks display, with explosions going on throughout the night. There were no casualties or fires outside the Citadel. It was one of the hazards of war, a lucky strike for the VC and a serious inconvenience for many of us.

Other issues came up for consideration on 3 November. Early that day a number of advisors met with staff officers of the 1/5 Infantry Brigade headquarters and officers from the 1/11th Infantry Battalion. The brigade staff and the battalion were putting their minds and efforts into assessing their contribution to the pacification plan. We provided a full brief on sector military assets, operations and responsibilities, and intelligence.

Later in the morning I was flown to headquarters 3rd Marine Division (Operations) to discuss an ARVN proposal for an RF battalion to take over an area of operations that was presently the responsibility of 3/1 ARVN. The 1/5 Infantry Brigade also had an interest in this initiative, and I discussed the issue with their staff the next day. Advisor support for the RF battalion also had to be arranged. On 4 November the switch came into effect, with the 3/1 ARVN moving elsewhere. In Team 19 this outcome was judged to be taking local forces in the right direction, as it moved the GVN military toward self-sufficiency on the ground at last. But there was a long way to go to general self-reliance. Lieutenant Ed Logan had the job of leading an advisory team formed to assist the RF battalion. I organized a UH-1H and escorted the team to Tam Hue, dropped them off, and departed. The precise location of the battalion headquarters was not known. As was expected, the team soon married up with the RF companies.

A report came from reliable sources to operations via intelligence that there would be a mortar attack on the night of 3 November. The CAP at Nhan Bieu One and a FO from 1/11 Infantry Battalion were detailed to move into the area, to the southwest, to take action against a possible threat. This teaming of a Marine CAP, a PF platoon, and U.S. Army direct support artillery to a district was for me a very pleasing outcome in a counterinsurgency situation. The mortar attack did not eventuate.

On 8 November the PSA, accompanied by my counterpart, Captain Cuu, and me, responded to a request from the district senior advisor at Cam Lo, Major Bill Healy, to act as intermediaries in a dispute that was developing there. On arrival we were met by Healy, his district chief, Lieutenant Chin, and his operations officer. It appeared there was a difficulty between the district chief and the RF company commanders. This was clearly a host country problem that was best resolved without advisor participation. The advisors listened initially and then left the local military to talk it though. They did so and reached a happy resolution. This meeting at Cam Lo raised questions in my mind: "Are we really doing what the Vietnamese need and/or want?" and "Are we pushing them too much?" Was it prudent to ask these questions? These were matters for the PSA to formulate. It was interesting and stimulating to chat with Mooney on such ideas.

Our operations center was reorganized to accommodate a FSCC team on 11 November. An RD team had been invited to join our burgeoning center, but did not make it due to a lack of initiative by civil/military RD advisors. The commanding officer of the 5/4 Artillery Battalion of the 1/5 Infantry Brigade visited his three soldiers who were setting up as part of the fire clearance authority.

I visited Jim Hill on 12 November at Huong Hoa for a brief on a 3rd Marine Division cordon and sweep with a battalion of the 2nd ARVN Regiment. A battalion group including tanks was to work into the cordon on the third day of the operation. RF/PF elements were to cordon hamlets, assisted by a NPFF platoon. Hill described the operation as a population control measure. Aircraft fitted for broadcast were to be used over the cordon to warn people caught up in the sweep that they were to move out of their houses for a documentation check. The intelligence estimate was that there was a company of Viet Cong in the area to the northeast in the Cua Valley. The outcome of the operation was not recorded.

Following the visit to Jim Hill the sector was requested to provide a further NPFF platoon to support the combined operation in the Cua Valley. This platoon was to come from Quang Tri City, where it had been deployed to provide security around the gas and electrical plant. The sector headquarters had to find other local troops to provide security to the plant. This use of the NPFF in the operation in Huong Hoa seemed to be a much more productive employment rather than the one in town. The troops probably thought otherwise. My job was to ensure that they flew out to the Cua Valley by helicopter the next day. That was achieved, thanks to the USMC.

A surplus prefabricated, mobile, office-type trailer had been found at Dong Ha. It was lifted by a flying crane to our local landing zone. With the assistance of a two-and-a-half-ton truck and a forklift, the trailer was moved to the area of the operations center. To his credit, Major Bernie Meisel (a logistics advisor) arranged the whole deal, which in the end was supervised by the redoubtable Lieutenant Colonel Nhan. While at Dong Ha the trailer had been stripped of whatever could be removed. Team 19 arranged for a Korean contractor to rebuild it. So, another scrounging effort paid off.

A luncheon was hosted by Colonel Mooney for a Red Cross representative from Sweden on 15 November. The representative had a British-made prefabricated hut for presentation to the local Red Cross. The intention was for the hut to be erected in the Mai Linh District headquarters compound. The PSA responded positively to the request to provide a supervisor to put the hut together. The lunch was a happy affair. The Red Cross representative visit prompted this written reflection at the six-month point of my time in Vietnam:

- The operational theatre of South Vietnam comprises both war and peace. When conflict comes into the populated areas peace disappears and warfare prevails. This leads to a general layered overview of power at play:
  - The machinery of the sovereign government of South Vietnam struggles to prosecute a war, seeking to achieve peace and freedom.

- The machinery of a well intentioned military super power guest, the USA, is here to help prosecute the war against armed aggressive communism.
- The machinery of a determined armed and aggressive communist enemy, some of whom work within the GVN, was in serious conflict with the Free World Forces.
- The first machine, the GVN, is weak tired and requiring full refurbishment, and does not provide a sound framework for the future.
- The second machine, the US eager and anxious, is militarily superior to the others but does not own or administer the government of South Vietnam.
- The third machine, North Vietnam is militarily inferior, logistically weak, arguably winning politically and psychologically, and is prepared to make huge sacrifices to reunify Vietnam.

The organizational structures of this complex war were described earlier in chapter 2. The above was my considered view of the conflict in November 1968. The overview summarized my thoughts then, and arguably reflected the conundrum carried in the minds of many of the allied leadership in South Vietnam and elsewhere.

The pessimism of the above reflection was mostly offset by daily events, with the likes of the PSA, Major Meisel, and Captain Black (Pay Corps) helping boost morale with good-natured banter. Team 19 evening meetings, around 5:00 P.M., were a clearinghouse for information and ideas. Some individuals were very entertaining, with Captain Black coming into that class, being bright and witty in presentation and performance. He was a good team member, and we all enjoyed his company.

Our direct support Huey flew us west for a liaison visit to Cam Lo and Huong Hoa on 20 November. Captain Cuu was in the group. At Cam Lo we listened to a debriefing on a PF contact with the VC. Casualties had been suffered. After providing reassurance, we moved on to the Cua Valley to visit leaders and staff at Huong Hoa sub-sector. Major Hill thought the place was in limbo, as the district chief was reluctant to accelerate pacification. When writing reflections that evening, the methods used by the VC were recorded succinctly:

Military tactics: raid, ambush and booby traps.
Political tactics: terrorism, psychological including propaganda.

At a routine Saturday weekly briefing for all available subsector advisors and staff on 23 November, Major Hill of Huong Hoa presented what I described as a "plea for help," as he was concerned about possible troop withdrawals from his district. By way of background, it was clear that some of the U.S. forces were going to be moving out of Quang Tri to the south, and perhaps thinning out was under way for a significant troop withdrawal.[3] The concern expressed by Hill was appreciated, especially after he related that fire support base J. J. Carroll was to close soon and that the U.S. advisors with the CIDG would be moving out from his area in January 1969. Already fire support bases A3 (north of Cam Lo) and C3 (close to Cam Lo) had been abandoned. These closures were consistent with the new concept of operations of the 3rd Marine Division, to be explained in chapter 18.

The broad question we were asking ourselves was "What does it all mean?" We knew the NVA was regrouping during its recovery from the Tet offensive. VC military action was relatively quiet. The Paris Peace Talks were under way, but it was early in the process. The military complex that was established at Ca Lu, with its advanced landing ground at Vandegrift, established for the relief at Kha Sanh, was also to close down. At the meeting we were informed that General Lam of I Corps had directed engineers to upgrade the road to the Cua Viet, through Trieu Phong District (Route 560).

It was a challenge to military leaders and staff in South Vietnam to keep the fighting spirit and troop morale at high levels. Answers would only come with the passage of time. The next day in our post-meeting discussions the local view of the advisors was that the thinning out of bases indicated that the Americans had some plan in mind for execution in the coming months. We noted that Richard Nixon had been elected president of the United States on 5 November.

The Blackcat crews were accommodated in the Quang Tri MACV compound from 23 November. The next day I accompanied the available crews to the 3rd Marine Division FSCC and the Division Air Support Center for orientation. A positive aircraft control zone had been established north of Hai Lang from early November. All aircraft within the zone except for helicopters and O-1s (Bird Dog aircraft) were to be on radar control for the whole time while in that zone.

I considered that a morale issue was in the making when I was requested to write up annual officer reviews on the U.S. Army officers who had come under my direct control over the past six months. The process in the U.S. officer system was known as "officer rating." I was not familiar with this reporting system. In the early stages of writing the required assessments I realized that I was not culturally attuned to what I had been requested to do. I discovered that the system lent itself to exaggeration, to a high degree. I appreciated that I would not be doing justice to the officers that I was to report upon because of my lack of familiarity with the nuances of the U.S. officer rating system. So as to avoid a morale mishap, I declined to undertake the task. This was accepted by the personnel officer.

Team 19 held a meeting for psychological operations officers of the 3rd Marine Division on 25 November. The meeting covered our mission and objectives. A seminar format was judged to be a useful way to formally communicate our pacification objectives to units, keeping in mind the frequent turnover of officers, normally on a six-month rotation.

Two days later I was in the Hai Lang district with my driver and interpreter to observe a sector operation. A recently arrived advisor, a U.S. Army captain, joined us for familiarization. The troops had covered the ground quickly. At the last objective the RF battalion had a serious contact with the enemy. In a rapid firefight eight enemies were killed and six weapons captured. Tactical skill was demonstrated to achieve the result. Soon we joined up with Lieutenant Colonel Nhan. The captain was introduced and in a short time they were having a discussion in French. Later I was told that they were discussing the merits of having another language. The cultural dimensions of mankind had a place on this particular battlefield. It was an enriching moment for those involved.

The Vietnamese forces were taking advantage of a lull in enemy activity about this time. I noted that this reduced activity was probably a convenient break for the Vietnamese, as they had been constantly at war for many years. I went on to note that their relative inactivity was no reason for advisor activity to be lessened. During the lull the generals were about, as were the advisors. The PSA and I went to Huong Hoa to meet up with General Drake and the chief of staff of the XXIV Corps headquarters. We then proceeded to Gia Dang on the coast, where the acting commanding general of the XXIV Corps, General Melvin Zais, and General Truong joined the group for a sector briefing on the Gia Dang project: Operation Fisher.

At the conclusion of that session we then proceeded to Cam Lo with General Drake. On return I obtained a vehicle and drove unaccompanied to Van Van hamlet, four kilometers to the east of the city. A police operation with the Territorial Forces was being conducted there. A combined information center had been set up for the operation. On the way to the center I offered a lift to two older gentlemen who were headed in the same direction. They appreciated the ride. On arrival at Van Van the first people to greet me were Generals Zais and Truong. It was a quiet day with nothing of significance going on. I was pleased to see the generals being involved at this relatively low level of activity. Driving back to the city I provided transport to seven children and four soldiers. I was prepared to provide this help to the locals despite the risk.

The mobile advisory teams were advisors to RF companies. Their time with companies was not designed to be of a permanent nature, as their role required them to upgrade the military skills with a company and then to move on to another. The advisor responsible for MATs in the province had done some research on this issue and found that it was time for some rotations. After consultations with Lieutenant Colonel Nhan and his staff, three MATs were to be reassigned to build up other companies and to freshen up themselves.

General Davis arrived unannounced on a courtesy visit to the province chief, who was out. The general informed me that he desired to see the province chief more often in order to get a better performance out of the Territorial Forces while the NVA were out of the province. By destroying VC and the VCI, the enemy would lose guides and organization to support the NVA if and when they came down from the north. The province chief had several U.S. counterparts to assist him in his mission

At the end of November I decided to rewrite the standard operating procedures for our operations center. The PSA and the executive officer supported the idea. As the review developed, the document evolved into a sector SOP. Following on from that effort the next staff exercise was to write an appreciation on Quang Tri Province roads. Lieutenant Ed Logan (Engineers) assisted me in this task by undertaking the road survey. Most of the visual inspection was conducted from a helicopter. The task was to do with repair and maintenance, to include a recommended priority order, and phasing over the next six months. The staff work was done in a couple of days, and the military system higher up the chain received the report. The province did not have the assets to do any of the work identified, and the advisors did not receive any feedback on the report that was submitted.

I accompanied Lieutenant Colonel Nhan on a visit to a sector operation at Nhu Le, six kilometers south of Quang Tri City, on 11 December. This was a joint effort with a cordon provided by two rifle companies of the 1/11 Infantry Battalion of the 1/5 Infantry Brigade, with the RF/PF and the NPFF working their respective search areas within the cordon. It was clear that the Territorial Forces were not doing any searching.

This was a typical anti-VC operation. Prior to such an operation a blacklist would be compiled of suspected VC/VCI within the hamlets to be searched. Nhan was informed that by mid-morning twenty-three suspects from the blacklist of forty-three names had been detained. In addition, villagers had handed in two grenades and a 75 mm recoilless rifle projectile. More broadly, there seemed to be no end to people being detained and to munitions being uncovered. Clearly there was divided opinion among the Vietnamese people about the future of their country, even this far from the political centers, be it Hanoi or Saigon. What an impossible dilemma it was for the South Vietnamese authorities. It was difficult to imagine the conflict being resolved to their satisfaction and on a basis of a guaranteed peaceful outcome.

Two days later I guided the PSA and the DPSA, Mr. Terry McNamara, on a visit by vehicle to Nhu Le, via Phuoc Mon, in the La Vang area. There were few men in the hamlets, and people knew little of VC activity there. This was consistent with a view often given by Nhan that only one man will know of each hiding place. Security was of prime importance for the VC. There were many young children in the area, giving rise to the question: "Where is your father?"

The VC military forces had not given up the resistance. They reminded us they were still about with mortar fire incidents. One night Mai Linh District reported several incoming rounds, without any loss, and the marine logistic base nearby had eight to ten rounds incoming, again without damage.

Early on 12 December I accompanied Lieutenant Colonel Nhan on a flying reconnaissance to Giao Liem, eleven kilometers to the north of the city in Trieu Phong. President Thieu was to visit the hamlet later that morning. All was in order for the visit. Later in the day the president officiated at the Gia Dang resettlement ceremony.

Census work.

The Cam Vu operation was not given the priority we were seeking. However a large-scale cordon operation in the Cam Lo area was being planned. On 15 December, in company with the PSA and John Cleary, we drove to the sub-sector headquarters to be briefed by the district senior advisor, Major Bill Healy. That night, a cordon operation involving three battalions of the 3rd Marine Division was to be conducted around the Cam Lo refugee camp. The search elements were to be provided by the 2nd ARVN Regiment. A combined intelligence center was to be established. What were described as "finger booths" were to be constructed with tin sheeting to allow people within the camp to point out, in relative secrecy, VC/VCI suspects who were to be paraded in front of them. It was noted that the Territorial Forces were not involved in this operation. Of more interest to me was that two of the marine battalions were from the 3rd Marine Regiment, located to the south of Da Nang. Also it was becoming clear that Lieutenant Colonel Giai, commander of the 2nd ARVN Regiment, was playing a role as a political leader in the northern districts of Quang Tri Province.

As Christmas was approaching I was back on the overnight TOC duty roster. The PSA directed that all field grade officers were to pull duty as the truce period of 24/25 December approached. At the request of the 124 RF Company, the 5/4 Artillery fired illumination rounds over Mai Dang to the southwest of the city. The company had contact with the enemy and reported three enemies killed and one friendly wounded.

To help celebrate the coming of Christmas the advisors organized a children's party for the Vietnamese who worked within the Citadel. A sense of fun started with the chief organizer pointing out the irony of a Jewish U.S. Army advisor arranging a Christmas party for people who were mainly Buddhist. The 3rd Marine Division Band attended the function, and their performance was superb, adding to the enjoyment of the day.

After an exciting day in Da Nang on Australian business I was into a night planning session with Mr. McNamara. I wrote in my diary, "It was pleasing to see the RD types involved in staff planning work." At 1:30 A.M. we experienced another mortar attack. Seven rounds fell on our area, with one being over the road from the PSA's house. Many slept through the short bombardment. The Nung guards were holed up in their bunkers, a sensible self-preservation action. Casualties that night amounted to seven wounded. The consensus the next day was that the rounds came from the same area as before, to the southwest of the city. The Vietnamese sector leadership planned to put four RF companies into the area to search for the mortar men, with perhaps a cordon being provided by the 1/5 Infantry Brigade. I wrote in my diary: "It will be interesting to see how thorough and inquisitive the search."

On 21 December I recorded that "the Vietnamese Sector FSCC was under way now, after experiencing delays in fire clearance." It was a long but worthwhile process to achieve this outcome.

As a pre-Christmas gesture to his troops, Lieutenant Colonel Nhan and his wife made a Blackcat tour, with me as escort, to outposts in the province. We dropped into Ca Lu, Gia Dang, Gio Linh, and Huong Hoa. At each stop 2,000 piastres were handed over to each RF/PF unit in that area. Where the money came from remained a mystery. Mrs. Nhan, a businessperson, had recently lost laundry contracts with the U.S. forces as it had been discovered that drugs were being pushed at her laundry enterprise at the Ai Tu combat base.

News came in from Gio Linh sub-sector that the advisors were getting into the Christmas spirit. Signalman Logan at Dong Ha subsector had drawn a sketch of Chuck Slaby as Santa on a buffalo, with a rifle in hand, and headed "Santa Rides on in the DMZ." This showed a good spirit within the ranks of Team 19. Word came back to us that Chuck had seven stockings hanging off the shelf of his sub-sector, one for each member of his advisory team. Gio Linh was a very hot spot. The advisors did not seem to be perturbed, much to their credit.

A temporary truce period was approaching with Christmas. On the night of 22 December, eighteen mortar rounds fell in the area of LZ Sharon in the marine maintenance base, again coming in from the southwest. Our artillery on the next night was active with harassing and interdiction fire, an arm of firepower whose effectiveness was very difficult to assess. Opinion within the advisory body was that this period would be favorable for the VC to attack, possibly causing our forces to overreact, and perhaps continue a battle into the truce period.

Christmas Day was relatively peaceful. The mail had come in. Eva's letter was a welcome one, accompanied by a Christmas parcel. I read *Exodus*, by Leon Uris, for most of the day. The midday meal was a special one, and much appreciated by all. I also devoted time to reviewing the sector operations SOP and giving my counterpart, Captain Cuu, a gift of a carton of cigarettes. At 5:00 P.M. it was back to reality. I was duty officer at the operations center. It was reported that there had been four incidents during the truce, events that one could do little about. More interesting was the news that on Christmas Eve the nominal VC hamlet chief of Nhu Le was killed in an ambush. Operations had been conducted in that area two weeks earlier. Vigilance had to be constant for each side.

At year's end I wrote a summary into my diary, reflections of the work done so far: "The year ends on a successful note. It has been satisfying for me under the circumstances of working for the Americans with the Vietnamese. It is a sad situation all round however. There is no end in sight for a long term settlement. The North seems to accept that with the USA here there will be no military victory. It will be in the political arena that the war will be settled, and obviously with US concessions. I wonder if it will be at the expense of the Vietnamese."

The next chapter covers the national pacification campaigns of 1968 and 1969, being two of the major policy initiatives that helped turn the tide militarily in favor of the allies in South Vietnam.

10

Pacification Campaigns, Strengthening the Spine

1968 and 1969

A province senior advisor (PSA) in South Vietnam had a very broad range of activities and programs within the scope of his responsibilities. There were 217 programs countrywide. In this chapter I will cover my involvement in some of the programs related to pacification. They have been grouped together here for convenience of presentation, as they all contributed to our drive for peace and a better way of life for the people of South Vietnam.

Military activity in Quang Tri Province had been intense in the first half of 1968. Allied forces operating in the area to the south of the DMZ had ten or more fixed defensive positions, which in some cases inhibited flexibility. Mobility of the allied combat force was somewhat limited with this design for battle. General Davis was striving to have a more flexible and mobile force structure. The NVA in some cases was able to take offensive initiatives on the ground of its choosing. However, by the end of May 1968 U.S. military operations had exhausted the enemy in Quang Tri, evidenced by a general withdrawal of enemy main force units out of the province.

As a GVN response to the enemy's February 1968 Tet offensive, a national Pacification Counter Offensive Plan was developed and implemented. At the early stage the concept was closely held by the PSA in Quang Tri, as I do not recall seeing or reading any documents during the preparation stage of the national plan. On 22 August, Bob Brewer, the PSA, briefed advisors on the general aims of the pacification plan. Termed a Special Pacification Campaign by the GVN, there were six interdependent campaigns:

- An intensive military spoiling campaign to destroy enemy organized forces and divert them away from populous areas of South Vietnam.
- An all-out effort to upgrade between one thousand and eleven hundred contested (D- and E-level) hamlets to at least C-level hamlet status before 31 January 1969.
- An accelerated Phuong Hoang campaign to neutralize at least three thousand VC each month. (Phuong Hoang was known as the Phoenix Program by the United States.)
- A stepped-up Chieu Hoi campaign to rally at least five thousand Hoi Chanh between 1 November 1968 and 31 January 1969.
- A widespread people's self-defense campaign to organize 1 million defenders and to arm at least two hundred thousand.
- An information campaign to demonstrate to the people and the enemy that the GVN had seized the initiative and was moving rapidly toward the end of the war.

I was of the view that the enemy had broken contact. It seemed that there could be some arrangement between the governments of North Vietnam and South Vietnam to bring about a cease-fire. Some liberation committees were being set up by the VC within South Vietnam. These committees were quietly coming into villages and hamlets as the GVN moved toward an anticipated cease-fire.

Bob Brewer invited Major John Shalikashvili and me to see a fortified hamlet at Thieu Phong District on 22 August. This was a well-defended hamlet, surrounded by layers of barbed wire and other obstacles, a model of self-defense. Mr. Brewer mentioned that he would like to see the hamlets in Nhan Bieu village resettled along the lines of this fortified hamlet. Nhan Bieu village was in Mai Linh District. Whether a resettlement could take place was a matter for the Vietnamese. At the time resettlement into a defended hamlet in Mai Linh District was not a priority issue for local Vietnamese authorities.

I noted the Soviet intervention into Czechoslovakia in late August. It was my thought that this put aside the policy of Russian "peaceful coexistence" for an indefinite period, coming on top of the 1956 intervention into Hungary.

From my new position as S3, I observed that the senior commanders were frequently in personal contact with each other. As an example, on 16 September Generals Stilwell, Lam, and Truong visited the province chief for lunch. Mr. Brewer was away for the day, and Mooney did not attend. Then on 27 September Mooney accompanied the province chief to an RD meeting in Da Nang with President Thieu and General Lam. Colonel Mooney later informed his team that the president impressed the gathering. The president had commented on HES and census figures. The RD effort for the pacification plan was to be concentrated in secure areas, as the RD teams had a very limited capacity to defend themselves, let alone to hold ground.

On 19 September Brewer, Mooney, and I went to Gio Linh District headquarters to discuss the pacification plan with the advisors, and sought ideas on the proposal for a relocation of the sub-sector headquarters to a safer place. I wrote to Eva that evening: "I had a remarkable experience today. We travelled to Gio Linh headquarters, three kilometers from the DMZ. One of our district teams is there permanently. As you can imagine it is not really 'settled suburbia' as far as the Vietnamese are concerned. Yet there we were discussing refugee problems and civic action projects right under the nose of the North Vietnamese. It was all very British, and indicative of the spirit of optimism that prevails here. I do hope it is a realistic view."

The reality was that leadership and effort by our military, both Vietnamese and allied, were holding the nation of South Vietnam together. The troops followed with loyalty. With a possible U.S. troop reduction the GVN was faced with the huge challenge of making plans to enable the nation to carry on into the future with less U.S. support. Concurrently the military capabilities of the ARVN needed to be expanded. Optimistic and pessimistic thoughts were often in my mind. The capabilities of the NVA and the intentions of its government were the sobering realities into the future. Being at Gio Linh, on the DMZ, was as close physically as one could be in a visual sense to the land interface of the opposing forces. This place was one of the iconic areas of the Vietnam conflict.[1] We lived in hope.

Mr. Brewer, at the completion of his tour, was replaced by Lieutenant Colonel Mooney at the end of September. On 2 October, Mr. Cross of CORDS came to Quang Tri for a briefing on the local pacification plan. The advisor viewpoint was that sixty hamlets could be upgraded in security assessment by 1 January 1969. The advisors at sector level had further discussions with the PSA. We were preparing a major briefing on the local pacification plan for the commander of XXIV Corps, Lieutenant General Stilwell. Our general view was that over the following three-month period the GVN and all agencies assisted by the United States needed to make up ground lost over the past fourteen years (since 1954). One local U.S. leader said of the GVN: "This is the last gasp of a defeated administration." Up to this point in Quang Tri all of the pacification planning by the advisors had been undertaken without any dialogue with our Vietnamese counterparts. Advisors needed to keep in mind that we were developing proposals.

The whole of the next day was devoted to preparing the briefing for Colonel Mooney, to be presented by him to the visiting senior leaders on 5 October in the afternoon. It fell to me to present the advisory staff conclusions to the PSA with Cleary, Cumming, and others in attendance. I felt it was a rather disjointed presentation. However, Colonel Mooney was ready to do the whole presentation himself.

Early on 5 October I visited the office of my counterpart, a routine call when in the headquarters. I noticed a chart on the wall that closely resembled our proposition for a new counteroffensive. In conversation with Captain Cuu it became clear that we had each been provided similar instructions from our respective higher levels, and each had been directed to keep the planning confidential. We agreed that we should inform our immediate superiors of this situation. It so happened that at the time the province chief was in Da Nang, at the headquarters location of the I Corps commander, General Lam.

Advisors of Team 19 had a very busy time that morning. All district senior advisors were in the Citadel to attend a CORDS Da Nang briefing on New Life Development (NLD), a term used to cover most of the pacification initiatives in the counteroffensive. The presentation addressed how the officials at district level were to administer the various programs that were essential to the GVN Pacification Counter Offensive Plan. This was a sound step, as it reflected a confident approach to nation-building. A table in chapter 5 shows the organization of CORDS in the province, including the components of New Life Development.

We were advised at 1:00 P.M. that General Truong would be attending our briefing that afternoon. Communications came in from higher levels requesting we work with our counterparts. This resulted in joint participation in pacification planning. The irony of this was that it should have been a Vietnamese planning exercise in the first place, with advisory assistance. Our PSA was disappointed with what had transpired. His disposition was not assisted by a chronic back condition and a heavy cold.

The afternoon briefing by Team 19 was made to an impressive audience. General Stilwell was accompanied by his deputy, General Drake, and they were joined by the commanding general of the 1st Air Cavalry Division, General George T. Forsyth, and the commanding general of the 1st ARVN Division, General Truong, and their staff officers. The Quang Tri sector's Vietnamese contribution to the Pacification Counter Offensive Plan was to upgrade thirty hamlets. Team 19 had identified eighty-six hamlets for possible upgrade, comprising 20 percent of the population of the province. Our priority list was made up of the following number of hamlets in various areas: Gia Dang (19), Cua Viet (2), Route 9 (23), Route 1 (21), Cua Valley (13), and Cam Vu (8). These hamlets were "must do" from a national and a security aspect, in the opinion of the advisors. The hamlets included the homes of many displaced Vietnamese people, including some of ethnic minorities, who were suffering severe disadvantage due to recent battles fought over their land. With projects already in place, we judged that fifty-six hamlet upgrades could be achieved.

After Colonel Mooney concluded his presentation General Stilwell had some words of encouragement. He addressed higher level policy considerations. In the development of the national strategy President Thieu and his cabinet held formal deliberations with the U.S. ambassador to South Vietnam and the commander of MACV, General Abrams. President Thieu had expressed the view that his government wanted a counteroffensive prior to Tet 1969. The United States supported this approach and wanted the campaign to be launched right away. So, the grand scheme of things was laid before us in Quang Tri.

As soon as the VIPs had departed, Lieutenant Colonel Nhan came to the advisors with his staff. It was common knowledge that he was not on good terms with the province chief. Nhan was often bypassed by him. The province chief communicated with Nhan's executive officer, Major Chua. After discussing the events of the afternoon Nhan informed us that he agreed to have a combined RF/PF and U.S. operations center, and a combined intelligence office. This was indeed good news, as it was a goal I had quietly set on coming into the S3 position.

A regional conference was conducted at Da Nang on 8 October, attended by the PSA and John Cleary. It was pleasing to receive independent feedback that the Quang Tri briefing had been an impressive one. We received later information that the province chief had accepted the proposals for Quang Tri as recommended by Team 19. As discussions progressed over the next week, advisors became puzzled by that information.

On the morning of 9 October all district senior advisors met in the city with the PSA. The agenda was short: the pacification plan and a new Revolutionary Development program. The reporting system was discussed. The HES report was a contentious document. After those who wished to express a view had done so, the PSA closed off the discussion. He acknowledged that faults might exist in the document, but firmly made the point that the formatted reporting system had to be accepted. The fact was that it was the only reporting system going at that time.

In the afternoon the province chief and his officers met with the PSA and his officers. This was a noteworthy meeting, as it was not often that district chiefs and advisors, including each DSA, met in such a forum at the province level. We were of the view that with a possible cease-fire North Vietnam could claim that the western half of South Vietnam was under its control. Thus, there was an imperative for the GVN to increase the area subject to its control.

The province chief presented his plan: thirty hamlets to be upgraded, employing fifteen Revolutionary Development teams. The Team 19 plan of eighty-six hamlets was presented, with a conservative number of fifty-six hamlets being included. After lengthy and open discussion, including ideas from district chiefs, the proposal from the province chief was for eighty hamlets to be upgraded. Some questions at the back of our minds relating to the counteroffensive were, first, the consequences of a halt in U.S. bombing of North Vietnam, and second, what was the ability of the GVN to contain the NLF and VC in the event of a cease-fire? The consensus arising from the joint discussion was pleasing to most in attendance. The future seemed to be bright on this day. There was general agreement that the key within the province would be the response of the RF/PF to the challenges to be faced.

A staff exercise carried out on 10 October focused on the details of each of the plans that had been developed: the sector local pacification plan and the Team 19 plan. Comparing the sector's amended seventy-nine hamlets (not eighty) against the HES report data showed that twenty of the hamlets were already at the required security level. Hence, on the basis of the U.S. reporting system the target was fifty-nine. Later that day the commander of the 1st Brigade, ACD, and his S3, Major Bob Canady, were briefed on the pacification plan and the Gia Dang project. Afterward they dined with the PSA, DPSA, John Cleary, and me.

On 11 October, I prepared a time phasing to show how the pacification offensive could be achieved. The PSA needed this quickly, as the III MAF headquarters required the information promptly. After one hour of effort I was able to hand a draft to Colonel Mooney. I noted that I enjoyed being involved in staff work, and expressed a hope that I could have further employment in a like field in the future.

Each DSA presented the general outline of a plan for his district in the pacification offensive on 12 October. Their presentations were well considered, realistic, and judged to be achievable. Overall, the PSA expressed his satisfaction that the plan was well on its way, and that it had every chance of being effective. Later that day General Drake visited and was brought up to date on the planning for the pacification offensive, and the Phoenix Program.

I considered the Phoenix Program to be the responsibility of others, and I felt that Colonel Mooney was inclined that way, too, although as PSA he had certain responsibilities to fulfill in that area. The CIA controlled the spies, RD, Police, PRU, the CIDG, and the Special Forces. There were some checks and balances along the way, but in the end the CIA in Vietnam only answered to the ambassador. The coup d'état against President Diem and his death was partly schemed by the CIA, and others. Stanley Karnow wrote in *Vietnam: A History*: "America's responsibility for Diem's death haunted U.S. leaders during the years ahead, prompting them to assume a larger burden in Vietnam."[2] November 1963 was a fateful month for the world. First President Diem was assassinated, and then Kennedy.

In mid-October I briefed the commanding officer of the 4th Combined Action Group, Lieutenant Colonel John Greenwood, on the likely sector response to the pacification counteroffensive. Greenwood had a very challenging command, with his troops dispersed among PF platoons in the sub-sectors and within the populated areas. He was well informed, so I requested that he provide feedback to the PSA after he had considered the proposed plans.

His company in Quang Tri could possibly have to respond to security rearrangements made to satisfy the objectives of the pacification plan.

The PSA sent me on 16 October to hear from three district senior advisors their views on the counteroffensive actions to date. Mai Linh, Cam Lo, and Huong Hoa were visited. Local plans were progressing as well as could be expected. In the afternoon Colonel Land, the G5 for the XXIV Corps, arrived seeking more information. I surmised that the G5 staff was verifying at source the information that was being passed to headquarters III MAF and MACV in Saigon, and to other staff sections in the XXIV Corps headquarters. About this time Lieutenant Colonel Nhan flew down to the RD National Training Center at Vung Tau. He was to be briefed at a two-day indoctrination course similar to that which I attended in August. This was a timely initiative, as he was not fully up to date with the possible consequences of the RD and pacification counteroffensive.

The province chief conducted a presentation on Revolutionary Development on 19 October. VIP visitors included those who had attended the briefing on 5 October, plus General Webster from the MACV headquarters. It was apparent early on that General Truong had already been briefed by Colonel Am, the province chief, in Hue, as there was little questioning on the Vietnamese side of the house. A question from General Stilwell highlighted that hamlet and village lists in the HES did not bear resemblance to the Vietnamese province lists of hamlets and villages. The general was probably aware of this and needed to make us aware that he knew it. Commanders and staff were becoming much more alert to the fact that VC/VCI numbers and names in hamlets had to be known for an effective transition in security grading. I thought the CIA brotherhood had some work to do countrywide, as did the Vietnamese authorities and agencies.

We were advised from higher levels on 21 October that only two provinces of the forty-four in South Vietnam were not required to go back to the drawing board for review and rewriting of their pacification plan for the counteroffensive. Quang Tri province was one of the two. Commanders and staff at all levels in the province, Vietnamese and American, were pleased to hear that, but lamented that so many others had to be reconsidered. That was not good news. At about this time our counterparts advised us that they had heard talk of a possible bombing halt. We awaited formal notification.

The commanding general of I Corps, Lieutenant General Hoang Xuan Lam, based in Da Nang, visited the city on 26 October for a commander's briefing to sector staff, both the Vietnamese and the Team 19 advisors. As a preliminary, the general was briefed on Operation Fisher, the resettlement project at Gia Dang, and local pacification planning. He then addressed the meeting, acknowledging that the two projects were of vital importance to the GVN, and to him. He explained that due to changed criteria over the past few days the number of hamlets in the pacification plan was to vary. In addition, there were a number of hamlets that would not meet the criteria as laid down in the HES.

The general concentrated on two of the campaigns within the counteroffensive. The target for Quang Tri Province was to be thirty hamlets for upgrade by the end of January 1969. He stressed the significance for South Vietnam of the neutralization of the VC infrastructure in the political war, the Phuong Hoang campaign. He expanded by saying that the Phuong Hoang campaign was essential, as by the time of a cease-fire the people had to be under the control of the GVN. He emphasized that the VC must be of negligible strength, because "when the shooting stops, we cannot shoot the VC." General Lam came and listened, spoke and departed.

My notes linked the GVN policies now being pursued to the Paris Peace Talks that were about to commence. I wrote on 26 October 1968: "Secret negotiations must be going on to allow this situation to develop." I further mused that the trend seemed to be to maximize GVN control as soon as possible; to push the VC underground, the living and the dead, to ensure that they had negligible strength; and to push the NVA out to allow for a cease-fire and peace in the February to April 1969 time-frame. Events in later years showed this to be an optimistic point of view.

The deputy for CORDS Da Nang, Mr. Cross, came to Quang Tri on 29 October to hear about progress with the pacification counteroffensive. He was well informed. He undoubtedly had participated in various discussions on hamlet upgrades, and in the case of Quang Tri the scenarios as to whether the target was eighty-six, or seventy-nine, or fifty-nine, or thirty hamlets. He endorsed the actions to be undertaken. He gave us the impression that he had had enough of the counteroffensive.

Over the next few days the main body of the 1st Air Cavalry Division commenced their redeployment to the south of the country. Remaining formations had to assume wider geographic responsibilities in Quang Tri Province, namely the ARVN Regiments, the 3rd Marine Division, and the 1/5 Infantry Brigade. During a staff visit to the latter, I encouraged the headquarters staff there to give consideration to affiliating their units with districts within their areas of operation. This had appeal, as it gave a simple linkup for the pacification planning and action.

On 6 November the province chief, PSA, and I traveled to Da Nang for a CORDS conference. Colonel Mooney attended the quarterly commanders' conference, where General Abrams and some of his staff were present. We found that the advisory staff in Da Nang did not build our confidence, and we left with the impression that they were not very effective. It appeared to us that senior staffs were not prepared to put issues to their superiors. One mused as to whether individuals had much of an understanding of the whole organization and their role within it. Mr. Cross covered the campaign elements of the pacification plan during an afternoon briefing that revealed little that was new. His attitude was similar to that which we observed on 29 October in Quang Tri. I sensed him to be disengaging.

We learned that planning had been going on quietly in the background on pacification initiatives for 1969, beyond 31 January. This had been running concurrently with the launch and implementation of the pacification counteroffensive. There was serious policy work going on behind the scenes, and clearly a lot was being held back from the operational level within provinces. This was sound planning in my view, and could explain the Quang Tri Province's goal of only thirty hamlets by 31 January 1969, and not a higher number. There was clearly scope for further hamlet upgrades in the coming year. The term to be applied for pacification work in the next year came under the project description of the Accelerated Pacification Campaign (APC).

I had returned with the province chief from Da Nang to Quang Tri in the Blackcat on 7 November. The PSA had briefed me in Da Nang on aspects of the APC. I now had to put forward a draft plan with briefing aids. A round of meetings was in the pipeline to assist in making detailed plans for 1969. The district senior advisors and staff of Team 19 were briefed on the APC. Arising from their feedback, further refinement was made to the data. More reports were compiled, and preparations for further briefings were undertaken.

A report on the APC was forwarded to I Corps at Da Nang. I noted that the reporting procedure was disjointed. CORDS Da Nang sought more complete information from us on the APC. The PSA was upset over our effort. Mr. McNamara and I were embarrassed by the situation. I noted that "all will be OK by tomorrow night."

I made field visitations to Cam Lo District and Dong Ha District. Discussions were held with fellow staff officers. The Quang Tri Accelerated Pacification Campaign report was then rewritten. I reflected that the report seemed to be oriented for computer minds, and lacked a facility for a field judgement or a personal touch. During the following week three hamlets in Dong Ha District were visited, as a staff check for the APC. It was becoming clear that officials of the GVN just did not appear to get down to hamlet level. For example, schools were overcrowded, needed repair, had little equipment, and some were without teachers.

Province-level GVN officials did not go into the field to see, to be seen, or to listen. The VC seemed to be better organized, and to work more closely with the people. In a moment of exasperation, one senior officer mused that we may have been killing the wrong people over the last few years. I drew two pyramid shapes in my diary in late November 1968 showing the GVN as inverted and the one for the VC being on a broad base, commencing at the hamlet level.

Earlier in June I had written to Eva: "Here is a conundrum. The US does not want to do everything for the Vietnamese. It wants to assist them. However it seems that since they are given so much by the US, the Vietnamese expect things to be done for them as well. I am sure the Vietnamese will only pull themselves together after the US has departed, whenever that may be." Five months later that view still prevailed.

I accompanied the province senior advisor and Lieutenant Colonel Nhan on 21 November for a further visit to Dong Ha District, on this occasion to three different hamlets. This journey was really a commander-level check on the hamlets in the context of the APC. At one of the hamlets a crowd of local people had gathered. The gathering was a local version of a town hall meeting, but in this case in the school hall.

Older men were in the front of the assembly wearing the traditional dress and hat. Some carried umbrellas. I presumed that these men were the backbone of the hamlet. One had a rag tucked in his belt under his outer garment, using it to wipe his nose and eyes. Each of the elders had goatees. One elder was given money by Nhan, as he was poor and had not been paid relief.

The hamlet officials were younger than the people in the front row, and spoke on behalf of the hamlet. A PF leader assisted. One older woman spoke about five orphaned grandchildren of hers that she was caring for. One of their parents, her son, had been assassinated by the VC, as he was a teacher. She had no income and needed help. Nhan said that his wife would start a fund. I gave her the money I had with me. This was a very sad case, but similar situations must have existed all over the country. A former soldier aged twenty-seven years with only one leg expressed his desire to work at the district headquarters. He realized it could be a temporary arrangement, but his point was that he wanted to help in the APC, and he wanted to lift the image of the GVN. One of the elders spoke, but he could hardly be heard, as his voice was so weak.

As the discussion continued the people present gradually packed in closely and crowded together in a way that was culturally alien to me; they were like sardines in a tin. The children present crowded in so much that they came between the elders in the front and took up sitting positions. Nhan ingratiated himself with the people by saying that he was a Quang Tri man, from Hai Lang District. One old man wanted to bring graves up from another province to Quang Tri for reburial. Nhan dismissed his request. Nhan later confided with the advisors: "I think I would make a good senator in the national parliament."

Afternoon tea was served to the elders and the visitors. The elders tucked into the food with reserved glee, a rare treat for them. Reflecting on the afternoon experience with the PSA, a number of matters were evident. The local people did not seem to be aware of their entitlements from the government and were not being assisted by officials. Provisions arising from Tet recovery programs and aid to refugees were two examples that were raised.

What we heard from the people indicated that the district chief and his staff were not performing. Perhaps the district, having only been created six months earlier, had yet to get properly established. It may not have been as easy as one imagined, motivating people to be politically active at the hamlet or village level in the prevailing conditions. Rural folk may not have held expectations for support to come out of the district, province, or regional level, let alone from

Saigon. Culturally the advisors were not in tune with these matters. The issues raised were political matters for the Vietnamese authorities. The civilian advisors had a job ahead of them in the pacification campaign, as did the military. The need here was for the province chief to get his officials closer to the people. At the time administrative visits to the people were not a priority matter to officials.

Pure and simple, survival seemed to be a paramount force. The older people had experienced successive waves of administration: the French before World War II, the Japanese, the French after World War II, Vietminh influence, U.S. influence, Viet Cong influence, and North Vietnamese military intervention. Exhaustion may have been a factor, certainly dislocation, leading to apathy. As outside observers, the advisors could reach the obvious conclusion that the people desired, wished, and prayed for peace. Our job was to help them toward enjoying freedom, achieving social justice, and gaining peace.

The people did not seem to be doing much for each other. To ask "What are the expectations to the people?" seemed to be a question that was based on ignorance, lack of thought and foresight. With peace and freedom, all else would follow. But this was so painfully difficult to achieve. Terror, and the fear of tomorrow, played a significant part also. We, the advisors, wondered how many VC/VCI were within the crowd on this day. It was a question we could not answer. I recalled a map of South Vietnam that was on the wall of the school hall where we had met. Dong Ha was at the top of the map. Saigon was a thousand kilometers to the south. North Vietnam, to the north of the DMZ, was fifteen kilometers away. We were well within the arc of fire of the Northern artillery. Despite the circumstances, the people lived in hope.

Another staff project was completed at the end of November. This was to do with a road works maintenance plan for Quang Tri Province for the next six months. Presentations on this exercise were being prepared for CORDS Da Nang and the XXIV Corps headquarters. The commander of the 1/5 Infantry Brigade called upon the PSA. He had some well-considered proposals, more broadly to do with pacification plans as well as items for the roads program. His major contribution was that additional district advisory teams be deployed to the presently inactive Trung Luong District and Ba Long District. The province chief had not shown any interest in either of these two districts. They were clearly in the "too hard" basket.

The novelty of the proposal for Trung Luong District was that it was within the DMZ, five kilometers north of the headquarters of Gio Linh District. The former district office was on the southern side of the Ben Hai River. The idea here was that during the anticipated Christmas truce period a district advisory team could be slipped into the old district headquarters. The argument was a presumption that if a cease-fire were agreed upon at the Paris Peace Talks the continuing presence in the once-abandoned Trung Luong District would be a political advantage. Whatever the merits, it was an unlikely prospect, as the South Vietnamese military and people had vacated the area some years earlier.

Ba Long District, to the southwest of Quang Tri City, was of little interest to the province chief due to a general lack of accessibility. It was in an attractive, remote valley in a heavily forested area. The road access was via Dong Ha, Cam Lo, new Huong Hoa, or further west along Route 9, then to Ba Long. I had been there by helicopter. There were about six hamlets in the valley. In addition to establishing a district advisory team there, the idea put forward was that a more direct route from the city to Ba Long be established. A map study showed that at least a fifteen-kilometer stretch of road needed to be surveyed before any roadworks could be undertaken. This had been identified in our study. The suggestion by the brigade commander added weight to our view. However, we all agreed that this was a project for "new works" rather than maintenance.

Thanksgiving Day was celebrated in the evening of 28 November. The Americans had a strong feeling for this day, with a sense of celebration similar to Christmas Day, in the company of family and friends. Colonel Mooney hosted a dinner, with guests being Colonel Am and his wife, Lieutenant Colonel Nhan and his wife, Terry McNamara, Cleary, Porteous, Tuttle, and me. The occasion was a happy one, reinforcing friendships.

I met with Mr. McNamara to discuss the 1969 RD plan on 3 December. The scope of the discussions was mainly about New Life Development program matters, but there were security aspects for consideration at the same time. During the discussions the group in attendance was informed of the intention to split the RD teams from a strength of fifty-nine members to thirty. This was a change of some magnitude, particularly from an RD team leadership aspect. The general view was that the initiative would have a positive effect for the RD effort, and therefore the pacification plan.

On 13 December there was a pleasing report to digest, and an annoying staff glitch to rectify. From higher levels we received reports that showed positive results for Quang Tri Province in the context of the pacification counteroffensive. Locally we judged that Operation Fisher at Gia Dang had made a significant contribution to the scorecard for upgrading hamlet security. It was frustrating to be advised that our pacification counteroffensive plan sent to the nearby headquarters of the 3rd Marine Division had been received by the G3 plans staff, and there it remained. Our Team 19 staff thought that we had kept all neighboring headquarters informed about our pacification plans. But we had not anticipated that the plans staff would not appreciate their significance. Fortunately, it became clear in conversation with G5 staff of that headquarters that they were not aware of our documents. The G5 had a major function to perform in pacification on behalf of the commanding general. I continued to learn that "to cover all the bases" there was a need to ensure the action staff each received copies of documents, even when they belonged to a separate formation.

I recorded on 16 December that military activity in the populated areas of the province had really slowed down. It was judged by our staff that the enemy was working with an emphasis on the political front, to make gains there. We were of the view that the VC was trying to gain as much as possible among the people. At the same time the GVN was trying to neutralize the VC, while concurrently striving to have as many people as possible in South Vietnam under GVN control.

Lieutenant Colonel Wallace, Major Brad Oliver, and I completed a further planning phase for Pacification 1969 on 19 December. The doubling of the number of RD teams was a new factor to add to the decision-making process. Opinions were tested when identifying hamlets for Pacification 1969. We achieved an earlier stated deadline, but were informed that it had been postponed. Internally, the military staffs of Team 19 at the sector level were of a view that the civilian CORDS staff was not cooperating with us. At the evening staff meeting I put the record straight for the military staff to the PSA. At a later planning session with the deputy province senior advisor and other civilian staff, little progress was made. My diary comment, perhaps out of frustration, was that the civilians "cannot treat a problem logically." We were of differing schools of thought.

With the approval of the PSA, I proceeded to Da Nang early the next day to attend a visit by the Chief of the General Staff of the Australian Army. I returned to Quang Tri refreshed, and after a quick evening meal attended a further planning session with Mr. McNamara and others. The air had been cleared during the day; the CORDS people were now doing the work expected of them.

The PSA on 21 December emphasized to all staff of the sector that we had to focus on the hamlets identified in the 1969 Accelerated Pacification Campaign, and to maintain a sharp interest on pacification in general, especially where a significant security component was required. Colonel Mooney went on to say that "the present high level of security in the province was a winning factor in the favorable position that existed." Our collective hope was for it to all hold up. We were not yet ready to present a proposed plan to our counterparts. There was another meeting with the DPSA that day on the APC planning. I noted that the end of this planning phase was in sight, and that planning was not a strong preference of the civil staff. By 23 December all the pieces fell into place for us. We had taken the 1969 pacification plan as far as we could, and now hoped that the Vietnamese staff would consider our proposals, in principle at least.

That evening the province chief hosted a Christmas dinner. General Davis was the senior guest. This was a gathering that not only gave recognition to the birthday of Christ, but was also an expression of appreciation by senior representatives of the Vietnamese people for the allied effort in Vietnam. The dinner embraced Vietnamese and French cuisine and included crab, soup, steak, mushroom, potato, and cake. Refreshments included lemonade, beer, and whisky, with tea at the end. The RD Drama Team sang and played music, and a magician performed. The entertainment overcame any language gaps. It was a memorable occasion.

The next day I put more effort into the military aspects of the Accelerated Pacification Campaign 1969. The commanding officer of the 4th Combined Action Group, Lieutenant Colonel John Greenwood, met the planning team to discuss the deployment of his CAPs to meet pacification campaign requirements. This was a significant meeting, as the USMC placed a lot of effort and faith in the concept and operation of the CAPs. Moreover, the marines took pacification seriously at all levels. By the end of the day we were of the view that thirty more hamlets could be added to the 1969 pacification plan. Most of the hamlets were in two districts: Trieu Phong and Cam Lo. The general mood was that the Vietnamese were visualizing that a truce might be upon us soon. That night I wrote home to say: "I have noticed a few more signs which indicate that peace is not too far away. I think it will be here by April. I hope I am not being too optimistic."

On Christmas Day the Blackcat helicopter flew hot dinners to the district teams that could not come into the city for the special midday meal. Over each drop-off point they air-dropped hundreds of leaflets expressing the Christmas spirit. It was very clever of them. They had been allocated from their parent aviation unit to support us. Their actions on this day reflected the close bond that they had built up with the advisors. It was very good for morale and reflected well on all involved. Thankfully, the truce over Christmas was uneventful, and the fine weather had returned to our area on that special day.

The next day I wrote a reflective letter to Eva:

> We have been busy over the past few days preparing a plan for Pacification 1969. This is our recommended plan for the Vietnamese authorities in Quang Tri province on how to conduct their business in the prosecution of the war for the next year.
>
> It is very interesting work, but at times I have a sense of futility, as the output will not be in the hands of advisors, as the execution is a Vietnamese responsibility. We can only provide advice in a way that we think is in the best interests of our hosts.
>
> With the incoming Nixon administration it is felt that there will be a general tightening of belts in the areas of manpower and expenditures. It is apparent to me that there is tremendous waste in the US effort here, and I guess the Vietnamese are going to feel the pinch also.

Ambassador Cross, CORDS Da Nang, came up for a visit on 27 December. He was happy with our 1969 APC plan. On 28 December our recommended 1969 pacification plan was presented to sector staff, district chiefs, and district senior advisors. Our ideas had been outlined. It was now for our counterparts to consider the plan. Our role now was to wait, be prepared to listen, be responsive, and see what happens.

The Vietnamese staffs at the sector level were awaiting recommendations from the district chiefs. An interesting joint mechanism for consultation was in place to help devise a plan. A joint committee was formed, made up of Lieutenant Colonel Nhan and the Province Revolutionary Development (RD) Council secretary, Mr. McNamara (DPSA), and Lieutenant Colonel Wallace (senior sector advisor). This was a well-balanced team comprising the senior officers of the province chief and the senior officers of the advisory team.

I drew up the 1969 pacification objectives in chart form for the PSA early on 30 December. At this stage the joint committee had not reached any conclusions. In the early afternoon General Davis, the commanding general of the 3rd Marine Division, visited our headquarters and was briefed by Colonel Mooney about the 1969 APC plan. Also discussed with the general was a proposed refugee resettlement project for the Cam Vu area. The general expressed the view that after a land-clearing operation was completed a decision on resettlement could be made. It was intended for Leatherneck Square, an area north of a line between Dong Ha and Cam Lo up to the DMZ, to be cleared commencing on 20 January. A separate chapter is devoted to the Cam Vu refugee resettlement project, named Operation Kangaroo.

Soon after General Davis departed, Generals Stilwell and Troung visited for two hours. The province chief joined them. General Truong spoke for some time, which was not his usual way. He expressed a view that security in his region of the two northern provinces was now similar to 1962/1963 levels. By this we thought he inferred that the initiative was with the South Vietnamese. No decisions were made, but the advisors and Colonel Mooney were of the view that the visitors were now much better informed about the situation and the probable scope of the 1969 pacification plan for Quang Tri.

We were informed on 2 January that Colonel Am (the province chief) and Colonel Mooney had been invited to visit Da Nang on 7 January to make presentations on the Quang Tri pacification plan. To assist in preparation, I undertook a further study of the guidelines for the 1969 pacification plan. This was to ensure that the PSA was fully briefed and prepared for his presentation to Ambassador William Colby, head of CORDS MACV. The ambassador, a title given to the office, wanted to hear what each province was planning for Pacification 1969. Colby worked closely with General Abrams and the U.S. ambassador, Ellsworth Bunker.

At a joint planning meeting chaired by the province chief on the afternoon of 4 January, military and civilian officials discussed and refined the 1969 Accelerated Pacification Campaign plan for Quang Tri. In the end the plan was based on the advisor proposal. It was accepted by the Vietnamese (our counterparts), as they could not agree on a common platform. The next morning the PSA and his staff rehearsed the presentation to be delivered to Ambassador Colby. In the afternoon our counterparts briefed Generals Stilwell and Troung on the plan. After the departure of the visitors Colonel Mooney expressed to the staff his appreciation for the effort put into developing the plan.

On 6 January the weather was foul, with low clouds and little wind. The Blackcats were not flying. Colonel Mooney had invited me to accompany him to Da Nang, so his travel problem was my travel problem: by what means could we get to Da Nang? Enquiries revealed that an Air America C-47 aircraft was arriving in Quang Tri that morning with rations and general cargo. We were successful in gaining seats on the aircraft for the return journey south. I was carrying charts showing geographic locations, Territorial Forces, and RD team dispositions. The aircraft was in cloud for the one-hour journey, breaking into clear sky eight hundred meters from the runway threshold. Ollie Olsen was the pilot. The PSA was accommodated that night at the residence of Major Ian Porteous, the senior Australian Army officer in Da Nang.

The next morning I met up with Colonel Mooney at an early hour to complete preparations for the briefing to Ambassador Colby, due at 10:00 A.M. The Quang Tri representative was invited to start the briefing. The plan was now referred to as the 1969 Pacification and Development Plan. Our plan was at the higher end of the scale when compared to others presented that day. Mooney later claimed that his briefing was ragged due to questions coming from the floor during his presentation.

Ambassador Colby had a fixation on a part of the pacification campaign, the People's Self-Defense Force, dubbed the self-defenders. He stated, "The country is to become an armed camp." This was an interesting idea. My private thought was that if implemented, it could lead to unintended consequences. The prospect of the VC gaining control of a percentage of the arms was one concern. In some areas the political aspirations of the people were questionable. Practical considerations came to mind: training in weapon handling, logistic support, and storage of ammunition. I concluded that the primary goal was to prevail, and that the people of South Vietnam, with their armed forces, were to be part of the fight against the aggressors from the North.

There was discussion about the RD teams. They were undergoing a role change, from being a paramilitary organization to a straightforward development team. The unanimous view was that members of the RD would embrace the new role. After all, it could be argued that most members of the RD were in that organization because they did not want to be in the armed forces of South Vietnam.

We returned to Quang Tri on 8 January, again in marginal conditions for flying. We were in an Air America C-47, initially flying up the coast at five hundred feet, just under the cloud base. We soon increased height and became enveloped by cloud. Under radar control we returned safely to Ai Tu Airport, just south of Dong Ha. The cargo for that flight was bottled propane gas for heating stoves. Life for us in Quang Tri went back to a normal pace. It was like returning home, as we were but visitors in Da Nang. Despite the conditions, Quang Tri was the place where you were relatively comfortable and happy in your work despite the negatives.

General Drake with staff of the 1/5 Infantry Brigade arrived at the Citadel on 9 January for an update brief on Pacification 1969. During the session we received an amendment to the province plan from our counterparts. There were minor changes, like fully committing all RD teams instead of having some of them in reserve. The essentials in regard to the hamlets that were to be upgraded were retained. One of the significant outcomes of the pacification planning effort over the past weeks was that the officers of the GVN were more committed to the Hamlet Evaluation Scheme (HES). The irony of this was that it raised the question as to who was to do the reporting, the GVN agencies or the advisors, or was it to be done jointly.

Later that day the PSA and the province chief set out for Da Nang, via Hue, to present the Pacification 1969 plan to the GVN. I reflected and noted: "In this theatre of war, keeping in mind the nature of the enemy, it is vital to maintain contact and cause the enemy maximum casualties. The enclave concept just does not allow that here. Logistics and the tail are wagging the dog. The standard of living here is good for all but the line troops. With talk of the war coming to an end the effectiveness of our effort here is likely to lessen our offensive spirit, and the degree of alertness required."

Toward the end of January 1969 a planning conference was held by Team 19 to devise recommendations for targeting members of the People's Liberation Committees in hamlets. It was known that the People's Revolutionary Party (PRP) was the primary agency that directed the VC insurgency in South Vietnam. The hamlet committees would encourage members to be active in other more open hamlet and village committees or associations. In VC-held areas the purpose of the People's Liberation Committees was to carry on the day-to-day government functions of administering the hamlets and villages.[3] It was known that committees could be supported legitimately by Buddhists in their efforts to bring about peace. The Buddhists in Quang Tri were not a publicly active political body during my time in the province. It was considered in the group that it would be very difficult to judge the motivations of local people in these local organizations.

In a letter to Eva on 3 February 1969 I wrote:

> This week is the commencement of the big effort for pacification in South Vietnam. Just how effective it will be depends on how much support gets down to the hamlets from the government, and how the hamlet and village chiefs handle things. The next month March is to be election time in many hamlets and villages. Only about 30% of the officials in place now have been elected by the people, the others have been appointed by District Chiefs. So there are interesting times ahead.
>
> To say that South Vietnam is run by a democratic form of government would be difficult to justify. There is no doubt that the Central Congress is elected by the people. However all Province and District Chiefs are military men appointed by the President, himself a former military man.
>
> There are very many problems here and it amazes and indeed it is amazing that the US has stuck with South Vietnam for so long. I firmly believe that our own government may not be fully conversant about what is going on here. We seem to follow the US regardless. This may be the price Australia has to pay for big brother protection! If our career public service people do not get

the experience that I have been fortunate enough to have had here, then we may never break loose of the USA, even if there is a good case to do so.

In early February the weather was wet and overcast. The days were as cold as winter in Sydney. Heavy clothing was required by day, with plenty of blankets at night. On 6 February we were informed that six tractors had been donated to the two northern provinces, Quang Tri and Thieu Thien, through funds collected by the enlisted men of the XXIV Corps. Major Harris had purchased the tractors in Japan at a price of $720 each. The vehicles were to be managed and operated on a cooperative basis. This was a generous and noble gift by the U.S. troops to the Vietnamese people.

On 9 February I wrote: "Things are dull and depressing at the moment, and we just do not seem to be getting anywhere. Do hope this picks up soon. There is still plenty to do." A week later I noted that in the frontline districts of Cam Lo and Huong Hoa pacification might take a step back. The Territorial Forces there were not meeting expectations. It was for consideration that CAPs might need to be deployed there to help give a boost to the RF and the PF. I recalled the warning signals given to sector by the district senior advisor of Cam Lo on 8 November and the district senior advisor of Huong Hoa on 23 November of their security concerns in their respective districts.

A very positive response was initiated by General Davis. The 2/3 Marines, deployed across the two districts, was given a special directive by the commander of the 3rd Marine Division. With thanks to the CO of the 2/3 Marines, I was given notes of his "Design of Action" in the Cua Valley. Guidance in the directive included:

- Work closely with the District Chief to accomplish the objectives of the national Pacification Plan.
- Upgrade the training and stimulate the initiative of RF and PF units to improve combat effectiveness.
- Integrate Marine units with RF companies. Live, train and conduct operations with District units on a permanent basis.

The 2/3 Marines' mission included:

- Institute a Pacification assistance program with the GVN Forces in the District.

- Conduct "Search and Clear" operations in coordination with District Forces.
- Establish permanent liaison at District HQ.
- Maintain security of GVN localities.
- Provide reaction forces to assist District Forces.

The 2/3 Marines' plan emphasized the role of the GVN in providing the protection of villages, and deemphasized marine participation in that particular program. Other elements of interest included in the plan were:

- Improve the security of populated areas to prevent VC/VCI interference with GVN pacification efforts.
- Upgrade the effectiveness of District Forces by integrating marines into units to assist in training and conducting combined operations.
- Provide forces and support for joint cordon and searches of hamlets to capture VC/VCI/VCS, caches and weapons, and to conduct accurate census for better population control.

The integration of marines into RF elements was along the following lines:

An RF battalion joined by a USMC company.

- Each RF company allocated a USMC platoon.
- Each RF platoon allocated a USMC squad.
- Each RF squad allocated a USMC fire team.

Each USMC officer or noncommissioned officer to be an advisor to the RF leader of the element to which he is assigned, and is also the assistant leader.
Each RF company assigned a "tactical area of responsibility."
Marines live with the RF element at all times.
Marine firepower and knowledge is to be distributed throughout the RF companies.

In the past, the transient nature of the USMC units' presence had created uneasiness; this had to be overcome. The marines had to develop mutual understanding and acceptance.

Evaluation some weeks later revealed that initial problems and obstacles faced were:

- Poor communication. As communication improved clearer understanding evolved. Detailed briefings were undertaken.
- "Village soldiers" were kept to the built-up areas.
- Keeping RF soldiers on the job during operations in the field. In some cases USMC soldiers accompanied RF soldiers when they took "time out" to return home.
- Overcoming fear of VC/NVA by improved field skills and firepower.

Accomplishments included:

- Integrating one USMC company with three companies in Huong Hoa District.
- Establishing much closer USMC leadership with the district chief.
- Increasing the confidence of the district chief, demonstrated by initiatives taken by him, with added aggressive action.
- Conducting search and destroy operations on an individual company and company group level.
- Increasing significantly the number of night ambushes.
- Upgrading training of individual and collective military skills.

On reflection the situation in the Cua Valley was probably unique in South Vietnam, certainly in Quang Tri. The area was isolated, remote, and arguably under-resourced. The NVA threatened from the north and from the west. Political decisions at the Saigon and Washington levels were being faithfully implemented. In the case of the Vietnamese plans, directions and orders had passed down at least six political and military levels for action at the grass roots: the president and cabinet, departments, corps and regions, divisions and provinces, to regiments/units and districts. In the case of the U.S. military forces it was similar: the Ambassador, MACV, force levels, corps headquarters, division headquarters, to regiment and action units on the ground.

The advisors acted as the oil and the glue in the "military machine," easing the large and small cogs together to ensure that an agreed and workable operational arrangement resulted. That was our command and staff contribution to help fulfill the objectives of the grand strategy in 1969. We can fairly make claim to have helped "strengthen the spine" in our area of South Vietnam.

On 20 February I briefed the assistant G5 at XXIV Corps headquarters on the security surrounding the elections, and the progress of the 1969 pacification campaign. The next day the advisors received information that in the pecking order of provinces on the U.S. HES score sheet Quang Tri held twelfth place among the forty-four provinces in South Vietnam.

National elections were about to be held. In Quang Tri Province the elections were for village council members and hamlet chiefs in 40 villages and 320 hamlets. Voting days were to be March 2, 9, 16, and 23. Overlays were prepared showing hamlets and villages. This would be necessary for keeping track of the security plan that was being developed for the election. I recorded some personal concerns: "How the GVN administration, in its very poor posture at the moment, could run an honest election is beyond credibility. It is a shame that a 'democratic' election organized by the GVN has excluded the opposition, who have been outlawed and made illegal. It is difficult to see how a sick administration could organize such a widespread election. However the various army field force formations, US and ARVN, are available to assist in providing security outside the populated areas."

On the brighter side of the equation it was anticipated that after the elections all the villages in the province would have elected councils of six to ten members, depending on their population. As a consequence of a positive outcome, each village would become eligible for 1 million piastres from the central government to add to its budget. There was a very large turnout by voters for the election. It was judged at the advisor level that the election process in South Vietnam would be well received by sections of the international audience and be a positive boost for the delegates at the Paris Peace Talks. A postscript to the elections was the question: "How solid will this democratic organization be in facing the challenges of this year, and of the coming years?"

More sobering reports came in. We were informed that propaganda leaflet distribution from VC/NVA sources was increasing in the province. Analysis of incidents was showing that more civilians were being killed in friendly ambushes each night. The circumstances of these actions were to be followed up by the respective District Intelligence and Operations Control Centers (DIOCCs).

In a letter home at the end of February I wrote:

> A Civil Guard [People's Self-Defense Force] has been formed recently. They complement the PF, but at the lowest end of the capability spectrum. I see them on our night patrols. They are here and there about the city. All together they are a sad and pathetic group, just like many of the people whom they are defending. Each man is obviously content to be with his family and seems not to be comprehending of the world outside his own area of interest. Just how long this will go on is the big question. But one can be certain that these folk are not going to contribute in any earth shattering way to the national cause. One has to admire their spirit and grit.

Later on a staff officer expressed a considered view that the People's Self-Defense Force could be classed as a psychological self-help group, giving the people some political security within the GVN tent.

At the weekly meeting with the district senior advisors on 1 March there was an optimistic view of the Territorial Forces' performance against the VC guerrillas in recent days. It was the view that the operations in the populated areas at that time were about counterinsurgency, not about limited war. The major formations—U.S. Army, USMC, ARVN—were providing the shield for the positive development of the pacification campaign.

On 7 March I drove to Nhu Le in Mai Linh District to view a new bridge built as a Civil Affairs project by the 1/5 Infantry Brigade. The bridge was declared open by the two main guests: the province chief and the brigade commander. This was a very positive step, as this village was clearly a contested village. With improved access for vehicles and motorcycles, and consequent communal benefits, it was hoped that this pacification effort would be a long-term gain for the GVN.

I drafted a briefing form for Pacification and Development 1969, Phase 1, reporting on 11 March. Information gathered from the districts allowed me later in the month to make up comparative overlays for 1968 and 1969 on some key measures: pacification areas and RD teams, and Territorial Force areas. Progress for 1969 over three months had shown pleasing gains against the 1968 assessments. At later briefings the advisors were pleased with the reported outcomes.

With the rice harvest season approaching, General Drake visited on 8 March to discuss rice denial, the operational plan to cut the VC out of gaining its rice resupply during the harvest. We had no details of plans at the time from I Corps or the 1st ARVN Division. So, the message was for the advisors to make proposals to the province chief to develop plans. It seemed to me that the U.S. involvement arose from their presence rather than from necessity.

There were other interesting and stimulating projects going on at the same time as the events just described. A refugee relocation initiative, Operation Fisher, is described in the next chapter.

11

Operation Fisher, Refugee Relocation at Gia Dang

September–December 1968

Being a displaced person within your own country during a war is a traumatic experience. For your own government to neglect you in that situation adds further torment to your life and that of your family. To have to dwell and survive in coastal sand dunes while displaced and neglected makes for a very bleak existence. So, helping to alleviate the circumstances of these Vietnamese people seemed to be a worthy task. Operation Fisher is an example of a well-executed pacification project, with objectives arising from national plans and professional implementation coming from a multinational team of Vietnamese and Americans in Quang Tri.

A proposal to give the people a better life by relocation required local allied leaders and staff to identify the major considerations before a concept plan could be developed. The preferred nearby vacant site at Gia Dang lacked infrastructure, but a coastal relocation area was essential to enable the people to sustain themselves by fishing in their traditional way. Movement of the people to the new site would be by walking or by fishing boat. Protection of the people from the adverse influence of the VC would require an extensive security operation. For commerce, an expedient fair weather roadway needed to be constructed to link the new settlement to the inland Route 555 (see map 2), and Quang Tri City.

The district chief at Trieu Phong had earlier raised with the province chief the plight of the coastal people in his district. District senior advisor Major John Shalikashvili[1] reported along similar lines to the then PSA, Mr. Bob Brewer. The people had to dodge the navy in the daylight to fish for their livelihood and were at the mercy of the VC at night. As an initial response the advisors arranged for the registration of the fishing boats. Procedures were set in place with the U.S. Navy and local police at the Cua Viet for the fishermen to have secure access to the sea for fishing.

Major John Hannon, the outgoing S3, on 9 September introduced me to the work done so far on what was at that time referred to as the Gia Dang Relocation Plan. He had booked a helicopter for later in the day to fly a small group of advisors over the coastal sand dune area where the displaced people were then located. Gia Dang was on the coast fourteen kilometers to the east of Quang Tri City. Several deserted hamlets made up the area of Gia Dang village in Trieu Phong District, abutting Hai Lang District, which was to the south. The displaced people were along the coast in a fifteen-kilometer strip to the Cua Viet waterway, and spread up to three kilometers inland. The sea area was part of the South China Sea, with the Gulf of Tonkin to the north.

The aerial reconnaissance group included Major Shalikashvili of Trieu Phong District, who was to play a key operational role in the implementation of this project. Most of the Territorial Forces involved were to come from his district. Security was to be at the forefront of our considerations.

From the air we observed people living in the most primitive conditions in huts, some facing the sea, others among the sand dunes. Shelters were made up of recyclables scavenged from timber crates, flattened can material, and other debris. We reckoned there were up to two thousand huts in the area of interest, most used for accommodation and some for work-related activity. The census tally after the relocation indicated that the number of displaced persons amounted to about fifty-six hundred.

There were many small, local fishing boats pulled up on the beach. One hundred and seventy-six boats were counted. This was to be expected, as it was thought that the displaced people, mainly from abandoned hamlets along the coast, were subsistence fisher folk. Being in a sand dune zone, there were no roads or vehicle tracks, and this lack of infrastructure was to influence our planning, preparation, and implementation.

There was a need now for Hannon and me to do some concentrated thinking. A whole set of factors needed analysis: military and civil aspects, an unusual environment, a foreign host country, an advisory-only organization, and displaced Vietnamese people in a predominantly VC-controlled area. A concept plan had to be prepared.

Low-level enemy action was judged to be the main military threat. The superiority of the friendly forces that existed in the province provided a general protective shield to the area of the project. The Territorial Forces would be involved in providing local security in each phase. It was the VC political campaign among the people that was the challenge, as it was nationwide. Our intelligence assessment was that we needed to be present and alert at all times to ensure an incident-free operation. Accordingly, a security supporting plan evolved. We were of the view that once the security elements were deployed, logistics would require particular attention.

Transportation needs were identified, mainly land and air. Also, a road survey team and combat engineers would be used to design and construct an expedient road of about six kilometers across the sand belt from the edge of the paddy areas to the coast, a connector road to link Quang Tri City to Gia Dang (see map 2). Prepositioning of supplies would be a requirement. The GVN civil administration was to play a vital part in helping achieve short- and long-term goals. Province officials were to be gradually phased into the operation. Town planning, provision of essential civil services, access to markets, and construction of housing and public buildings for up to six thousand people had to be catered for. Safety, health, education, and social services support had to be in place before the displaced people arrived. Registration and census taking had to be provided.

An outline of a concept plan evolved for a four-phase project.

- Phase 1: Preliminary operations during which the engineering tasks would commence and plans would be finalized.
- Phase 2: Operations prior to the resettlement of the people, including the clearing of the area of VC, the preparation of Gia Dang, and the screening of villagers to detect members of the VC infrastructure.
- Phase 3: Resettlement, and the continuing provision of security.
- Phase 4: Operations after resettlement, including the maintenance of security and the establishment of village administration.[2]

That evening John Hannon and I called upon the PSA, Bob Brewer, at his house. He accepted the concept. We visited the province chief the next day. Hannon did the briefing, and the province chief agreed to the concept. The planning then became my "baby," as John Hannon was preparing to move to another assignment.[3]

By this time the project had been given a new name: Operation Fisher. The day following the province chief briefing, the deputy commander of XXIV Corps helicoptered in for a visit and a briefing on the operation. General Drake was a charming man and had the gift of being able to put those in his company at ease. He liked what he heard and requested that an outline be prepared and sent to Colonel Land, a senior staff officer to the commander of XXIV Corps.[4]

Project guidance was passed down from the office of the province chief to the military and civil staff in the sector headquarters. Lieutenant Colonel Nhan, as commander of the Regional Forces, had certain security responsibilities within the sector. It was my task to brief Nhan on the project. He was a likeable fellow with a good grasp of English and the military art. He could be volatile, but earlier on I judged his bluster was more his way of being the leader of his troops. The brief soon evolved into a discussion of key matters of coordination. He accepted the plan but was concerned about the influence of inclement weather. Jumping ahead, I give credit to Nhan for pointing out that the monsoon season was upon us and that contingencies needed to be thought through, especially for wheeled transport in the wet conditions. He relished his "I told you so" opinion over the coming weeks as the weather influences came to bear on the activities within the project.

On 15 September I was in conference with Brewer and Mooney to settle on a briefing sequence for Operation Fisher. This was in preparation for an afternoon briefing that day to the leaders at the various levels of command:

- Lieutenant General Richard Stilwell, commanding general of XXIV Corps, and his deputy, Major General Drake, from Phu Bai in Thua Thien Province.
- Major General Ngo Quang Truong, commanding general of 1st ARVN Division, from Hue.
- Chief of staff of the 3rd Marine Division headquarters, from Quang Tri.
- Colonel Nguyen Am, Quang Tri province chief.
- Staff officers from the headquarters of the above commanders.

- Local advisors, both military and civil, who were to be involved in the project.

The operation relied on resource allocation from the commanders of the formations and units who were at that meeting, who in turn required the concurrence of their superiors in Da Nang and Saigon. More broadly, should the benign level of enemy activity change, then Operation Fisher could possibly be jeopardized.

One frustration in the staff preparation that day related to the simple matter of having the typing done on time. Usually the S1 (personnel) staff rose to the occasion when pressure was on, but for this effort the paperwork was not presented on time. Fortunately, the briefing notes and aids were ready, with the operation instructions being distributed after the meeting, which was not an unusual practice in any case.

The politics of Operation Fisher at this early stage of planning were noteworthy. My diary entry noted the significant number of organizations involved: MACV, CORDS, ARVN, Territorial Forces, I Corps, XXIV Corps, USMC, Merchant Marines, and the GVN, which was ultimately the beneficiary of our efforts. I was to realize in the coming weeks that once resources are assembled and applied to an operation like that required for Fisher, the organization arising becomes a kind of juggernaut, where individuals and groups of people rise to the occasion to earnestly strive for the achievement of set goals.

The province chief did not become involved in any of the discussion at the briefing. He sat in a central position with Generals Stilwell and Truong and took in all that was said. He let the U.S. personalities discuss the issues. On reflection, the role he played was a sensible one. With an obvious commitment by the U.S. representatives, who were embracing the challenges being set out, the objectives of all involved were convergent, so whatever outcomes could be achieved would be to the satisfaction of all concerned, including the representatives of the GVN.[5]

The briefing closed on a high note. All involved were to carry out the necessary command and staff functions over the next two weeks to get the huge machines of government and military in our part of South Vietnam to focus on a new operation.

While at Cam Lo on 26 September, I met a major visiting from the MACCORDS refugee staff section in Saigon. He was on a staff visit to the Cam Lo refugee camp. I was able to outline to him our province-wide plans on refugee support. He responded by stating Quang Tri was the leading province in the country for the planning and organizing of refugee relief. At a Team 19 staff meeting conference two days later Dick Cummings of CORDS described his vision for improving local administrative services to refugees in the province. He emphasized the special role that advisors had in working with their counterparts at the district and province levels on refugee matters.

Engineer representatives from the 1st Air Cavalry Division headquarters arrived in the Citadel on 30 September to undertake a reconnaissance of the proposed sand cement road to Gia Dang and to provide advice. Their assessment was sobering, being the first technical report that had been provided. One matter that was critical was whether an ARVN engineering unit had the capacity to undertake the construction of the road. The assembly of commodities was a significant issue, especially cement. We had been advised from higher levels that thirty-thousand bags of cement were on the water for the project. It was not known where the ship was located.

A few days later I flew into the area for a further reconnaissance. The beach was similar to that at Surfers Paradise, in southeast Queensland, with the water being warm. However, there was a total absence of beach lovers, surfers, and tourists. My notes described the plight of the people in the sand dunes there as being very basic. They were under VC control at that time. It was part of our mission to end that control by the end of the year, by ensuring that the government security forces and civil government agencies gained the ascendancy. Neglect by the GVN had given the VC the opportunity to gain influence. A continuing effective presence of the government was essential to win back the people.

The advisory leadership at Quang Tri City quickly appreciated that headquarters XXIV Corps was our best friend in the region in regard to Operation Fisher outcomes. So, Colonel Mooney and I flew to the XXIV Corps headquarters to visit Colonel Land and worked through the concept plan and supporting plans. Having arrived late in the day, we spent most of the evening on the details. It was made clear to us that Operation Fisher was high on the XXIV Corps commander's list of priority operations. A note about this time commented that this resettlement operation was not anticipated in the government 1969 Pacification and Development Plan. Nevertheless, it was low risk and with plenty of benefits to be gained. Not only was this project potentially beneficial for the refugees, but it could also add to the number of hamlets with improved security levels in the pacification campaign.

It came to pass that ARVN field engineers arrived on 7 October 1968. Their initial task was to undertake a detailed route reconnaissance for the road. Survey pegs were laid out. There was a concern that the pegs provided a temptation to be tampered with by friend and foe. Discussion arose on whether we, the friendlies, should booby trap the survey pegs. A view was expressed that the VC might do likewise. It was deduced that the engineers working on the road would soon know where the road was to be laid, pegs or no pegs, so the idea was dropped.

My role moved from being the planner, with others, to being a monitor of progress in the implementation of the plans. Essentially Colonel Mooney and I were there to look after the priority interests of the province chief, security and logistics, reporting back on activities. A control measure understood by all parties was the designated area of operation for each unit. Maps and traces showing boundaries were shared on a need-to-know basis. Advisors and liaison officers at all levels had the overlays. Radio communication between all parties was in place, with signal operating instructions again being issued on a need-to-know basis.

The PSA deemed me to be his roving operational staff officer. To help optimize that role, a liaison helicopter was generally available to me. This sophisticated aircraft enhanced mobility and communication. It was a multiplier. I made sure that other possible users in Team 19 could bid to make use of the aircraft if they had a need. The chopper provided much needed support to the advisors and counterparts. It was a vital and very effective mode of transport for us. The key advisor at the Gia Dang end, John Shalikashvili, was contacted frequently. The security part of the operation was central to a successful outcome, and the Regional and Popular Forces were the troops responsible in the main for security.

Liaison and general support helicopters were in demand. We did not "own" any air assets. We were reliant on commanders and staff to the rear and higher up the chain to allocate aircraft on a daily basis. Our salesmanship, the nature of the operation, and goodwill worked wonders. It seemed the enemy was in recovery mode from the setbacks they had received for most of the year, particularly since Tet 1968, and had broken contact to a large extent. This was one possible explanation for the availability of military resources to support Operation Fisher.

The deputy commander of XXIV Corps, General Drake, arrived at the Citadel pad in his helicopter on 8 October to hear how the operation was shaking out. The PSA and I joined him for what I termed a "see and be seen" activity. The general was doing his job in a command role: being able to observe that units were acting to plan, and providing to us and others in the field an opportunity to highlight any shortfalls that were being experienced, and which he might take back to his staff for remedial action.

We visited the engineers doing the preliminary preparations for the cement road, dropping in on a lone engineering survey party on Route 555 and then the sub-sector headquarters of Hai Lang District to the south of Quang Tri City. Hai Lang was not a dominant partner in Operation Fisher, but being on the southern flank we had to make sure that it was included in all relevant aspects of the operation.

The next day was spent coordinating boundaries from the coast to inland. U.S. Army elements from different formations were coming into the area to assist in the security phases. A unit came from the 1/5 Infantry Brigade and one from the 1st Brigade, Air Cavalry Division. The latter flew in troops with its organic helicopter fleet. The mechanized troops had their own ground vehicles. All activity went according to the plan, with troops keeping within their allocated boundaries. It was reassuring to work with seasoned troops, units, and full operational headquarters. Very wisely, the enemy kept a low profile. Contact with the enemy was light, with few incidents being reported.

The province staff announced details of the Gia Dang team for the sector Resettlement Control Agency on 12 October. In the plan it was intended this element would deploy on 15 October, after a sector RF battalion and an ARVN battalion completed their security operations. The province chief held a meeting for all parties involved in the Gia Dang operation on 13 October. This was a timely action ensuring that all leaders and staff saw each other, heard views, and allowed all attending to hear the views of the province chief directly. At this meeting we heard from the commanding officer of the ARVN's 101st Engineer Battalion.

The engineer commander, Major Diem, was very impressive. He had commanded the battalion for six years. It was reported that during the Tet battles earlier in the year he and his unit had been surrounded by the enemy for fifteen days. He had received training in the United States and had a good grasp of the English language. His confident approach to the road-building mission was uplifting. We felt at the end of the gathering that the operation had been launched in a very positive manner. We were looking forward to getting the job done.

More coordination and preparation was undertaken on 14 October. Lieutenant Colonel Nhan continued to argue against the launch of Operation Fisher. He was convinced the monsoon season would be detrimental to the conduct of the operation, a point he had made in mid-September. He was dogged in keeping up his attitude of "I told you so." Once a military operation with the complexity of Fisher is under way, a lone voice is just that, making little impact, despite the point of view having some merit. My diary entry for this day says: "pouring rain all day." Rainfall on 14–15 October was twelve inches.

We also heard that the province chief had expressed a view that he would like to commence movement of the people to be settled before the cement road was completed. The PSA clarified the issue by suggesting that the province administration staff should be set up as soon as possible, before resettling the refugees. The compound and my own accommodation were under four inches of water.

The next day the senior operations officer of the 1st Air Cavalry Division visited to discuss matters of coordination and further assistance for Gia Dang. For a key staff officer of such a high-capability military formation to have time to visit advisors reflected that the intensity of operations had slowed down in the northern provinces. The enemy was reconstituting itself. From the advisory point of view it was comforting to realize that our Operation Fisher was on the agenda of many friendly formations and units in our area. An outcome of the visit was reassurance that requests for helicopter assistance would generally be met, as long as due notice by way of bids for air support were provided through the agreed channels of communication. We could not ask for anything more; our highest expectations were being satisfied.

The monsoon rains were upon us. Lieutenant Colonel Nhan was against his RF being on operations in the wet. One reason for his position was that RF members were issued only two sets of fatigues. His opinion was puzzling, as only one set of fatigues was worn at a time. The VC/NVA would probably have had only one set, often worn to the point of being no longer usable. One could arguably conclude that the RFs under Nhan's command were a kind of well-protected species.

Two Regional Force companies were inserted into Gia Dang by medium-lift Chinook helicopters on 17 October. The district senior advisor from Trieu Phong accompanied the troops. The recent rains had left their mark. The land was saturated. The refugees appeared to be hardened by the very basic conditions under which they lived. Requests were submitted for further helicopter support for the next day.

Province administrative elements, troops of an ARVN engineer company, and other essential people for the resettlement flew from the city to Gia Dang in six sorties on 18 October. The transfer took over five hours. Many of the people flown out were probably experiencing their first helicopter flight, and the civilians were probably away from home and in effect camping for the first time. On the ground at Gia Dang, the place had the appearance of a picnic camp.

During this deployment the province chief flew out with staff officers (S3 and S4) of the headquarters of the 1st Brigade, Air Cavalry Division. The province chief seemed to have been energized by Operation Fisher. On the ground he mixed with the sector staff deployed there. This was very pleasing to see, and probably a great surprise to all involved. During my two return trips by helicopter to Gia Dang that day it became clear that heavy equipment and vehicles would be delayed in their deployment to the coast. Existing roads were under water, as were many houses.

The PSA assembled his staff that evening to review the progress of Operation Fisher. Despite the conditions much had been achieved on this day. We were thankful that our counterparts, the Vietnamese staff at province headquarters, had deployed their elements to the coast. We were all elated. It was judged to be a remarkable effort.

I was given the task of examining the possibility of moving the ARVN engineers and their equipment by road, river, and the beach to Gia Dang. The proposed route was by road from Quang Tri City north to Dong Ha (fifteen kilometers); from there via the Cua Viet waterway (fifteen kilometers) to the coast; and then southeast along the beach with USMC amphibious tractors (amtraks) and tank escorts to Gia Dang (fifteen kilometers).

Early on 19 October, I set out to visit the local U.S. Navy

Housing reconstruction, Gia Dang, November 1968.

headquarters ashore at Dong Ha. Back-loading ship capacity was available, as this was a main supply route for ship-to-shore bulk supply to the U.S. forces in Quang Tri Province. The necessary arrangements were thus made. Another problem was solved. Direct dialogue worked well. I am certain that being an Australian Army officer in such a position worked to the advantage of our advisory

Team and the South Vietnamese government agencies, be they military or civil. A feature may have been my Australian accent, or the Australian Army aviation beret.[6]

Later that day I flew out to Gia Dang with the local U.S. Refugee Agency representative, Mr. John Cleary, and Warrant Officer Deanshaw (AATTV) to familiarize them with developments, and in my own case to observe progress. It was reported that 374 people had moved into the developing village. A cache of rice in an earthen jar was discovered while we were there. This made a total of five jars found to that point. Opinion was that this was a prudent storage method in the event of food shortages. Charcoal to take up moisture was found in the rice. Each jar held about two hundred kilograms of old but edible rice.

Throughout the day of 19 October my assistant S3, Lieutenant Ed Logan, U.S. Army, supervised the loading and air-lift of material required to set up the Team 19 forward tactical operations center at Gia Dang. Steel planking, concertina wire, other defense stores, and creature comforts were uplifted. The quick-witted claimed we were setting up an R&R center for Quang Tri MACV people at Gia Dang. However, it was not going to compete with coastal Vung Tau, a short leave center farther to the south.

The next morning I flew to Gia Dang and then up the coast to the entrance to the Cua Viet. The opportunity to observe the scores of fishing boats and hundreds of huts gave me a sharp reminder of what Operation Fisher was about: giving the people here a start to a better life, in their own country. It was pleasing to observe the ARVN engineer battalion equipment already loaded on the landing craft at the Dong Ha ramp. Early in the afternoon the equipment was unloaded at the coast, where a USMC escort awaited them. The escort was composed of six amphibious tractors and a troop of three tanks. This was another welcome outcome within Operation Fisher.

Later that afternoon I attended a briefing at the headquarters of the 1st Brigade, Air Cavalry Division. A request was made to me to arrange for a boundary variation for the areas of operation of the 3rd Battalion, 1st ARVN Regiment (3/1 ARVN) and the brigade. This was a typical outcome of a routine staff liaison visit.

The next morning, 21 October, I flew out to Gia Dang with Major Brad Oliver, U.S. Army, MACV, our Regional Forces senior advisor. We enjoyed each other's company, especially when discussing the merits or otherwise of the various military situations we found our-

Amtrak on the beach, Gia Dang, October 1968.

selves in. Discussion was robust, particularly if opinions differed. We observed that the cement stockpile was growing. The cement was a critical item for the new road.

We noticed pilfering from the cement dump. The Vietnamese seemed to act as if it was their right to thieve bags of cement. Those involved were oblivious to the possible consequences of their actions. In conversation with Brad I referred to them as thieves. Surprisingly, my interpreter was moved to tears when he heard my comments. I had to ponder why he acted as he did. It was a rotten shame that the people were in such circumstances.[7]

In a letter to Eva on 21 October 1968 I expressed the view that work was very interesting. This was an understatement. The experience was just extraordinary. I went on to say that I thought that it might take time for me to settle down after moving back to Australia. I concluded by saying that I would depend on her to help me through, when the time came. Thankfully that was so. Two weeks later I wrote home to say that Operation Fisher was rolling along beautifully.

General Drake kept his visits up. These visits kept him in touch with the districts. When available I would accompany him. On 22 October we visited Gia Dang, Hai Lang, and Cam Lo Districts. We observed that the ARVN engineers were doing very well on the road project, and that they were ahead of schedule. Concertina wire was being flown in to Gia Dang for protection measures. After such visits I would brief the PSA, DPSA, and other staff on relevant matters that arose during such a visit.

The next day was a typical one, full of stimulating activity. The morning was spent with Logan getting essential Vietnamese staff out to Gia Dang. Included were representatives of the Vietnamese Information Service (VIS), Police Special Branch, intelligence staff, and advisors with returnees of the Chieu Hoi program. Late in the morning the PSA and I flew out to Gia Dang to meet up with Mr. McNamara and Major Chuu, who were on the beach. While we were discussing the project a U.S. Army UH-1H landed nearby, flown by the commanding general of the 1st Air Cavalry Division, Major General George Forsyth. He wanted to chat and catch up with the situation.

Being an aviator, I was able to share some matters of common interest with him. I was in awe of the capabilities of his formation and ventured to ask him about helicopter serviceability rates and effort available on a daily basis. He said on this particular day 43 percent of the aircraft in the division were flying. He explained that he wanted to cut usage by 33 percent to bring daily availability up to 55 percent as soon as possible. Colonel Mooney asked the general if I could do some flying with the Air Cavalry. As that idea was beyond the scope of my present appointment, I did not pursue what was a very tempting opportunity.

The province chief and Mr. Dick Cummings, of CORDS, in a village meeting at Gia Dang, October 1968.

During the afternoon at the nominated civic center of the growing Gia Dang village a short ceremony was conducted to present an award to a member of a Vietnamese armed propaganda team who led some soldiers of the Air Cavalry to two weapons buried in the sand dunes.

The province chief held a meeting at Gia Dang on 25 October. To his own staff Colonel Mooney pointed out "our feet are being kept to the fire, as we have got the Fisher project underway and now we have to give it real commodity support." The province chief informed us he wanted to bring his senior civilian officers out to Gia Dang in two days. This was another big step, and we had to ensure the helicopter lift was available to bring the province staff to the beach. To demonstrate to them the level of U.S. support being given to Operation Fisher, we arranged for a number of amtraks to be present.

That day Colonel Land, the G5 at XXIV Corps headquarters, arrived in Quang Tri City to overnight with Team 19, with a view to visiting Gia Dang. This was timely for him to be with us, as he was a friend in the "court" of our main patron, the commanding general of XXIV Corps. Other officers of the advisory staff accompanied Colonel Land to Gia Dang.

As a general comment, rotary wing aircraft were providing an admirable air taxi service throughout Vietnam. Surface movement, however, was the key—to both the Free World Military Assistance Forces and to the enemy. The enemy did not have any air-lift capacity in South Vietnam. The VC/NVA had to be admired for their tenacity and endurance against the firepower and airpower of the GVN and U.S. forces. To this point in Operation Fisher the weather and poor roads had caused us to rely on air support for a direct link to Gia Dang, even though only fourteen kilometers away by air and twenty kilometers by road.

With a break in the weather I took it upon myself, accompanied by my interpreter, to see how far one could drive by jeep toward the coast. If we lost our allocation of helicopter support we would then have to resort to the road, and vehicle movement. We headed northeast out of the city, through to Trieu Phong District and then headed east along Route 555. The land was flat, well populated, and paddy predominated. We were able to go to the point where Route 555 curved to the southeast, at the hamlet of Thon Tam Huu. Charlie Company of the ARVN's 101st Engineer Regiment had control here, as it was the western point (the start point) of the cement road. Traffic was not permitted to go further east toward the coast, six kilometers distant. The only other people at this place were two marine soldiers of a CAP team and four young Vietnamese lads. We carried a radio with us, enabling progress reports to be made to our operations center, which was very comforting under the circumstances. I was relieved and pleased to return to our start point in the Citadel. My briefing that evening was received with a measure of puzzlement, probably arising from individual perceptions of the security toward the coast. The PSA was happy to receive the firsthand report.

The fly out of the province officials to Gia Dang took place on 27 October. We had an Air America Huey in support. The people flew out in three sorties. Briefings were given by a number of Vietnamese military officers and officials. The province chief led the visitors through the resettlement area. The Air American helicopter had to be released to return to the South, so some quick problem solving was carried out to lift the visitors back to Quang Tri City. The commanding officer of 1/12 Air Cavalry came up with the air assets: a UH-1H and four sorties from a light observation helicopter.

We were informed that the rate of supply of cement had to be increased for the engineers to meet the completion target date. The logistics staff had to meet this challenge. Tents then became a problem, or rather a lack of them. In early planning, agreements had been made to satisfy a logistics staff advisory estimate for about 170 tents. They were to provide temporary shelter and working accommodation as the project at Gia Dang developed. When the promised supply of tents did not appear, the PSA was furious. Those who fouled up were the subject of his ire: "all promises and no results from the rear" was the cry. Our logistic staff officers were on the telephones.

As mentioned earlier in the story, it was about this time that the 1st Air Cavalry Division was given notice to deploy south. The focus of the Air Cavalry therefore was moving elsewhere. Thus our significant helicopter provider began phasing out. The CORDS side of the effort, through Air America, was filling the gaps on a daily basis when aircraft were available. Thereafter, a general support aviation company, call sign Blackcat, was committed to provide a UH-1H for direct support each day. Casualty evacuation was a separate source, on call and thankfully guaranteed.

Bagged cement started to arrive in the quantities required toward the end of October 1968. A consignment of five thousand bags was to come down from the Cua Viet area in the north in amtraks provided again by the marines. A load of six pallets came from the southeast, again along the beach, from Wunder Beach in Hai Lang District. The advisors were formally scrounging on a large scale for tents, cement, and to some extent air support. It really was a matter of saving face with our counterparts, who we were working with in tandem.

Hiccups happened as the tent saga was being resolved. Despite a lack of labor and transportation, we were requested to collect the first batch of fifty tents from a base some distance away. At the pickup point the logistics officer inspected the fifty tents; there were no poles. It was a maddening situation, but resolved by a persistent effort. By All Saints' Day, 1 November, we had the tents as promised: twenty-two from the 3rd Marine Division, seventy-five from the 1/5 Infantry Brigade, and seventy-five from base logistics at Camp Evans, in the vicinity of the XXIV Corps headquarters.

A few days later we airlifted province officials to Gia Dang to commence a land survey. That same day I flew out to Gia Dang to meet and talk with Major Shalikashvili, Dick Cummins (Refugee Service), Major Chuu, and Lieutenant Colonel Nhan. We agreed things were going well.

Meanwhile, out west in the mountains near Laos, in the abutting Thua Thien Province, the 101st Airborne Division had discovered an NVA rice dump in an enemy base area tunnel complex. On 8 November the delivery to Gia Dang of one thousand bags of rice from this huge cache commenced. The irony of this was that a line of logic could argue that the rice was a gift from the people of North Vietnam to the people of South Vietnam. Once it was consolidated, a ceremony was conducted to hand the rice over to the local officials for distribution to the refugees as they were resettled in Gia Dang. The rice was a nice bonus, but at a heavy cost to the North Vietnamese, the South Vietnamese, and the Americans.

My interpreter, Sergeant Long, entered into the spirit of Operation Fisher. He had artistic skills and gave some of his artwork to the Gia Dang project. It was his initiative, and it made a very positive impact on the minds of the advisors he was working with. His concept was within the context of the Accelerated Pacification Campaign. It was an impressive contribution by Long.

I accompanied the PSA to Gia Dang on 10 November. He spent the morning there, observing and clearly making mental notes of matters that required attention. To date the civilian advisors of Team 19 had not played a significant role in the Fisher project. Mooney let me know that some things were to change. He judged that complacency was evident among some civil advisors, and that they needed to "smarten up their act." The PSA on return to Quang Tri City called an evening meeting for the civilian advisory staff. The purpose was to bring their minds to the resettlement project, to get their imaginations going, and to ensure their collective energies and efforts would be well coordinated. The military staff was pleased with this approach, as the pressure had been on us for some time on this project, arguably to the detriment of other activities that deserved as much focus as Operation Fisher.[8]

While the PSA was at Gia Dang, Major Shalikashvili greeted him. The major was carrying with him the monthly Hamlet and Village Evaluation Report (HES). This reporting requirement had to be commenced at the district level and normally would be filled

The province senior advisor and the commanding officer of the 101st ARVN Engineer Battalion during road construction, November 1968.

out initially by one of the district team members. For good reasons Shalikashvili was doing the job. It was not a straightforward task in the case of Gia Dang village. He displayed diligence and a highly developed sense of responsibility. One could not miss the sense of excellence he brought to the job, and this of course had a positive impact on those near to him.

A Revolutionary Development team was due to arrive at Gia Dang on this day, but due to a lack of initiative by the civil RD advisors they failed to show. This added further justification to the action Mooney had taken with the civilian advisors.

Gia Dang was the center of advisor attention on 12 November. It was clear that Operation Fisher was being noticed at all levels to the south, including Saigon, by both the GVN and MACV. Mr. Cross, the CORDS ambassador from Da Nang, came into Gia Dang for a familiarization visit. A quartet of senior military officers then arrived. It was usual that visits by senior people were not announced, unless special security arrangements needed to be provided. The users of air transport had great faith in the safety of the helicopters allocated to them. The officers were COMUSMACV General Creighton W.

Command post area, Gia Dang.

Abrams, Lieutenant General R. Stilwell, General Drake, his deputy, and the commander of the 1st Division ARVN, Major General Truong. The province chief and the PSA attended to their needs. The visitors wanted to see and be seen. Their presence was stronger than words and written messages, and was an effective method of putting leadership and command into practice. This was another memorable day for Team 19.

Tented relocation center, Gia Dang, November 1968.

While these visits were going on, the province officials on the ground were preparing for a full dress rehearsal of the reception arrangements for the arrival of the refugees. We, the advisors, particularly Mooney, were delighted when a sole Vietnamese civilian entrepreneur from the city arrived in his truck at Gia Dang. He was a Coca-Cola vendor looking for business. He judged it to be safe to motor out to Gia Dang. To us, his silent action said a great deal about the security situation. It confirmed our assessment. Military activity was quiet, but we were not clear on what was going on politically within the hearts and minds. We had to persevere with our tasks.

The refugee reception rehearsal took place on 14 November. We were told that all went well. However, those officials who wanted to return to the city that night could not do so as the helicopter allocated for the day did not have time to pick them up. The formal refugee processing and relocation commenced the next day. I visited Gia Dang to be told that processing was going according to plan. The bad news was that the VC were running their propaganda program in the hamlets at night. This was a matter for the Vietnamese agencies to deal with.

While at Gia Dang on 16 November I walked past a police tent, where I observed the Police Special Branch people using torture to

Meeting of commanders, Gia Dang, December 1968.

get information from an old man. The technique being used involved a field telephone. The wires were connected to the person, and a crank handle was turned to generate an electrical charge. This was a deplorable scene, and not the way to win the hearts and minds. The officials were not very patient in this case, and the gentleman being interviewed might well have provided useful information without the torture now that a new way of life was being organized for his community. To ensure such measures ceased within Gia Dang, the local advisory network and counterparts were alerted about the incident.

The following day three senior officers called into Gia Dang: General Stilwell, Major General Truong, and the commander of the 1/5th Infantry Brigade, Colonel Richard Glikes. They walked through the new village designated Gia Dang 1. It was pleasing to observe the RD team members dressed in their customary black uniform, and the Regional Force soldiers assisting people in building houses.

The new houses were being constructed with frames made of bamboo or cut timber, tin and thatch roofing and walls, with a sand floor. Kitchens were basic. Communal toilets were built. Some of

Housing reconstruction, Gia Dang, November 1968.

the refugees recovered materials from their former shelters to help improve their dwellings. Overall the dwellings were simple and adequate for the conditions. It was most gratifying to see the joint activity taking place. The local culture appeared to differentiate classes. The Vietnamese people on the ground were mostly women and children, with a few older men. The people seemed happy, yet a little hungry.

The 3/1 ARVN was involved in the security operations in Gia Dang with the Territorial Forces. The area of operations was not exclusive to any unit. This was a joint policy of Generals Stilwell and Truong at work. It was a sound one for joint operations, provided liaison officers were in place with reliable communication links. The interest displayed by the senior visitors was partly motivated by their desire to see their policies being applied in the field.

Our sector advanced operations center was working well, being co-located with the other deployed agencies. Our soldiers, mostly specialists in communications and weapons, deserved the highest praise for the manner in which they were conducting themselves in a new setting and in difficult conditions.

I wrote home on 18 November to say that:

> The people are moving into their new homes at Gia Dang. Fourteen hamlets are to be relocated into this central area. The move started three days ago and was expected to take about two weeks. Thankfully the weather of recent weeks has been excellent. Sergeant Long and I had driven each way to Gia Dang as a helicopter was not available.
>
> The people have been neglected over the years, and at last the GVN is now giving them something, with considerable US assistance. Family size averages about four people, and as is usual there are not too many men. The men are either with the VC, working with the GVN in some form or another, or have been killed over the years. It is a sad situation, but we are making the best of it for them. The people moving into Gia Dang appear to be really overawed by the generosity of the government.

In my notes I expressed a hope that Australia "would not get involved in this kind of war again, especially on a US scale. For effectiveness and efficiency all support in a theater needed to be under military control. How South Vietnam can successfully recover from a long French and American presence, to achieve self-sufficiency and security appears to be improbable."

Gia Dang was now on the visitor circuit. The next fly-in was by Under Secretary for the Army David McGiffert on 18 November, accompanied by his support staff. The Vietnamese sector military staff made a presentation on local affairs, which was well received. In the new hamlets small shops were starting up and the people seemed happy. For the McGiffert visit the province chief, PSA, and I made the return trip to Quang Tri by road, along Route 555. It was an uneventful road trip in a four-wheel-drive vehicle.

About this time the PSA, Mooney, was appointed to the rank of colonel, a well-deserved promotion and timely from the point of view of all in Team 19. I accompanied the new colonel and Mr. Puckett on 21 November to the hamlets at Gia Dang. We were advised there that the resettlement was proceeding well. My notes included: "The move of people is progressing in grand fashion. The officials can process 105–110 families per day."

A report received on 25 November from Hai Lang District was sobering. That morning the local RF/PF had captured twenty-five persons to the west of Route 1, the principal north-south highway.

Suspected VC recruits from Hai Lang and Gia Dang.

It was further reported that the operation was initiated on advice from a Chieu Hoi. Those captured included fifteen young Vietnamese men who were classed as recruits; twelve came from Gia Dang and three from the local VC K8 Battalion. In addition, there were three guerrillas and four carriers, with only one weapon between them. The captives were transported to the sector headquarters at 5:00 P.M. It was reported that interrogation commenced with water treatment, with all captives present. This was very crude, with a tape recording being made of a volunteer captive for later playback into an area where a further one hundred other suspects were thought to be hiding.

At 5:20 P.M. that day Generals Stilwell and Truong came in to be briefed on the captives and the surrounding circumstances. The two commanders were continually seeking information and feedback from people in the field. Intellectual curiosity was a necessary element in the intelligence process. Their example was impressive.

Only one and a half kilometers of sand-cement road remained to be completed as of 27 November. We were advised by a staff officer of the 3rd Marine Division headquarters that the corps commander, General Stilwell, wanted the road completed quickly. The word was that he wanted to show President Thieu the work done at

Planners at work, Gia Dang, November 1968.

Gia Dang on 1 December 1968, so that he could go on R&R leave on 2 December. Completion by that date was not possible.

Major Ian Porteous, AATTV, Da Nang, was in the province on 28 November, and he accompanied the PSA and me to Gia Dang. Yet again we met up with Generals Stilwell and Truong. They were brought up to date with the project's progress. Approximately fifty-six hundred people had moved and been resettled. The Trieu Phong District part of the relocation had been completed at Gia Dang, on time. There remained three hamlets at the northern end of the coastal strip to be relocated to a place near to the Cua Viet.

General Stilwell visited Gia Dang beach on 2 December to present a Bronze Star to Major Diem for the road-building achievement. This recognition reflected well on his unit, who were then taking a well-earned rest. It was noticed that surplus bags of cement were being redirected onto the local market, to the financial advantage of unknown persons.

The PSA went to Gia Dang on 3 December to meet with Vietnamese officials to discuss and plan for the provision of public infrastructure for the two district areas, Trieu Phong and Hai Lang.

The main needs discussed were schools, dispensaries, toilets, and markets. These were the basics and were probably typical of family needs throughout the world. While these discussions were being held another helicopter arrived. General Davis had landed, accompanied by Joseph Alsop, a syndicated American columnist. Mooney excused himself from the meeting to brief the visitors. The colonel had a sense of theater about him and rose to the occasion, knowing that what he said would most likely be news on the U.S. networks in a short space of time.

The next day in Quang Tri City I had a conversation with a Catholic priest, Father Ai. I told him of the happenings at Gia Dang. He was generally well informed about affairs in the province and was always an interested listener. His opinion was always worth hearing. He was of the view that the people being resettled were only happy because of the material things they were gaining. He added that "psychologically they were not at a similar level of contentment; the material aspects at present were stronger than that of the heart and mind."

We were informed on 11 December that President Thieu would be in Quang Tri Province the next day. The local Vietnamese authorities had plans organized for this occasion, so preparations were promptly put into action. With the president and other VIPs in attendance, a special security arrangement had been implemented by the ARVN forces in the province. Warrant Officer Doug Hill, AATTV, was deployed on the beach with his artillery battalion command post. Fortunately there was no enemy interference. The cynic in me thought that the effort to concentrate the people more closely in Gia Dang could perhaps make the propaganda campaign of the VC easier to carry out.

Earlier in the morning I had taken a small boy with his mother to the dispensary. The webbing of his hand had split. The hand was washed, bandaged, and he was asked to come back the next day for further treatment. The boy was obviously in pain but did not fuss. I had met another boy, a ten-year-old, during the morning who had received treatment on a U.S. hospital ship off the coast. He had been wounded by VC rifle fire in the arm and elbow, with two shots to the chest and one injury in a leg. He had no love for the VC. Food bags from the United States, but enclosed in bags marked GVN, had been stacked in the ceremonial area for the president to give to the people in the new settlement.

Welcoming President Thieu, Quang Tri Province, 12 December 1968.

Official ceremony at Gia Dang, 12 December 1968.

For the official ceremony the people walked into the VIP area in the village in columns at 12:30 P.M. on 12 December. All had flags and had rehearsed cheering earlier, being led by Captain Vong. A helicopter park had been provided for the fly-in. A fleet-like group of eighteen helicopters had lifted visitors in for the occasion. President Thieu was accompanied by Ambassador Colby and others from Saigon. Other senior people present included Generals Lam and Truong and U.S. generals Cushman, Stilwell, Zais, Davis, and Carney.

The new cement road had come into its own, but was showing wear and tear already. It was also used as a pedestrian way. Fish were being taken to inland hamlets, and people inland were bringing out fruit and vegetables for sale. About three hundred boats were now fishing, without any restrictions. This day of public celebration was as good as you could get in a war-torn country.

On the night of 12 December 1968 I wrote a long letter to Eva:

> The President of Vietnam visited Quang Tri Province today. He called into a village to the north of us firstly, and then visited Gia Dang. The resettlement of the people has been completed, as has the road (40,000 bags of cement) from Route 555 to the coast.
>
> The people were previously not under GVN control and probably provided shelter and food to the VC. The President pointed this out to the people in his speech. He also told them that he realised that the young men have gone to the mountains to join the VC or to North Vietnam for training. He now expected the people to support the GVN, and not the VC, and said he had visited them so that they could see him and know who was delivering government support to them.
>
> In all, it was a successful day with no problems reported. The whole project has been blessed with perfect weather. You may recall that two months ago I was sure the monsoon was with us; well since the three heavy rains in September and October we have been having fine weather. For two hours today after the ceremonies I sunbaked and swam in the South China Sea. It was beautiful and now my skin is no longer white, as I was determined not to come home for R&R with pale skin.

Housing reconstruction, Gia Dang, November 1968.

The swim gave me a feeling of having washed away the efforts of the recent past, and allowed me to draw strength for the challenges of the coming months. On top of that the thrill of the Team 19 achievement passed through me like a warm spring breeze. I had been refreshed.

The Vietnamese military and civilian staffs at province and district levels were pleased with the outcome of Operation Fisher. So too were the advisors of Team 19. Quang Tri was showing positive results from the GVN point of view, especially in the general pacification program and with the recent refugee resettlement.

On 14 December 1968, Mr. McNamara, Major Shalikashvili, and I visited Gia Dang and walked through the hamlets. The people appeared to be happy, as were we. The RDs were assisting in the construction of homes. Fresh water was being won from wells, from a depth of about five feet. Each hamlet had at least one television set.

Our limited resources within Team 19 were beginning to show the strain of our intense activities. The vehicles we had at Gia Dang were out of service. Major Brad Oliver went out with an assistant to make repairs and towed one vehicle without brakes to the Citadel. It was an achievement to tow it for twenty kilometers, bringing the towed vehicle to a halt by having it bump to a stop against his own.

Within a week of the ceremonial launch of Gia Dang the road showed signs of breaking up, particularly in the paddy area. The quality of the construction work deteriorated toward the end of the project, perhaps arising from the pressure on the engineers from higher levels. The local motorbike traffic, which offered low-cost access, was finding it difficult to make the trip to the coast. I was saddened by this turn of events.

Generals Stilwell and Truong inspected the stretch of cement road to Gia Dang on 19 December. After an on-the-ground examination General Stilwell expressed his disappointment over the condition of the road. Lieutenant Colonel Wallace, the sector military advisor traveling with the generals, said that he thought the trouble may have been caused by the target dates and the rush for completion. He had missed the point that it was Stilwell who had directed it to be thus. The generals were also informed about the price of fish and seed. Seed was being provided to the new arrivals to help them become self-sufficient.

Being security and safety conscious, I thought the situation was more than novel, to observe this on-the-spot inspection by the generals. A corps commander and a divisional commander were striding up and back along the road without organized protection. As a backup the two helicopters had engines running and rotors turning while the generals were walking. This was high-stakes risk management by our highly regarded senior leaders. The generals departed safely, but probably not altogether satisfied.

A report came from the Gia Dang village complex that a small cartridge had been handed to the advisors by a child. The story presented by the child was that a VC person wanted to lure a U.S. soldier to an isolated area, where he would be ambushed. Routine was returning to village life, where the chance of conflict and harm was always close at hand.

On the afternoon of 22 December the two generals were back at Gia Dang. The province chief, the PSA, and their staffs were in attendance. Award presentations were made to a number of Vietnamese and U.S. soldiers. The conditions were uncomfortable, with strong winds and rain belting in from the sea. This recognition was timely and deserved. Time was available that day for the generals to visit the three hamlets being reestablished at the Cua Viet to the north. Major John Shalikashvili was there, allowing due recognition to be given to him for a job well done. General Drake visited the

Citadel on 24 December with Congressman Montgomery from Missouri. The PSA and the agricultural advisor gave them a short briefing on local matters, and then they headed to Gia Dang.

Late in January 1969 a report critical of Operation Fisher was delivered to Colonel Mooney. The author was a major of the G5 staff of XXIV Corps headquarters. He raised points of contention about cordon and search operations during Fisher based on his observations over three days. It was not accurate or fair, giving reason for Mooney to give Colonel Land, the G5, his views. We thought that the major would be reluctant to return to this territory for some time.

The lesson from this entire episode was that the movement of refugees was clearly a factor to be considered in diplomacy, governance, and the planning and conduct of operations, in peace and war. I concluded that humanitarian considerations needed to have a high priority.

The scars and shadows of the enemy offensive at Tet prevailed throughout 1968. Early in 1969 top-down consideration was being applied to the forthcoming Tet period. The next chapter outlines my experiences in undertaking the contingency planning for the approaching Tet 1969.

12

Contingency Planning for Tet 1969

January–February 1969

A series of friendly force initiatives during Tet 1969 indicated battlefield dominance rested clearly with the allies. Command, staff, and troop efforts were rewarded by a relatively peaceful period. Any repeat of an enemy offensive along the lines of Tet 1968 was thwarted. Here is how Team 19 contributed to the contingency planning to achieve this outcome.

The counteroffensive by the GVN and MACV was gaining traction during the second half of 1968. Implementation of the national pacification plan was continuing. Within the allied forces there was a consciousness that the NVA and the VC should not be allowed to gain ascendancy, either politically or militarily, in the coming months.

The policy threads of a possible U.S. downsizing have been mentioned earlier in this narrative. There was a clear need for the GVN to fill out the military where necessary to minimize the effect of a thinning out by the U.S. forces. Full mobilization had been declared by the GVN in June 1968. The armed forces were to be expanded from six hundred thousand, eventually reaching 1 million.[1]

Within this framework we were facing Tet 1969, to be celebrated on 16–17 February. Like the Chinese, the Vietnamese people celebrated Tet at the beginning of each lunar year, which falls approximately in January or February of the solar calendar. Tet was an occasion for the Vietnamese to rest and celebrate as compensation for the many days of toil and hardship. Tet was also an opportunity for them to remember their ancestors and to refresh the bonds of family and social relationship. Tet was a time to put aside past conflicts and differences, so as to welcome together a happy and hopeful New Year.

Hence, while the host country was preparing for a significant cultural event, the allies were busy planning for a worst-case military scenario, a possible repeat by the enemy of Tet 1968. I consider the USMC involvement in this period in Quang Tri Province to be one of the highlights of this phase. The planning experience over the two months showed me, first, how command arrangements could be adjusted to meet a need, both in single service and joint operations, and second, the value of regular staff officer liaison with other headquarters.

The 3rd Marine Division had embraced the pacification objectives. After the 1st Air Cavalry Division had departed in early November 1968 the marines had demonstrated flexibility in adjusting to wider responsibilities in the province. The USMC was not a stranger to pacification, as the Corps had a sound history and doctrine in operations of this kind. With the temporary disengagement of the NVA, the marines in Quang Tri had the capacity to put more effort into the populated areas. Nevertheless, they had to be constantly vigilant, as their area of operations touched two major infiltration borders, from North Vietnam and Laos.

One initiative of the 3rd Marine Division in preparing for Tet 1969 was to create a provisional company. These troops were required for deception purposes. The company came out of the Quang Tri Combat Base and was deployed to represent a battalion. There was a lack of communication equipment for the provisional company, and an attempt was made to obtain the necessary radio sets from Vietnamese resources. My diary note of 24 January expressed an expectation that "problems may be ahead for us on issues arising with this company." Lieutenant Colonel Wallace and I visited the G3 (Plans) at the 3rd Marine Division headquarters to further develop relationships. We discovered that in Quang Tri Province the marines had only one battalion in reserve and that it was presently deployed, and arguably committed.

The provisional company came into Quang Tri City on 29 January. The command post for the company was located in the Citadel for the night, with two platoons dispersed in Mai Linh District. Ideally, from a unity of command standpoint, the command post would have been better located in the sub-sector center at Mai Linh. But due credit to the marines, the dispersion may have achieved the purpose by showing a marine presence in several places, creating the impression that the force was more than a company. There were no contacts with the enemy.

On 31 January 1969, Team 19 learned that our leader, Colonel Mooney, had been admitted to the hospital. He had not been in good health for a month or so, and hospitalization was necessary. At the same time, it would give him a break from the demands of his position. His absence led to some surprises, with respect to responses at several levels. Jitters about Tet 1969 were to become evident.

Prudent precautions were being introduced in the event of any serious intervention by the NVA or the VC. As a contingency, advisor duplicates of maps and overlays and other essential operational information were compiled. These were the basic items for an alternate operations center, and were put into a secure safe of another friendly agency, in a bunker. Our wish was that they would not be needed. Within the Citadel, advisors were working on priority tasks to help build up protective measures. Our staff, drivers, and interpreters spent an afternoon of manual labor, mainly filling sandbags. These were placed around our generator and trailer, a sensible precaution. This was an overdue response to a mortar threat.

With PSA Mooney out of action, F. T. McNamara became acting PSA, and Lieutenant Colonel Wallace became the acting deputy province senior advisor. At this time General Stilwell, the commanding general of XXIV Corps, U.S. Army, was acting commanding general of the III Marine Amphibious Force.

On 5 February our S2, Major Paul Laski, gave a military history briefing on the local 1968 Tet battle to advisors and staff of the 63rd Maintenance Battalion. Five enemy battalions, with support, failed against one ARVN battalion, one Ranger battalion, and elements of the 1st Brigade, Air Cavalry Division. One VC battalion had moved twenty-five kilometers overnight to be in position for action. According to CIA reports on Tet 1968, the province chief was prepared to leave Quang Tri City if enemy efforts had continued for another twenty-four hours. It was considered that he was aware of VC intentions. Fortunately, he remained in place.

At the staff gathering at the end of the day I briefed the assembled advisors on Quang Tri City defenses, as provided to me by my counterpart. A range of contingency plans had been prepared by the sector staff for a variety of counterattack scenarios, including key points in the city and sub-sector headquarters. The Territorial Forces were well prepared to counter the threat.

On 6 February the acting leadership of Team 19 was energized, due to a high-priority telephone call from Da Nang. Something was afoot, as the acting PSA, the DPSA, and others visited Colonel Mooney on the hospital ship off the coast. It was clear that something was of concern to them. We, the advisory staff, were not briefed on the ship discussion, but as events unfolded we were able to deduce the essential elements. A message arrived informing us that General Stilwell had arranged a secondment of the 3rd Marine Division headquarters' G5, Colonel Corrigan, to Team 19 as acting deputy province senior advisor.

This change came as a surprise to us in Team 19, as it probably did to the acting PSA, Mr. McNamara, and to his acting deputy, Lieutenant Colonel Wallace. Wallace had been coping well in the absence of Mooney. It seemed that this initiative had come about due to concern of a possible enemy Tet offensive, and a situation with the RF/PF at Cam Lo District. The commanding officer of the 2/3 Marines had reported to General Davis that at Cam Lo the number of ambushes and patrols by night had been reduced. This had been passed on to headquarters XXIV Corps, and thence to the 1st ARVN Division headquarters, at Hue. General Truong, the commander there, was informed. Our information at the sector operations center showed that this information about night activity was inaccurate. Our formal reporting system, the Brass Report, recorded the official facts.

We now had high-level command interest in RF/PF activities at Cam Lo and Huong Hoa, brought about by an opinion on facts that the sector considered ill-founded. No checks had been requested on RF/PF activities of our staff at the sector operations level. Particularly felt was the absence of staff interest at headquarters 3rd Marine Division and the 1st ARVN Division headquarters in these issues.

Our troops in Team 19 were not clear on the scheme at play. I suggested to the acting PSA, Mr. McNamara, that all ranks be put in the picture as soon as possible. This he did at 9:30 P.M. on 6 February 1969 by gathering E5s and above to a briefing. My conclusion from the briefing was that CORDS, for the present, would no longer be as influential in military matters in Team 19, but that headquarters XXIV Corps would remain involved through Colonel Corrigan. We hoped that McNamara would keep the Team 19 flag flying.

Key staff members of Team 19 gathered to brief Colonel Corrigan on our activities: the S2 (Intelligence), Major Paul Laski; the RF/PF advisor, Major Brad Oliver; and myself as S3 (Operations). We quickly established a sound professional and personal relationship with Corrigan. Major Laski said that there were no indicators for another Tet offensive. I inferred from the brief that the marines should take care of their own contingency plans, overlooking the obvious fact that we were now part of the marine team, being directed by the USMC and headquarters XXIV Corps, a fact we had yet to get our heads around.

During this busy and unusual day Generals Stilwell and Truong arrived for what was a longer than usual visit. Our Team 19 leaders were with the generals. There was clearly high-level command interest in Quang Tri Province. In a way, it was reassuring, as they had the overall responsibility in this area of South Vietnam. Later that night I wrote that I had felt a bit depressed over the last few days. Major Brad Oliver felt much the same, as we reviewed our relative positions. We agreed that there was a sense of futility prevailing about the overall effort, there being no light at the end of the tunnel. That was our professional view. From a personal perspective, the end of our respective tours of duty provided the light at the end of our individual tunnels, provided we survived.

I accompanied Corrigan and Wallace on a visit to the headquarters of Marine Task Force Bravo at Ai Tu on 8 February. Colonel Clarke was the commander and commanding officer of the provisional company. It became obvious that Clarke did not have a clear understanding of the Vietnamese situation locally. He seemed to have assumed that the Vietnamese would perform as marines do. District boundaries had to be explained, including the political and military implications. This visit was a wake-up call for me, particularly in the areas of personal communication and mutual understanding.

Later that day we went to Huong Hoa, accompanied by Major Bill Healy from Cam Lo. Healy advised us that the local forces had increased their number of operations. At Huong Hoa we met with the commanding officer of the 2/3 Marines and discussed local security issues and RF/PF matters. He was "right on the ball." His battalion continued to be dispersed. He had companies at Huong Hoa, Cam Lo, fire support base C2, and on a land-clearing operation in Leatherneck Square, above Route 9, providing protection to the engineers. In the event that any of his deployed elements came into enemy contact, his reserve—or reaction force—would have come from a company not in contact. This was a demanding role for a battalion in this area, and was an example of the 3rd Marine Division's contribution to pacification. The district senior advisor at Huong Hoa stated that within local military resources the "Strikers" of the Special Forces camp were earmarked to provide a reserve at sub-sector level.

A marine engineer survey team visited on 9 February to discuss land clearing proposals around key government infrastructure in the city. The general idea was to focus on close-in defenses, such as flattening all areas within wire barriers and for two hundred meters outside them, and to improve fields of fire. The idea had merit. The weather might prove to be an obstacle.

During the day General Drake visited to talk to McNamara about a briefing to take place the next day, to be given by Major Nguyen Luu De, successor to the recently relieved Lieutenant Colonel Nhan. I mused that the chain of command did not seem to be particularly relevant to the generals as they flew here and there in their helicopters. In some cases the colonels acted similarly. The concept of unity of command was being tested. At the same time Colonel Land, from XXIV Corps headquarters, was in attendance to sort out a problem arising from a visit by General Stilwell to Hai Lang the day before. Some sense of meaning and relevance had been lost in the transfer of messages. The enquiry appeared to have been a Vietnamese problem, now on transfer to the advisors. The advisors were unable to assist Colonel Land.

Later on 9 February the Corrigan, Wallace, and Millie team traveled to the 3rd Marine Division headquarters to discuss Dong Ha city defense. The G3 (Operations) thought the existing arrangements to be satisfactory. Colonel Corrigan said he had a problem with the defenses but was unable to define the nature of the problem. The concept of the defense was on mobility for reserves, the uncommitted troops, with key installations in a permanent state of defense with static defenders. Thus concentration of force could be brought to bear wherever the threat appeared. We were advised this day that the marine provisional company was to be redeployed from Quang Tri City to work north of Dong Ha in the 2nd ARVN Regiment area of operations. The company was replaced by another USMC company within a week.

The next day Colonel Corrigan continued his quest for knowledge about the city defense. He was briefed on the advisory communications networks. He was searching for the nub of his problem, with his mind not yet clear on some fundamentals. The advisors could not help him; it seemed that we were at a loss as to what more we could do. Then General Drake and Colonel Land came in for a flying visit. Major De gave the officers a security and defense posture briefing. The Vietnamese briefers found it difficult to respond to questions put to them in a verbose manner by the U.S. officers, and some questions were not answered, either because they did not understand the questions or because they judged it to be prudent to avoid answering.

There was a flurry of staff officer activity over the next two days. This arose from a visit by General Davis to the police headquarters in Quang Tri City. He had a conversation with Major Dick and Walt Bayling, the police advisor. Their conversation covered not only police issues, but included the defense of the city and tactics. Davis took this information back to his headquarters and directed his staff to investigate. This led to the 1/5 Infantry Brigade's S3 and a pair of USMC colonels from the 3rd Marine Division's G3 staff headquarters joining up with Colonel Corrigan at the sector headquarters. Bayling and Major Dick had not been speaking on behalf of the PSA or his deputy, yet General Davis had his staff moving on his discussions with them. Perhaps that was part of the motivation behind this command-driven activity. Discussions were inconclusive.

Later Colonel Corrigan and I went by road to the G3 staff at headquarters 3rd Marine Division for further discussions about city defenses, without any decisions arising. In the evening the advisory staff met with Corrigan for a long and detailed discussion about the matter. A range of questions arose for which we did not have the answers. Most of the issues were to do with the Territorial Forces. We, the advisors, relied on the Vietnamese forces for our security within the city and environs and had been encouraging the development of their military skills and minor tactics since taking up our appointments.

Corrigan seemed not to have a feel for the Vietnamese, or their tactics, nor did he seem to appreciate the position of advisors in the situation in which he found himself. We concluded that night tours of the city by advisors might be helpful for all concerned. Thus we toured the city in rosters, at 11:00 P.M. and 3:00 A.M., to help better appreciate the city defenses and preparedness. I agreed to go out at 11:00 P.M., but not anything later, unless it was coordinated with the Territorial Forces, with adequate protection provided. This was a very depressing situation, but such was the lot of an advisor. We were spending more time with the U.S. military than with the Vietnamese. As a result of this preoccupation, it was noticeable that at our local level the number of operations was decreasing. Perhaps the cultural and social aspects of Tet were becoming the focus of the Vietnamese people, whether civil or military. After all, they were the hosts.

On the night of 11–12 February the advisor vehicle patrols commenced in Quang Tri City. In company with Corrigan, Wallace, and the police advisors, we toured the city. We were accompanied by a beefy enlisted man who was tasked to ride shotgun. His primary job was that of interpreter with the Civil Affairs platoon. He appeared to be "under the weather," from alcohol, and was on his first night trip out into the city. There was an "all is normal" report for the two excursions that night, at 11:00 P.M. and at 3:00 A.M. Mr. McNamara accompanied me on the second patrol.

USMC elements in the city were allotted to be under the operational control of Team 19 on 12 February. I thought this arose as a result of Colonel Corrigan's being present in our ranks, and as an outcome of our city patrols. The marine elements with Team 19 were defined as Task Force Charlie. This was a clue toward a continuing USMC presence during Tet.

During the day my counterparts in the operations center requested that the marine platoon located within the Citadel be relocated to the NPFF area, situated outside the Citadel. As the current deployment had been agreed upon by the province chief, I judged that it would be a proper protocol for the province chief to make that request to Colonel Corrigan, who by then had operational control of the marines. The request made sense, and was duly agreed upon by Corrigan when it came from the province chief.

General Davis visited the acting PSA on 13 February and expressed his view that he wanted to put marines on all installations likely to come under VC attack, to have patrols in Quang Tri City, and to provide assistance whenever required. He awaited a considered view from Team 19. With our counterparts we reviewed the local situation, worked out troops to task, and concluded the defenses required one additional platoon. We identified a gap in a vulnerable area, Nhan Bieu Two, to the southwest of the city on the west side of the Thach Han River. Colonel Corrigan and I then visited General Davis at his headquarters. The general decided to send down an additional company, as he wanted to have a reaction force available.

Major General Raymond G. Davis, commander of the 3rd Marine Division.

My record for that meeting noted: "Seems 1/5 Infantry Brigade will be tasked to provide a company. This is likely to upset them as they have only seven rifle companies." This speculation proved to be just that, as a marine company was allocated. A further note was that a principle of war, public opinion, was a key factor behind our Tet preparations. The U.S. military command, and commanders, did not want any further adverse publicity at home over likely VC activities in the Tet period. I went on to write that "to keep credible with the Vietnamese military forces and the GVN, the allied forces should stay here in Vietnam until after any NVA/VC offensive has been destroyed."

Marine Company M/3/4 arrived in the city early on 14 February to undertake the tasks outlined earlier. This company of Task Force Charlie based up at the elementary school, and deployed one platoon to the abandoned village of An Don the next day, two kilometers distant. This platoon was covering the southwest approach to the city, on the other side of the river. My diary comment was one of admiration for the U.S. Marines: "The 3rd Marine Division moves companies around in a very flexible way. The G3 and staff get involved in company deployments." Our operations center had to make a request to the III MAF headquarters for the radio frequencies to be allocated to Task Force Charlie. This requirement was placed on the advisors by headquarters 3rd Marine Division. This was puzzling to us, but we got on with the task. The chain of command that now existed could only be understood by the initiated.

All squad leaders and above from the marine elements in Quang Tri City were provided with an aerial visual reconnaissance of their areas on 15 February. This was an ideal preparation for the role that they had to perform. They also had the opportunity to patrol their areas on foot, to become familiar with details, and to let the VC know of their presence. This would give the VC a great deal to think about, particularly if they wished to mess around with us. That morning I traveled to the Marine Corps' Quang Tri Combat Base to brief Colonel Michaels and Brigadier General Canny on Quang Tri City defenses. I then moved to the headquarters of the 1/5 Infantry Brigade and made the same presentation to the S3 operations staff. My two visits were just in time, as the brigade commanders were preparing their presentations to the corps commander and division commanders that day.

The advisor compound held a social to celebrate Tet with our counterparts and friends on 15 February. The gathering was a very happy and relaxed occasion. On the face of it we were all friends, facing up to a common foe. We had much in common to share. The general view of the advisors, after the celebration, was that it was probably the most successful social occasion held of this nature. Later that day we heard that the 3/3 Marines had returned from Da Nang after sixty days in the mountains to rejoin Task Force Bravo. This was good news for the 3rd Marine Division, and for Team 19.

I sat in on a sector police briefing on present and future operations on 16 February. After thirty-five minutes of briefing in the Vietnamese language the two marine company commanders in attendance walked out of the meeting. This action drew the attention of the hosts, who quickly made amends, reconvening with the marines present and covering the briefing points in English. Some reservations about the extent of Territorial Forces leadership involvement in the current joint military affairs had been growing in my mind over the last few days. No Vietnamese unit commanders attended this sector briefing.

I judged that the Territorial Forces leadership was being insensitive toward the marines. Despite the Vietnamese military's having the responsibility to provide security to the Chieu Hoi hamlet, they failed to do so. A platoon from M/3/4 was allocated the task on the evening of 15 February. Perhaps the Vietnamese military had opted for the festival spirit of Tet instead of the perennial rigors of military security.

Advisor doubts about Major De were growing. The ARVN battalion from the 1st Regiment had not yet been relocated to La Vang. This battalion was a major component of our city defense plan. Without a battalion there, the southern approach to the city was wide open. It was probably beyond De's control, but he was the "go to man." The last resort for the advisors would be to contact the 1st ARVN Division advisors in Hue and ask them to approach General Truong on the matter.

A message came down from the GVN and MACV in Saigon about the approaching Tet: Curfew for the military and civilians was to be from 1:00 P.M. on 16 February to 6:00 A.M. on 17 February and there was to be a truce from 6:00 P.M. on 16 February to 6:00 A.M. on 17 February.

My diary entries for 16 and 17 February read:

> All is very quiet. Should be interesting to see and to hear what happens at midnight. Traditionally it is noisy, with firecrackers and the like. Last year the celebrations were of assistance to the VC, as a noisy cover to their assault. The Province Chief visited the Sector Military Hospital and gave a small monetary gift to each of the 80 patients.
>
> It was a very peaceful night in Quang Tri city. During the day I/3/3 Marines relieved M/3/4 Marines who were redeployed to Vandegrift [Ca Lu]. Aerial reconnaissance of the city by the relieving troops could not be undertaken.

As the Tet season continued, the acting PSA and acting DPSA required that reports of incidents be passed by the operations center to them as they happened during the night. My notes indicated some frustration: "Why would a senior commander who cannot influence things in any way whatsoever, want to know about relatively trivial matters? A poor show and would probably soon wear them into the ground." Perhaps night calls from their senior officers further back may have stimulated them. In a letter home dated 17 February 1969 I wrote: "The Vietnamese Tet passed peacefully. A very noticeable feature was that the people, adults and children, were dressed in their best clothes on this day, usually white for the young ladies."

The I/3/3 Marines, less a platoon, withdrew from the city. The significant USMC presence was brief, from 29 January to 19 February. Priorities seemed to have changed after a quiet Tet. Task Force Charlie disbanded on 4 March, ending a five-week USMC presence. They did a good job and helped maintain the morale of the Vietnamese people.

Colonel Mooney, PSA, was discharged from the hospital ship on 20 February and was welcomed back to Team 19. Within a few days he was undertaking the full duties of his position.

The operations center received an Alert III message from the III MAF headquarters by a Flash Confidential signal on the evening of 22 February. The source of the information was not known, but the message warned of the threat of attack between 11:00 P.M. and 6:00 A.M. the next day. There was no unusual activity in our area. A note of 23 February included: "Curfew is to be at 4:00 pm today, and is then to be at 7:00 pm each night."

On 23 February the MACV compound formed a provisional platoon of thirty-two, composed of all ranks. The role of this platoon was to be a reaction force to meet any contingency in Quang Tri City. An ad hoc group of drivers, cooks, bakers, clerks, and storemen was very good in a barracks role, but to perform as infantrymen, without rehearsals, in what could be urban fighting was an interesting prospect. Thankfully the platoon was not put to the test.

Later that night General Stilwell telephoned the duty officer at our operations center requesting hourly situation reports from sector. "Yes sir," we said. All the necessary information was routinely passed to headquarters 1st ARVN Division in Hue. It was assumed distilled reports would go to the XXIV Corps headquarters. We thought that maybe the general was cross-checking the contents of various reports that came to him.

Two days later, Chuu and I, while on the night beat, visited the home of the local Vietnamese Military Security Service chief, Lieutenant Minh. He was the proud father of seven children. He lived in a solid cement house at Tri Buu. His home was well appointed, including a refrigerator, with the walls adorned by many religious pictures. During our patrol we came upon a well-prepared machine gun bunker, sited under a street lamp. Chuu attempted to shoot out the globe but missed. I thought it noteworthy that many of the PSDF were seen on the streets. It was also encouraging to see people out and about, armed and prepared. There were many rats and mice on the streets, possibly in plague proportions. The marines at the town water pump site were fully alert and eager to talk. They were doing their job well, and made it clear that they were working harmoniously with the Vietnamese. The night was free of incidents.

I drafted a letter of appreciation on behalf of the province chief on 7 March. The letter was to Major General R. Davis, 3rd Marine Division, expressing the heartfelt thanks of all the people in Quang Tri Province for the work done by the USMC throughout Quang Tri Province and particularly in the city during the recent Tet period.

Reports came into the operations center on 9 March of a full-blooded firefight going on to the north and northwest of Cam Lo. Contact ceased and relative calm was resumed. The 3rd Marine Division continued to dominate the western part of the province.

Supporting my earlier observation about the rats, an outbreak of plague was declared in Quang Tri City on 10 March. A total of seventy-six cases were reported over a three-week period, with twenty deaths resulting. It was thought that the plague was of the bubonic type. The municipal authorities were now endeavoring to clean up garbage, particularly in the monsoon drains, which were continuously blocked with other filth. Rats were also to be targeted. The plague was a serious health hazard to all.

I patrolled the city streets with Major Chuu on the night of 10 March. At the posts occupied by the NPFF, those sentries expected to be alert were asleep. At the RF/PF posts the soldiers were barely alert. I wrote in my diary that the hopelessness exhibited by some of the Vietnamese was not encouraging.

A closer working relationship between headquarters 3rd Marine Division and our Team 19 gave rise to our attendance at the daily briefing at the division headquarters. Colonel Corrigan, who had left us upon Mooney's assuming full duty, may have been an influence in this initiative. General Davis judged that our attendance there would be beneficial for all. We agreed.

During my time with the U.S. forces in Vietnam I attended many briefings. The command and staff briefings of a combat division were very impressive occasions. Detailed preparation, stage management, and performance were evident. The commanding general had the biggest rotating chair. His chief of staff was close by, as was the aide to the general. These three officers had center stage. Immediately in front of the general was a further row of ten chairs, one for each presenter. The main body of the audience was composed of about sixty staff officers and liaison officers. The presenters addressed the whole gathering, but clearly their focus for the delivery was General Davis. He probably knew as much about the subject areas as each of the presenters, which kept them professionally sharp. One of the purposes of such briefings was to ensure that all in attendance had the operational news of the day, heard any directives of the day, and had the opportunity to ask questions.

The briefing took about thirty minutes to cover the operations of the division, down to company level, by areas of operations. There were no questions, there were no interruptions. Members of the audience knew it was their professional responsibility to keep principal staff officers informed on relevant matters, and that the divisional briefing forum was not the place to raise items for the first time.

Our Team 19 group in attendance had a part to play on this particular day. Colonel Mooney was accompanied by John Cleary, Hassler, and me. The general invited Mooney to brief on a combined operation being developed for Cam Vu, to be discussed in chapter 14. Cam Vu was on the north side of the east-west Cam Lo River, on Route 88 between Cam Lo and Dong Ha, twelve kilometers south of the DMZ. General Davis endorsed the operation. He reminded us that twelve NVA regiments had been identified just above the DMZ, estimated to be but six hours from us. His final word was that we must press on with optimism.

With the concerns of Tet 1969 behind us, other present and future demands now had our focus. The advisors had been clearly sharpened up by the recent attention given to us by U.S. Army and USMC commanders and staff officers, in a contingency plan that was not put to the test. Colonel Mooney was refreshed and was already under pressure from anticipated coming events. We were all in the business of helping the Vietnamese prepare for their future without U.S. support, whenever that might be.

The next chapter follows the scheme of chapter 9, where my experiences in sector operational life at Quang Tri in 1968 are told. My "oil and glue" role as a field operations staff officer continued into 1969. Pacification had been the name of the main game for Team 19 for most of 1968, and that continued into the coming year.

13

Sector Staff Work

The Oil and the Glue

January–April 1969

I pick up the story from Boxing Day 1968 by way of introduction to the activities of 1969. A coordination meeting was held for a cordon and search operation for the next day. We were informed that "block" was to be the term to use instead of "cordon." The joint operation had the hallmark of the Stilwell/Truong doctrine. The 1st ARVN Regiment, elements of the 1/5 Infantry Brigade, and sector forces were to participate in the operation. The advisors present at the meeting had an observer role, as we were not to be involved in the operation. Planning was done by committee, with the most persistent voices being the people who influenced the shape of the plan. The discussion took two hours. The operation was uneventful, but a positive note was the experience to be gained by the ARVN and the Territorial Forces in a joint operation of this kind. The GVN forces were being prepared for their future without U.S. support.

Later in the day there were further discussions about a fire support coordination center for the area. The main participants were the commanding officer of the 5/4 Artillery (U.S.), the commanding officer of the 11th ARVN Artillery, and Lieutenant Colonel Nhan. Each was in agreement about the idea, and there did not appear to be any technical problems in implementation. The location of the center seemed to be the only matter to be resolved. I had reached a personal view that the 1/5 Infantry Brigade headquarters wanted the center to be in its area, but I judged that the Citadel (sector headquarters) could finally be decided upon.

The hosting issue for an area center continued for about a month. I attended a conference of artillery officers from the 3rd Marine Division, the 1/5 Mechanized Brigade, and the Quang Tri Combat Base on 27 January. A potential impasse was overcome with a simple and agreed solution. The decision was that the commander responsible for an area of operations, be it at a regiment or brigade level, was to be responsible for fire clearances into or out of the respective areas of operation, and to obtain GVN clearance as well. The sector staff agreed to the procedure, which was really a confirmation of what was a past practice.

Sector staff had informed advisors on 31 December 1968 that all of their priority and routine air medical evacuation requests were to be passed to the Hue operations center in order to have the South Vietnamese Air Force more involved in the action. The policy was to apply to Vietnamese medical cases. Vietnamization of the war effort was being introduced in a gradual way.[1]

I collated the operations procedures manual for the assistant sector advisor to review. Some relief was provided on New Year's Day when advisory staff available celebrated S4 advisor Major Bernie Meisel's thirtieth birthday with cheese, biscuits, and beer.

On some days advisor operational staffs were committed to tasks away from the center. As key advisor operations center staff were committed elsewhere on 3 January, the center became my place of duty. Fortunately, no challenging issues arose, allowing me the time to familiarize myself with the radio networks and other details within the center.

At the next Saturday advisors' meeting the new police advisor, Mr. Walt Bayling, spent fifteen minutes telling us of the strengths and weaknesses of the police in Quang Tri Province. He related to us highlights of his eight years of service in South Vietnam. Bayling had undertaken a personal inspection of all the districts in the sector and had reached certain conclusions, which I did not record. His performance was impressive, and most of us looked forward to hearing from him of developments over the next few months.

The highlight of my next night of duty at the operations center was to have talented Vietnamese soldiers in the combined center preparing charts and overlays for presentations by advisors on the pacification plan the next day.

The four Ps were listed in my notes on 5 January. A planned operation in Trieu Phong District would not get under way on time due to adverse weather and road conditions, factors known to exist during the preparation. Hence the four Ps: piss poor prior planning, later to be known as the seven Ps: proper planning and preparation prevents painfully poor performance. Helicopters did not fly on this day or the next.

Major Ed Thomas, U.S. Army, arrived at the Citadel on 8 January en route to replace Jim Hill at Huong Hoa. He had spent the first part of his tour of duty in Da Nang, where he was the advisor for railway security. A few days later I visited Ed in the Cua Valley. He was settling in, knowing he had little choice. It was always prudent to make the best of a bad draw.

A staff officer from MACV (a lieutenant colonel) arrived at the Citadel on 9 January to assess the USMC Combined Action Program (CAP). He was a member of a CORDS evaluation team in Saigon. He was to hear many points of view, including mine. In summary, my opinion was that, considering the number of troops involved, judged against results, the program could not justify the effort allocated. More than 70 percent of the 104 CAPs in I Corps had been with platoons for months. It should not have taken that amount of time to upgrade trained soldiers to make an effective platoon. Later observations confirmed my conclusions.

A few days later PF Platoon 62 in Mai Linh District, with a CAP, was the subject of suspected foul play. Against the advice of the CAP leader, the third in command of the PF platoon conducted a night patrol. In what appeared to be an inside job of treachery, the patrol was ambushed, suffering ten soldiers killed and eight wounded. There were no marine casualties.

Weeks later it seemed the CAPs were not receiving the full cooperation from the PFs. One case, by way of example, was in the notorious Nhu Le area, and a second was to the northwest of Cam Lo. Advisors were required to intervene in these two cases. It appeared that district chiefs and their PFs were being coerced into reacting to Combined Action Group policies. A general view of advisors was that the CAP operations had to be more understanding of PF operations. Advisor incident reports from sub-sectors to sector about these matters caused some concern for the commanding officer of the 4th Combined Action Group. A further complication to these relationship matters was highlighted in April. A report came in from another district that a recent CAP/PF contact was a friendly fire incident, not one of enemy action. It was stated that a PF leader and a CAP leader were fired upon by their own troops when returning from a night out with females in a nearby hamlet. This liaison by the junior leaders was taking friendly relations, good neighbor policy, and winning the hearts and minds too far. There was more than a discipline problem here. The USMC and MACCORDS consequently had a problem, one among many. I pondered whether the U.S. scheme of Army mobile advisory teams (MATs) with RF companies had similar issues.

The S2, Major Paul Laski, had warned us that this period of relative quiet could be the time the VC/NVA would undertake reconnaissance and preparation for an offensive. He pointed out that commanders conduct their reconnaissance well forward in time and place. Further, he suggested that the enemy could be arranging guides and having sand model exercises in preparation for battle. This methodical approach to battle deployment could have the enemy at that stage now. This was a timely reminder by Paul that vigilance was always needed in a theater of war. We were comforted by our elimination in 1968 of Bui Tu, Phan Thi, and other VC leaders. Loss of such leaders would have set back enemy planning and organization locally.

I attended a briefing on 10 January at the 1/5 Infantry Brigade headquarters to help coordinate a major operation due to commence on 12 January. Troops to participate included five PF platoons, the 3/1 ARVN, the 1/61 Mechanized Battalion, and a troop of 11th ARVN Cavalry. The main aim of the briefing was to ensure sector and ARVN elements were coordinated, and that the role of the U.S. units was understood by all participants. The brigade commander was disappointed that Lieutenant Colonel Nhan was not in attendance. I shared his disappointment.

A reconnaissance was undertaken to determine the location for the combined information center. I was able to influence the site selection and the composition of the center. Lieutenant Colonel Nhan was able to attend a final coordination meeting for the center on 12 January, where the Vietnamese S2, Captain Nong, chaired the gathering. This was an encouraging start to the operation for the Vietnamese. The next day I prepared to go home to Australia on R&R leave.

The period away from Quang Tri on leave was a wonderful tonic. Team 19 had runs on the board. Operation Fisher had concluded in December, pacification planning was settled, and my tour of duty was two-thirds complete. I was in good health, and my family was to have their share of husband and father. I felt blessed compared to the lot of some, those who had made the supreme sacrifice or been wounded. The Vietnamese were not able to take a break out of country, a sobering thought. I also had a break from diary entries. A diary was not required to remind me of the joy to be with Eva and our two sons for five days.

Air travel legs each way for leave were from Da Nang to Darwin to Sydney by World 707. Eva met me at Sydney Airport. At the time she was away from our home in Queensland on a Christmas visit to her family. The next day we flew to Coonabarabran, in the central west of New South Wales, to link up with our sons. We were hosted by Eva's mother, Mary, and her brother, Patrick, who lived on a farm to the west of Coonabarabran. The season was mid-summer; the days were hot and dry. Time was spent talking and having enjoyment around the children's paddle pool. Our sons were aged two and one year. With grateful thanks to Eva and her family, I found my family happily settled. We were enriched by the short visit. My stay was at an end when we bade each other farewell at the Coonabarabran airport for my return to Vietnam.

Upon returning from leave on 22 January, I traveled from Da Nang to Quang Tri by an Air America Porter aircraft, a forty-five-minute flight. The pilot informed me that three days earlier an Air America C-47 had crashed into a hill to the southeast of Hue. The aircraft had been flying in fog at low level. All on board had been killed. On hearing that sad news I was relieved that this flight was in fine weather. At the same time it was a reminder that leave was behind me and that my mind now had to focus on the reality of the tasks I was to deal with on the ground in Quang Tri, a place that was now a special part of my life.

That afternoon Team 19 received a new advisor to fill the appointment of S2/S3 (Air). Captain Porter Angel, U.S. Army, had ten years of service to his credit and had been commissioned after his first tour in South Vietnam. He had a quaint habit of sucking on an unlit cigar. I was very pleased to be able to brief him on his tasks. He was a quick learner. Lieutenant Colonel Wallace was working hard in his executive role, and I thought he saw an opportunity in gaining some extra officer support now that Captain Angel was with us.

A dedicated operations and intelligence communication advisor net was established in the Citadel on 24 January to link us with Hue and Da Nang. This was a surprising initiative, as there had been an absence of prior coordination and information on this regional link between operations and intelligence. The new net was potentially a useful communication link. My note was that we were in a kind of limbo for the moment on this one. What was surprising was that the military machine to our rear had judged that this link was necessary at a time when preparations were under way for a phasing out of U.S. military assets. My entry on 5 February indicated that the newly introduced operations and intelligence net for I Corps Advisory had closed down over the past two nights. A clarification on this matter was requested, and the next day we were informed that the net was now not a twenty-four-hour-a-day operation. The earlier thoughts Team 19 advisors had about this net had come to pass. The link was not required.

The next day I visited Huong Hoa sub-sector with Major Ed Doran, an FSCC officer of the 3rd Marine Division, to talk about fire clearances with the district chief, the DSA, the Special Forces A-Team leader, and the ARVN Vietnamese Special Forces commanding officer. The main fire support shortcoming for the units in the Cua Valley was that they did not have a direct support artillery battery allocated to them. Hence, they did not have a dedicated artillery communication and fire observer present. Despite having simple procedures in place for artillery support, they involved attention to detail and took time to be executed. The people in this valley were seeking timely artillery support, if a need arose. Experience indicated they had a good case.

A GVN initiative backed by MACV to establish a People's Self-Defense Force (PSDF) gained momentum in the second half of 1968. The PSDF was a post-Tet 1968 response by the GVN. Reporting on the PSDF to Saigon became mandatory from the district level up. The report had several purposes, and I was moved to write in my diary: "One purpose was to provide guidance on a management information system for the subject program." The report document came out of CORDS, with the reports going to GVN agencies. One wondered how the results were to be managed and acted upon. The assumption seemed to be that a significant part of the population in South Vietnam would be armed. There were built-in risks here.

On resuming the role as a duty staff officer in the operations center I noted the following log book entries on 25 January. They represent a typical night of incidents:

2115 hours: Hai Lang mortared.

2125 hours:	Citadel mortared with six rounds. Five children wounded.
2300 hours	Tracked vehicles of 1/61 moving to a "Block" in Mai Linh sub sector on Route 1 were shot at by RFs on Nhung Bridge. No casualties.
2329 hours:	111 PF Platoon east of Dong Ha at Phu Le attacked by a Viet Cong platoon, withdrew, and came into an ambush. Outcome: Fourteen own KIA, five civilians injured. No known enemy casualties. Also lost: eleven weapons and one radio set PRC10.[2]

Reports indicated that the local Territorial Forces were not operating effectively in the southwest of Quang Tri City, the suspected location of the enemy mortar base plate(s). Procedural problems continued in obtaining clearance to fire into the Quang Tri Combat Base area, a marine area of operations, but also an area of particular interest to the ARVN. The marines and the combat base disallowed requests from the Vietnamese to fire into their area. The outcome here was procedurally correct, as the commander of the area had the right of refusal. Perhaps there were good reasons to disallow requests. More dialogue was needed to keep people calm. Later it was reported that the Vietnamese would not give fire clearance to the marines seeking to fire from Quang Tri Combat Base on targets outside their area. One hoped this was not a tit-for-tat game.

Later in the day I made a quick visit in a Blackcat helicopter to the site of the ambush in the Dong Ha area the night before. The incident was two kilometers east of Dong Ha. General Truong, Colonel Giai, and Lieutenant Colonel Nhan were there also. There was little they could do, but their presence was necessary under the circumstances. This was a very serious blow to the local people, as the soldiers killed would have all been local lads. More attacks of this nature could not be ruled out. It was the second occasion that week of an attack on a PF platoon.

U.S. mortar fire from LZ Sharon within Quang Tri Combat Base fell on a CAP at Nhu Le on 27 January. This was a friendly fire incident, with nine marines and four PF soldiers wounded. This led to a diary comment: "At present we seem to be spending more time on after action matters than on before action planning."

An Explosives Ordinance Demolition team was allocated to Huong Hoa District on 28 January with directions to blow up unwanted concrete bunkers and items of ammunition. Sector was informed that the explosives had made little impact upon the old French fortifications in that area. The colonial forts had survived but not the French; was this an ominous sign for us?

I was duty officer in the operations center on 29 January. A report was received of a sighting of thirty VC at Nhu Le. The Territorial Forces did not react. I expressed a view to Captain Cuu that one would have expected a response from the local security forces. The next day an RF company was tasked to work in the Nhu Le area. This response was a matter of "face," but also of "the oil and glue" at work.

The VC political infrastructure in South Vietnam was guided by the People's Revolutionary Party, whose existence was officially acknowledged in January 1962.[3] A complex network reached all the way down to communist local committees and to VC local force units, which were directly controlled by district military headquarters. Work commenced on the targeting of local committees.

A sector planning conference was convened with the task of formulating recommendations for targeting members of the People's Liberation Committees in hamlets. These committees, communist led, had the job of carrying on the day-to-day governmental functions of administering the hamlets and villages for the party. For local organizations, villagers could easily be involved in communist-inspired interest groups with front guises. It was a local view that Buddhists could be attracted to an activity established by the liberation committees. In such circumstances it was very difficult to separate party members from nonpolitical aspirants. This was a task for the Vietnamese agencies to work at. The advisory organization was there to support and to resource the GVN in this kind of intelligence work. The Phoenix Program was designed to neutralize the VC.

Local operations continued. A combined RF/PF operation to the east of the city, out of Mai Linh District into Hai Lang District, proceeded without contact. The VC could not be drawn into action during daylight on our terms. An intelligence report informed us that a recently captured courier was carrying a message from the 6th Front

(NVA) in Thua Thien Province. The message included a request for ammunition and other supplies. Forward air controllers reported sightings of trails cut for the laying of telephone lines from Laos into Base Area 101. The effort for such an endeavor would have been considerable. Action was being taken to destroy the lines. One skeptic offered a view that the trail could have been a dummy.

Evidence that earlier combined operations were having a positive influence on the Territorial Forces became apparent when the 1/5 Infantry Brigade could not provide troops to work with the Territorials. The RF companies were now conducting their own "block and search" operations. Advisors judged these operations to be satisfactory. With the police, combined information centers had been set up for processing purposes. These were small steps in self-sufficiency and self-reliance.

The evening of 5 February was spent reviewing our province brief. The assistant sector advisor had been given the task of preparing a folder of local information for the PSA, and for visitors to the province. This was a useful tool, and all advisors had made contributions. Confidential parts included a description of Quang Tri City defenses and relief plans for a variety of contingencies in the event of any need for counterattacks on key parts of the city, or any subsector headquarters. The brief in draft became a hefty document.

The causeway to Trieu Phong was put out of service on 7 February. A low loader carrying a bulldozer, a class 35 load, attempted to use the crossing, a class 12 Bailey bridge. Naturally, the bridge collapsed. This was on the route to Cua Viet along the road that General Lam had earmarked for upgrading.

Major Nguyen Luu De, Nhan's replacement, was settling into his new appointment. First impressions upon meeting De were positive. He was an energetic type of fellow, and it struck me that if he could keep his spirit up he would do a good job for all of us. Our first excursion together was to the Cua Viet, where a combined NPFF/USMC operation was under way. At the Cua Viet, on the south side, a hamlet had been cordoned off following intelligence reports. It was thought that VC activities in the hamlet, and suspected caches of munitions, could lead to enemy activity against navy vessels on the waterway. Major De was only interested in the military aspects of the operation. He kept clear of the villagers and hamlet chief, and in particular he did not want to be involved with a vocal homeowner who belonged to a particular sect of Buddhists.

He confided to me that it was for the district chief to be involved with his people, not him.

We then flew south to the Gia Dang settlement. De was primarily interested in the defenses there. He judged that more defense stores were needed to bolster the security and safety in some spots. Accordingly, De set in action the delivery of twenty thousand sandbags for bunkers on the wire perimeter, and also additional concertina barbed wire for the area occupied by the advisors. He was an action man.

Later that day, 9 February, De, Cuu, and I took a vehicle to Hai Lang District to attend a Tet party. Our hosts were the district headquarters staff and an RF company. An RD vocal group provided the musical entertainment. The function was a happy one, with whisky in particular being forced upon the guests. The organizational leadership was excellent and morale was up. Attendance seemed to be 100 percent of all ranks.

Despite the province brief book's being completed in draft form, the assistant sector advisor was not prepared to hand the draft to typists. It seemed that there was a lack of expertise among the typists to present a reasonable draft. The problem arose due to a lack of uniform presentation, as the originals came from a number of Army and USMC officers and a disparate group of civil agencies. It was just as well that we were only dealing with the English language in this document. In the past we may have required a Vietnamese and possibly a French language version as well. I noted that staff papers written in the U.S. Army had a different presentation format from the Australian and British systems, where papers used headings with crisp, short sentences. The U.S. papers were more of an essay narrative form with an absence of headings. Whatever—if an idea had merit, and was well argued, the presentation style was not of consequence.

I flew to Huong Hoa in a Huey on 16 February to sit in on a military conference. In attendance were the district chief and his advisor, the commanding officer of the CIDG and his advisor, and the commanding officer of the 2/3 Marines. The open forum was about capabilities, defenses, and offensive operations. The CIDG was responsible for an area of operations within the district but could not cope with the responsibilities. Again of major concern was the lack of direct support artillery. It was agreed that most of the Vietnamese hamlets supported the VC. The district chief was concerned about security and gave his view that most of the area should be allocated as a tactical area to the 3rd Marine Division.

General Stilwell visited Gio Linh on 17 February to discuss a "phantom mortar." This was a surprise to the advisors. Staff in the operations center thought that a report of little substance might have originated in Vietnamese channels and found its way to headquarters XXIV Corps, via the 1st ARVN Division in Hue. Generalship, in this case by Stilwell, was displayed in many ways in the combat zone. In this case it was a matter of attention to detail.

Our operation center was advised on 21 February that during the night enemy naval sappers attached mines to three landing craft at the Cua Viet. One friendly was killed, and scuba equipment had been found. Damage included one craft sunk and two damaged. All craft were reported as repairable. I had wondered about the effectiveness of the operation up on the Cua Viet two weeks earlier.

I visited Gio Linh District headquarters on 25 February with Major De. We flew up in the Huey, much smoother than by vehicle. De was expansive, discussing the coming GVN election and security matters. He went so far as to ask the advisors our opinions on sector staff, and other Vietnamese matters. We advisors kept clear of sharing our views on any of those issues, sensing that egos might be involved, as well as areas of responsibility. That evening I recorded the following considerations: "Operational appreciations these days are not only a study of the ground and the enemy but also of population and lines of communication: surface, air and electronic. To be really effective in counterinsurgency one needs not only current intelligence but also considerable troop density, a purposeful attitude and above all a clear aim."

I visited the G3 plans staff at the headquarters of the 3rd Marine Division. Three senior staff officers were on duty. They appeared to be very tired. I pondered on where they had come from prior to taking up their present appointments. They pointed out to me that the division was moving farther to the west, into the Da Krong Valley, south of Route 9. Elements of the 9th Marines were in an NVA base area close to the Laotian border. This activity was part of Operation Dewey Canyon.

While I was duty officer in the TOC on 26 February a report came in that a MAT group at Huong Hoa, while in the team hut, had been subjected to a rocket-propelled grenade attack. Two rounds had hit the hut and wounded five members, two of whom were evacuated by helicopter. This was a reminder to all of the constant threats around us. A soldier in another MAT team received a Red Cross message informing him that his wife had given birth to a healthy baby. This happy news was soon turned on its head, as the soldier had not been home for twelve months. He was given leave to travel home. An intelligence report came in advising of Russian voices heard on a tactical communications net. Our view was to not take action against any site identified, but to let them keep going, in order to gather information by listening.

I made a routine staff visit by vehicle to the headquarters of the Quang Tri Maintenance Base (USMC) and to the headquarters of the 1/5 Infantry Brigade on 27 February. These visits had to do with relationship building and needed to be frequent, due to the fluidity of events and the roll-over of officers in staff appointments. I learned that the U.S. forces in the area of the Quang Tri Combat Base numbered eleven thousand. The marine strength within that number was fifty-five hundred, including Marine Air Group 39 at Ai Tu.

Over the first nine days of March I recorded a range of thoughts and observations:

> 1 March (Saint David's Day): The war has provoked the following in my mind:
>
> - The problems arising from a nation (USA) at peace, and the military at war.
> - Have we really fully developed the techniques required for counter-insurgency warfare?
> - Have we decided that communism is bad, democracy is better? Can we give the South Vietnamese a better deal than the communists?
> - Unity of Command. Despite sovereign national responsibilities, unity of command is a must: for unity of purpose, for economy of effort and simplicity.
>
> Finding it difficult to become enthusiastic and motivated to work. [This was a passing mood, which lasted less than a day.]
>
> The radio operators in the operations centre continue to accept responsibilities beyond that of their appointment. A

typical case was not advising the duty officer of Vietnamese operations registered with the operator.

Vietnamese co-ordination of RF/PF operations is very poor, such as at the Ga Bridge and Nhan Bieu. At the bridge is an RF company, two PF platoons, one with a CAP, and an intelligence platoon.

Narcotics used by troops causing a degree of inefficiencies in US units. Military Police action may be required to control trafficking in drugs.

5 March: An NVA 2nd Lieutenant from K8 Battalion taken as a PW in Trieu Phong. He had walked from Base Area 101 to the coastal plain.

Mines and booby traps are causing casualties; a significant number of these devices are made up from ordinance of US origin.

6 March: We have been informed that Mr McNamara, deputy PSA, is to open a US consulate in Da Nang in May. He was pleased with the news. This is a good promotion for him.

8 March: The operations centre is being remodelled by Captain Angel. I hope it is finished by Sunday night.

9 March: Slept to 9:15 am. A glorious rest. Out on patrol last night with Major Chuu. Bayling on patrol also, under the weather.

In Huong Hoa District on 9 March the resident Marine Company had a significant contact at 7:00 am. It was reported that 21 NVA were killed, with three marines wounded in action. The Blackcat helicopter evacuated the wounded.

Working within a mix of military and civilian advisors, the USMC, the U.S. Army, and a variety of Vietnamese units and agencies presented me with a fascinating military experience. Then to add more to the mix, advisors were informed the PSDF membership was increasing in the pacified areas. This was good news for the government. However, some advisors thought it incongruous that arms should be provided to people in pacified areas, where the Territorial Forces and the police were in control.

Work on improving the operations center continued. Our Vietnamese counterparts in the center watched and pondered on our efforts. Continuous improvement was our mantra and a key driver in our efforts. I had observed that the Vietnamese operations center had not changed a jot since I arrived on the scene six months earlier. Our hosts seemed to approach their working area on the basis of it being a temporary work area, so why make improvements? Insularity prevailed, perhaps waiting for the inevitable to happen.[4]

I noted on 12 March that the day was very quiet, and hoped this trend did not continue. In retrospect, thoughts of this kind alerted me to the fact that it was time to be creative, to lift the motivation, and to earn one's keep. With the pacification program gaining traction, one post–Tet 1969 initiative by local U.S. military formations was novel and informative. American military vehicles involved in direct support to the Vietnamese people were signed in such a way to show their role in pacification work. Signage was in the Vietnamese language for all Civil Affairs and psychological activities. As an example of signage, the 3rd Marine Division Band vehicle showed a first aid post and a dispensary.

The early hours of 16 March 1969 will be long remembered by the people of Kam Dau hamlet, two kilometers north of Dong Ha. A platoon of enemy sappers attacked 78 PF Platoon and a CAP at 2:00 A.M. Friendly casualties were high, with six marines, one navy chief petty officer, six PF soldiers, two hamlet chiefs, and one village chief being killed. Four marines and ten PF soldiers were wounded. There were no known enemy casualties. The attack took ten minutes. Explosives used included bangalores and TNT with pull friction fuses. The compound was blown to pieces in the attack. A conclusion after the attack was that reconnaissance by the sappers had been thorough. I noted that a static defensive position invites attack. The argument for more mobile operations and patrolling was self-evident.

In the case of the defenders, the fundamental shortcoming was to do with inadequate security. A Vietnamese boy aged fourteen years had been acting as an interpreter with the CAP. He was being interrogated by the sub-sector and sector intelligence staff. It was alleged he had been captured during the attack and then escaped. The question was whether he had been acting for the VC. I did not hear any further outcome of those interviews. The village and hamlet chiefs who died in this attack had been elected on 2 March 1969. They were in the village headquarters compound next to the CAP and PF platoon. This attack was a blow to the GVN and to the advisors.

The evening of 17 March was spent with Major Chuu on patrol

throughout the city of Quang Tri. We met up with the Mai Linh District chief and his communications officer at the city water works. Pleasantries were exchanged. It was an uneventful night. I had a discussion with Lieutenant Colonel Wallace about the Team 19 compound defenses earlier that day. Now that a "provisional platoon" had been formed, there was capacity to provide clearing patrols and listening posts around our advisor area. This initiative was long overdue. There was no room for complacency in regard to security measures in a hostile area. Care now had to be taken that patrol routes were varied constantly, to keep the patrols from becoming an ambush target for the VC.

Security at the hamlet at Nhu Le continued to be a puzzle. The perimeter fence, a defense measure, had been cut by the VC fifty meters in front of an ambush position. A VC propaganda team entered the hamlet for its night work among the people. We were perplexed by the inability of the RF/PF to deter such enemy activity. Naturally, the unit of the 1/5 Infantry Brigade sharing this part of the tactical area was as much concerned as the advisors.

Staff discussions with the PSA were frequent. In mid-March RF/PF capabilities was a topic of successive evening meetings. My contribution was to prepare a review paper for consideration by Colonel Mooney and the assistant sector advisor, Phoenix advisors and RD advisors, and our intelligence officer, Major Paul Laski. On the third day the paper was redrafted over a two-hour period to reflect a collective view. The PSA needed the document and supporting slides for a G5 briefing to be held at the III MAF headquarters, and at the headquarters of the 3rd Marine Division. One significant conclusion was for the integration of the RF/PF into the ARVN structure. In more detail the paper said: "As an overall view, RF/PF should be integrated with the ARVN. If better organized into the traditional structure of companies, battalions and regiments the RF/PF strength could continue the same mission in the same areas, and be termed as an example, the Quang Tri Regiment, ARVN. The advantages, in the framework of the Principles of War, would be in the maintenance of the aim, economy of effort, administration and cooperation."

Other advantages of a Principles of War nature included concentration of force as required, security, and flexibility. It was not until late 1971 that this recommendation was implemented. This delay in implementing the obvious had tragic consequences. The U.S.

ground forces had been thinned out, as had the advisory structure. The significant regrouping and training needed was delayed until attack by the NVA across the DMZ was inevitable. This continues to be a matter of sadness to me. Other topics in the discussions included a reduction in Team 19 strength in the context of a U.S. withdrawal and the April Rice Harvest Protection Plan. Liaison officers from the 1/5 Infantry Brigade would participate in the rice harvest planning.

On the night of 21–22 March, the headquarters of XXIV Corps was hit by mortar shells. There was an absence of a front line in this war.

With my counterpart, Captain Cuu, we developed a plan to bring out hundreds of tonnes of rice discovered by elements of the 3rd Marines in the remote west of the province, near the border to Laos. The marines had commenced Operation Maine Crag there on 15 March.[5] The RF had to prepare a landing zone for the rice to be transported out to the Vandegrift Combat Base, near Ca Lu on Route 9. Two PF platoons were to be employed there, loading the rice onto trucks for eventual distribution to the people.

Four USMC CH-46 helicopters transported the 125 RF Company to the cache area on 25 March. Interpreter Long was late at the departure point but did not miss out on being deployed. The company strength flown out was less than expected. A total of 105 troops were promised. The count was 80. It was noted that the troops were not equipped for the job they were to undertake. More stores were lifted out in a sling at 2:45 P.M. for the troops. During the day a report was received from the marines informing us that the cache complex might contain up to a thousand tonnes of rice.

The next day a progress report advised that nineteen tonnes had been lifted out to Vandegrift. It was also reported that one of the deployed PF platoons did not take rations with them. This highlighted the unintended consequences of employing PF in a situation outside its role. Then, to further dent the reputation of the Territorial Forces, 125 RF Company at the cache site, now known as LZ Saigon, indicated that it was preparing for a return to Quang Tri City the next day. The company claimed its briefing prior to departure was for the deployment to be for three days only.

On the third day of Territorial Forces participation in Operation Maine Crag the province chief expressed interest in visiting the rice cache. The commanding general of the 3rd Marine Division took

Rice, NVA base area, western Quang Tri.

him out in his helicopter in the afternoon. Earlier in the day our Lieutenant Colonel Wallace went out by Air America to LZ Saigon and Vandegrift. The rice recovered now totaled seventy tonnes.

Representing our advisory team at LZ Saigon was Captain Porter Angel. Sergeant Long, the interpreter, was with him. I was able to visit them on 29 March. Angel and his group were doing a great job with the RF. Long was not familiar with hard physical work and was not happy at the cache area. Angel, with a wink, claimed that at last Sergeant Long was eating rice. On the same day 149 RF Company relieved 125 RF Company. The estimate of the weight of the rice cache was revised down to three hundred tonnes. The initial estimates were high because the cache, extending over a wide area, had been discovered by two separate marine elements, which

Cache, NVA base area, western Quang Tri.

reported different location coordinates, understandable in rugged, forested terrain.

Angel pointed out old well-established NVA tunnels comprising part of a base complex in the area. It was remarkable that the enemy would go to such lengths to prepare for extended operations toward the coast at a later time. The NVA had to position its supplies in forward areas prior to mounting operations, whereas the allies had shorter in-country lines of supply. Several CH-47 and CH-53 helicopters carried slung loads of up to sixty-five bags of rice at a time. With each bag at about 45 kilograms, a slung load was in the order of 2.5 to 3 tonnes.

There was a large contingent of marines in the area, including infantry, tanks, dozers, and tracked 106 mm, self-propelled M50 Ontos.[6] The terrain was hilly, forested, and in some areas burned out. The 3/2 ARVN Battalion was in the area with the 3rd Marines. Later in the day I returned to Quang Tri City via the combat base, but not before listing the types of battlefield aircraft that were supporting the troops in this particular operation. Helicopter types I identified at Vandegrift were: UH-1H, OH-6, AH-1G, CH-46, CH-47, CH-53, CH-54, and CH-34. Fixed wing types on the ground were O-1s and OV-10s. This amount of support provided an enormous mobility capability to the operational commanders and units.

By now the Territorial Forces effort at Maine Crag was developing a kind of folklore of its own. The advisors at sector from the PSA down were referring to the deployed group as "Angel Force." Adverse weather intervened, delaying the concluding part of the operation. By the close of 31 March there were six slings of rice to be extracted.

Sadly, the operation ended on a disastrous note. A CH-47 with Vietnamese soldiers on board crashed on liftoff from LZ Saigon on 2 April. One crewman and twenty-two soldiers were killed. The casualties were all from 145 RF Company. The balance of "Angel Force" was evacuated in two helicopters. The final tally of rice extracted was 230 tonnes.

Later on 2 April General Drake visited the Citadel in Quang Tri to see the rice. The sector Vietnamese S4 acted as guide for a visit to the commissary. The bags of rice had printing on them, including Chinese script, indicating that the rice was a gift from the People of China to North Vietnam. This was similar to aid given to South Vietnam via the USAID program.

The next day Lieutenant Colonel Wallace and Major De went to the crash site by CH-46 to recover the bodies of 145 RF Company. None could be recognized. The *Pacific Stars and Stripes* reported in an April 6 edition that the tragedy was "the worst copter crash of the Vietnam war."

To formally conclude the rice recovery operation, a ceremonial rice handover to the needy was held by the province chief on 12 April 1969. This was a big event, attracting high-level commanders. Gunship-escorted helicopters carrying Generals Lam, Truong, Nickerson, Stilwell, Davis, and Jones arrived at the Citadel for the occasion. The visitors and other dignitaries helped make the day memorable. There was a somber moment when reference was made to the soldiers who had been killed in the course of their duty for their country.

While the rice recovery was under way to the west, other activities continued in the sector. On the night of 26 March five mortar rounds landed in the city near the entrance of the Citadel. Four local soldiers were killed, and four people were wounded. The FSCC was able to confirm that the enemy mortar base plate was to the southwest. Our allies at the Quang Tri Combat Base at Ai Tu reacted with mortar fire into the suspected enemy mortar base plate position within four minutes. The base casualties were evacuated by helicopter to the nearest U.S. Army surgical hospital. A reconnaissance company was deployed to the southwest in an attempt to find the enemy mortar team, without success.

At the end of March an evening entry in my diary outlined what was planned for the next day: "We have six big choppers here at 8.00 am to lift out 120 soldiers for an operation. A visiting general is coming in for a briefing at 1.00 pm. A briefing is to be prepared for another visitor in a few days hence. A trip by helicopter in the pm is to be made out to the Laotian border, Operation Maine Crag. There are several other lesser things to do. It all makes for a full day, with time passing quickly."

An accidental discharge of a small arms weapon occurred in the Team 19 compound in Quang Tri City on 2 April. This was a matter for the compound commander to investigate. Usually accidental discharges happened through carelessness. No one was injured. Later that day there was a further incident at the secondary school just outside the compound. Two grenades were thrown from the school onto the road approach to our MACV compound. Fortunately they did not explode. The next day two students were arrested by the police over the incident. The PSA made a comment that there may well be a case for having police in the school, just as was happening at home in the United States.

There was a series of high-level visitors to Quang Tri in April. On 3 April we had a visit by Brigadier Long from the office of CORDS, within the staff of COMUSMACV. The usual advisory staff briefing for our visitor was conducted. During the presentation General Davis came in for a five-minute visit. A week later General Kauffman, J4 (logistics), MACV, visited the sector headquarters with General Drake. During this time the deputy commander of MACV visited Trieu Phong District for a briefing on sector and sub-sector activities. These high-level visitors were welcome.

Generals Stilwell, Drake, Truong, and Davis and their staff officers attended a Rice Harvest Protection Plan meeting for the April/May crop. The province chief and his staff led the discussion. It was clear that we, the MACCORDS people, did not have a feel for the economic and commercial aspects of rice marketing in the Vietnamese economy. The military task was to protect the integrity of the harvest.

A week later the province chief had a lunch gathering to bid farewell to General Davis. Accompanying the PSA, I attended the 3rd Marine Division change of command ceremony at Ai Tu when General Davis handed over to his successor, Major General William K. Jones.

I visited the A2 outpost on 2 April. The Reconnaissance Company of the 1st ARVN Division was operating out of this fire base into the DMZ. AATTV member Captain David Savage, an advisor to the Reconnaissance Company, was at A2. He was not authorized to enter the DMZ with the patrols. It was always a pleasure to meet a fellow Team member when deployed. Two patrols from the reconnaissance company were in the DMZ at the time. David informed me that it was very quiet on the DMZ. There was an American 8-inch artillery piece in A2, which was firing at a slow rate into North Vietnam. Counter bombardment by the enemy was not being applied. If it had been, we would not have been observing things in the open at A2. By the use of binoculars a huge red flag could be seen flying at Freedom Bridge, on the Ben Hai River. The flag was that of North Vietnam. It was lit up at night, making it a useful landmark for navigation.

There were about five hundred troops in this A2 outpost, two hundred of them being Americans. The layout appeared to be an uncoordinated mess. Bunkers were on top of the ground. My perception was that they should have been underground. A further note in my diary related to observing a Vietnamese soldier being given field punishment. Fellow soldiers from his platoon were giving him two whacks each with a piece of bamboo while he lay on the ground. It seemed to be a hard way to be taught a lesson.

Sector conducted a briefing for an operation named QT12 on 10 April for a deployment the next day. The operation was sizeable, and was to be conducted in Hai Lang District. A representative from that sub-sector was not at the briefing. My assistant S3, Captain Angel, and Sergeant Burdett were assigned as the advisors for this operation. My task was to be the duty officer at the operations center. There was no enemy contact on the day of the operation.

A week later there was a further sector operation into Hai Lang sub-sector along the Route 555 axis. Major De conducted a good briefing on 17 April. His concept for the operation was sound. Troops to be involved were two RF companies, three PF platoons, a mechanized platoon, and an intelligence platoon. This operation was to be in much the same area in which the French conducted a large-scale operation in July 1953 with five battalions.[7] There were no contacts with the enemy on 18 April 1969.

In mid-April a second case of malaria was reported from the group of advisors on the rice recovery operation. Lieutenant Waters, U.S. Army, was medically evacuated for treatment.

We advisors had to keep our composure at all times despite the daily aggravations and frustrations being experienced in working with our counterparts. Our thoughts had to be internalized, shared with close friends, or written into a diary. Events up to 18 April led me to make this entry: "Vietnamese officials pathetic. The military chief De is not the man for the job. The police chief is ineffective. The people are not motivated." Such was my view of a few matters that day.

Defoliation operations were contentious due to the application of a range of herbicides. There was a high level of awareness about the impact of defoliation agents. My first introduction in Vietnam to these operations was in Da Nang, in August 1968, when I observed four C-123 aircraft returning to the airfield after an early morning spraying operation.

My first close encounter with herbicides and defoliants was in the Gio Linh area. There was a large group of advisors with Chuck Slaby on a reconnaissance to an abandoned village with a visiting senior U.S. official. By chance we observed a C-123 undertaking a spray operation in the northeast area of Leatherneck Square. After the aircraft departed we discovered a gentle wind bringing a mist of spray toward our group. The mist passed through and away from us with the prevailing breeze.

In the first half of April 1969 there was a long overdue flurry of staff activity on herbicide requests. Sector advisory staff had a small but important role in the processing of herbicide requests within the province. The herbicide policy document outlined the responsibility of the PSA. Colonel Mooney discussed the policy with Major Harry Bell, my successor, and me. The PSA in effect was the Quang Tri watchdog of Vietnamese and U.S. interests for spray operations.

We reached a shared personal and professional view that for the longer term, herbicide use was not worth the effort. There appeared to be minimal benefits alongside possible detrimental and negative outcomes.

One of my last staff tasks was to discuss the MACV protocols for the processing of requests for herbicide operations with Major Bolger of the 1/5 Infantry Brigade headquarters. Many staff channels of U.S. and Vietnamese military and civil agencies were involved in the clearance process for such operations. It was our duty to implement the policy. My particular task was to present requests to my counterpart, who processed the document through Vietnamese agencies to the province chief for his endorsement or otherwise.

The new commander of the 3rd Marine Division, Major General Jones, teamed up with the province chief for a familiarization of the sector. I was nominated to accompany them. Each sub-sector was visited. The province chief was back in his shell, playing it cool, and gave a constant display of not being too involved with events around him. Within Quang Tri City the general displayed a keen interest in all the projects that were shown to him, including the Kit Carson Scouts at the Chieu Hoi center, the high school, and two hospitals for children.

In concluding this segment of my narrative, the eight months spent in "the oil and glue" role as a planning and operations staff officer was a most stimulating professional experience. This was a period of personal growth, of challenge, and of gaining wisdom in a multifaceted environment.

The next chapter describes how the planning for the resettlement of refugees to Cam Vu evolved. Mention has been made earlier of a proposal to resettle displaced Vietnamese back to their rural lands when certain security conditions had been met. General Davis agreed to the resettlement. I was part of a staff team tasked to undertake the planning of Operation Kangaroo in early 1969.

14

Operation Kangaroo, Cam Vu Resettlement

December 1968–April 1969

Planning on the pacification counteroffensive had commenced in early October 1968. One specific Quang Tri Province project was founded on an area named Cam Vu, a rural village complex six kilometers to the west of Dong Ha. Eight evacuated hamlets had been identified for resettlement. The number of displaced people to be returned to their residences was estimated to be about six thousand.

The people of these hamlets had been evacuated from their homes during the enemy Tet offensive in February 1968. They were presently in a temporary camp near Dong Ha township. Province officials believed that a relocation of the people back to their fertile, irrigated lands would be to the advantage of the people and the GVN. A local CORDS position paper for the project had been presented to the PSA on 5 October 1968. Due to the uncertainties of the security situation, a start date was not nominated. A timed phasing was written for the relocation project, based on a D-Day. That was the easy part. Gaining the necessary security and material resources was the challenge.

On 3 December, Quang Tri CORDS advisors Cleary and Cummins took up the initiative for an operation in the Cam Vu village area. The village was seven kilometers to the east of the Cam Lo District headquarters, on the north side of the Cam Lo River, astride Route 88. Staff of Team 19 was supportive of the idea, particularly as the prime minister of Vietnam was to visit Cam Lo later in the month. At this point, due to security imperatives, we had to gain the support of the 3rd Marine Division and the ARVN. This required approaches to the 3rd Marine Division commander and Major Gen-

Damaged fuel tank, Cam Vu, 1968.

eral Truong, via General Stilwell. The irrigation system in the Cam Vu area was designed to feed water from the Cam Lo River. The scheme had been financed by Australia under the Colombo Plan in the 1950s. I flew over the irrigation channels to familiarize myself with the land during an air reconnaissance on 16 December. Due to battle damage the channels were not in use and needed repair. However, the paddies in most places were being worked, a reflection of the resilience of the people. I also found the pump station. On closer inspection I discovered the pumps had been made in Australia. This gave me an added incentive to focus on the project.

A Cam Vu planning conference was held in Quang Tri City on 18 December. A number of issues had to be sorted out before any commitment could be made. That afternoon a further aerial reconnaissance was carried out. All seats on the Huey were occupied by staff involved in the planning. The canals and roads were checked out from the air. The Blackcat landed us close to the pumps. Earlier, as a safety precaution, the site had been checked for booby traps, and declared clear. The inspection was very useful and uneventful.

On 30 December the PSA briefed Major General Davis on the preliminary work we had carried out on the proposed Cam Vu project, in the context of the pacification plan for 1969. The general said marine engineers were to carry out a land clearing operation in "Leatherneck Square," the area to the north of the Cam Lo River to the DMZ, the corners generally being Gio Linh, Dong Ha, Cam Lo, and Con Thien. The work was due to commence on 20 January, and any decision could not be made until the land clearing was near to an end. The general summarized the discussion by saying: "Resettlement would depend on the military posture at the time. The elements that caused the people to evacuate would have to be negated to validate a return to former areas."

During the second half of January and into February the land clearing operation proceeded, moving from west to east, above Cam Vu. The marine equipment was secured by the ARVN at night, and the operators flown in and out each day. An incident on 5 February gave us an insight into NVA reconnaissance methods.

A land clearing party uncovered a bunker occupied by two NVA soldiers. Their equipment included a Chinese radio, binoculars, paper, and pens. They had a listing of allied units in Quang Tri, from east to west. This reflected a recognized characteristic of NVA/VC operations, the gathering of sound information prior to offensive operations. The enemy in South Vietnam had limited mobility and communications. Any offensive operations by the enemy could be expected to be inflexible, but would be executed in a fearless and determined manner.

In response to a request initiated by Team 19, Major Ian Porteous in Da Nang advised me that a representative of the Australian embassy would be in Quang Tri City on 15 February to visit the Cam Vu irrigation scheme. The official did not arrive, which was a disappointment. Headquarters Australian Force Vietnam, in Saigon, was requested to follow up on this matter.

Land clearing continued throughout February, at a reported rate of five hundred acres per day. General Stilwell continued his relentless visit schedule. The sector military staff briefed him on 26 February. The marine engineers had been doing some preliminary repair work, and restoration assessments on the Cam Vu pumping station. Two pumps were operational, with a pumping capacity of sixty thousand gallons per hour. Staff work continued on the project in several areas. On 3 March, I prepared briefing aids on Cam Vu for the PSA. Our DPSA, Mr. McNamara, when in Saigon, visited the Australian embassy to contact the action officer. This was a good

Irrigation pumps, Cam Vu, Quang Tri Province, 1968.

move by McNamara. He discovered the contact was a Canadian employed by the embassy.

Officials in high places then became involved in the procurement of parts for the pumps. A junior Seabee was to go to Australia to purchase the necessary items. Word came back that the fare was to be arranged by a ministerial decision. In the meantime, a seat on an aircraft to Australia had been arranged on a "sergeant to sergeant" basis. CORDS in Da Nang was also involved. A small issue was becoming a big issue. The humor in all this was that our local aid-in-kind fund could have covered the costs to purchase the items required. We persisted in the belief that some civil aid money from Australia would be appropriate. By early March the land clearing had been completed at Cam Vu. We discovered that little work had been done on the east-west road, especially in places where people had cut irrigation ditches across the road to provide passage for water flow. Bridges had not been repaired, but bypasses had been improved.

In a collaborative exercise with our counterparts, the operational plan for the security and relocation of the people to Cam Vu had been completed. On 15 March, Major Chuu had been appointed to command this sector operation. It was to have been Major De,

Nhan's successor, but the PSA had some reservations about the appropriateness of De's involvement due to his province-wide responsibilities. Colonel Mooney had a discussion with the province chief about the appointment.

At a briefing about the Cam Vu plan with the commander and his staff at the 3rd Marine Division headquarters on 16 March, the general shared his thoughts with us. Leatherneck Square had been a battleground for the marines against NVA regiments in 1967 and 1968. Although an enemy presence was not evident south of the DMZ, it was known that there were twelve NVA regiments close to the DMZ on the north side, within six hours' marching time. General Davis, despite his reservations, agreed that the operation should commence. Team 19 agreed that we must press on with optimism. For the GVN there was political advantage to have the people return to their homes and land, thus reestablishing their hamlet communities.

On 17 March we were informed that Major De would command the Cam Vu operation. Major Chuu was to attend a Territorial Forces conference in Da Nang for three days. Our advisors deployed to Dong Ha on 18 March with their Vietnamese counterparts. Operation Kangaroo had commenced. The next day I drove up to Dong Ha to visit the command post for the operation. Major De was reveling in his new role. He was shirtless and involved in whatever was his whim. He was "king" in this show. Meanwhile, the responsibilities of his prime job as commander of the province Territorial Forces were being neglected. General Drake visited the district headquarters of Dong Ha and Cam Lo to see and listen.

On 21 March the Australian ambassador visited Quang Tri City. Major De delivered a presentation on Operation Kangaroo and accompanied the ambassador on a flight over the pumps and the Cam Vu area. The sector officers gave him a further briefing at the Citadel. We then proceeded to lunch with the province chief. The embassy staff man for aid, Jim Donovan, and I called on Mr. McNamara to discuss a range of topics, including pump parts. The embassy was to fund certain works at Cam Vu. This was a pleasing outcome. Also on this day the relocation to Cam Vu commenced, with 230 people being interviewed prior to return.

There were reminders as to the cost in lives and equipment for road security and relocation in this part of the province. Two recovery vehicles hit mines on Route 88 as they attempted to recover a three-quarter-ton vehicle wrecked the previous day. Apparently the road had not been swept to ensure it was clear of mines. Then the next day two more recovery vehicles hit mines. A sweep team hit a mine later that day. The 11th Engineers lost one soldier killed and one wounded. It had been a torrid few days on Route 88. A later intelligence report stated that the mines were improvised, being made up from expended American canisters. They were obviously very effective, as they were able to disable a recovery vehicle and a three-quarter-ton vehicle.

On 29 March the province chief, PSA, the G5 of the 3rd Marine Division, and the commanding officer of the 4th Combined Action Group visited Cam Vu. The chief and all available staff held a meeting with representatives of the displaced people of Cam Vu. A spokesman for the Cam Vu villagers petitioned the chief to allow them to stay in their camp. He explained that the people were not happy with security in their future hamlet area. We knew that on the previous night the pumps had been attacked. Our forces had sustained seven wounded in action, with enemy losses of three killed and three wounded. This was a relatively pleasing outcome, but the spokesman needed further assurance on security. He was a very impressive person and made a moving speech. The spokesman was backed up by two elders who also spoke well, and with feeling. The province chief responded by promising security to the people, but confirmed that the relocation was to be undertaken as scheduled.

A company group had been formed. Three RF companies were to make up the group, with Captain Nong in command. In addition, a MAT from Hai Lang District was to join the company group the following day. An operation was conducted the next day, 30 March, to start off the military security plan. The contribution by the Territorial Forces was not impressive. An RF blocking company was two hours late getting into position. It also appeared that the advisors were not with the Vietnamese—in fact or in spirit. My diary note was that Captain Weary, the district advisor of Dong Ha, was doing his job well, assisted by John Cleary (CORDS refugees) and Major Richard Mottel (S4, Logistics). The advisors needed a local director of operations. I was able to discuss my concerns with the PSA.

Some pressure was being put on Major De, but I felt that he needed to be given a fair chance to work through the challenges he was facing without advisor interference. Then it was discovered that Major Chuu still had a role in the Cam Vu operation. Apparently he was to command when Major De was not present. This was indeed a muddle. I apprised General Drake of the issue when he came through Cam Lo and Dong Ha that afternoon. That would ensure the commanding general of XXIV Corps would also be informed, which would then get to General Truong and the province chief. This was an example of wartime military politics in South Vietnam.

Following discussions on 31 March with the PSA, I visited the advisor command post at Cam Vu. I set about fine tuning—otherwise known as reorganizing—the advisor setup, and perhaps also the local Territorial Forces. Up until this point the command post was not co-located with the sub-sector headquarters. As a transition arrangement the advisor command post was to close down the next day, 1 April, and be reestablished at the district headquarters. The RF company group was to deploy to the field. There was a need for the PSA to speak with the province chief, and for an advisor to be appointed to the RF company group led by Captain Nong.

During the day the 2nd ARVN Regiment made a request to Major De for two RF companies to remain with the 3/2 ARVN Battalion. De indicated that he might agree to the request. This did not make sense, as it undercut the company group arrangement decided upon with De during the planning stage. As De seemed to be departing from the earlier agreed arrangement with the PSA, an early resolution was required. Colonel Mooney made a point to me that he would consider pulling the advisors out if the Territorial Forces were not readily available to provide protection and security to the people being relocated. There were no enemy contacts on the night of 31 March and 1 April.

The PSA led a group comprising John Cleary (CORDS), the now returned Major Chuu, Captain Weary (DSA, Dong Ha), two XXIV Corps headquarters liaison officers, and me into Cam Vu on 1 April. We conducted a visual air reconnaissance of the area and landed at the pumps site. This site had been secured so the Seabees could bring the pumping station into full service. The group then went to the Cam Lo District headquarters to discuss issues with the district chief there.

Next day, Major Brad Oliver relocated from the sector headquarters in Quang Tri City to Cam Vu, to control the deployed advisor effort and to advise Nong and his company group. This was a necessary advisor appointment, to correct a gap in the advisory organization and give further standing to the level of support that the United States was providing to the pacification effort in this part of the province. Brad was the right man for the job. He had a hearty and wise approach to the military art. The PSA and staff were of a view that the shortcomings identified three to four days earlier had been corrected. On 4 April 1969 we received the news that the Australian government would contribute $3,000 to purchase the spares required for the pumps. The Seabees were continuing their work on the site. A trial run of the engines was expected in the next few days.

During April Mr. Firfer accompanied Mr. Hitchcock, the refugee director, Saigon, on a visit to Quang Tri. Our CORDS people took them for a guided tour of the main refugee groups in the province: Gia Dang, Ha Thanh, Cam Vu, Cam Lo, and Huong Hoa. The visitors acknowledged the security and humanitarian efforts being conducted for the refugees. They also stressed the importance of economic productivity. It was noted that in South Vietnam 30 percent of the population had been displaced, these people being classified as refugees. The GVN administrative effort allocated to refugees policy and programs amounted to 2 percent of the national budget.

Major De was of concern to many advisors. We did not hear any comments from the Vietnamese about this eccentric man even though he managed to rub many people the wrong way. For example, De ordered Major Meisel out of his office over a difference of opinion on one occasion. As time went on De remained, while others moved on. My successor, Major Harry Bell, developed a very sound relationship with De, who was promoted to lieutenant colonel in 1969.[1]

Efforts continued on the resettlement of the Cam Vu area during April. The marine engineers had a Class 60 ferry working on the Cam Lo River. This ensured water access from Cam Vu to the coast. My interpreter, Long, was temporarily transferred to the Cam Vu area to provide his skills to the marines and CORDS advisors working with the people. Returnees were moving slowly from the haven of the Cam Lo River to the north, back to their former homes. The advisor mission was accomplished.

As I often wondered how life evolved for the people of Cam Vu, I decided to visit Quang Tri Province in May 2012. In the Cam Vu area rural life was thriving. I met the supervising engineer for the irrigation system on the north bank of the Cam Lo River, now renamed the Song Hieu. He told me the Australian pumping site was in operation from 1969 until it was destroyed in 1972. After reunification a new pumping site was built, which has operated for each rice season since. At the time of my visit the irrigation pumps and the general system were undergoing routine maintenance. I was able to examine the present pump site, and was guided to the former pump site, about five hundred meters further to the west. Forty-four years later only some concrete remnants of the previous site could be seen among the rich, verdant growth. The people were now focused on the present and the future.

During my time among the people of Quang Tri in 1968 and 1969 the spirituality of many, quietly demonstrated, had a strong impact on me. Many faiths and beliefs were evident. I decided to devote a chapter, "Faith at Work," to describe my experience.

15

Faith at Work

May 1968–April 1969

Little did I realize before taking up my post in Quang Tri that a significant part of my time as a military advisor would be spent in both urban and rural environments, working mainly on issues that were the core of the counterinsurgency and pacification effort in South Vietnam. This chapter arises from my experiences with people of many faiths and practices in the province.

In Quang Tri, I had the opportunity to participate in the celebration of the Mass in a number of Catholic churches in the city and environs. Within a few weeks I was comfortable, from a security point of view, to walk or drive to Mass unaccompanied. The local people attended services in large numbers. It was reassuring to me that those in attendance shared my faith and beliefs. Taking those thoughts further, I realized that I was relatively safe within the community in which I was working. Further, in their struggle to live in a conflict-filled environment some Vietnamese people came to me seeking assistance and help. I assumed that, as an unintended consequence of my church attendance, it could be construed by the local people that I might possibly be a useful man to approach. I hold to this day that the empathy created with the people helped them and me in the pursuit of our pacification goals.

I accompanied Michael Casey on 19 May 1968 to view the La Vang Basilica, constructed around 1925. The site had long been an esteemed place of pilgrimage. Vietnamese Catholics had been gathering at La Vang since about 1800. In August 1960 the president of the Republic of South Vietnam with a large entourage dedicated the future of Vietnam to Our Lady of La Vang.[1] I visited the basilica on a number of occasions during my time in Quang Tri. The priest in charge of the basilica took me on a tour of the church and grounds

La Vang Basilica, Quang Tri, 1968.

in June. In the 1960s a two-hundred-bed retreat house had been constructed, with a dispensary attached. The gardens around the basilica were extensive and included a grotto. In more peaceful times up to ten thousand people assembled from all over Vietnam, some staying for up to two weeks. One particularly impressive outdoor amenity was an elevated one-hundred-place squat toilet, made of masonry, over a ponded area.

While in Hue in May I attended Mass at a local church. The people there were in recovery mode from the enemy Tet offensive in February. It struck me that Catholics in Hue and similar groups throughout the country, including freedom-loving Buddhists, would be influential in keeping anticommunist nationalism alive in South Vietnam. It was a moving experience to hear the national anthem sung, with gusto, after the communion. Just before communion I noticed the priest gently biff a boy who was approaching the communion rails from the wrong direction. The action by the priest reminded me of some of my experiences growing up.

Back in Quang Tri in late May 1968, when settled into my district advisor position in Mai Linh, some nuns from a local school

The grotto at La Vang Basilica.

approached me for assistance. They were in need of seven hundred sandbags to construct a bunker for their protection. Funds were available from U.S. sources for this kind of support. The sandbags were provided as requested.

A protestant church was adjacent to the Mai Linh District headquarters compound. Pastor Phillip was in charge. He was caring for eighteen orphans and had five children of his own. The church building was in good order, with accommodation for the orphans nearing completion. The advisors were attempting to assist by providing roofing materials for the orphans' home. A U.S. soldier, Private Cook, had an interest in the orphanage and told me that his congregation at home was providing support. Later, I was to see Pastor Phillip riding a bicycle around the district, dressed as an English gentleman. I thought this to be a class act.

Michael Casey guided me to a small abbey at Tri Buu on 2 June. We were accompanied by my interpreter, Binh; Warrant Officer Fitzgibbon (AATTV); and two U.S. Army doctors. Their presence gave me food for thought, as I gathered they might have been providing material assistance to the abbey. I had to quietly work out the extent to which these fine fellows were supporting the abbey before I could respond to any subsequent request for assistance.

Binh later guided me to Father Ngoc, a priest who came to Quang Tri from North Vietnam in 1954. At partition he led ten thousand people from the North to the South. He informed us that only four thousand of his people remained in Quang Tri. In addition to being responsible for his parish he cared for orphans. Food was his main concern, rather than anything else. Part of his afternoon routine was to chew betel leaf, a habit of some people which I first noticed when working in Papua New Guinea in 1960. Two weeks later Father Ngoc called upon me to help him with his church. He needed twenty bags of cement and forty sheets of iron. I promised to provide the materials, and did so. After delivery we shared a small glass of "liquor" (altar wine), a pleasure we each enjoyed. Ngoc, in passing conversation, said that the land occupied by the refugees at La Vang was gifted to the church by President Diem in 1954. It had once been forested land and had been cleared by the people. Other refugee areas established in the province in 1954 were allocated on a hamlet area basis by the then province chief.

A Vietnamese Sacred Heart brother, Gabriel Duong Van Ngheim, called on me and requested some assistance on 18 June. This was in a way a confirmation that word had been passed around that I was a practicing Catholic. His school had a speech day coming up on the following weekend. The teachers were short of prizes for deserving students. I responded to the request by saying that I would see what prizes I could arrange. An invitation to the prize giving

The Reverend Mother in front of Tri Buu abbey, July 1968.

was accepted. The brother was about my age, very well educated, and fluent in English. He came from a local family in Duong Loc, in nearby Trieu Phong District. I organized some appropriate prizes and delivered them to the school.

At the prize giving I was treated as an honored guest, welcomed in English, and invited to assist in the prize giving to the students. Apart from the school families I was the only visitor present. The occasion was a reminder to me of the importance of a sound education for the youth, to enable talents to be discovered and developed.

The local representative of the U.S. Catholic Relief Service in Quang Tri called on me on 6 June. Father Do-Ba Ai carried a letter of introduction from a longtime friend of mine, Matthew d'Arcy. (More is to be mentioned of Ai and d'Arcy shortly.) It was of interest to me to recall a conversation with the district chief on the previous day. It had come up in conversation that CRS relief programs had created some dissent among the majority of local Vietnamese. My understanding was that aid should be for the benefit of all, on a needs basis and not on a basis of religion.

Matthew d'Arcy was a classmate of mine at the Royal Military College at Duntroon, in Australia. We had each been allocated to the Infantry Corps upon graduation. Matthew had served in South Vietnam as a captain with the Team in Da Nang for eighteen months from February 1966. He resigned from the Australian Army in 1967 and came back to Vietnam as head of the Catholic Relief Service for Region 1. He had married a fine lady from Cholon, a suburb of Saigon. Over the next few months Matthew was an occasional visitor to Quang Tri, and I was able to visit him at his home in Da Nang in August.

Father Ai was an impressive character who was working earnestly for his flock, mainly refugees. He was fluent in English and French and had plenty of charm. In mid-June 1968, I attended a Sunday Mass that was concelebrated by Father Ai and a newly ordained priest who was his godson. After Mass, Ai invited me to a celebratory breakfast, which I had to decline due to a planned visit to the recently wounded Peter Wooden on the hospital ship. A few days later I was to meet the godson, Father Tran Van Doan, who offered a Mass for Father Ai's father, who had been assassinated by the VC some years before.

Later in mid-July, d'Arcy came up to Quang Tri City on business, giving Father Ai an opportunity to host a luncheon. So the three of us, plus Father Cong from Hue and three others, enjoyed a delicious meal together, sprinkled with interesting conversation. This gathering gave me an insight into how the clergy were operating. The priests I met were very active men, giving their parishioners good leadership and direction. The people seemed to be rich in faith, but were materially poor.

During lunch it was revealed that Ai had published a book in 1961 based on a lecture series he had given to men. The theme was "Life Was Worth Living." Further, he had traveled to fourteen countries, mostly in Asia. It was pointed out in the table talk that Buddhists made up about 85 percent of the population of South Vietnam. The Vietnamese view at the table was that this figure was an arguable statistic. The point was made that if the Catholic population was 15 percent, it did not necessarily follow that the balance of the population was made up of Buddhists. Catholics clearly had a lot of influence within government circles, particularly in the Diem period. Buddhists resented this situation, particularly when and where they thought they were being ignored. Confucianism was an influence, as was Taoism. Within households there could be an overlap by way of reverence to elements of other religions.

I passed on to Eva in June 1968 my analysis of the religious and social situation:

> In this province there are approximately ten to fifteen per cent Catholics among the population. They receive a fair amount of food, clothing and the like from overseas. This aid is arguably going to a minority group, and significantly a group that is fully behind the Government of South Vietnam. The majority of the people in Quang Tri could possibly not be receiving the same handouts as the Catholics here, and it is this majority group that the GVN is vitally concerned about. They must win their "hearts and minds" to continue their platform. If these handouts are upsetting the majority, the Catholic Relief Service may not be providing a benefit to the whole. So the point being made is that the CRS should direct aid to the people, not to just a particular section of the community.
>
> Bringing down the above to a factual account I want to point out an attitude of the Vietnamese that is now common in the province, and could apply to the whole

> country. Ships that bring aid to South Vietnam drop cargo off at points up and down the coast. Here in Quang Tri it is at a beach complex, about twenty miles from the city. The U.S. authorities then advise the Vietnamese authorities that the goods are ready to be collected. And do you know what? The Vietnamese say they have not got the transport available to carry out the task, and ask the U.S. people to do it. Of course the U.S. agencies pick up the cargo and deliver the goods. So that is the extent of thanks to those providing the aid to this point. The providers of the aid have already donated, packed, shipped, unloaded and transported the goods to the recipients. Then I would say the locals are tardy even with their own distribution.
>
> For the past six days we have been trying to gather emergency goods for twenty refugee families who are about one mile from us. The items required are tin for roofing, food and the like. The Vietnamese officials just do not seem to care about the needs of their own. If it was not for the advisory effort the refugees would go without. I feel the Vietnamese want the US to stay, even though a distasteful side issue is the war.

I then said to Eva that "I felt a lot better for having written this particular letter, and that I only hope it does not depress you. I think you should know about this."

I was soon to discover that Father Ai had an interest in a laundry service. He asked me to arrange a meeting for him with the Mai Linh district chief. The district chief agreed to the meeting. The point of the laundry was to provide work for refugees, and Ai was seeking the district chief's endorsement in the hope that it would help his sales pitch to U.S. unit quartermasters. The meeting with the district chief lasted ninety minutes. Father Ai stressed that he was making every effort to find work for the poor and the refugees. The district chief reminded him that the laundry needed to be attractive in appearance, with a good service. Others were operating successful laundries.

The laundry manager, Ai, Ramos, Binh, and I talked through a business plan for the laundry operation for an hour. The going price for a shirt or a pair of trousers was 30 piastres (dong) per item. The main input was from Ramos and Binh, who were streetwise. They gently pointed out to Ai that an assumption in a financial plan was 50 percent of takings for the workers and 50 percent to the business for other costs, such as disbursements to go to the province chief, the commander of the 1st ARVN Regiment, taxes, and other business costs. Ai had in mind 80 percent for the workers, 20 percent for the business. He admitted that letters he had drafted up were unrealistic. He understood the problems confronting his business. We, the advisors, could do no more. The manager and Father Ai had to review their plan. During discussion Ai said he had a list of five hundred people seeking work. The warehouse project was discussed in an earlier chapter. Five people on Ai's list could be provided temporary work there. I heard a few days later that upon his receiving a request from the neighboring headquarters 1st Brigade, ACD, for five laborers he had sent six. I was to learn from Father Ai that he had a brother who operated an ice factory. The price for a block of ice to the local Vietnamese people was 90 dong. To the U.S. military the price was 300 dong.

Father Ai was a charismatic man. I noted many interesting observations about him, including the following:

> Ai travelled around the city on a motorbike. In July I noted that he was living at the Caritas office. He was disappointed that a brothel was operating directly opposite his Church.
>
> At Mass on 30 June his sermon was about the universality of the Church, referring to Father Doolan (Australian visitor) and me being blessed by Father Doan at the invitation of Father Doolan.
>
> At the Abbey, Father Ai was teaching philosophy to the nuns. Next day he was preparing children for their confirmation.
>
> An American military chaplain used me as an intermediary to Father Ai in vetting Civic Action projects recommended by Ai for his unit to support and fund.
>
> His attitude was one of optimism and I often wondered about his positive and happy disposition. Clearly he had no doubts spiritually and perhaps ideologically. He wrote letters to President Thieu about his views of the situation in Quang Tri. I did not hear from Ai as to whether he received any replies from Saigon.
>
> In discussing the conflict, he emphasised that all involved

on each side of the conflict were fellow human beings. However I gathered from Ai and some other Catholics that they were determined not to have any compromise solution with the VC or with the North. This was to be a fight to the death one way or another from their point of view.

On 27 October I organised a helicopter to take Ai on a visit to Ca Lu, and return.

A CA officer of the 1/5 Infantry Brigade made a commitment to Ai to fill land at the hamlet of Long Hung to the west of the Basilica. The project was intended to create a refugee hamlet. I reserved my thoughts on this project as fewer paddies resulted, there were to be no extra farms, a work plan was not presented, and the project could provide more opportunities for the VC.

For Christmas Eve Mass, Marine chaplain Father Anderson arranged for a medical evacuation helicopter to take Father Ai to midnight Mass with the US Marines. The pick-up was at 11:00 pm.

He invited me to his office on 26 January. He handed over three B41 rounds and fuses found by the hamlet chief at My Thuy at Wunder Beach. Ai would be paid an amount of money by the S2 for the hand-in of these munitions.

Two priests from Thua Thien Province stated their bishops (at Hue) felt that Buddhists would support the NLF in elections if their candidates were permitted to stand. The impression given to me was that if the GVN accepted the NLF, the elections would be a follow up. These notions did not come to pass.

Father Ai woke me at 7:15 am in the MACV compound on 9 February to check on a helicopter flight which I had arranged for him to visit the refugees relocated at Gia Dang. He went out to Gia Dang as arranged with another priest, two nuns and a large quantity of packed items.

As I was preparing to leave Quang Tri I had my farewell lunch with Father Ai and four of his priests. He was a leader among leaders. I do hope my views above are a fair description of this fine human being.

I went to schools at Tri Buu and La Vang on 24 July 1968 with Lieutenant Grey of the 41st Civil Affairs Unit. The purpose was to assess quantities of timber required for repair work. There was a need to follow up on these material needs with the contractors who were to do the work. On the same trip we visited the refugee hamlet at Thach Mon, with a population of about three hundred people. This hamlet required two wells. As a temporary measure they were taking water from the river to meet their needs. We also checked on their site for a village school whose approved plan was ready to proceed to the building stage. U.S. material aid distribution for projects of this nature was being encouraged by the PSA, Mr. Brewer.

My notes contained a number of entries about the basilica at La Vang. I was able to scrounge up twenty-five sheets of iron for the priest there, and he was very grateful for the materials. The use was at his discretion. He gave me a small souvenir saucer as a token of thanks, which I later passed on to my mother. I accompanied Binh and some sisters from the La Vang abbey on a visit to the priest at the basilica on 26 July to discuss some matters to do with the school at the abbey. This particular visit seemed to be a discussion about protocols concerning requests for support.

It appeared to me that the Catholic religious with whom I was talking reflected the terrible dilemma that faced their country. Their commitment to their respective vocations required them to be brave and stoic and true to their calling. They, however, were in a situation that tested their personal and professed convictions to the limit. The reality of the situation was that they were under intense pressure. They were not materialistic in outlook but were looking for support from outside their respective religious communities so that they could continue to pursue their callings in peace and tranquillity. Most of those in the community of eighty nuns in the abbey had come down from the North in 1954. They, like many others, were probably praying hard and with earnest hope that peace would be upon them soon. I in turn was very concerned about their plight. They needed both security and material aid, and the military was well placed to do this for them.

The next day I noted: "Very irritable today and short with the Vietnamese especially." When reflecting on the experience of the day before with the basilica and abbey people, I felt within me the anguish of the Vietnamese people who had been occupied by foreigners for decades. My judgement in regard to the host country was not warranted and was insensitive. My hope was that my colleagues and I could help satisfy their expectations. I noted that the day before was the feast of the Mother Superior at the abbey. At the end of my thoughts I concluded that at the micro level the religious had their job to do and I had mine.

A priest from the basilica visited me at Mai Linh on 8 August. He invited me to an ordination to be presided over by the Bishop of Hue. He asked, if possible, for assistance from the Air Cavalry Brigade for security that day. The security request included the provision of troops to be placed in the church tower at night. These requests were passed on to the 1st Brigade, ACD, headquarters. As an aside, a seminarian accompanying the priest said that the priest had in the past been captured by the VC and escaped. He no longer had the confidence to live at the church, but stayed in a nearby village at night.

The ordination day arrived on 22 August. Chaplain Jim Coghlan and two interpreters had also been invited. We were led to the front row seats by Father Ai. The Bishop of Hue was assisted by seven priests on the altar, with fifty other priests in attendance, robed and in the procession. Many people had walked from Quang Tri to witness the ceremony, which was held outdoors at the grotto. Proceedings commenced at 7:30 A.M., concluding about two hours later. The singing was led by the nuns and brothers. Thousands of people were in attendance. The only unpleasant aspect of the day was the wind. Security was provided behind the scenes but was not called upon. The ordination of this priest was moving and colorful. Later I sent a letter of thanks to the basilica in appreciation of being able to be present for the occasion in such stressful times.

Contact with the nuns at the abbey happened in a variety of ways during my four months at Mai Linh District. Mother Themasa, the sister of my interpreter, Binh, was Superior of the convent. Binh conducted English classes there at 1:30 P.M. on Tuesdays and Fridays. He asked me to help him with the class, primarily to assist with pronunciation. There were thirty-seven nuns in the first session I attended with Binh, in late June. They were all very interested in their subject. It was not difficult to support him with such a wonderful group of people. The feedback from the group was that they thought I spoke very clear English. That was a nice message to receive. Later I conducted a one-hour English pronunciation class with the nuns. I found the exercise to be a tiring mental activity, but good fun and worthwhile.

The chapel at the abbey was under repair. The request came to me, from Binh, to provide new beams. This was a "materials (manna) from Heaven" request if ever there was one. The leadership at the abbey was alert and did not let opportunities go by. In early July, I was escorted to the chapel to observe that the roof had been removed and the ceiling was about to be raised. The carpenters to do the job had come to the Mai Linh compound earlier to check on the timber for the chapel.

The school run by the nuns at La Vang also was undergoing a rebuild. The Revolutionary Development effort that was initially allocated was no longer available. I had a site meeting with the nuns and the contractor. Binh did the talking for me, having earlier discussed the project with me. Binh fortunately had skills in design and construction, so he was able to make clear the materials that advisor sources might be able to provide. Through scrounging and purchase on the market, assistance was provided for the school and the chapel roof project. Sand fill was being trucked in at no cost to the nuns. I noted that the nuns must have had some wealth behind them and that they were not afraid of the VC. On 30 August I observed that the work on the school at La Vang was nearing completion, but there continued to be a need for more corrugated iron and cement to finish the job. I noted that this was a very sad time for the Vietnamese people, and that life for the nuns was very tough.

During August I decided to make a break with the nuns. The final load of timber had been delivered to La Vang. I requested that should they require any further material assistance, a priest should do the business on their behalf. I added that I would come by from time to time to see how matters were progressing. There was another reason for making a break—factionalism, to be described shortly.

In early July I made two official calls on local Buddhist leaders. Binh was with me, as my interpreter. In each case I was received with the utmost politeness in a simple setting. These men were impressive and more formal than the priests. Despite a reserved calm, they expressed material needs similar to those of the other clergy. Two pagodas and a school were under repair, and materials for completion were hard to come by. My diary note concluded: "Shall see what I can do about that."

I asked my assistant, Captain Bill Coviello, to be the helper for the Buddhists. We were able to create order forms for the various groups that we had promised to help in Mai Linh, both Buddhists and Catholics. The civic action program within the 3rd Marine Division had funds available for us to purchase materials on the open market. How the market had U.S.-supplied materials for sale was another story, and beyond my area of responsibility. The marines were pleased to provide the funds for legitimate orders, and the advisors were happy to advance the pacification program by assisting the local Vietnamese. The scope of the justification for the requests came under the heading of "Well Being Projects."

On an evening walk in Mai Linh through a housing area I observed a Buddhist at prayer in his home. He was standing still before a table with two lit candles, and he held burning red incense sticks. I assumed he was in mourning. It was a very moving and thought-provoking scene. Further along the street I noticed in a number of houses that people were asleep sitting at their tables. Life was going on, in many and varied ways.

Visits to Quang Tri City by military chaplains were always stimulating. Most were very interested in the plight of the local people. While with their assigned units, or areas, some were not in contact with the Vietnamese people. Australian Army chaplain Father Frank Doolan, on his rounds from Vung Tau to AATTV members, was keen to meet an ARVN chaplain. We found our way to Father Tu, chaplain to ARVN forces in Quang Tri sector. The two priests struck upon a common interest, the role of the chaplain supporting the wounded and sick, in this case with the 31st ARVN Clearing Station in the local city. Tu expressed a view that he was not receiving the support expected from his fellow ARVN officers and men in completing a school he was sponsoring. School rebuilding seemed to be a common theme. GVN schools were also in need of assistance, both in materials and teachers.

Doolan and I then visited the casualty clearing station, and the morgue. Father Doolan was very committed to and anxious about the souls of the men. Later that day he said Mass in the compound dayroom, where the other chaplains also held services occasionally. Time was found for us to call upon Father Ai. Chaplain Kevin Hoffman and Father H. F. Brennan, Australian Army, had a short stay on 16 August and had similar interests to Doolan.

Marine chaplain Father Mignon, from the 3rd Marine Division, said Mass in the dayroom on 2 March 1969. He was having a short break from field duty. He was assigned to the 1/3 Marines and was keen to return to his troops. Mignon expressed his greatest admiration for NVA soldiers, a comment frequently made by those who had close involvement with the enemy.

I wrote to Eva of some interesting experiences relating to faith at work:

> It is difficult for me to establish the accurate starting time of any Mass here. It seems to be the Vietnamese custom to be vague about time, as I have previously mentioned. For instance the 9:00 am Mass has started at any time between 9:00 am and 9:40 am. It seems to depend upon how many people attend, or priest availability, or probably one of many other unknown factors.
>
> I went to Mass on Sunday and arrived early for confession. I looked for a priest in the sanctuary area. The head priest provided assistance. He could speak reasonable English, but slowly. He asked me to write down my confession, which I did, so that he could better understand what I was confessing. That went fine. He then escorted me from the back of the altar to the front pew, where he indicated a seat. I noticed that the church was packed with parishioners, and I felt honoured and embarrassed by his concern for me. I thought perhaps I could claim this pew on other occasions when attending Mass at this Church!

Eva had mentioned to me that I should not be involved in factionalism. This was an excellent observation, as arguably I may have been giving too much of my time to Catholics, although they seemed to be the more organized and progressive. This comment prompted me to call on the Buddhists leaders, on the basis of my being a district advisor and as the senior Australian in the province.

Diary comments arising from calling on the Buddhists, and also some research, revealed that Buddhism had its origins in India over twenty-five hundred years ago. Confucianism arrived in Vietnam with the Chinese. The two philosophies exist side by side in many Vietnamese homes. Taoism also came from China. Christianity arrived in Vietnam about three centuries ago.[2] Clearly Buddhism was ingrained into the Vietnamese culture, with other influences. These earlier and older philosophies could possibly have meant more to the Vietnamese than either Christianity or communism. I wondered how the early Christian missionaries achieved their influence over the dominant culture and customs. Foreign participants in the series of occupations and interventions over recent centuries, and from other cultures, have come and gone. They needed much wisdom and learning to become effective partners with the Vietnamese people. There are possible fertile areas here for scholars to examine. My clever interpreter, Binh, likened the Buddhist and Catholic problem in Vietnam to his notion of the Caucasian and African American relationship in the United States. In the last chapter I describe some later happenings related to faith in Vietnam, in the context of my 2012 visit to Quang Tri Province.

I end the chapter of this very enriching part of my life with an extract from a letter I sent home to Eva in early August 1968. It is about my prayer life:

> Attending Mass is the highlight of my Sunday and the week for that matter. I will probably get along to some week day Masses as my present routine may allow me an occasional 6:30 a.m. Mass. The discipline of prayer is excellent as it helps keep everything in perspective. You and the boys are always in my thoughts during my prayer time. I have prayed the rosary when possible. Sometimes it takes up to 15 minutes to get through the rosary, when thoughts come up that cause me to digress from prayer, yet at the same time cause me to examine my conscience. So in all it helps me to behave in a better way, hopefully.

By now a reader would be aware of a prevalent sentiment for a peace settlement in Vietnam. Advisors, our counterparts, and the people were very interested in the negotiations going on in Paris. The next chapter relates what I describe as the ripple effects that flowed down to us in the forward areas at the early stages of the talks.

16

Paris Peace Talks and Ripple Effects

May 1968–April 1969

The doors were opened to commence peace negotiations when the president of the United States of America made his surprising announcement on 31 March 1968. The conference of diplomats opened in Paris on 10 May 1968.[1] The talks were to continue throughout my year in South Vietnam and for some years thereafter. The prospect of a peace by negotiation fuelled hopes of an early settlement of the war, certainly so for the troops. The talks in Paris cast shadows over our efforts in Vietnam, some pleasant, most dark. They had what I describe as a ripple effect on some of our thinking and actions. A sobering question was put to me soon after my arrival in Vietnam: "Who is going to win the war?" The answer to that question has remained with me since: "the Vietnamese."

President Thieu had a basic policy with respect to any negotiation with North Vietnam, the "Four Nos" discussed in chapter 2. I cannot recall if that policy was known to the Free World Military Assistance Forces in South Vietnam in 1968. Some elements of policy flowing from the GVN position were understood, like the banning of some opposition political parties in the national elections. Clearly, the "Four Nos" created a conundrum for the negotiators in Paris.

The moral purpose of being involved in the war was raised again in my mind with the peace negotiations under way. To what extent should nations pursue warfare when the outcomes are so uncertain? The belligerents had their respective negotiating positions. The issues arising were to test and expose their ethical positions. These matters were up for debate in Paris, as well as in many other capitals, as the negotiations unravelled. Reputations of nations and individuals were at stake. Leaders and officials were to be tested. Meanwhile the military forces continued their operations.

Two weeks after my arrival I recorded two of the key current measures of success on the battlefield: how many kills and how many weapons captured. The thinking was that the NVA and the VC had a manpower advantage over the ARVN and U.S. Forces. A consequence of this was the view that the shooting war would be inconclusive and likely could end only with a negotiated settlement. The voice of public opinion, particularly in the United States, was pressuring the president and his administration to bring the troops home. The future rested with the negotiators. This was the mood after Tet 1968.

I made this assessment of the people in Quang Tri in early June 1968. It was apparent that individual Vietnamese, their families, and indeed their government were accepting handouts and goods in generous amounts. The people seemed to have set aside their pride. Their attempts at self-help appeared to be minimal. A mood of dependency may have set in. The United States was really bleeding itself of funds, for what return? My diary entry concluded that I would have to wait and see. My anguish was shared by my American colleagues.

From my experience of but one month with the Americans in South Vietnam I sensed that I was working within matrices of multilayered organizations, overlapping and somewhat confusing. It was clear that the United States did not want to do everything for the South Vietnamese. It wanted to assist them in a deadly serious environment. However, it seemed that since they were given so much by the United States, the hosts expected things to be done for them as well. I was sure that the "Vietnamese will only pull themselves together after the US has departed, whenever that may be." The same idea was expressed in a later letter home: "With their present attitude, the Vietnamese are reluctant to rebuild, and to get works under way. This is a big problem for the Americans right now and for me too: as I have to help them pursue their policies."

The psychological war was ongoing, influencing the attitudes of people worldwide in regard to the war and the peace negotiations. The North Vietnamese representatives in Paris proclaimed that the NVA was not in South Vietnam. Sadly, many believed this lie to be a fact.

In August there was a report of a temporary cessation of bombing on North Vietnam. We were aware that the NVA could, under these circumstances, bring military divisions up to the DMZ and hold there for a thrust south, at a time of its choosing. My notes included: "Hope the bombing halt gets results in Paris." Concurrently, the United States' domestic politics were part of the equation. My American friends expressed a view that the bombing pause would continue until the new president was elected in November.

The pacification campaigns in 1968 and 1969, discussed in earlier chapters, were integral to the future of a sovereign South Vietnam. Upgrading hamlet security, eliminating VC and VCI, holding populated areas, and destroying the enemy organized forces, both NVA and VC, were key pathways for the GVN in seeking an acceptable end to the war.

There was a flurry of discussions locally as news trickled into Quang Tri about progress at the talks. A message arrived in Quang Tri from the MACV headquarters on 1 November 1968. We were informed that a bombing halt was to take place north of the southern edge of the DMZ. At the same time enemy artillery rounds were coming from north of the DMZ throughout the day onto Dong Ha and Gio Linh. The previous day the sergeant major of the 3rd Marine Division had been killed in a freakish way. A 130 mm NVA artillery round hit the mess hall within the marine base complex, with a piece of shrapnel killing the sergeant major. From the enemy point of view this was good shooting. From our point of view it was a serious misfortune.

That evening Colonel Mooney invited McNamara, Cleary, and me to dinner. We listened to President Johnson's address. We were informed that on 6 November at the commencement of the expanded peace talks the National Liberation Front, although not recognized by the Saigon government, would be represented at the negotiations in Paris. We awaited the response from the GVN to that piece of news. President Thieu advised Ambassador Bunker in Saigon that he "would join the conference if the VC were not a separate negotiating delegation."[2] On 26 November the South Vietnamese foreign minister announced that the GVN had decided to participate in the Paris talks.[3]

The bombing halt would allow NVA regiments and divisions to reinforce, rest, reequip, and retrain in a safe area and allow them to pause above the DMZ for further offensives.[4] For those of us in Quang Tri, we just had to grin and bear the thought of how we would fight the battle should the NVA thrust south. On the other hand, the bombing effort could be applied to the NVA resupply routes through Laos. Our counterparts naturally had a high level of self-interest in what was going on in Paris, and justifiably so. There was a conundrum, one of many about the consequences of a cease-fire: would there be civil disobedience or civil war?

For the United States, the big conundrum was to bring about a peace deal, with honor. There was a self-imposed perception that the prestige of the United States was at stake here. It seemed that American prestige was a dominant national interest. The political pressure in the United States was strongly in favor of finding a way to bring the troops home. For South Vietnam the purpose was to preserve the nation, and to free itself of communism. The enemy was extraordinarily tough and ruthlessly determined to have a united Vietnam, seemingly regardless of the costs of trying to achieve that goal.

The United States had by November 1968 built up a logistics base to support a force of about 1 million troops. The U.S. Army had done the work to support an increase in manpower in South Vietnam to well over five hundred thousand. But the tide was turning against South Vietnam. In a letter home I expressed an opinion that there appeared to be a significant waste in assets and of manpower. Further, some of the supporting programs that were manpower intensive were just not worth the effort. I commented that there were good lessons here in Vietnam for Australia.

An indicator of the interest in the Paris Peace Talks was seen in Quang Tri on 8 November 1968. The province chief, Colonel Am, hosted a lunch for senior military leaders at his residence. Guests included Lieutenant General Hoang Xuan Lam, I Corps (ARVN) commander; Major General Ngo Quang Truong, 1st ARVN Division commander; Lieutenant General Richard G. Stilwell, commander of the U.S. Army's XXIV Corps; and our province senior advisor, Colonel Harley Mooney. Later in the day Mooney shared some of the lunch table talk with his Team 19 staff. One significant point reported by Stilwell was that should a cease-fire be put in place, law and order would still need to be maintained. This was to ensure that the VC/VCI internal threat could be contained. Government agencies in South Vietnam would have to carry weapons to preserve the peace.

The next day the U.S. Armed Forces newspaper in South Vietnam, the *Stars and Stripes,* carried a columnist contribution on this same issue of law and order. I noted that there was widespread interest within all ranks in the negotiations in Paris. In a letter home, I dumped my anguish about the dilemma in South Vietnam on Eva:

> If a cease fire comes, there is going to be a problem in the maintenance of law and order as the VC may still want to fight on: i.e. a civil war situation. It's very difficult to see a true and meaningful settlement coming about. The whole country and people are a series of contradictions. It is a beautiful country and potentially rich, yet very poor and not self-supporting. The young people are good looking, but the older folk are worn and haggard.
>
> All of the people are after peace, yet secret societies abound. Corruption is being resisted in places, yet flourishing as well as ever, especially in the black-market. The South Vietnamese are a people who require our assistance, yet few go out of their way to help us. So that clears my liver for the better. The Vietnamese right now are a pain in the neck to me and many others. I am very glad that we do not have to live with them here; working with them is hard enough.

One was also mindful that the South Vietnamese may have had similar thoughts about Americans and Australians, myself included.

My record on 9 November indicated that the GVN military forces, ARVN and Territorials, were under-resourced in combat support and combat service support capabilities. The logistic effort provided by the Americans was enormous. With a gradual phase out of the American troops and the rightful placing of greater responsibility onto the GVN, a hurry up was needed to put in place structures to allow the ARVN/RF/PF and VNAF to be self-sufficient in logistics as well as combat power. Later events were to show that these shortcomings were not met.

Further, by way of contrast, there was a paradox facing the U.S. Navy and MACV in Saigon. The need by the U.S. ground forces for naval gun fire support was decreasing. Naval gunfire liaison officers were seeking targets from the ground forces to keep the warships in action. The concern of the navy was that the justification for the present level of naval support might not stand up to review. At the time the battleship *New Jersey* was firing into Base Area 101 to the west, but was soon to be withdrawn.

On 10 November a National Police Field Force (NPFF) company at Quang Tri was put on standby for possible deployment at the Ben Hai Bridge within the DMZ on Route 1. The province chief had

Visit by Vice President Nguyen Cao Ky.

issued the warning order on direction of the president of South Vietnam. It was viewed by the advisors that the task was beyond the NPFF. Nothing of substance followed the warning order.

By mid-December 1968 military activity had slowed down. Locally, it was considered that each side was working on the political front to make gains. It was thought that the VC was trying to gain as much success as possible with the people. Concurrently, the GVN was trying to neutralize as many VC as possible while working toward having more Vietnamese people under its control. The pacification programs were showing their positive effects among the people. Vice President Nguyen Cao Ky made an informal visit to Quang Tri Province on 21 December 1968.

The sector headquarters was advised on the last day of the year that the GVN had called off a twenty-four-hour truce due to an incident with the enemy during the Christmas truce. The VC had earlier agreed to a seventy-two-hour truce for the New Year. I thought that the GVN was not being very positive in calling off a short-duration truce.

A new U.S. leader had been elected, with the inauguration of President Richard Nixon being held on 20 January 1969. Proposals for thinning out were being mooted. The U.S. troops in Vietnam were restless. The home fronts were restless.

By mid-February 1969 reports indicated that two new NVA divisions were now in areas adjacent to Quang Tri Province. One division was to the north of Gio Linh. It had been earlier established that there was an NVA division to the west in Laos.

Toward the end of February my notes recorded that things were quiet in the populated areas of the province. However, the marines were in contact with the NVA near the Laotian border in NVA Base Areas 101 and 110. Although we were aware of disturbances all over Vietnam, we were of a view that the NVA did not want to draw attention to the DMZ area. Perhaps the NVA was endeavoring to show the world that the present strife was internal to South Vietnam.

While on a staff visit to the Dong Ha area on 19 March 1969, I was called back to the Citadel to help prepare a briefing and presentation on the Territorial Forces activities and capabilities for the period 1 November 1968 to 28 February 1969. Lieutenant General Fred Weyand, the senior military negotiator for the United States at the Paris Peace Talks, was to be briefed by the PSA at the headquarters of the 3rd Marine Division on 24 March. Colonel Mooney wanted an early discussion on a draft for the evening of 20 March. The senior advisory staff then considered the draft brief, and Colonel Mooney asked for a rewrite. After his consideration a further revision was completed on 22 March. On 23 March I accompanied the PSA on a visit to the 3rd Marine Division to set up the briefing.

At the briefing we were informed by the marines that the division had been in contact with five NVA divisions in the last year. When in contact, friendly casualties were about two hundred troops killed in action each week. In quieter periods USMC losses were about twenty troops killed per week. In his address General Weyand stressed that the commitment must be continued. He asked rhetorically: "How could our Nation and Armies live with the fact that we pulled out before the job was completed, and before our promises to the GVN were fulfilled? Public opinion could change things at home, but it is up to us to change that and to inform the people of what it is all about." As the U.S. Army chief of staff back in the States, General Westmoreland toured the country promoting the purpose of the mission in Vietnam.

General Weyand continued by saying emotionalism needed to be managed. He pointed out that casualties and the cost of the war were the heartburn issues. He added that the presidential changeover from Johnson to Nixon was a slow process, as there was no shadow government in the U.S. political system. The deep fundamentals of the U.S. involvement in Vietnam were covered. His words were sobering.

I found the generals of the U.S. Army whom I met to be impressive men and outstanding leaders. Their unswerving loyalty to the United States and to their commander in chief, the president, was rock solid, embedded in them through their heritage, education, respect of the law, character, and commitment to their profession. I was aware that at least four commanding generals in Vietnam had a son serving there during my time.

The peace talks in Paris continued for another four years. The allied ground forces supporting South Vietnam withdrew in phases, from 1969 to 1972. A peace agreement was concluded in Paris on 23 January 1973. The cease-fire came into effect on 28 January 1973. However, North Vietnam did not give up on its aspirations for a united Vietnam.

Others have written about the long-running negotiations in Paris, the peace agreement reached in 1973, and the consequences. The final outcome in 1975 was conclusive, and I was very disappointed at the time. Afterthoughts in 1975 included:

- Professional instincts were constantly pressed by personal instincts.
- Winning on the battlefield, the winning of the hearts and minds of the people and the compromises of the diplomacy have been scarcely recognized.
- The above were being overarched by the national interests of the belligerents, ending in the nightmare of a dud peace settlement.

In the preceding chapters the way in which senior American and Vietnamese leaders carried out their respective responsibilities in the field has been a constant thread. The next chapter provides a perspective of the way senior Australian leaders went about their responsibilities in the field in Vietnam. Special efforts and personal risks were some of the issues leaders had to consider in deciding to travel to Quang Tri. Their presence was appreciated by the advisors.

17

Australian Leaders in South Vietnam

May 1968–April 1969

The Australian Army hierarchy, from Canberra to the headquarters in Saigon, had a high degree of interest in the deployed AATTV. In 1968–1969 the Team provided to MACV more than ninety highly skilled and experienced advisors throughout South Vietnam. Australian leaders, from the AATTV's commanding officer upward in the Australian chain of command, spent quality time on visitation to deployed Team members in South Vietnam. There were considerable benefits for higher ranking Australians in traveling the country. Also, Australian visitors provided a morale boost to Team members, as well as sustaining an invaluable network of U.S. military leaders throughout South Vietnam. I wish to express my grateful thanks and appreciation to the many Vietnamese and Americans who welcomed Australian visitors to Quang Tri Province.

Commanding Officers of the AATTV

Few allied commanders in Vietnam had a unit such as the AATTV to command and administer. With Team members deployed throughout South Vietnam, it required a special effort by the commanding officer to see and be seen by his troops. Any visit by the CO was valued by all ranks. Lieutenant Colonel Ray Burnard, whom I first met when I was passing through Da Nang on 16 May 1968, made a routine visit to Quang Tri on 19 June.

The CO arrived at Ai Tu in an RAF DH.104 Devon aircraft, a version of the British-built twin-engine de Havilland Dove, an eight seater. The host for his trip was Lieutenant Colonel Peter Varwell, the only British serviceman in South Vietnam, who was doing his rounds within the country with Burnard as his guide. Varwell informed me that earlier the British Defense staff at the embassy in Saigon totaled three officers. When the UK press became critical of this level of British Defense involvement in Vietnam the minister directed the withdrawal of the Royal Navy and Royal Air Force officers.

A busy schedule of visits was made to the sector headquarters, to Dong Ha, and then back to Ai Tu. From there a Chinook helicopter from Marine HMM 161 Squadron flew the two colonels and me to the hospital ship USS *Repose.* We visited AATTV member Peter Wooden and other seriously wounded soldiers on the ship. Souvenirs of NVA origin, two helmets and a belt, were gifted to the ship. The skipper of the *Repose,* Captain John Drew, provided dinner, shared with three senior medical officers and three nurses. We flew off at 7:00 P.M. for Quang Tri City. The two colonels met up with Team members at the compound.

During the evening Warrant Officer Alf Hunter, advisor to 3/7 ARVN Cavalry, let the colonels know that his armored personnel carrier unit might be called out early the next morning. The colonels were keen to deploy with Alf, so they declined the air-conditioned comfort of the CORDS residence and stayed at the compound in the event of a call-out, which did not occur. Early the next morning the colonels visited sector headquarters, where the police chief presented captured NVA and VC flags to them as gifts of appreciation to the Minister of the Army and the Hall of Flags. The colonels departed mid-morning, flying Air America on this occasion.

The CO had an administrative conference the morning after the Team birthday celebration in Da Nang on 31 July. The military secretary in his role as manager of the officers of the Australian Army was also in attendance. Brigadier Freddie Whitelaw had one-on-one interviews with each officer present. Future career paths were discussed. This was an impressive effort for the brigadier to attend to such matters while the war was going on.

While I was passing through Da Nang on 23 August I met up with Lieutenant Colonel Burnard. He was visiting Team members in that area. Major Ian Porteous was our host. There was always plenty to talk about, ranging from Team matters to our own and enemy tactics. I was on my way south to attend the Revolutionary Development National Training Center at Vung Tau. Lieutenant Colonel Mooney in Quang Tri had also encouraged me to spend a few extra days at Nui Dat with the Australian Task Force.

AATTV members, Da Nang, ANZAC Day 1969.

The CO was back in Quang Tri on 3 October with the director of infantry, Colonel David Thompson. Lieutenant Colonel Varwell accompanied them. A Huey was available, so the visitors were able to visit Dong Ha, fire support bases A1 and A2, Task Force Hotel at Ca Lu, and the sector headquarters. Colonel Mooney kindly hosted the visitors to a light lunch at his house. Available warrant officers were able to meet the colonels after lunch for discussions. On 5 November I was in Da Nang with the province chief and Colonel Mooney. As the visit coincided with a CO visit to Da Nang, I was able to join him and Porteous for the evening.

Another occasion arose for further conversations with the CO when an Australian Forces Overseas Fund hut-opening ceremony was held in Da Nang on 29 December.[1] I had traveled to Da Nang with Major Jim Hill by an Air America Pilatus Porter. For me this was a welcome in-country break. The ceremony was a big social event for the AATTV. Australia House at Da Nang had some shortcomings, so a contribution by the Fund to provide a recreation hut for our use was most welcome. The amenities provided gave us a home-away-from-home free from the host and U.S. environments. The CO had traveled north from Saigon with COMAFV Major General A. L. MacDonald. They were accompanied by Lieutenant Colonel G. Thompson and Lieutenant Colonel Swift, both from headquarters AFV. Team members gathered formally for the opening ceremony.

The commander of I Corps, General Lam, was the principal guest and officially opened the door of the facility to a luncheon. The general was accompanied by his protocol officer, Major Xuan. An Australian concert party entertained the gathering for two hours. The VIPs departed at 3:00 P.M. My return to Quang Tri was by Air America C-47 along the coast at five hundred feet. That evening I wrote a letter of appreciation to the Fund on behalf of the Australians in Quang Tri. At the same sitting I wrote to three families in Australia who sent Christmas cakes to "Soldiers in Vietnam." Their gifts and the thoughts behind them were full of kindness. In a letter home I wrote: "Before the break I felt jaded. Now my enthusiasm has returned and I should be back to normal form soon."

During a visit to Da Nang on 7 January 1969 I met up with the CO again. Then at the end of the month a routine changeover of command of AATTV from Burnard to Lieutenant Colonel Russell Lloyd brought about a visit by the two colonels to Quang Tri. I flew south to Hue in an Air America helicopter with Warrant Officer Bill Deanshaw to meet them at what was termed the province pad. We then flew to LZ Nancy, where the command post for 1st ARVN Regiment was located. The regimental commander, Colonel Hanh, briefed the visitors on current operations. This was of special interest to Burnard and Lloyd, as the AATTV provided a warrant officer to the U.S. advisory teams working with each of the four battalions of the 1st Regiment. Colonel Hanh stated that the present operation had been going for 142 days. The regiment had earlier contact with the NVA 6th Front, which was replaced by the NVA 7th Front. He informed us that recently captured documents indicated that the enemy forces in the area were running out of ammunition. A courier moving to the west carrying written messages had been captured a few days earlier, providing the source of the information. Over the period of the operation the number of NVA killed amounted to 820, with ARVN troops killed in action numbering 150. Medical supplies, equipment, and many weapons had been captured, including mortars, rockets, machine guns, rifles, and ammunition, which were destroyed in place.

From LZ Nancy we flew to Cam Lo sub-sector, where the district senior advisor, Major Bill Healy, briefed us on the situation. Warrant Officer Ken Chester guided the colonels to a PF housing project and to a water reservoir project which had been constructed to provide water to the refugee camps in Cam Lo. From there we proceeded to A1, via the Cam Vu water pump project. At A1 we were met by Warrant Officer John Barker, a member of the 1/2 ARVN Battalion advisory team. Barker ran proceedings here, not allowing his U.S. captain to get a word in. The Australian flag was flying, and a photograph of the queen was displayed in the bunker. His predecessor, Warrant Officer Jim Geedrick, had a similar passion for such things. Despite being in such a hot spot as the Gio Linh area on the DMZ, these two soldiers performed with élan and professionalism.

From Gio Linh we proceeded back to the Citadel for a Quang Tri sector briefing in the operations center. Dinner was at the PSA's house, where we were hosted by the acting PSA and the acting DPSA, Mr. McNamara and Lieutenant Colonel Wallace. There was plenty to talk about. I noted that the discussion was centered on discovering the common elements that dictated national policies. This was an esoteric informal agenda for such an occasion!

After dinner we proceeded to the Quang Tri MACV club, where the colonels met up with Warrant Officers Kevin Gabriel, Ray Purton, Bob King, Bill Deanshaw, and Herbert Beezley. The Australians departed via the compound gate at 10:50 P.M., a little late for the compound commander. I stood beside him as this was happening, reassuring him that the occasion was a kind of demonstration of third-party nationalism. We remained on good terms. As a unit, the

AATTV was proud of our contribution in South Vietnam. The bulk of the Australian Army presence was in Phuoc Tuy Province to the south, so our Team members were inclined to claim (or brag) that we contributed a lot to the V of the Australian Force Vietnam.

Lieutenant Colonel Lloyd assumed command of the AATTV on 11 February 1969. His next visit to Quang Tri sector was on 4 March. His comprehensive approach to his task was not unexpected. I had first met the colonel when he was adjutant of the Corps of Staff Cadets at the Royal Military College, Duntroon, in 1956. The CO planned to join warrant officers in the field while they were carrying out their advisory duties with the U.S. teams attached to ARVN units. This allowed him to gain firsthand experience with the employment of the warrant officers. At the same time the operational effectiveness of the ARVN units being supported could be assessed.

After arriving on an Air America Porter, Lloyd had a discussion with Colonel Mooney. Following lunch at the MACV compound, we proceeded to the command post of the 2nd ARVN Regiment, where the senior advisor, Major Coleman, outlined the situation in the area of operations. Then the Blackcat helicopter flew us to 3/2 ARVN Battalion, where Warrant Officer Max Stack was located. Perhaps the pilots were distracted by the artillery rounds that were going out—and coming in—as it took a little extra time to find the landing pad we were seeking. The sortie was completed successfully. Lloyd was dropped off. An ARVN soldier wounded in action was evacuated with ten enemy weapons. On the morning of 6 March I dropped off Warrant Officer Ron Gurney at 3/2 ARVN, then at an abandoned hamlet known as Dao Xuyen. Ron was to replace Max Stack. Lieutenant Colonel Lloyd joined me in the Blackcat.

The CO shared his views on the employment of team members, especially at the sub-sector level. With MATs under the control of a district senior advisor, the role of a warrant officer as an assistant advisor to RF companies and PF platoons was limited. It was clear that the CO was having a hard look at AATTV deployment and employment to ensure that the best use was made of the Australian warrant officer talent pool in the Team.

During breaks in interviews I was able to discuss other matters with him. He expressed a view that the Australian Task Force in Phuoc Tuy had been doing a good job against the main force enemy units. However, he was concerned about the Australian contribution to pacification. I was able to share my experience to date in the staff planning of the pacification campaigns of 1968 and 1969. He was able to take away a number of ideas, but had to find a way to get any considered views into each of the headquarters of the AFV and the 1st Australian Task Force.

Lloyd visited Major Shalikashvili at Trieu Phong sub-sector, and then proceeded to 2/1 ARVN Battalion at My Chanh in Hai Lang District, on the border with Thua Thien Province. Warrant Officer Kevin Gabriel was rejoining the advisory team with that battalion, so he was able to accompany the commanding officer on a road and boat journey to meet up with the unit. Gabriel was given a big welcome when he arrived with Lloyd. In jest, the CO observed that the return of Gabriel was like a "Chieu Hoi" in reverse. In appreciation of the Australian contribution to the battalion the executive officer presented a regimental plaque to the AATTV, a thoughtful gesture.

At the Team 19 evening briefing on 7 March Lieutenant Colonel Lloyd was the guest of the PSA. They had developed a close, personal bond by now. Mooney was impressed by the way Lloyd was approaching his responsibilities within the AATTV and establishing relationships with the U.S. Army and ARVN organizations. Invited to address the gathering of MACCORDs people, my Australian commanding officer was diplomatic, not being drawn into debate on the pressing issues of the time.

Lloyd departed for Hue early on 8 March, accompanied by Warrant Officer Henry Stuttard, advisor to the 1/11 ARVN Cavalry. Lieutenant Colonel Lloyd had impressed all ranks with his presence and friendliness and was an exemplar of the maxim to see and be seen.

ANZAC Day 1969 was approaching, 25 April being the anniversary of the Australian and New Zealand Army Corps' 1915 landing on the Gallipoli Peninsula in Turkey during World War I. It was the annual occasion for the AATTV to gather available members formally, in Da Nang. The CO addressed members present in the advisors' hut at Australia House on the eve, sharing his views about the unit role. He was firm and clear in his oration and left little to doubt. One of his observations was of particular interest: that the warrant officer rank did not fit in with the rank structure of the U.S. Army. Australian warrant officers had officer status while serving with the U.S. Army in Vietnam. The CO saw the mismatch as a matter that had to be lived with, but was a consideration in deciding upon Team member employment. More broadly, though, he concluded it was the best way for Australia to provide our operational experience to the Vietnamese and U.S. effort.

Seventy members attended the ANZAC Day dawn service at Australia House. Warrant Officer Class 1 Jack Morrison, DCM and Bar, acted as the parade marshal. We all had a soft spot for Jack, one of the characters of the Australian Army. He was a veteran of earlier wars and on his second tour in Vietnam. He had helped aspiring Team members on special courses of training at the Jungle Training Centre, Canungra, in Queensland. Chaplain Kevin Hoffman conducted the service, and the CO gave a short address. Principal guests were Generals Lam, Hay, Nickerson, and the commander of the 2nd ARVN Division. It was a long day. Breakfast comprised hot dogs, coffee, and rum, then beer. The band of the III MAF played during the morning: drums, bugles, and trumpets. Staff Sergeant David Cairo was a dynamic bandmaster. A barbecue lunch followed, then "two-up," with some stalwarts keeping the game going. Then sad news arrived.

The CO passed on to us that Warrant Officer John Albert Bond had been killed in action early that morning. He was serving with the 7th ARVN Cavalry Regiment, operating out of Hue. His unit was involved in an action one kilometer southwest of the former Special Forces camp at Lang Vei, in Quang Tri Province. His death happened during an NVA mortar attack on his unit. Letters to the next of kin followed. This was a melancholy duty that commanding officers had to face from time to time, in war and peace. Escorts were arranged to ensure that the body was in safe keeping for its return to Australia.

Although Quang Tri was a long distance from Saigon, successive COs of the AATTV diligently kept in touch with their men in the most northern provinces of South Vietnam. During my 1968–1969 tour, AATTV members had an opportunity to see the CO in the north on eleven occasions. This personal contact was of good value for personal morale and unit esprit de corps.

Senior Australian Visitors

The Australian Army's director general of medical services, Major General C. M. Gurner, visited Quang Tri on 9 July 1968, accompanied by Lieutenant Colonel John Dunn (Medical) and Captain Peter Ray (AATTV). My fellow team member Warrant Officer Gordon

Fitzgibbon[2] (Medical) was keen to make the visit a memorable one for the general. Fitzgibbon took ownership of our task and was determined to give the general "the whole lot."

The visit included tours of USMC medical units, government military and civilian hospitals, and a call on the province chief. Dr. Hong gave a very good presentation of his work in the scheme of things. He was rightfully pleased with himself, as were we of him for helping our visitor take in what he did in the five hours he was with us.

COMAFV Major General A. L. MacDonald was the next Australian senior officer to visit Quang Tri, on 24 July 1968. He arrived at Ai Tu, and we proceeded to the headquarters of the 2nd ARVN Regiment. Unfortunately the regimental commander and his senior advisor were out on a joint operation with two battalions of the regiment and the marines, working out of Ca Lu on Route 9. The regimental executive officer did his best to brief the general on current operations. Four warrant officers were at the Quang Tri stadium pad to meet the general, a stimulus after a relatively disappointing visit at Dong Ha. A call on the province chief was duly carried out. The 1st Brigade, Air Cavalry Division, headquarters was the next call for lunch. The divisional commander, Major General Irby, and the brigade commander, Colonel Stannard, hosted the visitors, who included Lieutenant Colonel Hanh, commanding officer of the 1st ARVN Regiment, and his senior advisor, Major Ferguson. Other staff officers of the ACD were in attendance. This was a good visit for COMAFV, as he was at ease. General MacDonald then visited a fire base before he was bade farewell on his way south.

During a visit to South Vietnam, General Sir John Wilton, chairman of the Chiefs of Staff Committee (Australia), included a stopover at the headquarters of XXIV Corps. Lieutenant General Richard G. Stilwell extended an invitation to me to join his guests for lunch on 24 October 1968, which I accepted. A thirty-minute helicopter flight carried me to Phu Bai to join the group. Warrant Officer Deanshaw traveled with me. I was the junior officer at this special gathering. Those joining the host and his guest were Major General Melvin Zais, commander of the 101st Air Mobile Division; the deputy commander of XXIV Corps, Major General Drake; Major General Truong; Major General Schwitser, chief of staff; COMAFV; and two brigadier generals. The story of the day at the lunch was about the experience General Wilton had during the morning. He had been winched down from a helicopter to visit a warship off the coast. Later he was to learn that the captain of the aircraft had been undertaking his first winch operation on that flight. The general was lifted off at the due time and was delivered safely back on land. There were smiles all around on hearing that yarn over a well-earned pink gin. I flew back to Quang Tri with General Drake. Colonel Land was dropped off at Hai Lang, and I was dropped off at the Citadel with Deanshaw.

Following on from the director of infantry visit on 3 October, the director of military training, Brigadier G. Solomon, visited on 13 November, accompanied by the CO of the AATTV. As the brigadier had an artillery background, I had arranged for him to visit the 3rd Marine Division Fire Support Coordination Center. (More detail about this center is provided in the next chapter.)

COMAFV arrived in Dong Ha for his second visit on 26 November. He was accompanied by the Team commanding officer and Major Ian "Digger" Campbell of the AFV headquarters. His two-hour visit was spent with the commander of the 3rd Marine Division. General Davis invited the visitors to join him on his morning rounds in a U.S. Army helicopter. The group traveled west to Vandegrift combat base to visit the headquarters of TF Hotel and the forward logistic base surrounding the extensive landing zone. The land around the zone was divided up to provide slices for the forward combat units, where unit representatives prepared loads for the helicopter resupply to their units. Daily resupply from the coastal maintenance areas to Vandegrift at that time was 400 tonnes by road and 170 tonnes by airlift, using C-130s and helicopters. This met the needs of the two marine regiments in the hills farther out. Shore parties organized the operation of the landing zone.

From this forward base we flew over the recently abandoned Khe Sanh base. Leaving this desolate place, we flew to the southeast, down the Da Krong Valley to LZ Dick, where the headquarters of the 9th Marines was located. The battalions of the regiment in searching for the NVA were further deployed away from the landing zone. Companies of the battalions were allocated four map squares to search at a time (i.e., two thousand meters by two thousand meters). This was tough work for the marines. Each base was being mutually supported by artillery. When cloud and mist closed off air resupply, the going got tougher. The NVA had its advanced logistic bases in these remote areas, usually underground. The marines were searching for them methodically, with success. This privileged battlefield tour provided us with a brief and firsthand view of the shield at work. Early in our journey I noted a chase helicopter accompanying our party as a backup. This was reassuring for our group. I privately wondered how the Australian Defense Force would cope if Australia was committed to an operation of this kind nearer to home. Our track record indicated that we would prevail, but scenarios would need to be analyzed.

I was to meet up again with COMAFV in Da Nang on 20 December. The occasion was a visit to the Team by the Chief of the General Staff, General Sir Thomas Daly, accompanied by his staff officer, Lieutenant Colonel John Murphy. The chief arrived at 1:00 P.M., and at 2:00 P.M. he was on his way to Hue. He spent the time talking with the warrant officers, many of whom had served with him elsewhere in the Australian Army. For Team members the visit was too short, but we realized that his time was also short. However, he was here and we saw him. This was an occasion where a leader can do his best by listening, by seeing, and by being seen. I was to see COMAFV Major General A. L. MacDonald on 11 February 1969 during his final visit to Quang Tri when he was accompanied by Major General Long, army chief of personnel.

The Australian ambassador to South Vietnam, R. L. Harry, visited Quang Tri on 21 March 1969. He arrived at 10:00 A.M. in an RAAF C-47 at Ai Tu, accompanied by Colonel Jim Norrie, the Australian defense attaché, and three embassy staff. Norrie had been my commanding officer when I was posted to the Pacific Island Regiment in Port Moresby, Papua New Guinea, in January 1960. The province chief was host for the day and made sure that a pleasant five hours was had by all. The morning was spent in the Cam Vu project area. Major De briefed the visitors, and then came a helicopter view over the pumps and the irrigated area. Before lunch a sector briefing was provided by the Vietnamese military staff. Colonel Am, the province chief, hosted lunch. The visitors were then flown by helicopter to Gia Dang to observe the progress on the relocation scheme. The ambassador left from Ai Tu for Kontum. Before he departed he indicated that there was to be no reduction in the Australian forces in South Vietnam for the foreseeable future.

In a letter of appreciation, the ambassador wrote: "Major Johnston and Major Millie exercised their imaginations and exerted their influence to make our visit to I Corps a tremendously interesting one. The opportunity to use helicopters and visit such places as LZ Nancy, the forward post at LZ Davis where we met Warrant Officer Bill Tillet, the irrigation resettlement area at Cam Vu and the resettlement fishing village on the coast was most acceptable after a series of somewhat dull briefings we had received in other areas."

About this time I noted that there were not many more visits to go before my departure from Quang Tri.

Major General Bob Hay, COMAFV designate, visited Quang Tri on 27 March 1969. As well as an official call, his desire was to meet as many warrant officers as he could during his two-hour visit. We met at Ai Tu, and the Blackcat took us on quick calls to the province chief, where a small guard of honor was provided, and to the PSA. From the Citadel we proceeded to Cam Lo, A2, and the 2nd ARVN Regiment headquarters, meeting warrant officers in each location. At 2nd Regiment the general met Colonel Giai, the commander. We completed the visitation circuit at the Quang Tri Citadel pad. The general then flew south to Hue.

In the evening I received a request to return a telephone call to General Stilwell, commander of XXIV Corps. I felt as though another visit was to be upon me. Instead, the general wanted to talk about the policy concerning U.S. awards to Australian soldiers serving with the ARVN. He had been advised by COMUSMACV that it was a "negative" due to Australian policy. My response was that we could receive foreign awards but were not authorized to wear them. I mentioned that the commanding officer of the AATTV had recently discussed the idea of a citation being awarded to the unit. The general agreed with that notion, and continued by saying that we should get both. I then informed the CO by letter of the discussion.

Other Australian Visitors

To assist Team commanders in their work, staff officers, chaplains, and couriers had a visitation role to play in supporting Team members in the field. Ian Porteous and Frank Johnston were frequent visitors from Da Nang. Standing arrangements were in place at Team headquarters in Saigon for a pay and mail run at least monthly to Quang Tri, via other places. The adjutant did this run on a quarterly basis. On other occasions people from outside the Team acted as the courier. News came in, and news went out. Visitors at times were loaded up by members with various items to go south, and beyond.

ANZAC commemoration service conducted by Chaplain Kevin Hoffman, at Danang, 25 April 1968. (Original image provided by Australian Department of Defence, Copyright Australian War Memorial, AWM LES/69/0254/VN.)

The visits were all a good tonic for morale. Army chaplains came to Quang Tri frequently. The Army Chaplaincy Service has a wonderful tradition in the Australian Army. Usually the visiting chaplain came from the Australian Logistic Support Group base at Vung Tau.[3] During my year in Quang Tri, Chaplains Hoffman (five visits),

Doolan, Brennan (two visits), Badcock, and Gorman were welcome visitors. On one occasion in July Kevin Hoffman spent four days with us. These chaplains were good friends to most of us, confidants when required, and special advisors to COs and other commanders. I judged that the chaplains did help the commanding officer in managing the welfare of his men. Visiting chaplains helped me on occasion.

With Headquarters 1st Australian Task Force

Having completed duty in Quang Tri, I traveled to Nui Dat in Phuoc Tuy Province after the Da Nang ANZAC Day gathering. I was to become a visitor. I had been allocated for temporary duty to the 1st Australian Task Force headquarters from 26 April to 4 May 1969. The deputy commander of 1 ATF requested that I research and give him suggestions on how the task force could best participate in pacification. To commence my enquiries I spoke with the staff officers involved in operations within the headquarters. From there I went to 9th Battalion, Royal Australian Regiment (9 RAR) and met with the commanding officer, Lieutenant Colonel Alby Morrison, and the officer commanding C Company, Major Laurie Lewis. The company was preparing to provide training for three battalions of the ARVN at the "Horseshoe," an artillery base outside of Nui Dat. Six weeks had been allocated to train each battalion. The next day I read into the pacification files held at the task force headquarters.

At the task force operations center I renewed my friendship with the commander, Brigadier Sandy Pearson. I had last served with him in 1 RAR in 1963 and 1964. He wished me well. He explained that he would ideally like to have had a plans officer and an executive officer on the establishment of his headquarters in order to free up his present senior staff to "run the show." Based on my experience with the U.S. forces, I fully agreed with him.

Over the next few days I visited some Australian units, including the task force maintenance area, the Logistic Support Group at Vung Tau, and the Civil Affairs Unit. ARVN units visited included the National Training Center for the RF/PF of III Corps and IV Corps at Van Kiep, the Infantry Specialist Training Center, which included the Australian-run Long Range Patrolling Wing, and the local sector headquarters at Baria. I met up with Lieutenant Colonel Lloyd at Luscombe airfield in Nui Dat during my rounds. He was visiting Captain Bob Guest and his warrant officers, who provided a cadre staff to the 18th ARVN Division Training Center, near Nui Dat. I gained essential information from these visits to help me to provide useful advice to the Australian officers at Nui Dat. The gist of my suggestions was essentially incremental points arising from my Quang Tri experience to add to the policies and processes already in place in Phuoc Tuy Province.

A further meeting on pacification was held with the task force commander and Lieutenant Colonel Peter Gration, commanding officer of the Civil Affairs Unit. More detailed discussion on my suggestions was held with Peter Gration the next day. To conclude my detachment to 1 ATF, I met with the deputy commander to provide him with my conclusions. These conversations marked the completion of my formal duties for the Team, and I traveled back to Saigon on 4 May 1969.

During the week at Nui Dat I had my third and final visit to 161 Reconnaissance Flight, an army aviation unit with 1 ATF. I considered these visits to be a professional necessity, as on return to Australia I was to command 16 Aviation Squadron at Oakey, Queensland. This squadron was the source of most of the Australian Army pilots posted to Vietnam. Having an awareness of where the pilots were going and what they were expected to undertake allowed me to develop training programs in Australia to help prepare them for their operational role in the war zone. My passion for Army Aviation was well satisfied by the flying time I had while in South Vietnam. I was in an aircraft on 170 days, totaling two hundred flying hours. There were hundreds of landings, arising from short-duration helicopter trips. I sincerely thank the air crews, ground crews, and aviation units for each and every flight, all undertaken safely and without a mishap.

The Shield

The brunt of the ground warfare in South Vietnam was borne by the combat troops outside of the populated areas, and the bulk of the security for pacification activities was provided by U.S., ARVN, and other allied combat forces in this shield. The following chapter gives an overview of the protective shield in Quang Tri Province.

18

The Shield in a Limited War

May 1968–April 1969

During my orientation into Quang Tri Province and the northern region in May 1968 I quickly realized that I had to become professionally and mentally adjusted to the enormous military campaign that was under way. My earlier preparation had been soundly based. Now the reality had to be understood so that I could become an effective member of MACV and AATTV. The experiences described so far happened mostly in the populated areas. The combat forces of the allies provided an outer protective shield. The following is a snapshot account of the shield in Quang Tri Province.

The NVA had refuge in its base areas on the Laotian border to the west and in North Vietnam above the DMZ. The Tet offensive and the mini Tet were over. Procedural meetings for the peace negotiations in Paris were under way. The Khe Sanh experience caused the military leadership on each side of the conflict to review their respective situations and to decide on some conceptual changes in their methods of operation. Top-down command changes in the U.S. military structures were taking place at the highest level of MACV, at III MAF, and at XXIV Corps. Major General R. G. Davis was appointed to command the 3rd Marine Division in May 1968. Earlier in Washington, Clark Clifford had assumed the appointment as secretary of defense on 1 March 1968, replacing Robert McNamara.

General Davis introduced a new design for battle after assuming command. His scheme was to close with the NVA and provide a continuing shield to the populated areas in Quang Tri for the next twelve months. A higher level of mobility was to be achieved, with less reliance on the fixed defenses of bases. Davis laid down some ground rules for his division: "Unit integrity would be reestablished; not only would organic battalions work with their parent regiments, but this would also apply to normal support units, particularly direct support artillery. Unessential combat bases and strongpoints would be closed, and those that were not closed would be made defendable by no more than one reinforced company. The reconnaissance effort was also to be upgraded, with from 30 to 35 teams to be kept out in the field at all times."[1]

This concept broke away from the anti-infiltration system that had previously influenced marine and ARVN ground operations south of the DMZ. Those advisors who were involved in the counterinsurgency and pacification programs, projects, and operations were to have a closer interface with the units and formations in the shield. Major Casey at the outset had ensured I was given a thorough introduction to the units of the 3rd Marine Division.

The two marine combat support bases between Quang Tri City and Dong Ha town were the first places to be visited by Casey and me. At a medical facility we were informed that 258 casualties had been treated in the previous twenty-four hours. This was my first contact with casualties on this scale. Included among the casualties were NVA soldiers and injured civilians. I noted that war had little to commend itself as a method for settling disputes. The marine dead were moved by vehicle to the local airfield and then flown to Da Nang. From there bodies were flown to a number of destinations in the United States. The bodies of NVA soldiers were buried locally. The ARVN dead were processed by available means to their home areas. The G5 staff at the 3rd Marine Division rear headquarters then welcomed us. Lieutenant Colonel Thompson made it clear, on behalf of the USMC, that the marines were determined to push through with civic aid to the Vietnamese. The point was made that for security reasons Vietnamese were not permitted onto the combat bases.

We visited fire support base C1 on 22 May 1968. This strongpoint was then occupied by the 4/2 Marines. The observers in a tower at C1 were able to point out a suspected NVA bunker across the DMZ, which was probably directing fire into Camp J. J. Carroll. Later that day, at about 4:30 P.M., enemy artillery targeted the 3rd Marine Division base south of Dong Ha. Ammunition points were hit, and secondary explosions and fires resulted. The fires lit up the night sky. Minor shock waves were felt in Quang Tri City.

While the ground war went on, the psychological war was being played out across the globe. In Paris the North Vietnamese delegates were telling the world that the NVA was not in South Vietnam. Hanoi Radio was beaming the same great lie to the South Vietnamese. At the sharp end and above Dong Ha an NVA scout left a message on a roadside advising ARVN soldiers as to how they could surrender. As a countermeasure the 3rd Marine Division arranged a 1 million–leaflet airdrop on likely enemy areas the next day, followed up by voice messages from aircraft. The results of these endeavors are not known.

The USMC had Marine Air Group 39 located at Ai Tu, on the east side of Highway 1, in the Quang Tri Combat Base. I was invited by a helicopter unit to be the group's guest for the night on 22 June 1968. They were good company, with an esprit de corps common to pilots all over. The CO invited me to fly with his squadron. I was not prepared to put that request to my American and Australian commanding officers, as I judged piloting of aircraft to be outside the terms of my present employment. Helicopter squadrons of this kind were providing the battlefield mobility that General Davis needed for his division to close with and disrupt the NVA in Quang Tri. The flexibility helicopters provided enhanced the effectiveness of the shield.

I received an invitation from Major Rusty Hansen in mid-August to join him for an official opening of the officers' club at MAG 39. Warrant Officer Bill Deanshaw came along with me. The commanding officer, Colonel Sienko, explained that the numbers were low in the club as many of his pilots were deployed at that moment on tasks supporting two separate marine rifle elements that were in contact with the enemy. One company was surrounded near Khe Sanh. The aircrew was awaiting a break in the weather so it could fly in supplies and bring out casualties. The other situation involved a marine battalion in contact with the NVA to the west of Gio Linh. Reserve troops were on standby to be flown in as reinforcements. Life for the marines was one of constant action.

For the first week of July the enemy above the DMZ in the coastal plains area was subjected to an intense bombing attack by available U.S. naval and air forces. Operation Thor helped minimize shelling from North Vietnam into Quang Tri, giving relief to the marines and the 2nd ARVN Regiment, based at Dong Ha.[2] During Thor, with a northerly wind prevailing, the shock waves of the blasts could be felt in Quang Tri City, thirty kilometers to the south.

The MACV command changeover of Westmoreland to Abrams

formally occurred on 10 June 1968. As Abrams had been deputy to Westmoreland for about a year, the transition was smooth. Policy decisions to be announced had been flagged quietly with commanders during that time. The closing down of the Khe Sanh combat base in early July 1968 was such an event. Another event of significance in Quang Tri was the arrival of a fresh U.S. Army brigade on 31 July 1968.

The 1st Infantry Brigade, 5th Infantry Division (Mechanized), commenced training and acclimatization to the east of Quang Tri City. Soon they were to deploy to the northeast of Dong Ha, relieving the marines in that area, which included the Gio Linh area. This brigade was a formidable formation numbering more than forty-five hundred troops, grouped into the following units: a mechanized headquarters, the 1/11 Infantry Battalion, the 1/61 Mechanized Infantry Battalion, the 1/77 Armored Battalion, the 5/4 Self-Propelled Artillery Battalion, a support battalion, the 4/12 Cavalry Company, an engineer company, and technical combat service support elements.

With the 2nd ARVN Regiment, the 1/5 Infantry Brigade was to cover the coastal area astride Highway 1 on the south side of the DMZ. This was the most direct land route for the NVA to approach Hue and Da Nang. Another formidable U.S. Army formation was farther to the west, the 1st Air Cavalry Division.[3] Operation Pegasus had tasked the air cavalry, 1st Marines, and the ARVN Rangers to relieve Khe Sanh and open up Route 9. After advancing west for a week from Ca Lu, the link-up was achieved on 6 April. The 1st Brigade of the ACD was in the area of Mai Linh District when I arrived in May.

In August changes were made to some high command positions. On 1 August, General William B. Rosson handed over command of Provisional Corps Vietnam to Major General Stilwell. On 15 August that corps was redesignated XXIV Corps, with Stilwell promoted to Lieutenant General. General Cushman continued as commander of III MAF. The headquarters of III MAF at Camp Horn, near Da Nang, was acting as the command and control center for the equivalent of a field army. In the northern provinces the XXIV Corps headquarters came under the operational control of III MAF. XXIV Corps formations in Quang Tri under operational control were the 3rd Marine Division and the 1/5 Infantry Brigade. This latter brigade, after settling in over July and August, was ready for more demanding operations throughout the province. The brigade had responsibility in the Cua Valley and the DMZ area from 26 August 1968.

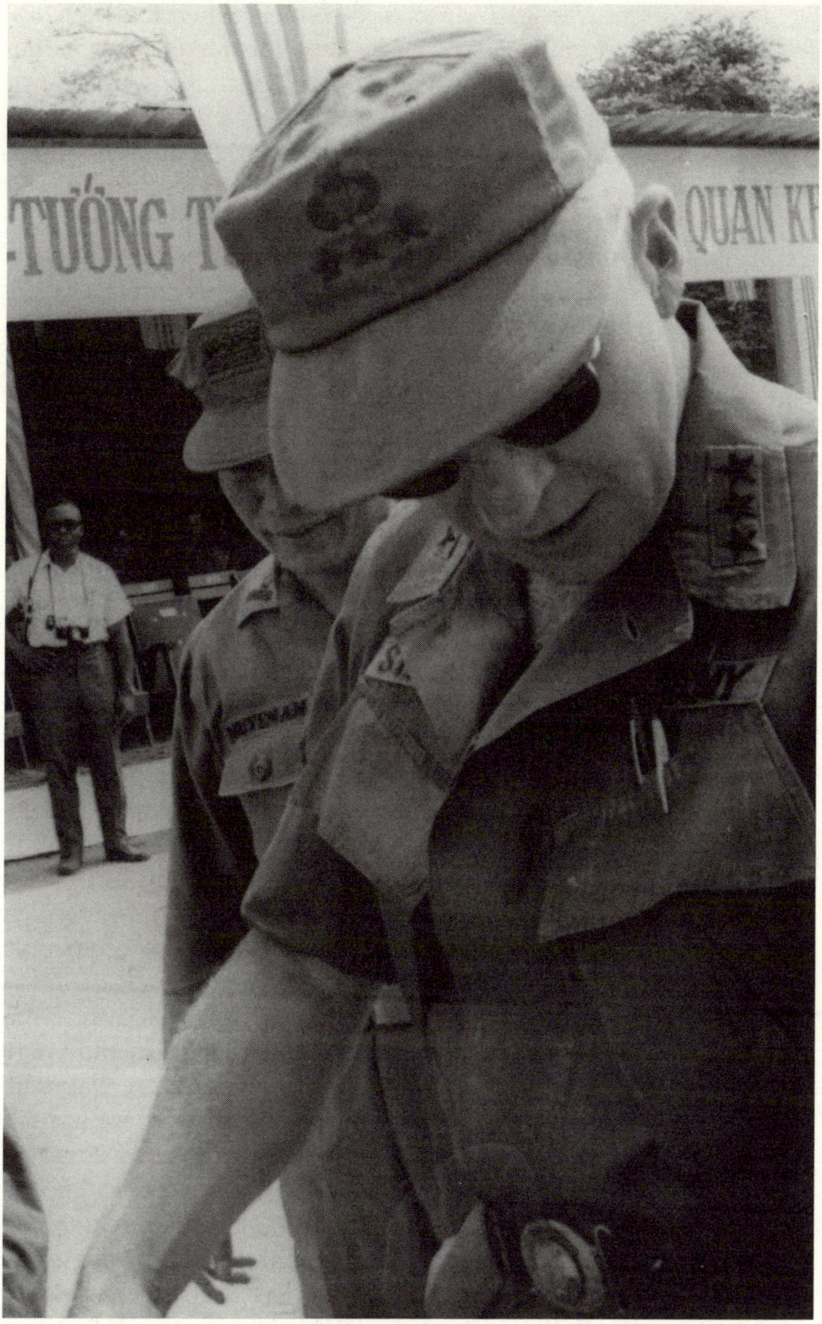

Lieutenant General Richard Stilwell and Colonel Nguyen Am.

Further firepower was added to the shield when the USS *New Jersey* took station off the DMZ on 29 September 1968. This battleship carried nine 16-inch guns and twenty 5-inch guns. The range of the 16-inch guns was about forty kilometers, a naval gunfire fan as far inland as Cam Lo.[4] The *New Jersey* was tasked out of Vietnam waters in March 1969. It is noteworthy that the battleship came out of the mothball fleet in mid-1967, was given an overhaul, and was recommissioned in April 1968. She was decommissioned in December 1969. Due to a U.S. Navy manpower shortage her crew members were needed to man more important ships.[5]

As in most wars, it is the soldiers—particularly the infantry—who bear the brunt. One tragic case reported to me on 17 September involved the marines on the DMZ, northwest of the Rockpile. The day before at 3:30 P.M. 282 rounds of 82 mm mortar fell on a landing zone, killing 21 marines and wounding 150. This was a shock to many.

In an earlier chapter I outlined the events of 1 October, when detailed plans were worked through at Vandegrift for a joint operation. Operation Pegasus had been launched from this site, on Route 9 in April. Route 9 in the Ca Lu area ran in a north-south alignment, with high ground on each side. An airfield capable of operating C-130 transport aircraft was abutting and parallel to Route 9. This forward combat base was essential for the conduct of further marine operations to the west and south. The headquarters for Marine Task Force Hotel, a key element in the shield, was based here. The joint operation was to be conducted in the Cua Valley, to the east of Vandegrift. It made eminent sense for the marines to be satisfied that enemy forces were not swimming in the sea of displaced people living in the relocated Huong Hoa District.

I had an opportunity on 10 October to visit the 3rd Marine Division combined fire support coordination center, which included fire direction and fire support information. This was a very elaborate setup, necessarily so, as it was the hub of control and application for all the firepower available in this sector of operations, covering Quang Tri Province and the abutting areas. It was a clearinghouse for all fire support in the province. At the time the allies had thirty-five battery-equivalent artillery fire units in the area. Naval gunfire support was processed through the center, as well as offensive air support from the flying units of the USAF, USMC, and U.S. Navy. Arc Light strikes by B-52s were also processed by the center. The

Colonel Vu Van Giai, 2nd ARVN Regiment, and Mr. John Cleary, CORDS.

center had overlays of all areas covered by the various fire plans that were current. It stretched the imagination to take in all the firepower available. For the NVA artillery, ranges were 27,000 meters for 152 mm guns, 17,000 meters for 130 mm guns, and from 9,000 to 11,000 meters for rockets. Enemy artillery was capable of causing damage in the northern areas of the province. Comparative ranges for the U.S. artillery are listed in Appendix B.

My visiting the center arose from a concern expressed by the district chief at Cam Lo, via the district senior advisor, Major Bill Healy. The district chief was unhappy that requests cleared by him for fire support in his district could be subject to veto by Lieutenant Colonel Giai, the commanding officer of the 2nd ARVN Regiment. Following my visit to the coordination center I had to advise Healy that the district chief would need to accept the status quo. The 2nd Regiment was part of the shield, and Giai had more clout in military matters and in Vietnamese affairs than a district chief. A later fruitful outcome from my visit to the center was that two of the duty officers came from Dong Ha to the Citadel to discuss artillery procedural matters that were of concern to them. A cruel paradox was that the firepower available to the NVA and Viet Cong was like a relatively "bare cupboard" compared to the military force that they were against. On my hypothetical table of comparison, say on a scale of 100, the allies in the South could be at 90, excluding nuclear, to the NVA and Viet Cong at about 20. Despite this, the North Vietnamese persisted heroically.

I wrote up reflective notes on 12 October. One was about the effectiveness of U.S. firepower against the NVA. The pressure of the shield preserved a military status quo due to firepower, more so than numerical relative strengths. The NVA and its deployed troops in South Vietnam always had the option to withdraw to Laos or North Vietnam if the pressure on them was too threatening. They knew that pursuit could not be exercised by the allies due to the rule of engagement that did not permit U.S. land operations across international borders.

The forward operational base at Ca Lu/Vandegrift/Rockpile appeared to be as vulnerable as the now abandoned Khe Sanh base. There was high ground in the area that may have been tempting for the NVA to occupy. The mobile operations now being applied by General Davis were likely to keep the NVA off balance. Concurrently, should the NVA occupy high ground for tactical reasons, the full weight of the allied artillery and airpower could be applied against it, in a devastating manner. I concluded that a military solution to the war, as seen from Quang Tri, would be a near impossibility to achieve under the conditions prevailing.

Generally wars of the past were based more on the control of terrain and territory. In 1968 in South Vietnam it was now a psychological battle as well as a land battle, with a political battle being waged around a table in Paris and elsewhere. The political and the psychological were being influenced also by public opinion on the home fronts. Arguably the land, air, and sea battle had been won by the U.S. forces and the ARVN in 1968, but there was more to this war than the battle area of South Vietnam.

The shield forces were advised late in October that the ACD was to go south. This made sense, as the air mobile concept was best suited to battlefield circumstances that matched the capability. Operation Pegasus earlier in the year was such an example. Usually ground was not held, as the destruction of the enemy was the main object. With the units generally being lightly equipped, it was not desirable for them to stay in one area for too long a period. Further, because the formation had a large number of helicopters organic to the division, there was an imperative for these high-value assets to be utilized. The division needed to be kept moving. In Quang Tri, the area that had been the responsibility of the ACD now had to be covered by the 3rd Marine Division, the 1/5 Infantry Brigade, and the two ARVN Regiments.

I visited the operations staff at the 1/5 Infantry Brigade headquarters on 4 November and had discussions with the S3. The staff had experienced a rigorous orientation, having worked up for the whole gamut of limited war in Quang Tri: the shield (main forces), the counterinsurgency, and the pacification. An artillery officer from the 1/5 Infantry Brigade came to see me at the Citadel on 7 November. He was seeking to register targets for harassing and interdiction fire programs. One of his goals was to keep the U.S. Navy employed, as the staffs were concerned that warships could be redeployed farther south, resulting in a reduction in indirect fire support. The COMUSMACV General Abrams had another view; restraint in the use of firepower was being encouraged. To that end the battleship *New Jersey* was taken off station in March 1969.

A week later the S3 of 1/5 Infantry Brigade came by to advise of a three-battalion operation in the area of Thuong Xa, a village five kilometers to the southeast of Quang Tri City on the east side of Highway 1. The next day, 15 November, Colonel Mooney and Lieutenant Colonel Nhan visited the brigade headquarters to discuss the concept. A full briefing was to be held there the following day. At the briefing the brigade commander, Colonel Richard Glikes, informed the group that participating units in a cordon and search operation would be the 1/11 Infantry Battalion, the 1/9 Marines, and two battalions of the 1st ARVN Regiment. The marines were not represented at the briefing, which immediately raised the role of guides for 1/9 Marines once they arrived by helicopter at the landing zone. The village of Than Mai Dong on the other side of the highway was to be included in this cordon. It was clear by the end of the day that liaison and communication between all players needed to be improved.

On 17 November I made another visit to the brigade headquarters for final coordination of the operation. Colonel Hanh, the commanding officer of the 1st ARVN Regiment, was at that time conducting a briefing twenty kilometers south for the battalions and district chiefs (Mai Linh and Hai Lang) on the same operation. Sector level advisors were now in the role of responding to questions related to this operation, mainly coordination detail, such as boundaries and Vietnamese field headquarter locations. There were important benefits arising from this operation, as Operation Fisher was well under way farther to the north and northeast. Our southern flank was being covered, which was very reassuring. Later that day the commanding officer of the 1/9 Marines visited and some issues were clarified. The 3rd Marine Division was arranging the helicopter lift of his battalion to the landing zone, which was to be secured by a platoon of the 1/5 Infantry Brigade. The guides were to be provided by Territorial Force troops from Hai Lang District.

I visited the information center on 18 November with Lieutenant Colonel Nhan. All units involved in the operation had deployed. An underlying concern of U.S. commanders in joint deployments was security. When American units worked with ARVN units there was a view that early notice of intentions gave opportunities for the VC/VCI to be warned of the operation. Much earlier General Davis had expressed this concern, observing that he would prefer for U.S. troops to deploy first, and then to advise the Vietnamese authorities. This approach relied upon one commander for each phase of the operation. In my time in Quang Tri I do not think this ideal was achieved for a joint operation.

The operation at Thuong Xa ran for several days. I do not have a record of the results of this joint operation. On 22 November I accompanied the PSA on a visit to the combined information center at the headquarters of the jump command post of the 1/5 Infantry Brigade. The 1/11 Battalion was to leave the cordon that day, with the 1/9 Marines maintaining the cordon at the northern end. Mooney discussed future intentions with Colonel Glikes, who agreed to a further operation to the east on Route 555, south of the hamlet of Co Luy.

Smaller cordon and search joint operations were conducted over the last week of November in Trieu Phong and Mai Linh districts. In December two additional cordon and search operations were conducted in Hai Lang. At each, information centers were established, but not cleverly. In the first case the 192 people detained (including children) had to walk six kilometers to the center. Representatives of the DOICC and Phoenix were not in attendance at the center. Generals Stilwell and Truong visited each of these operations. The 1st ARVN Regiment and the 1/5 Infantry Brigade were involved in the two operations. For more than twenty years the local people had lived under a succession of military administrations. One wondered where their allegiance rested now, and in the future.

To see out the year, a combined information center was established at Tich Tuong, four kilometers south of the city, near La Vang, to support a joint operation involving RF/PF/NPFF and a battalion each from the 1st ARVN Regiment and the 1/5 Infantry Brigade. During this operation a U.S. soldier was killed by a booby trap and a suspected VC was taken into custody.

The commanding officer of the 1/5 Infantry Brigade was doing his best to facilitate a better working relationship with the Territorial Forces leadership (Lieutenant Colonel Nhan and his staff) and the ARVN regiments. This was a critical time for the Vietnamese, as it was clear that with the marines gradually thinning out and the air cavalry no longer in Quang Tri, they could well be on their own soon. During the preparations for another "block and search" joint operation an information center was involved, with Lieutenant Colonel Nhan conducting a sound briefing for representatives of all units and agencies involved. The perseverance displayed by Glikes was paying off. At the end of December Colonel Richard Glikes handed over command of the brigade to Colonel James Gibson.

By the end of January the 1/5 Infantry Brigade units were in contact with the NVA in Base Area 101. Lieutenant Colonel Wallace was keen to keep in contact with the headquarters of the brigade. Captain Nong (sector S3) and I went to Quang Tri Combat Base to catch up with brigade staff officers. The liaison was worthwhile. It was clear the 1/5 Infantry Brigade was now participating in serious combat against the NVA in the shield to the north and to the west.

Within the shield, counterinsurgency and pacification work was continued by the Territorial Forces and civil agencies, supported by the advisory network. At this time the GVN claimed control of 69 percent of the villages and hamlets in Quang Tri. These assessments indicated that there might be some hope for the Vietnamese to have a future based on freedom, rather than totalitarianism.

Along with the rough and tumble of military operations, some positive personal interactions occurred, making life a little easier for a few, for a short time. One such event involved Captain Williams, a U.S. Army advisor with the Cam Lo District advisory team. Williams had a brother serving in the USMC who was deployed with the 2/4 Marines. This battalion was north of Cam Lo, responsible for security along a fourteen-kilometer frontage on the DMZ. The headquarters for the 2/4 Marines was at Con Thien. Williams asked if I could get him to Con Thien so he could have a short time with his brother. There were good operational reasons for such a visit, as his district and Quang Tri sector could become fully aware of the situation further north. So, after receiving the necessary clearances we helicoptered in on 4 February. Williams met his brother, and I was to see and hear of the operations that were under way.

Four marine rifle companies were all deployed into their respective areas of operation on the DMZ. One platoon defended the A4 base. The companies each set up squad-sized patrols, setting ambushes in such a way as to achieve contact if there was NVA infiltration. There had been no contact during the previous twenty-four hours. Artillery support was guaranteed, up to 8-inch guns being available. Rules of engagement allowed patrolling up to the Ben Hai River. Ground navigation was not easy due to the terrain and vegetation. A ready reaction rifle company was on standby at Vandegrift should any reinforcement be required. A rifle platoon of the company was at the ready, to be flown in as an immediate response, with the balance of the company to follow. We returned to Cam Lo happier and wiser. We agreed that the marines had to be admired for the sacrifices and sufferings experienced in the course of their duties on the DMZ.

The ARVN regiments in Quang Tri were highly regarded, but suffered trials and tribulations similar to those of their allies. On the night of 13 March 1969 a company of the 3/2 ARVN was subjected to a sapper attack, suffering twenty soldiers killed, fifty-four wounded, and ten missing in action. Opinion was that a relatively small group of sappers had been involved in the assault, possibly assisted by an inside element of VC sympathizers. Another downside for the ARVN was the smoking of marijuana by soldiers in the field. Advisors reported that smokers could be identified by a look at their eyes. Hunger was considered to be the main reason for smoking the drug, with the soldiers freely admitting to its use.

A liaison visit to the headquarters of the 1/5 Infantry Brigade revealed that six battalions were presently under its operational control: 3/3 Marines, 3/5 Marines, 1st Amtrak Battalion (Marines), and brigade battalions 1/11, 1/61, and 1/77. The area of operations extended from the coast to Ca Lu, a distance of about eighty kilometers. A direct support artillery battery of self-propelled 105 mm guns was deployed into the Cua Valley. The balance of the 3rd Marine Division was operating up to the Laotian border and to the south in the Da Krong Valley, supported from Vandegrift.

In mid-March I made another visit to headquarters 1/5 Infantry Brigade to brief on Operation Kangaroo, the Cam Vu operation near to Dong Ha. There was a sector need for a shield reaction force should the security situation get beyond the resources of the Territorial Forces committed to the operation. While recognizing the commitments of the brigade, an agreement was reached for the 3/5 Marines to be allocated to this task. Our advisors at Cam Vu were pleased to receive this news. One limitation on the task was that a rehearsal would not be undertaken, as it was judged that it could compromise the plan.

My next visit to the 1/5 Infantry Brigade headquarters, then at the Quang Tri Combat Base, was with my replacement, Major Harry Bell, on 6 April. The next day Harry and I drove down to La Vang, the home of the 1st ARVN Regiment, to meet the regimental commander, the commanding officer of the 11th ARVN Artillery, and the senior advisors with those units. Australian advisors of the Team were members of the MACV advisory teams supporting the various ARVN units there.

Also at La Vang was the command post of the 1/77 Armored Battalion of the 1/5 Infantry Brigade. The commanding officer, Lieutenant Colonel Milia, was just back from leave and was preparing to go farther west to join his task force. He explained that his unit had taken up its own bridging going west along Route 9. The colonel went on to say the brigade had been regrouped to cover a frontage to the DMZ, allowing the 3rd Marine Division to keep in the mountains to the far west. The task force organization of units by the 1/5 Infantry Brigade was appropriate for the prevailing conditions. It permitted balanced forces to work as required in their areas of operation. My last visit to the brigade headquarters was on 13 April. The final staff matter I considered there was to do with herbicide operations, as outlined in chapter 13.

The main body of the 3rd Marine Division was committed to the Laotian border area now, and the 1/5 Infantry Brigade was becoming familiar with its operational area. General Davis had commenced mountaintop fire base operations after the Khe Sanh area had been cleaned out by the USMC. To ensure the Khe Sanh area was clear of the NVA, Operations Robin North and Robin South were conducted in the first half of June 1968, mainly against the 308th NVA Division. These operations confirmed also that the 304th NVA Division had withdrawn. Khe Sanh was evacuated by 5 July. Camp J. J. Carroll was deactivated by 28 December 1968.

By late 1968 it was known that the NVA was building up in the southwest corner of Quang Tri. This was in the Da Krong Valley in what was described as Base Area 611. Two major operations were conducted in this western area by the marines during the first quarter of 1969, using fire support bases in this mountainous and forested area to support multi-battalion marine deployments. Operation Dewey Canyon ran from 22 January 1969 to 19 March 1969. Large enemy caches were found and destroyed. Operation Maine Crag was then launched, from 15 March to 2 May, in the area south of Khe Sanh. To complete this round of mobile operations, Operation Virginia Ridge was conducted above Cam Lo toward the DMZ at the end of April 1969.[6]

As an example of the intensity of these operations, in the first month of Dewey Canyon the 9th Marines killed approximately eight hundred NVA soldiers. Marine casualties were one hundred killed and five hundred wounded in action. A mass burial site was discovered, revealing the bodies of 185 NVA soldiers. It was thought that these deaths were caused by B-52 strikes on 4 February 1969. Captured NVA hardware included two 122 mm towed artillery guns, one 12.7 mm wheeled antiaircraft vehicle, and one five-tonne tracked prime mover.

These operations by the friendly forces in the shield were providing the security for the Vietnamese authorities to get on with counterinsurgency and pacification without enemy main force interference. VC military activity in the populated areas was minimal. The counterinsurgency effort and pacification initiatives were having a positive effect, protected by the shield. The people and the ARVN were soon to see the gradual thinning out of the U.S. forces. Concurrently they were being kept abreast of the Paris Peace Talks. The future of South Vietnam was taking an uncertain direction in 1969, which was further reinforced by the phased withdrawal of the 3rd Marine Division, with thinning out commencing in mid-1969.

In summary, two U.S. military formations provided long and meritorious service in Quang Province. The 3rd Marine Division landed in Vietnam at Da Nang in May 1965, deploying to Quang Tri in July 1966. The three years in Quang Tri were hard not only for the division, but also for III MAF and the USMC as a whole. The other major entity was the 1st Brigade, 5th Infantry Division (Mechanized), which arrived in Quang Tri in July 1968. By the end of 1969 an allied regrouping was executed, as a response to the withdrawal of the marines from Quang Tri. Additional units included three ARVN battalions, a fourth battalion for the 1/5 Infantry Brigade, and two airmobile battalions of the 101st Airborne Division. Redeployment of the 1/5 Infantry Brigade back to the United States commenced in July 1971.

On 6 April 1969, Mr. Green, Under Secretary of State for Far Eastern Affairs, came to Quang Tri to be briefed on past and present security. The briefers were General Davis and Colonel Mooney. In very simple and clear terms the general gave an excellent presentation, covering points earlier described in this chapter. He was able to describe the advantages of helicopter mobility, firepower, and enemy intelligence as the key, not the holding of terrain. In detail he described the fire support base concept with infantry company deployments in battalion or brigade areas of operations, and the positive results achieved. The consequences of the prohibition of crossing the international borders by our land forces were highlighted. For sound political reasons the American president imposed this leg iron on the U.S. ground forces. The NVA took full advantage of this geographic limitation by establishing safe havens across the border in Laos. Despite this limitation, the conclusion was that the present U.S. concept of operations must cause the NVA to reevaluate its own methods of operation. Mooney and I left the briefing wondering if Mr. Green had understood the presentation.

For the combat soldiers, knowing that if you became a casualty you would be treated well and quickly was a key morale issue. I saw enough of the medical system from battlefield evacuation to hospitalization to be able to reach an opinion that it was first-class. The casualty evacuation system operating in Quang Tri was comprehensive and around the clock. One special component was the work of the hospital ships. The USS *Repose* and USS *Sanctuary* were tasked offshore during my time there. On two occasions I visited the *Repose.* Captain John Drew was in command of the ship. On one occasion he kindly guided me all over the ship during a daily round, including the hospital component. The hospital had a maximum capacity of up to 700 cases, working best at 450 cases. The captain explained that when on station with *Sanctuary* there was more flexibility with case management. Staff included sufficient doctors, thirty to forty nurses, and two Red Cross people. One CH-46 USMC helicopter arrived while I was on board the *Repose.* Six battle casualties from the 9th Marines on Operation Dewey Canyon were received. Four dead were taken off. The death rate of patients on board was 3 to 4 percent. From the *Repose,* patients would be flown to Da Nang for further treatment and processing.

The shield was a mighty effort by all involved, whether on the ground, in the air, or at sea. The combat power applied by the allied shield was far superior to that of the North Vietnamese Army. The regime in North Vietnam faced significant capability deficiencies while U.S. military forces were involved in Quang Tri, on the DMZ, and in the Laotian border area to the west.

My story now moves back to mid-August 1968, when Lieutenant Colonel Harley F. Mooney arrived in Quang Tri to take up the appointment of deputy province senior advisor. As the narrative unfolded I realized that the significance of his performance as province senior advisor deserved special consideration. I also judged a study of his role as a commander and leader would help complete my memorable story within Team 19 in Quang Tri Province, South Vietnam.

19

Colonel Harley F. Mooney Leads the Way

August 1968–April 1969

What are the qualities required of a commander in a multicultural, multidisciplined conflict environment? Character, leadership skills, knowledge, experience, skills in the organization of people, common sense, communication skills, adaptability, diplomacy, management skills, and abilities as a teacher and mentor may be some of the key qualities. Professionalism of a high order is an essential ingredient. A province senior advisor needed to be a master of facilitation to motivate and bring together a committed group of people from a variety of cultures, to achieve goals set by two governments, the United States and the GVN. In Quang Tri Province, on the DMZ, Colonel Mooney was the leader of a province advisory team at the interface with a monolithic North Vietnam. We were constantly aware of the prospect that our goal of preserving the nation-state of South Vietnam might not be achieved.

Lieutenant Colonel Harley Mooney, U.S. Army, arrived in Quang Tri on 14 August 1968. He was to take up the appointment of deputy province senior advisor (DPSA), replacing Lieutenant Colonel Thrasher, who was completing his tour of duty in Vietnam. Over the next eight months we were to develop a close commander/staff officer relationship, one that was professionally effective and personally rewarding for me. I have judged that his efforts and achievements deserve particular recognition in this narrative.

A "Stand To" was ordered at the MACV compound on 15 August when a small arms firefight broke out at the hamlet of Tram Ly, three kilometers to the east. The uniformed people moved in a desultory manner to their positions. There was a careless attitude to what should have been a smart drill. The colonel was not impressed with the turnout of all ranks. He kept his counsel for a later day.[1]

Mooney held a military staff meeting for Team 19 after lunch on 17 August, having waited for Thrasher to depart, a matter of courtesy. He gave the assembly a comprehensive briefing on the role of the advisory team, covering also his ways of doing business and his aims. His approach was refreshing, a new broom, which I interpreted as an intention to revitalize the newly designated Team 19, excised from Advisory Team 4, the 1st ARVN Division advisory team.

This was Mooney's third tour in Vietnam. His wife was at home caring for their five children. Such were the demands on the U.S. military and their families. Mooney's style was impressive from the start, and he energized the staff. His predecessor was not as firm or as decisive. Our new leader showed he was all of that and more. On his second day in Quang Tri Mooney visited Mai Linh District headquarters with the deputy commander of XXIV Corps, Major General Drake. This was my first formal contact with these two leaders. After three months I was well and truly settled into my position as a district senior advisor and looked forward to the discussions that were about to commence. Preparing for the visit, I had encouraged my counterparts, Captain Phong and his staff, to take part in the briefing and discussions with members of my advisory team. The meeting ran for an hour, with the visitors being satisfied with the session. Mooney advised me later of a comment by the general: "I liked the style and the presentations." All at Mai Linh were pleased to receive this feedback.

A further routine staff change came about on 18 August. Major John Hannon came from Cam Lo sub-sector to be sector operations advisor and the Team 19 plans and operations officer. Major Bill Healy, on an in-country change of appointment, replaced Hannon. Within a month I was to succeed Hannon.

During August, in a letter to Eva, I endeavored to describe the impact Colonel Mooney was having on his team with his leadership style: "Mooney is really making his presence felt, and he has got a lot of people thinking. That is a positive. My end is OK and I hope it stays that way." At the end of August I recorded: "DPSA Mooney is still pushing the staff and some thoughts are that he may not get the PSA job. Military, CORDS and Vietnamese channels are all at work over the Brewer successor. The developments will be interesting."

Lieutenant Colonel Mooney came to Mai Linh District to congratulate the district chief and the advisors on the outcome of a recent contact with the enemy. The visit followed a PF operation where three platoons were involved, with seven VC killed. The two of us then sat down for a long conversation, with Mooney doing most of the talking. Naturally, he was anxious about the confirmation of his succession as the PSA. He had undertaken special training in the United States to fill such an appointment. I was hoping he would be appointed. He was waiting for Brewer to leave. One operational matter that we agreed on was that the USMC Combined Action Program procedure of having an area of operations for platoons was not sound. For the time being this was an operational anomaly that we had to live with.

I had lunch with Mooney and a U.S. chaplain, Father Anderson, of the Benedictine Order, on 3 September. We then went to the colonel's room, as he obviously wanted to have people to talk to in confidence. Mooney really let off steam over some of his frustrations. He had our sympathetic ears, and minds, and we each felt richer by the dialogue. Mooney was clearly a passionate man in private, and in public played the role of the leader in command.

As covered in chapter 8, my appointment to the planning and operations position in Team 19 at the sector headquarters level was approved on 9 September. I was happy about that, as was Mooney. My involvement started immediately, John Hannon handing over his responsibilities to me on 11 September. I now had to perform. I wrote home saying: "As you can imagine the colonel is one for details, and I think I can keep up with him."

Two small actions by Mooney gave me an insight into his temperament in mid-September. The first was about a helicopter booking that was made for him to visit Camp Evans, near Hue. It got fouled up, causing him to cancel the appointment. However, it actually suited him not to go, as he was anxious to have a meeting with Bob Brewer. Nevertheless, he let all and sundry know of the no-show by the helicopter. Second, he was putting pressure on local civilian CORDS staff. They had quietly showed their displeasure toward him by not embracing some of the sector activities planned in their respective areas of responsibility. This was a disappointment and surprising, as what was being expected of them was consistent with policies that were emanating from MACVCORDS in Saigon and were in accord with GVN policies. This did not augur well for some in regard to their future in Quang Tri.

Mooney showed his private thinking on a major issue in the province. The district of Huong Hoa was overrun in January 1968 by the NVA. The GVN administration decided to keep the district alive, in name at least, by reestablishing its presence in the Cua Valley south of Cam Lo. The Americans were to meet the bill, leading Mooney to say: "Nothing is too good for Huong Hoa, and that's what they have been getting." Thereafter more attention was given to the struggling district of Huong Hoa.

It was customary for Team 19 to have a meeting every two weeks for all of the staff who could attend, military and civilian. The briefings and discussions had become rambling and tedious. Mooney was not happy with the format and asked me for suggestions on how to improve the meeting content and order of business. As we each knew how a battalion commander conducted meetings, I responded along those lines, as the model was proven and could be adapted to meet our local needs. Thus the stage management of these gatherings was changed to a new model. It worked and Mooney was happy, as was the staff—and I also.

On 13 September in a letter to Eva, I wrote:

> My main concern at present is that Mooney does not pressure himself out of the PSA's job. He is the deputy at the moment. The present PSA [Brewer] is due to go home next month. He has some powerful friends on his side from lieutenant generals down. Mooney's opposition is probably from the civilian side, possibly the State Department in particular. Brewer is a CIA man. We will know of the new appointments in a matter of weeks.[2]
>
> Mooney is a determined man, very quick mentally, exercises sound judgement and is sharp in his decision making. He is critical of both the civil and military efforts here, and naturally the civilians do not like having themselves criticised. He is a good man to work for and with.

In mid-September Mooney told me he had a bad back, which was giving him severe discomfort from time to time. He said to me: "I admired Jack Kennedy for his endurance with the back condition he had."

My earlier military education, experience, and reading had prepared me for the role I now had to play. General John Monash, a leading Australian commander of World War I, had set the tone for Australian staff officers: meticulous attention to detail in the planning, preparation, and conduct of operations.[3] A week later I wrote, "All is well in the new job. The colonel is really a live wire and very refreshing. So far I have kept up with him and hope to continue to do so." I noted: "My routine has not yet been reestablished, so everything I seem to do is rushed. I will have to get a grip on myself in the next few days and concentrate on the important things."

The senior CORDS official in the region, Ambassador Cross, came up from Da Nang for a visit. In conversation I suggested to him and Mooney that consideration could be given to making the senior advisor position in Mai Linh District a civilian post. I came to that view as the assistance needed in the district was predominantly of a civil nature. The Territorials were in my opinion competent. Here was an opportunity for the United States to demonstrate to the local authorities that the time had come for them to assume greater responsibility for their affairs. The idea was tabled, with a military person continuing in the role, no change.

Before Mooney was confirmed as the next PSA I was invited to a long chat with him. He was in a pessimistic frame of mind at that moment. He expressed a view that after the cessation of the war in Vietnam the United States might tend toward being isolationist, with a significantly reduced army. He thought that there would be a reduction in the size of the officer corps, with many to be made redundant should a significant downsizing take place. He went on to say, as a talking point: "Let's declare a victory, a success, and leave it to the South Vietnamese, Thailand, Korea, and Australia to sort out the future of this country." Mooney's was a proverbial voice in the wilderness.

Team 19 was formally advised on 23 September that Mooney was to be the PSA, beginning on 1 October. The staff officers of the team in particular were pleased with that announcement. I was delighted. However, the colonel was inclined to be subdued, especially in the evenings over the next few days. Unfortunately, Brewer kept some crucial information to himself, probably sensitive CIA matters. By not taking Mooney fully into his confidence Brewer was judged negatively on this matter by the staff at my level. We respected the "need-to-know" rule, but we were disappointed that there were some gaps in the handover.[4]

In a letter home on 24 September, I wrote: "The work is demanding but I am thoroughly enjoying my new job. It is exhilarating. New experiences come each day. Mooney keeps the morale up. The sector team is now to a point where we are beginning to see the difference from where we were six weeks ago and to where we can aim for in the future."

On the first day in his new appointment I saw Mooney performing at his best. The events of that day have been described in chapter 8. A State Department officer, Terry McNamara, arrived on 13 October to take up the post of deputy province senior advisor. This was a fortuitous time for Mooney, as McNamara would be taking up the responsibility for the CORDS elements of our MACCORDS team.

We needed to travel to Hue on 28 October for a meeting with Mr. Cross, but our direct support helicopter was not available. Road travel was the only way to solve our problem. To my knowledge, Highway 1 traffic to Hue usually involved armored vehicles only. Up to this day administrative traffic to Hue was judged to be out of the question due to uncertain security. We were going to put to the test the notion developing post-Tet 1968 that the enemy forces had suffered a serious military setback and were not a dominant threat, especially in the coastal areas. The PSA was determined to attend the meeting. Two vehicles were organized for our party of four, Mooney and I in one, and Hal Cottrell and his driver in the other. In effect we were testing not only the condition of Highway 1, but also the security, especially from Hai Lang to Hue. We carried flack jackets, weapons, ammunition, and radio communications. The distance was thirty-five miles (fifty-six kilometers). The main security and safety issues in the forefront of our minds were buried mines, booby traps, ambush, and an enemy contact of some sort.

During the journey we found the road to be cut up. There was no sign of any recent maintenance. We were relieved that the weather conditions were dry, as it would have been impassable in the wet. The journey to Hue took an uneventful one hundred minutes. The weather in Hue was perfect. The city had a charm, but had not yet recovered from the severe fighting experienced over a number of weeks in February, the Tet offensive period. Mooney had pleasure in describing our journey to the assembly. He had a point to make about security. There is nothing to match a personal eyewitness account.

While we were in Hue the intended relocation of the Air Cavalry Division (ACD) from the north to the southern area of South Vietnam was announced. The PSA said that General Truong, commander of the 1st ARVN Division, when advised of the pending deployment, looked like he had been hit by a bucket of offal slops. The ACD had worked closely with the ARVN in the two northern provinces. Troung quickly understood the security implications of such a move. We felt for him and his people. Our return road journey was without incident. This day was logged as a very interesting one.

Any visitors who came to Quang Tri City had a meeting with Mooney if his schedule permitted. He could lay on the charm and provide a gripping narrative of the situation in his area of responsibility. His briefs were modified to fit the background and responsibility of the visitor. If there was a chance of gaining some benefit for his advisory team or for the province, he would argue a persuasive case. One such visitor was the commanding officer of the marine shore party, on 29 October. With the 1st ACD leaving Quang Tri, a shortfall in helicopter lift capacity was inevitable. The USMC in Quang Tri was an obvious possible future supplier of helicopter support. Aerial resupply was a hot issue at this time due to the weather conditions. Our particular concern then was about Huong Hoa District to the west. The PSA made our needs known to the shore party leader.

Visiting journalists were given an opportunity to meet the PSA. An earlier visit by Creighton Burns has already been described. On 3 December Joseph Alsop, a syndicated American columnist, had a discussion with Mooney. On 19 December Bob Jones, of NBC News, arrived for a story on Operation Fisher. Then on 14 April 1969 the PSA and Dick Cummings had a joint discussion with *Time* magazine reporter Burton Pines.

Whenever a senior officer was departing Quang Tri, Colonel Mooney was more relaxed and expressed his appreciation of their contributions. Lieutenant Colonel Davis, the 3rd Marine Division G3 plans officer, was concluding his third tour of Vietnam, and the PSA invited me to join them for a light lunch at his residence. It was a pleasant interlude to the daily routine. Davis was to complete his military service in the United States and was then to settle in South Africa.

Monthly reports caused us to concentrate our minds. Some of the contributors to the report had difficulty in writing their story. I was introduced to the term "murder board," where draft reports were worked over. Within a short time I was able to grasp what Mooney required. Within a few months, however, the deputy province advisor and the senior sector advisor were carrying the presentation responsibilities of the monthly report.

By early November 1968 I discerned that the PSA was employing a gentle psychological campaign on me, trying to get me to extend my tour of duty. This gave my ego a boost, as I appreciated that we were working well together as a team. It obviously was a tempting prospect to continue to work in a challenging appointment and place for a longer term. Without consulting the commanding officer of the AATTV, I decided the issue had to be quickly resolved. My Australian successor in the Team had probably been identified. My wife and family were expecting me home after a year away. My next appointment in the Australian Army was probably already in train. It was hoped that the Paris Peace Talks could come to some kind of settlement during 1969. So, on balance, I decided to decline Colonel Mooney's invitation. He graciously accepted my point of view.

A visit to the PSA by a senior officer of the 525th Military Intelligence Group on 6 November raised some eyebrows among the advisory staff.[5] The visitor asked me on his arrival where he could find Colonel Mooney. He was full of nervous energy while he explained that it was a very important issue that he wanted to discuss with Mooney. He was not smiling when he was going through these preliminaries. The advisory staff did not receive any feedback from the PSA on the visit. There was no point in speculating, as there was plenty of work going on to keep advisors busy, and clearly the exchange was on a need-to-know basis. It was more than a year later when I received a letter from my successor, Major Harry Bell, that a possible link could be made on some issue related to the military intelligence visitor. Formal U.S. investigations during 1969 revealed that certain American advisors and some Vietnamese military officers were involved in selling U.S. aid material on the local market. This was disappointing to read but not a surprise.

Some Team 19 people had not yet reached an understanding of the team culture. I was not familiar with the formal process of integrating U.S. civilians into the joint organization of MACV. For civilians going through the process on the job it was hard work. Some military people also found the going difficult in a multidisciplined organization. Three examples follow. The case of Ted Law, discussed in chapter 9, fitted into this work culture theme. Second, at an evening staff meeting at the sector headquarters, the Phoenix coordinator, a CIA person, had a stand-up difference of opinion with Colonel Mooney. To most of us present this was judged to be poor form. The Phoenix man did not have the wit to avoid a public confrontation. I thought it would have been prudent for him to have bided his time and sought a private meeting with the PSA. The general view among the military staff advisors was that the Phoenix man had put his tenure at Quang Tri at risk. Another well-intended officer, a major employed in the psychological warfare branch, received a jolt when a leaflet he presented for consideration was criticized. He informed the assembly that it had taken him three months to produce the item. He deservedly received a word of caution from Mooney.

The PSA said to me one morning in November that he had been listening the previous evening to a radio broadcast of cricket. He explained that he could not understand the cryptographic-like broadcast. So, at the evening staff meeting I commenced a brief introduction to cricket to help the Americans become better informed about the game. Player locations on the field were explained at a second session. Bill Deanshaw had crafted a bat to demonstrate the art of hitting the ball. A comparison with baseball was noted. Interest was not high. Cultural differences were accepted in this difficult and remote part of the world. There were no further sessions on the great game of cricket.

The general idea of a proposed joint ARVN/Territorial Forces/ Marine Corps operation in the populated area to the north of Dong Ha was passed to the sector headquarters. The proposal led to a 14 November liaison visit to Colonel Spark, the commanding officer of the 3rd Marine Regiment, at Camp Carroll, to the southwest of Cam Lo. Major Paul Laski, the sector S2 advisor, and I accompanied Colonel Mooney. From that location we proceeded by helicopter to the 2nd ARVN Regiment headquarters at Dong Ha. The marines were keen to conduct a cordon operation at Ha Thanh with the ARVN. The hamlet was north of Dong Ha, astride Highway 1 and the railway line, three kilometers south of the Gio Linh District headquarters. Paul Laski was of the view that the intelligence preparation was poor, being based on minimal evidence. He advised Colonel Mooney that from the sector point of view there were insufficient grounds for the sector to be involved in the operation. We flew Colonel Spark back to Camp Carroll and proceeded back to the Citadel. The proposed cordon of Ha Thanh did not proceed. The marine intention was consistent with MACV and GVN national policies, but had been critiqued and not supported. Joint clear and hold operations were being encouraged, but there had to be a justification to mount such an operation.

On or about 20 November 1968, Lieutenant Colonel Mooney was promoted to the rank of colonel. All ranks were pleased for the PSA. The promotion of Mooney was important for our team. He was a proven leader of fine character, and he had a thorough understanding on the conduct of operations required in this war.

The PSA had me accompany him to Huong Hoa District on 27 November. On arrival he gave the district senior advisor there a pep talk on operations and the general slackness that seemed to prevail. It was evident that the marine network had passed back some observations and commentary to Mooney about security in the Huong Hoa area. The message, commander to subordinate, was for the district senior advisor to lift his performance. Significantly, there was a lack of information about the enemy in the area. One way to rectify this was for the military elements in the valley to increase patrolling in order to establish enemy dispositions and intentions. The district senior advisor was urged to get the military forces in his area to be more active and less passive.

Thanksgiving Day was given due recognition by Colonel Mooney, who hosted a luncheon for invited guests: Colonel Am and his wife, Lieutenant Colonel Nhan and his wife, Major Ian Porteous, up from Da Nang, and four others, including myself. To Eva I wrote: "I would say it is a very special day for the Americans and celebrated in a way similar to our Christmas Day. It was rather sad for the men to celebrate this day away from their families."

Toward the end of the month two more members of Team 19 received the Mooney treatment. A junior officer in a psyops section failed to carry out a direction of the PSA. He was promptly relocated south. The second case involved a civilian officer in the refugee service. He had written to his Da Nang office saying that he wanted a transfer from Quang Tri, as he was not happy. When the PSA heard of this the officer was called from the field for an interview. He was advised to write to the PSA requesting transfer, who then had him out of Quang Tri that day on the next Porter aircraft. In two months five officers had been transferred out of Quang Tri. Mooney was not prepared to hold back anyone who was not settled in. He had a high regard for all ranks under his command. It was a measure of his leadership that this was reciprocated by his men. Two favorite catchphrases of the PSA seemed to be appropriate to the events just described: "Accentuate the positive, eliminate the negative" and "the train is about to leave the station."

The exercise of command is a paramount power vested in a military leader. It is not to be used in an arbitrary manner. Sound judgement needs to be applied to the facts of each case before making a decision. Mooney was exemplary in his exercise of command. He showed this in each of the personnel cases mentioned above.

In a much wider sense I was favorably impressed by commanders at all levels in the U.S. Army in their exercise of leadership and troop management. Unit commanders and commanders further up the chain have responsibilities which are special to the military, and to the uninitiated the responsibilities could appear to be intimidating. In particular the U.S. Army is an ethnically diverse institution, reflective of the parent nation. This mix of peoples in uniform on the face of it would seem to be more than a handful to lead and manage. From my observations, manage it they do, to the credit of all ranks and to their families. I was impressed by American soldiers, ethnically diverse, working in harmony with one another. There was a unity of purpose in their diversity. I had the honor of being in the company of U.S. Army members Coviello, Ramos, and Hogg in the Mai Linh advisory team. I recorded some experiences of an ethnic flavor in my year with MACV that made an impact on me. My diary included only three instances where serious and deep interpersonal sensitivities were displayed among army people, not necessarily members of Team 19. They could be considered as minor frictions related to ethnicity. They highlighted to me the heavy responsibilities commanders could face, should there be a breakdown in respect between uniformed colleagues within a unit. As a privileged observer, I judged these separate cases to be worthy of mention.

An African American sergeant knocked on the door to the club at the MACV compound asking for a doctor to attend to a man cut by concertina wire. All present had a look on their faces that conveyed the following nonverbal message: "What are you doing here, man? Take your problem elsewhere." There was no immediate reaction from members present until Lieutenant Lowe (U.S. Navy) and I went to get a doctor. Later in the evening a major called on me, questioning my response to what I thought was a reasonable request by the sergeant. I quietly responded to him by explaining that

I was disappointed with the lack of initiative shown: here was a junior leader concerned for his man, and the officers did not approach him to get the facts. As time passed nothing further was heard of the occurrence.

An African American lieutenant from a regimental advisory team had a promotion party coming up. He informed me he was only going to invite Australians because of the way he felt about Caucasians in his army. On top of that he said his young son had been killed recently in riots in the United States. He was coping with his grief. I was not invited to the celebration, nor did I expect an invitation.

Another African American lieutenant also shared his thoughts and feelings with me. He said: "Some soldiers in the compound would shoot some of the senior officers there if the opportunity came along." Fortunately there were no incidents of that kind. In my experience all ranks were treated equally and equitably.

With further thought about the above, I reflected on my own possible Caucasian prejudices. For example, when uniformed people gathered together for conversation I could conceive of a number of topics that might be under consideration. A simple explanation could be that they were enjoying their own company as friends at that moment, whether as a group of African Americans or as a group of Caucasians or as a group of African Americans and Caucasians together. The work of the mind can be deceptive. The only generalized and reasoned conclusion I have reached on these isolated experiences is to marvel at the way in which most Americans get on with life, and with respect to each other. Any national army reflects the country from whence the members are recruited. Due regard needs to be given to human frailties, with exceptions like the above arguably proving the rule.

Colonel Mooney shared some of his personal disappointments with me. I touch on them now to highlight the human heart and soul of military life. Mooney had expected to meet up with his family in Hawaii during a planned R&R break. Some promises made to him about these matters had been broken. In response he sent a letter to Da Nang requesting his tour of duty be reduced to one year in view of his leave arrangements not being satisfied. He later informed me that he had been notified that he was to go to the Industrial War College in July 1969. If that had happened his tour of duty would have been one year. Instead, Mooney stayed in Quang Tri to the end of 1969. Senior commanders experienced similar trials, as did their soldiers and other officers in their personal and professional lives.

With a Christmas truce approaching, our procedures and degree of alertness were examined to ensure that Team 19 would not be caught off guard by any surprise actions by the VC. Our pacification campaign was a work in progress. The VC would be aware of it and would relish an opportunity to strike a blow. Mooney, in the week leading into the truce period, directed that field-grade officers (majors) were to be rostered for duty officer at the operations center. Our counterparts needed little encouragement to be on guard, with the last Tet experience relatively fresh in their minds. My first night on was a struggle, as I discovered that I was very tired. The PSA had done me a favor by not permitting me to be on this roster at other times.

In an expansive mood after Christmas, Mooney shared his thoughts with his officers on some of the possible options that the recently elected President Nixon could pursue with his new administration. One scenario was that economies in spending and manpower in Vietnam could be examined. There was a nodding of heads in agreement within our group. We were aware of the generous military resources available, especially with regard to air support and artillery. Isolated Special Forces forward operating bases also came to mind; their usefulness was worth questioning. Advisory effort was clearly at the optimum level. Our helicopter availability had been reduced to four hours per day, from the earlier eight to ten hours. Fuel to energize the whole effort could be scaled back should activity and force levels be reduced.

At the start of the New Year it was evident that Colonel Mooney was not enjoying good health. His pace had slowed a little. It was a coincidence that military activity levels had slackened at the same time. It was of interest to compare our two senior officers. The U.S. military deputy to the PSA, Lieutenant Colonel Wallace, did not come across as being as highly motivated as Colonel Mooney. But Wallace perhaps was offering, by his example, how the PSA should go about his work. In the end I judged that it was really each to his own, a matter of personality.

After an intensive group effort in early January 1969 to prepare the Accelerated Pacification Campaign, Colonel Mooney expressed his satisfaction with the staff. He expanded by saying that the Vietnamese now had full ownership of the Quang Tri plan. Their presentation to Generals Stilwell and Truong on 7 January convinced the PSA that they were "up to speed" on what was to be done, and how it was to be done. Then Colonel Mooney said: "I have decided not to be province chief any more." To me this was a statement worth remembering, and one that I understood. Mooney had come in fresh to Quang Tri in the middle of August 1968. In a general sense the Vietnamese in August were still recovering from the Tet experience, where the ARVN/RF/PF in Quang Tri had acquitted themselves well.[6] Now, Mooney judged the Vietnamese military to have recovered from the Tet experience.

The PSA and others had put a lot of effort into helping the Vietnamese recover and in many ways provided the leadership to enable the recovery. Advisors in a broad sense were assisting their counterparts in the performance of their duties. Now a less assertive role was to be played out by Colonel Mooney, supportive to the Vietnamese but leaving new initiatives to the local authorities, military and civilian. This was one small local step in what was hoped to be a phased U.S. withdrawal from South Vietnam, and the GVN's taking up of the full burden.

The PSA had the ability to put a humorous spin on some events that he participated in. Mooney debriefed the staff of Team 19 after the 9 January meeting of province chiefs in Da Nang. At the meeting the Ministry of Information provided further guidelines for the new pacification campaign. Apparently all the province chiefs except Colonel Am had offered their thoughts and comments on matters raised by the briefer. After the meeting concluded, General Lam, as an aside, complimented Colonel Am on his acceptance of the changes put forward. The cryptic summary by Mooney was: "There was a case of a 'negative response' paying dividends." My diary note of 22 January was that the PSA was not in good health.

The next day, with the deputy and me, Mooney expressed the view that he was keen to keep an Australian staff officer as a follow-on to me in the S3 position. We dined well that evening on steak and Australian beer. In appreciation of his hospitality I had brought along a packet of tea for his pantry.

By the end of January Colonel Mooney was in poor health and was admitted to the hospital for a checkup. He had earned a break in any case. The members of Team 19 were going to miss him. A few days later Lieutenant Colonel Bibb, Lieutenant Colonel Nhan, and Captain John Pitts, our personnel officer, visited Colonel Mooney on the hospital ship *Repose.* Mooney was expected to stay in hospital for a week or more, but he was not able to break free of his responsibilities. On 6 February Mr. McNamara as acting PSA, with his secretary and some other key staff, took a helicopter ride to visit Mooney on the ship. In hindsight, it was to do with command rearrangements while Mooney was absent, in the context of the security preparations for Tet 1969, as discussed in an earlier chapter.

The next visit to Mooney on the ship was led by Terry McNamara, with Brad Oliver, Paul Laski, and me in company. The ship was not far from Quang Tri at the time. We found the colonel to be in good spirits, and he was looking forward to coming back to Quang Tri on 20 February. An initial assessment of his condition was "ulcers." To our knowledge his complaint had not really been isolated. The PSA was cheered by a letter he had received from Lieutenant General Weyand. These two men were good friends and were keen to meet up as soon as circumstances allowed. They had earlier served together in the 25th Infantry Division in Vietnam.

Mooney did return to duty on 20 February. It seemed he had a bile problem and had to keep clear of fat in his diet. Within a few days he was fully engaged. On 24 February he spoke to all available Team 19 members. This was a very emphatic way to let us know that he was back and in command. His message to us was to be confident, demonstrate competence in our work, and maintain our commitment. My thoughts were about his health. I noted: "May be rather difficult here; time will tell." Fortunately he continued in good health.

The next day, Mr. Fritz, of III MAF headquarters, was given a full province brief by Mooney. One memorable statement put by the PSA to Fritz was noted: "Any Team 19 member who did not fit in here would go south by road to Da Nang, through pacified Thieu Thien Province." As with most of us, there was a deep bitterness here on a range of issues to do with the conflict. Mr. Fritz had a memorable briefing.

The commanding officer of the AATTV visited Quang Tri on 4 March to catch up with as many of his Australians as possible. Lieutenant Colonel Lloyd had a ninety-minute meeting with Mooney. One of the matters covered in that discussion would have been about an Australian staff officer succeeding me in Team 19's S3 position. Happily, a very experienced officer was under consideration, and as events proved, Mooney accepted the Lloyd recommendation of Major Harry Bell.

The G5 of the 3rd Marine Division had a morning discussion with Mooney on 6 March. The PSA briefing to him was very frank, showing that an element of pessimism persisted. After that I had a quiet lunch with Mooney, where we reviewed world affairs. I hope that I was a useful confidant to him.

Captain Black (S5) and I joined the PSA on 11 March to prepare a presentation on pacification to Mr. Firfer, the CORDS head for refugees. Due to the weather conditions it was not possible for him to fly into Quang Tri. The CORDS refugee chief for Region 1 was to accompany him. The latter had not, to our knowledge, been to Quang Tri during our time in the province. For such an important agency, it was difficult to understand why he had not visited this area, which had a significant refugee population. With deadpan irony, Mooney had this to say: "I'm glad he did not show up, as we would have seen that it was the end of an era."

The incoming commanding general of III MAF, Lieutenant General Herman Nickerson Jr., visited the Team 19 headquarters in Quang Tri on 18 March. He was accompanied by Generals Stilwell, Davis, Drake, and Truong. Nickerson had earlier served in senior marine appointments in Region 1 in 1966–1967. The PSA briefed the visitors on pacification activities. The visitors were very well-informed leaders and battle hardened through various command appointments in Vietnam. Mooney was at his best for this presentation, demonstrating that Team 19 was doing its best for the cause. The big disappointment for the advisors was that the province chief did not attend the gathering.

One evening in March some staff officers gathered with Colonel Mooney for a chat about future prospects in our sector and in Vietnam. There was a general view shared by all that there would probably be little change in the situation in the coming year. This made me feel flat. The likelihood of an early negotiated peace settlement was low. The next day, at the Saturday morning Team 19 gathering of all available staff, Mooney expressed his disappointment with the whole effort in South Vietnam. He sincerely felt that the Vietnamese in South Vietnam would collapse within a few months if and when the United States pulled out. He continued by pointing out that the people in Quang Tri just did not seem to realize what they were being given by the Americans and the troops of the 1st ARVN Division. He concluded by saying that if the situation in the other four northern provinces of Region 1 were similar to that in Quang Tri, then these folks would be overrun by their enemies.[7]

At the end of March one of the battalion commanders from the 1/5 Infantry Brigade lunched with the PSA at his residence. Lieutenant Colonel David Hartigan was the commanding officer of the 1/61 Infantry Battalion, a unit with an authorized strength of nine hundred in all ranks. The exploits of the 1/5 Infantry Brigade are worthy of formal research and recording in the annals of military history. Some years earlier Mooney and Hartigan, and Colonel Jim Norrie, the Australian defense attaché in Saigon, had been classmates at the Command and Staff College at Fort Leavenworth.

In early April the PSA by his public actions demonstrated his uneasiness with and about CIA people. He was critical of the CIA, in the macro sense, in that it had built up an empire but did not appear to be doing anything with it. At the micro level in Quang Tri Mooney wanted a young officer assigned to the CIA to be relocated to another place of residence. The supervisor to the young officer was not happy about the decision and challenged the Mooney request. The supervisor was called in for a personal meeting with Mooney. Relationships and pecking order were quickly established. The young officer relocated as Mooney had required.

In March and April Mooney kept a firm hand and eye on Operation Kangaroo, the refugee resettlement at Cam Vu. This operation was not an easy task for the Vietnamese military at the sector level or for the administrative officials within the various agencies involved. It was a severe test for the advisors involved, and for the 2nd ARVN Regiment, which was providing the area with outer security. In addition, the advisors had to keep abreast of the pacification aspects with the refugees and of local security with the Territorial Forces. After some initial settling in problems, Mooney was satisfied that the best possible advisory arrangements had been set in place.

In mid-April I had to request the assistance of the PSA to sort out an Australian problem in one of the districts. The AATTV had been providing advisors to this district team for a number of years. In recent times a succession of warrant officers had passed through the Trieu Phong District advisory team, some of the personnel movements being scheduled, but some not. I was unable to resolve a particular matter with the district advisor, which was my preferred option, so I sought the assistance of Colonel Mooney. Fundamentally the issue was about how to gainfully employ our Australian warrant officers in the district team. There were also personality issues within the district team that were difficult for the warrant officers to accommodate. Fortunately, Mooney was sympathetic to the district senor advisor and the warrant officers. The DSA was responsive to matters raised in our three-way discussion and harmony was restored from the Australian point of view.

The time had come for me to hand over to Major Harry Bell (AATTV). We visited Gia Dang by road on 8 April. All was found to be calm from my point of view. The fisher folk appeared to be very healthy, and action was being taken to keep the already deteriorating road in service. About three hundred people were out on the road clearing sand off it, as a preparation for a "snow" fence to be erected. The visit with Harry was my adieu to Gia Dang after an involvement of seven months. I revisited Gia Dang in May 2012, an experience described in the next chapter.

My last effective day of work in Quang Tri was on 23 April 1969, as I was to leave for Da Nang the next day. At the evening brief, as was customary, a departing Team 19 member was given a plaque as a memento of the time spent with the unit. It remains on my office wall to this day. Mooney in a brief speech said to me that he was bidding farewell to a professional friend, one with whom he had developed a rare personal relationship. This was a great compliment to me. I felt the same of Mooney, a highly regarded soldier, respected commander, and good friend. Such is the lot of military life. That evening a farewell dinner was held at the Mooney residence. Others who attended were Fred Elfers, Bernie Meisel, Richard Mottel, Paul Laski, Dick Cummings, and Mr. Ford, men whom I had worked with closely over the past eight months. Together we had all done our best. Major Harry Bell was to join the Mooney team. Harry was to be in good company.[8]

As I left for Da Nang I reflected on the Team motto, "Persevere." I was very content with the thought that I had persevered in meeting my obligations to the best of my ability. Serving in Team 19 and with my fellow Australians in Quang Tri was a unique life experience. I thank them all for the privilege.

On the evening of ANZAC Day 1969, in Da Nang, I wrote up my diary and included a review of my year in Quang Tri. I was leaving, on my way south. My summary was a reflection of my opinion of the South Vietnamese problem in Quang Tri, a fresh retrospect:

Gia Dang–Quang Tri Road, December 1968.

> There is no national unity, nor is there any prospect of it being achieved.
>
> The people of Quang Tri have been overcome by the environment in which they are living, and despite the support provided by outsiders they are not able to fully grasp the opportunities presented.
>
> Enemy information is a key component in a counter insurgency situation.
>
> The GVN military and uniformed services need to be rationalised. Economy of effort is necessary to overcome inefficiencies and to make the organisations more effective.[9]
>
> A military solution to the war as seen from Quang Tri without the support of US ground forces will be a near impossibility for the South Vietnamese to achieve in the prevailing conditions.

My story concludes in the following chapter with an outline of some of the major events in South Vietnam in the 1970s, and some later and related personal events. I end with impressions gained during a private visit to Quang Tri in May 2012.

20

The Omega and a New Alpha

1970–2012

As a teenager I enjoyed swimming, often in the ocean surf. As a veteran I can equate the highlights and low points of my Quang Tri experience to some of the attributes of body surfing. In the sea, waves roll toward the shore in a never-ending cadence. At the entry, known surface currents and unknown undercurrents are hazards that need to be managed. The approaching crest of a wave is a decision point for the rider, to go or to back off. Occasionally in Vietnam I felt I was in a big wave, as some of the major events in my tour had the ambiance of a big ocean wave. It could be exhilarating. Storms arose and rogue waves arrived unannounced, some dumping the surfer from the wave, some carrying the surfer within turbulence to the safety of the shore. The challenge when standing up after the beaching was to go back for more. In many ways such was life in Quang Tri. Looking back at the conflict, I have a professional regret that I was not in Quang Tri with my allied comrades and friends in 1972, and 1975, to help confront the very nasty waves that came from the North, swamping the South. A retribution of tsunami proportions then followed. Any short-term prospect of democracy for the people of Vietnam was washed away by a totalitarian regime.

On return to Australia the army posted me to an aviation command appointment at Oakey, Queensland, again a once-in-a-lifetime experience, as officer commanding 16 Aviation Squadron. Three years later, in 1973, I attended the British Army Staff College, at Camberley, Surrey, England. On return to Australia I went into the military bureaucracy of the Department of Defence, Canberra.

The 1972 Communist Spring Offensive

Quang Tri was one of the three fronts that bore the brunt of a well-coordinated combined NVA and VC assault on 30 March 1972. The province capital fell to the communists on 1 May and was occupied until September 1972. General Ngo Quang Truong replaced General Hoang Xuan Lam as the I Corps commander of the ARVN forces during the early stage of the counteroffensive.[1]

The North Vietnamese had limited military objectives in this campaign, as their main objective rested within diplomatic settings beyond the borders of Vietnam: in Paris, Washington, Moscow, and Beijing. In land operations the communists wanted to outlast the Americans and the South Vietnamese, believing small gains on the field of battle would eventually lead to political victory. By early May 1972 the North Vietnamese claimed "Quang Tri Province was entirely liberated."[2] Cam Lo was proclaimed as the Zone of the Provisional Revolutionary Government of the South Vietnam Republic in Quang Tri.

The ARVN commenced a counterattack in June 1972. In the face of overwhelming bombing, the NVA stoutly defended the Citadel for eighty-one days. Quang Tri City and the Citadel were destroyed in the process. Many thousands of soldiers, of the South and North, were killed in the fighting.[3] The ARVN troops recaptured Quang Tri City and the Citadel on 15 September. The NVA regrouped and planned for the next phase of this epic struggle.

At the end of January 1973 the peace settlement document included an agreement that the DMZ at the 17th parallel would remain a provisional dividing line, with eventual reunification of the country "through peaceful means."[4]

The 1975 Conquest of South Vietnam

The northern provinces were again assaulted by the NVA in March 1975. The GVN military and civil authorities collapsed. Quang Tri, Hue, and Da Nang fell to the NVA before the end of March.[5] The NVA soon had the initiative on all fronts and moved on Saigon. The GVN forces offered resistance, but were not up to the fight against their determined enemy. In essence, the South Vietnamese did not have the resources or the infrastructure, civil and military, to withstand an invasion by North Vietnam.

It was North Vietnam's communist conventional military forces who invaded and overran the South Vietnamese, not the Viet Cong insurgents. On 30 April 1975 the chief of state of two days, General Duong Van Minh, surrendered South Vietnam to the conquerors from the North.[6]

A Retrospective and a General Conclusion

I thought it sad that the people of South Vietnam, very bright and well educated, succumbed to the North. The United States of America and the other free world allies involved in the conflict to the end of 1972 gave their all to help the South Vietnamese in their struggle for freedom. In the end, the North Vietnamese military forces overran the South, reuniting Vietnam in their image. Many people left Vietnam, fleeing terror and oppression, to seek a better way of life elsewhere.

In the post–World War II period, the threat posed by communism to democratic ways, personal freedom, and peace was a significant global security issue. The Iron Curtain was in place in Europe, China had become a communist state, and a settlement of the war in Korea had evolved. From 1954, North Vietnam was a communist state with a leadership determined to reunify Vietnam on its terms. In Southeast Asia the general view was that communism posed a threat to stability in South Vietnam, Thailand, Malaysia and Singapore, Laos, Cambodia, the Philippines, Indonesia, and Australia (the possible dominoes).

In Europe NATO faced the Warsaw Pact. The United States was the democratic super power. The Americans took over from the French in Indochina as a committed supporter of South Vietnam in the fight against communism. Politically and militarily, Australia joined the United States in Vietnam in 1962. Earlier, Australia was an original member of the Colombo Plan (Cooperative Economic and Social Development in Asia and the Pacific), which was formed in 1950 with a primary focus on human resource development. Soviet actions in Hungary in 1956 and Czechlovakia in 1968 reminded the world of the evil of communism. The Soviet policy of "peaceful coexistence" seems to have been put aside in the case of the Czechs.

It was a tragedy for the people of Vietnam that their country became a battleground for a stand against armed aggressive communism in Southeast Asia. In the 1954–1975 period, while the war was being waged in South Vietnam, other states in the region were given time to build up their democracies, to act against insurgents, allowing their peoples to live in peace and freedom. This was a significant beneficial consequence of the stand made by the United States and its allies in South Vietnam.

My story may help the reader to understand why I have reached the following general conclusion on the conflict in Vietnam. World bodies and governments in the post-1945 period should carry some responsibility for the tragedy that came to bear on the peoples of Vietnam. They had representatives who experienced the Second World War, the Cold War, and the Korean War. It can be fairly asserted that they were well informed about the consequences of war: carnage, the dislocation of humanity, destruction, the sense of loss, grief, and sadness. However, in the 1950s grave decisions were left to a few leaders of the belligerents. Their judgements led to the events that were so devastating that any benefits that may have arisen from engagement in warfare could not compensate for the losses. How much have national leaders worldwide learned since then? Are there better ways for groups of nations to mediate and mentor aggrieved nation-states, so as to assist in the avoidance of armed conflict? Government leaders and their diplomats should do better.

In time it can reasonably be expected that the central authoritarian control of communism in Vietnam will unwind, as has happened in some other former communist states. In the meantime I pray that the people in Vietnam and the nation will move toward democracy through peaceful processes.

Refugee Settlement in Australia

Australia has provided a new home for many refugees from across the world. I was involved in one part of the history of human migration and settlement into Australia in the 1970s and 1980s as a consequence of the Vietnam War. The Indo-China Refugee Association (ICRA) was formed in South Australia in 1975. The purpose of the organization was to render humanitarian assistance to refugees from the aftermath of the conflicts in Vietnam, Cambodia, and Laos. This assistance took the form of aid to people in the refugee camps in Southeast Asia, and those settling in Australia. In 1977, ICRA was established in Victoria, New South Wales, and the Australian Capital Territory (ACT), and later in Queensland. Eva and I joined ICRA (ACT) in 1979.

Unlike the other Australian capital cities, Canberra did not have a local migrant hostel, which was the usual initial point of reception for arriving refugees. In 1977 an astute group of dedicated volunteers in Canberra drafted the aims of the ICRA (ACT) during a series of afternoon meetings. The aims decided upon were:

- To provide a self-help organisation for the communities of Indo-China refugees who settled in Australia;
- To urge the Australian Government to provide refuge for as many refugees from Indo-China as can effectively be settled in Australia;
- To assist the Indo-China refugees in the process of settlement in Australia in co-operation with the Government departments and other voluntary agencies concerned with the settlement of Indo-China refugees; and
- To provide awareness of the situation of the Indo-China refugees within the Australian community and to seek within the Australian community support for the Indo-China refugees.

In mid-1979 the committee of management of ICRA (ACT) made submissions to the Department of Immigration and Ethnic Affairs (DI&EA) seeking direct settlement of refugees from camps into the local Canberra community. The DI&EA agreed to a pilot scheme being undertaken by ICRA (ACT) on behalf of the local community. One of the committee invited me to become involved in this challenging and ambitious project. At my first meeting with the committee it became evident that a planner was needed. I offered to plan the project, as a spare-time activity. The offer was accepted. I was appointed as the voluntary director of the project, named Operation Camplift.

The overall scheme was described by the immigration department as the Community Refugee Settlement Scheme (CRSS). Community settlement groups affiliated with ICRA (ACT) were soon formed. For Camplift One, eighteen groups were organized between July and October 1979. For Camplift Two (November/December 1979) twenty-three groups were formed. With about fifty people backing each community settlement group, the number of citizens participating and being influencers in refugee settlement was considerable. Over one hundred refugees were settled into the community by ICRA (ACT) by the end of 1979.

A host group and a support group were formed within each community settlement group to get the job done. The number of citizens in Canberra and nearby Queanbeyan who wanted to help refugees from Indochina to settle into our community was impressive. Not only was there a great amount of goodwill to help those who were in serious need, but there was generosity in time, material, and money.

Further, our fellow citizens demonstrated strength of character and quiet but determined perseverance that gave one great hope for the further successful settlement of refugees. Something beneficial was also happening to Australians who were involved in the Community Refugee Settlement Scheme. Differences had been put aside, new friendships were developed, and boundaries that were the creation of humankind were being crossed and perhaps set aside. In summary, political, religious, racial, social, and economic boundaries had been overcome in order to accomplish the noble task of settling refugees. On top of that, when the new settlers realized the scope and nature of the support being given to them, it brought about a realization in them of the positive qualities of the people who were assisting them voluntarily in their settlement in their new country. That appreciation made all of the effort worthwhile. Despite the setbacks experienced in leaving their home country, the migration put an end to the past (the omega), making way for the beginning of a new life (a new alpha). The people from Cambodia, Laos, and Vietnam who came to Australia have entered into many walks of life and continue to make valuable contributions to our nation.

In a letter of appreciation to me as the president of ICRA (ACT), the Minister for Immigration and Ethnic Affairs included the following about the CRSS Program: "I am sure that the personal involvement of you and your group members in the welcoming and settling of refugees has left a lasting impression in the minds and emotions of the people whom you have befriended. The results of your help and kindness will have far reaching effects both in their own lives, and in the life of the community at large."[7]

To be involved in the settlement in Australia of refugees from South Vietnam after my active service there was a most rewarding and satisfying experience.

Quang Tri Province, May 2012

A seven-day private tour to Quang Tri in May 2012 was made all the more enjoyable as I was accompanied by my third son, Peter. The tour objectives were centered on friendship, pilgrimage, and veteran curiosity. We were ably assisted by a first-class guide and interpreter, Tam, and a conscientious driver, Thanh. We arrived at Da Nang airport on Sunday, 21 May, and drove over the Hai Van Pass to Hue, and then to Dong Ha, our base for the next four nights. On the return part of the trip we had a day at Hue and a day at Da Nang. The visit exceeded my expectations. Here are some observations from the trip.

The administrative boundaries for Quang Tri Province had been modified. Quang Tri City, virtually destroyed in 1972, is no longer the province capital. Quang Tri is now designated as a town, with the town boundary encompassing the former Mai Linh District. The head office for the province administration and the seat of the Provincial People's Committee is located in Dong Ha City, the province capital.

With the demise of the DMZ, Vinh Linh District to the north of the Ben Hai River has been reinstated into Quang Tri Province. The former district of Trung Luong has been absorbed into Gio Linh District. The districts of Cam Lo, Gio Linh, Trieu Phong, and Hai Lang continue. Huong Hoa District, to the west on the Laotian border, has been reinstated, with Khe Sanh being designated as a town and district center. The former Ba Long District and part of Huong Hoa District have been absorbed into a new district of Dakrong, centered on the town of Krong Klang, known in the 1960s as Ca Lu. Dao Con Co, an island thirty kilometers off the coast, is designated as a district.

In my earlier period in Quang Tri, I was only able to observe the flood plain of the Ben Hai River from the higher ground at Gio Linh to the south. I felt a degree of comfort during our drive through the flood plain and across the river, an imaginary peaceful crossing of the Rubicon experience. On the northern bank we visited the museum and observer buildings (1954 onward), and viewed there the great monuments and memorials. The achievement of reunification is quietly and proudly celebrated here. On the southern bank of the river, at the end of the old bridge crossing, stands a large statue of a mother and child, symbols of a family awaiting the return of a loved one.

A few kilometers north of the Ben Hai River, on the coast, are the Vinh Moc tunnels. I was surprised to realize that they existed during the conflict, virtually under our noses. Three levels of underground tunnels developed by hamlet people, military, and specialists in mining and survey were on display. The subsoil is of clay, allowing the tunnels to be self-supporting. The tunnels had eleven access and exit points, with three of them providing concealed openings to the foreshore. After walking comfortably through the three levels, I have to say the tunnels make up a stunning place, worthy of preservation.

Little remains of the military infrastructure of past wars in Quang Tri. Remnants of block houses are more likely to be from the French period than the more recent. Native vegetation and rural and industrial development now dominate the landscape. The former Dong Ha airfield land is now a residential precinct of an expanding Dong Ha City, with a population of about eighty thousand people. In each district there are reminders of the sacrifice and suffering during and since the conflict, referred to by some of the Vietnamese as the American War. Veteran cemeteries, memorials, and monuments commemorate the dead, and the feats of soldiers. Museums devoted to local heroic deeds are open to the public, from Khe Sanh airfield in the west to the Citadel in the East, and from the Ben Hai River in the north to Hai Lang in the south. Remnants are not obvious. Any materials that had a recycle value at former airfields or bases were stripped away by commercial scavengers. Sensor relics from north of Khe Sanh were for sale at the local scrap merchant yard. The items were too large to be carried home as souvenirs.

At Dong Ha, by chance, I met a U.S. team from the Joint POW/MIA Accounting Command (JPAC), which has the responsibility to account for the more than eighty-three thousand Americans still missing from past U.S. conflicts. The team I met was one of eight recovery teams based in Hawaii that deploy to Vietnam. They search for Americans who remain unaccounted for from the Vietnam War, some two thousand individuals. The Vietnamese have about three hundred thousand individuals listed as missing. Information exchanges take place to assist searchers, Vietnamese and Americans.

We visited the Cua Valley, south of Cam Lo, where the overrun Huong Hoa District was relocated in early 1968. The Cua is now part of Cam Lo District. The valley is a peaceful and beautiful place, where vegetation, farming, housing, and supporting services have taken over. Without any reference points, except instinct, I asked the driver to stop and for the interpreter to inquire with the local people observing the strange visitors as to whether U.S. helicopters landed near here in the past. We had hit the spot. We were within one hundred meters of a former Special Forces FOB and advisory team compound. While on our walk from the car along a side track, and being led by a crowd of children and mothers, we were asked to wait in order to meet an important local senior citizen.

We were introduced to Captain Sat. He pointed fifty meters toward the edge of a rubber plantation and said: "that is the spot." As expected, there were no remnants, but we all sensed that an interesting exchange of conversation was about to commence. We were informed the captain was an authentic national hero. When others had completed their introductions, the eighty-seven-year-old veteran related his story. He was a fighting man for thirty years, taking up arms against the French in 1945. After the cease-fire in 1954 he went to North Vietnam for further training and education. He returned to this area six years later, in 1962, to continue the resistance as a VC leader. Pointing to the mountains, he said he lived in the forests for the next ten years, often observing the Americans in the valley with his binoculars. He participated in battles at Hue in the 1968 Tet offensive. He operated in the Ashau Valley, to the south of the Cua Valley, from 1969 to 1971. He claimed he was involved in the Quang Tri Citadel battle in 1972. During this period he was recalled to Hanoi to be formally recognized for his achievements on the battlefield. The journey was of epic proportions, walking over eight hundred kilometers to Hanoi, four months there and four months to return. I thought his travels were more than a sabbatical. After the North conquered the South in 1975 he returned to his big family in the Cua Valley to enjoy his retirement. Captain Sat had earned a break.

The national and local road system has been transformed. Wide, sealed roads and new bridges have been built to meet growing demand. Bridges span each of the river estuaries, the Ben Hai and the Cua Viet, at the coast. The coastal sandy strip of the province has been opened up. Gia Dang village has been transformed by modest development. Despite some setbacks in the period 1972–1975, the main body of refugees settled there by Operation Fisher in 1968 have become Gia Dang folk. Some people there were happy to share their stories with us, including two former NVA soldiers, a former female guerrilla, a widow, a fisherman, and younger people. The expedient road built in 1968 on the coastal plain had a short life, being replaced by a new road a few kilometers north. Our guide, Tam, was a gem in this wonderful experience. Fish farming on land is flourishing. In each city and town of Quang Tri Province schools and hospitals have been built to meet the population growth.

The Hanoi to Saigon unification railway is in full operation, for freight and passengers. Few police were seen in public places, less than at home. The military were not seen in numbers, except in barracks and traveling to work. Commercial road vehicles appeared to be in greater numbers than motor cars. Motorbikes and bicycles are the popular forms of personal carriage. Bus services link villages to towns and cities. Cuisine, whether in the home, café, restaurant, or roadside stall, was pleasing to the palate.

Our visit coincided with the dry season in Central Vietnam. In the paddy areas the rice had been harvested, the stubble cut and placed in the sun to dry. The growth of other crops, plantations, and flora was evident. Farmers, now members of cooperatives, were prospering. Capitalism is being embraced, although state ownership of key industries continues. Market-oriented socialism appears to be working in a developing and growing economy.

The Communist Party is the sole source of power. Political dissent is not tolerated, but the people are skilled in being discreet. There is stability, but I was unable to discern at what cost. The majority of the people are focused on the present and the future, the war being a memory. I think the pride of the Vietnamese people remains intact, perhaps growing because of recent achievements. I was advised that overseas Vietnamese are returning, and that their investments are contributing to progress.

I had been thinking that one possible way to measure a degree of freedom in a one-party state is to assess the extent to which public worship is tolerated. Belief objects were evident in homes, hotel foyers, work places, temples, pagodas, and churches. We enjoyed a lunchtime meal at a pagoda. Tri Buu Church in Quang Tri town was visited. Destroyed in 1972, the parish completed a reconstruction of the church in 2000. Other buildings on the site indicated a thriving community. The annual national pilgrimage to the partially rebuilt La Vang Basilica on 15 August attracts huge crowds. A Sunday morning Mass at Da Nang Cathedral attracted an overflow congregation. These were signs to give hope for the future. I hope there is cultural and religious freedom for the people beyond the public places.

The Citadel in Quang Tri holds a special place in my life and clearly is the heart and soul of commemorations for many Vietnamese to mark the national liberation. The interior of the Citadel has been cleared and developed as memorial parkland, providing a setting for monuments and a museum. Now a recognized national relic, it is likely to be a magnet for Vietnamese of all ages to visit for reflection and remembrance. One entrance has been restored. The two-kilometer-long wall is an esteemed relic. Although the walls of the Citadel have been severely damaged, the surrounding moat has prominence, acting like a protective mantle to a precious place.

My visit to Vietnam in 2012 has put my mind to rest on one important matter. For the rest of my days I will no longer be wondering about how the people in Quang Tri Province are living. Since 1975 the future of Vietnam has been the sole responsibility of the Vietnamese people. I hope they continue to live in peace, and with justice and prosperity.

Epitaph

The Cross of the Sacrifices Made
By Those Involved in Vietnam
Is Carried by Many
Across the World
They Weep
Still

Acknowledgments

This writing and research project based on my Vietnam diary commenced in 2007. Without the unfailing support of my wife, Eva, the emerging manuscript would not have matured into a publication. Other people played an invaluable part in the journey, and I thank them for their part as members of a large support team, albeit one that has never gathered together.

My handwritten first draft was typed by Liana Gray. Simon Millie assisted with research and advice on word processing and storing. Bruce Davies critiqued the chapter about the Australians in Quang Tri. Single chapters were critiqued by Dr. David Horner and Nina Valentine, who encouraged me with their expert comments.

Along the way a local literary discussion group, including Garry Spry, Wendy Owen, Eva Millie, and Bruce Davies, helped keep my motivation up, as did occasional conversations with the Geelong Writers, especially Garry Kinnane. A 2011 version of the manuscript was peer reviewed by Ken Francis, Daniel Millie in the UAE, John Moug, Julian Millie in Melbourne, Frank Alizzi, and Peter Millie in Brunei. Many thanks for their time and effort. Ian Teague, Brian Day, and Matthew d'Arcy commented on single chapters. Chris Crook did the cartographic work. In the United States, I am grateful for the assistance provided by Bill Coviello and David Sciacchitano in responding to my requests on a range of topics.

In late August 2010, Brigadier General Harley F. Mooney, U.S. Army (ret.), contacted me by email, our first communication since 1969. We resumed our friendship with ease, and I thank him for his encouragement to complete my story. We were a fine team then, as narrated in this book, and still are now. Thanks to Lieutenant General Richard G. Trefry, U.S. Army (ret.), who passed on my draft manuscript of 2011 for consideration by the Association of the United States Army Book Program. I am indebted to the Association for its assistance, and in particular to the director of the book program, Roger Cirillo, Ph.D., Lieutenant Colonel, U.S. Army (ret.).

In May 2012, accompanied by my son Peter, I spent five days on a return visit to central Vietnam. Thanks to Michael Francis in Hanoi for making the necessary arrangements, and for organizing our guide and driver. Thanks Tam and Thanh for your professionalism and friendship during our travels and for the wonderful meetings we experienced in Quang Tri Province. At the final stage, in October 2012, Carmel Murphy, Geoff Braden, Jim Cope, and Laurie Muscat helped me to format the files for submission.

Sincere thanks to the staff of the University Press of Kentucky and its contractors. During the submission stage the director's staff eased me gently into the publication project, particularly Allison Webster, who was the pleasant voice at the other end when I called by telephone from Australia.

Harley Mooney and Jim Geedrick have given me permission to use their photographs, and I acknowledge that the originals of the photographs came to me from Australian Department of Defence sources during the Vietnam conflict. Further, I acknowledge the Australian War Memorial, publisher of the book *The Team* by the late Ian McNeill in 1984, for its permission to use the same images in this work.

Guidance from copy editor Derik Shelor was invaluable. The work of the indexer will help readers find their way through the narrative. Frederike Ramm created a website for the book (www.team19vietnam.com). To the people who assisted me in this work and who have not been mentioned here, I thank you also for your kindness and support. Finally, I take full responsibility for the contents of this book.

Appendix A

Some of the Characters, 1968–1969

Advisory Team 19 (Quang Tri)

Province Senior Advisors	Mr. Bob Brewer Colonel Harley Mooney
Deputy Province Senior Advisors	Lieutenant Colonel Harley Mooney Mr. Terry McNamara Mr. Fred Elfers
Assistant Sector Advisors	Lieutenant Colonel Thrasher Lieutenant Colonel Julius Schelhammer Lieutenant Colonel Wallace
Staff Advisors	
S1 (Personnel)	Captain John Pitts
S2 (Intelligence)	Major Paul Laski
S3 (Plans and Operations)	Major John Hannon Major David Millie (Australia) Major Harry Bell (Australia)
TOC Supervisor	Sergeant Burdett
S2/S3 (Air)	Lieutenant Ed Logan Captain Porter Angel
S4 (Logistics)	Major Bernie Meisel Major Richard "Dick" Mottel
S5 (Civil Affairs)	Captain Black
RF/PF Advisor	Major Brad Oliver
Compound Commander	Major Robert "Bob" Phillips
District Senior Advisors	
Cam Lo	Major John Hannon Major Bill Healy
Dong Ha	Captain Weary

Gio Linh	Major Simpson
	Major Charles "Chuck" Slaby
Huong Hoa	Major James "Jim" Hill
	Major Ed Thomas
Hai Lang	Major Paul Fitzpatrick
Mai Linh	Major Mike Casey (Australia)
	Major David Millie (Australia)
	Captain Huntley
Trieu Phong	Major John Shalikashvili

Mai Linh District Advisors

Deputy District Advisor	Captain William Coviello
	Sergeant Bob Hogg
	Sergeant Ramos

CORDS (Quang Tri)

Director	Mr. Terry McNamara
Refugees	Mr. John Cleary, USAID
	Mr. Dick Cummings, FSO
Projects	Lieutenant Colonel John Bibb (ret.)
Police	Mr. Dick Peterson
Phoenix Program	Mr. Riddell
Montagnard Affairs	Mr. Bob Hendy
MILPHAP	Lieutenant Steve Lowe (U.S. Navy)
Others:	Mr. Hal Cottrell, Lieutenant Colonel Fox, Mr. Coughlin, Mr. Ford, Mr. Hassler, and Mr. McKie

Quang Tri Province

Province Chief	Colonel Nguyen Am
CO, Territorial Forces	Lieutenant Colonel Ngo Thanh Nhan
	Major Nguyen Luu De
S3	Captain Cuu
S4	Major Chuu
Interpreter	Sergeant Long

Districts and District Chiefs

Cam Lo	Nguyen Van Rao
Dong Ha	Le Quong Khiem
Gio Linh	Le Thanh Thong
Huong Hoa	Tinh A Thi
Hai Lang	Phan Van Thu
Mai Linh	Ton That Phong
Trieu Phong	Nguyen Duc Nhiem
Ba Long	Inactive
Trung Luong	Inactive

Mai Linh District Staff (Quang Tri Province)

District Chief	Captain Ton That Phong
Executive Officer	Lieutenant Sang
S1	Warrant Officer Sung
S2	2nd Lieutenant Huu
S3	Warrant Officer Nhan
S5	2nd Lieutenant Hung
Security	Sergeant Thi
Communications	Sergeant Nhi
First Sergeant	Sergeant Phuc
Interpreter	Binh
Housekeeper	Ba Le

Army of the Republic of Vietnam (ARVN) I Corps

Military Region 1 (Headquarters at Da Nang)

Commander	Lieutenant General Hoang Xuan Lam
Territorial Forces	Colonel Vinh

1st ARVN Division (Headquarters at Hue)

Commander	Major General Ngo Quang Truong
1st Regiment (La Vang)	Lieutenant Colonel Hanh
2nd Regiment (Dong Ha)	Colonel Vu Van Giai

III Marine Amphibious Force (Headquarters at Camp Horn, near Da Nang)

Commanders	Lieutenant General R. Cushman Jr.
	Lieutenant General H. Nickerson Jr.

Corps Deputy for CORDS	Ambassador Charles T. Cross

Provisional Corps Vietnam (redesignated as XXIV Corps on 15 August 1968)

Commander	Lieutenant General William B. Rosson

XXIV Corps (was Provisional Corps, Headquarters at Phu Bai)

Commander	Lieutenant General Richard G. Stilwell
Deputy Commander	Major General Clifford B. Drake, USMC
Senior Staff Officer (G5)	Colonel Roy Land

3rd Marine Division (Quang Tri Province)

Commanders	Major General Raymond G. Davis
	Major General William K. Jones

1st Brigade, 5th Infantry Division (Mechanized)

Commanders	Colonel Richard J. Glikes
	Colonel James M. Gibson

4th Combined Action Group (USMC, Quang Tri)

Commander	Lieutenant Colonel John Greenwood
Company Commander	Major Jim Brown

1st Brigade, 1st Air Cavalry Division

Commander	Colonel John F. Stannard
Operations Officer	Major Robert Canady

Australian Force Vietnam (AFV, Headquarters at Saigon)

Commanders	Major General A. L. MacDonald
	Major General R. A. Hay

Australian Army Training Team Vietnam (AATTV, Headquarters at Saigon)

Commanding Officers	Lieutenant Colonel Raymond L. Burnard
	Lieutenant Colonel Russell D. F. Lloyd
Staff Officers, Da Nang	Major Ian Porteous
	Major Frank Johnston

USS *Repose*

Captain	Captain John Drew, U.S. Navy

Forward Air Controllers (USAF, La Vang)

20th Tactical Air Support Squadron Detachment	Major Robert Ball, KIA Major David Dahl Captain Linwood O. Grant

282nd Aviation Company (Assault Helicopter)

Detachment of "Blackcat" crews

Air America (Da Nang Station)

Pilots of various aircraft types

Revolutionary Development (National Training Center, Vung Tau)

Commandant	Colonel Be

Viet Cong, KIA

Senior Officer Quang Tri Province Top Ten List	Bui Tu Phan Thi
Hamlet Chief Nu Le	Unknown

Appendix B

Aircraft and Weapons

Fixed Wing Aircraft

Transport
C-7 Caribou
C-47 Dakota
C-123 Provider
C-130 Hercules

Attack
F-4 Phantom
B-52 Stratofortress

Utility
U-21 Volpar (Beech)
Pilatus Porter

Observation
O-1 Bird Dog (Cessna L-19)
OV-1 Mohawk
OV-10 Bronco
Cessna 180

Helicopters

Transport
CH-34 Choctaw
CH-46 Sea Knight
CH-47 Chinook
CH-53 Sea Stallion
CH-54 Tarke (Skycrane)

Attack
AH-1G Huey Cobra

Observation
OH-13 Sioux
OH-6A Cayuse (Loach)
OH-58 Kiowa

Utility
UH-1H Iroquois (Huey)

Search and Rescue
HH-3E Jolly Green Giant

Artillery

U.S.	Maximum range (m)
105 mm towed M101	11,000
155 mm SP M109	18,000
8-inch (208 mm) SP M55	16,800
175 mm SP M107	32,800

NVA	Maximum range (m)
rockets	9,000–11,000
122 mm	12,000
130 mm	17,000
152 mm	27,000

Mortars

U.S.	Maximum range (m)
60 mm	1,500
81 mm	3,625
4.2-inch	6,000

NVA	Maximum range (m)
60 mm	1,500
82 mm	3,000
120 mm	5,670

Appendix C

Chronology, 1968 and 1969

1968

March 31	President Johnson announces that he will not seek reelection.
May	Procedural meetings commence for peace negotiations in Paris.
May 14	Arrive in Saigon.
May 17	Meet Mr. Bob Brewer, province senior advisor, Quang Tri.
May 19	Uncle Ho's birthday.
June 1	Province chief promoted to colonel.
June 6	Assassination of Senator Robert Kennedy.
June 10	MACV command changeover.
June 12	Warrant Officer Peter Wooden, AATTV, wounded at Cam Lo.
June 18	Generals Lam and Cushman visit Mai Linh District Headquarters.
July 5	Khe Sanh combat base closed.
July 11	Advance Party 1st Brigade, 5th Infantry Division (Mechanized), briefed.
July 16	Captain Bui Tu, Viet Cong, killed.
July 22–29	Four FAC sorties with 20th Tactical Air Support Squadron.
July 24	COMAFV Major General A. L. MacDonald visits Quang Tri.
July 31	1st/5th Infantry Division (Mech) deploys into Quang Tri.
August 14	Lieutenant Colonel Harley Mooney arrives to be DPSA.
August 15	Provisional Corps Vietnam redesignated XXIV Corps.
August 19	Top ten-listed VCI Phan Thi killed by district troops.

August 22	Bishop of Hue conducts ordination at La Vang Basilica.
August 25	Two-day course at the RD NTC at Vung Tau.
August 28–29	Four sorties with 161 Reconnaissance Flight at Nui Dat.
September 9	Appointed to S3 (operations officer) for Advisory Team 19.
September 20	Minister for Montagnard Affairs visits Cua Valley.
September 23	Lieutenant Colonel Mooney confirmed as PSA.
October 1	Mooney appointed to province senior advisor, Quang Tri.
October 2	Floods continue.
October 12	Operation Fisher commences.
October 13	Le Loi Festival. Mr. Terry McNamara arrives to be DPSA.
October 27	Notification of 1st ACD redeployment to Tay Ninh.
November 1	National Day. Bombing halt on North Vietnam.
November 12	COMUSMACV General Creighton W. Abrams visits Gia Dang.
November 20	Mooney promoted to colonel.
November 20	Australian CGS General Sir Thomas Daly visits Da Nang and Hue.
December 7–9	Four sorties with 161 Reconnaissance Flight at Nui Dat.
December 12	President Thieu at Gia Dang Refugee Settlement.
December 21	Prime Minister of South Vietnam at Cam Lo.
December 24–25	Christmas truce.
December 24	Viet Cong hamlet chief at Nhu Le killed in ambush.
December 27	Warrant Officer Peter Garrigan, AATTV, drowned at Trieu Phong.

1969

January 7	PSA briefs Deputy CORDS Mr. W. Colby in Hue.
January 14–22	R&R leave in Australia.
January 29	USMC provisional company deploys into city.
January 29	General Lam relieves Lieutenant Colonel Nhan.
January 31	Colonel Mooney to hospital ship USS *Repose.*
February 6	Colonel Corrigan, USMC, appointed acting deputy province senior advisor.
February 6	Major De takes over from Lieutenant Colonel Nhan.
February 11	COMAFV Major General A. L. MacDonald visits Quang Tri.
February 14	Second USMC company boosts security in city.
February 16–17	Tet 1969 truce.
February 20	Colonel Mooney returns to duty.
March 7	Bridge at Nhu Le opened, a 1/5 Infantry Brigade Civil Affairs project.
March 16	Village chief and two hamlet chiefs killed at Kam Dau, Dong Ha District.
March 18	Operation Kangaroo at Cam Vu commences.
March 21	Australian ambassador to South Vietnam visits Quang Tri.
March 27	COMAFV designate Major General R. A. Hay visits Quang Tri.
April 2	145 RF Company in CH-47 disaster at LZ Saigon.
April 4	Assassination of Dr. Martin Luther King Jr.
April 14	3rd Marine Division change of command ceremony.
April 16	Mr. Hitchcock, Refugee Director, Saigon, visits five camps in province.
April 18	New DPSA Mr. Fred Elfers arrives in Quang Tri.
April 24	Handover to Major Harry Bell, AATTV.

April 25	ANZAC Day. AATTV commemoration ceremony at Da Nang.
April 26	Detached to Headquarters 1 ATF at Nui Dat.
April 27–30	Seven sorties with 161 Reconnaissance Flight at Nui Dat.
May 3	Visit to Vung Tau.
May 4	At Headquarters AATTV, Saigon.
May 7	Tour ends. Departs Saigon for Sydney.
June 8	President Thieu meets President Nixon at Midway Island.

Appendix D

Abbreviations and Terms

AATTV	Australian Army Training Team Vietnam
ACD	Air Cavalry Division
AFV	Australian Force Vietnam
AIF	Australian Imperial Force
APC	Accelerated Pacification Plan
APTs	Armed Propaganda Teams
ARVN	Army of the Republic of Vietnam
ATF	Australian Task Force
AWM	Australian War Memorial
CA	Civil Affairs
CAP	Combined Action Platoon (Marines and a PF platoon)
CG	Census Grievance
CGS	Chief of the General Staff (Australia)
CIA	Central Intelligence Agency
CIDG	Civilian Irregular Defense Group
CIT	Counter Intelligence Team
CO	Commanding Officer
COMAFV	Commander Australian Force Vietnam
COMUSMACV	Commander U.S. Military Assistance Command Vietnam
CORDS	Civil Operations and Revolutionary Development Support
COSVN	Central Office for South Vietnam (Hanoi directed)
CRS	Catholic Relief Service (U.S.)
DCM	Distinguished Conduct Medal
DMZ	Demilitarized Zone (Vietnam)
DOICC	District Operations and Intelligence Control Center
DPSA	Deputy Province Senior Advisor
DSA	District Senior Advisor

FAC	Forward Air Controller
FFV	Field Force Vietnam
FO	Forward Observer (artillery)
FOB	Forward Operating Base
FSB	Fire Support Base
FSCC	Fire Support Coordination Center
FWMAF	Free World Military Assistance Force
G	Staff Level, Division and Corps Headquarters
GVN	Government of the Republic of Vietnam (South Vietnam)
HES	Hamlet Evaluation System
HQ	Headquarters
J	Staff Level, Above Corps
KIA	Killed in Action
LPH	Landing Platform Helicopter
LZ	Landing Zone
MACCORDS	Military Assistance Command Civil Operations and RD Support
MACV	Military Assistance Command Vietnam
MAF	Marine Amphibious Force
MAG	Marine Air Group
MAT	Mobile Advisory Team (U.S. Army)
MILPHAP	Military Provincial Health Assistance Program
MPC	Military Payment Certificate
NLD	New Life Development
NLF	National Liberation Front (communist)
NPFF	National Police Field Force
NTC	National Training Center (RD)
NVA	North Vietnamese Army
PF	Popular Forces (platoons)
PRP	People's Revolutionary Party
PRU	Provincial Reconnaissance Unit
PSA	Province Senior Advisor
PSDF	People's Self-Defense Force
PX	Post Exchange (supermarket)
R&R	Rest and Recuperation
RD	Revolutionary Development/Rural Development

RF	Regional Forces (companies)
RF/PF	Territorial Forces
ROK	Republic of Korea
RVNAF	Republic of Vietnam Armed Forces
S	Staff Level, Unit and Brigade/Regiment
SAR	Search and Rescue
Seabees	Construction Battalions (CBs), of the U.S. Navy
SOPs	Standard Operating Procedures
Tet	Vietnamese New Year's Day
TOC	Tactical Operations Center
USAF	United States Air Force
USAID	U.S. Agency for International Development
USARV	United States Army Republic of Vietnam
USMC	United States Marine Corps
VC	Viet Cong
VCI	Viet Cong Infrastructure
VCS	Viet Cong Suspect/Supporter
VIS	Vietnamese Information Service
VNAF	South Vietnamese Air Force
WIA	Wounded in Action

Notes

1. Leaving Home for War

1. John S. Bowman, gen. ed., *The World Almanac of the Vietnam War* (New York: Pharos Books, 1985), 200.

2. In 1965 the Military Board at Army Headquarters Canberra issued the *Pocketbook: South Vietnam*. The preface was of three paragraphs. These words in the preface provided the Australian Army mission in South Vietnam at the time: "By helping the people of this proud nation repulse the aggression of the Communist Viet Cong you will strike a telling blow for democracy and add greatly to the strength of freedom throughout the world."

3. "Team" was the short name given by Australians to the AATTV, and not to be confused with the MACV U.S. Army advisory teams that Team members were allocated to for duty.

2. The Big Picture

1. Bowman, ed., *The World Almanac of the Vietnam War*, 37.

2. Millie diary, 2 January 1969. The ARVN Order of Battle: 1st, 2nd, 5th, 7th, 18th, 21st, 22nd, 23rd, and 25th Divisions, 42nd and 51st Regiments, Ranger and Airborne units. Regional and Popular Forces are grouped as Territorial Forces.

3. GVN, *The Viet Cong Infrastructure, Modus Operandi of Selected Political Cadres (U)* (GVN, December 1968), 3.

4. Nguyen Tien Hung and Jerrold L. Schecter, *The Palace File* (New York: Harper and Row, 1986), 36.

3. Travel to Quang Tri and Orientation

1. Adrian Nesbitt died in 1987.

2. Until August 1968, Quang Tri advisors were grouped into MACV 1st ARVN Division Advisory Team 4. I went to Hue for a Team 4 introductory briefing. Later Team 19 was spun off from Team 4. As the majority of my time in Quang Tri was with Team 19, I have chosen to use that designation throughout my story.

3. The Viet Cong Infrastructure (VCI) was defined by the GVN as all VC political and administrative organizations established by the Communist Party, which went under the name "People's Revolutionary Party" from the cities to the countryside. The COSVN was the highest level steering organ of the VC in South Vietnam, which directed these political and ad-

ministrative organizations through the various echelons of the People's Revolutionary Party of South Vietnam, and the National Front of Liberation of South Vietnam, from central level down to the hamlet. In addition, the communists planted a number of cadres to direct and control other parties and organizations, such as the Progressive Socialist Party, the Southern Democratic Party, the Alliance of National Democratic and Peace Forces, the Revolutionary Liberation Committee, and similar organizations of the future.

4. Staff levels are identified by S, G, and J, referring respectively to Unit and Brigade/Regiment, Division/Corps, and above Corps. The level designations are followed by a numeral to denote the Staff function: (1) Administration, (2) Intelligence, (3) Operations, Training, and Planning, (4) Supply, (5) Civil and Military Operations, and (6) Communications.

5. MACV Team 19 Brochure, Quang Tri Province, 1968.

4. Australian Army Advisors in the Province

1. Larrikinism, especially Australian: rowdy behavior; hooliganism.

2. Bruce Davies and Gary McKay, *The Men Who Persevered* (Sydney: Allen and Unwin, 2005), 217–369.

3. AATTV War Diary, AWM 95, 1/2/54, dated 7 July 1968, 2.

4. Lieutenant General Sir Thomas Daly, Chief of the General Staff, Australia, 1966–1971, foreword to *The Team: Australian Army Advisors in Vietnam 1962–1972*, by Ian McNeill (St. Lucia, Qld.: Australian War Memorial, 1984).

5. Counterinsurgency in Mai Linh Sub-Sector

1. Presentation on "The Roles and Achievements of the Australian Army Training Team, Vietnam," Chief of the General Staff's Exercise, Canberra, 13 August 1970.

2. Captain Kilroy was a U.S. Army advisor killed in action in Quang Tri in 1966.

3. Early 2009. Our youngest son, Simon, aged thirty-two years, was suffering a terminal illness. He had been living at home for about two years, with Eva and I being his caretakers. In the early hours one morning when I was reading to him, he asked: "Dad, how did you cope with the possibility of death during your time in Vietnam?" After some reflection my response was: "Once I accepted my own self-sacrifice, my own possible death, I did not feel the fear of death anymore. Naturally, the likelihood of death crossed my mind from time to time. But I was ready and got on with the tasks at hand."

Simon died on 10 May 2009, surrounded by his family.

4. Mark Leepson, *The Heart and Mind of USAID's Vietnam Mission* (Washington, D.C.: American Foreign Service Association, 28 May 2008), 2, 3.

6. Pacification in Mai Linh District

1. This demonstration was written up in the 10 July 1968 edition of the U.S. Army newspaper:

> Rice Threshers Aid Harvest. Quang Tri (USMC). There's a new addition on the rice harvest scene in the 3rd Marine Division's area of operations.
>
> Instead of the age-old process of using water buffaloes for threshing the rice, farmers of Mai Linh district are now utilizing rice threshing machines.
>
> Fifty such machines were received by the division's Civil Affairs Section and are being made available to the farmers.
>
> The simple, drum-operated, foot-pedal machines were purchased by funds donated through the U.S. Marine Corps Civic Action Fund.
>
> Prior to the introduction of the machines, an experiment was conducted which showed the local farmers that the machines can accomplish the job in half the time it takes by having a water buffalo do the threshing.

2. A typical menu for a day at the Quang Tri Field Ration Mess included:

Breakfast	**Dinner (Lunch)**	**Supper**
Chilled Juice	Onion Soup, Crackers	Sandwiches
Stewed Prunes	Beef Patties	Brown Gravy
Cereal	Fried Potatoes	Mashed Potatoes
Hot Oatmeal	Buttered Corn	Buttered carrots, or
Eggs to Order	Assorted Salad	Buttered Beets
Fried Bacon	Hot Rolls	Assorted Salad
Fried Sausage	Butter	Bread, Butter
Hotcakes, Syrup	Fruit Gelatin	Apple Crisp
Toast, Butter	Coffee	Coffee
Jam or Jellies	Ice Tea	Ice Tea
Coffee, Milk	Ice Koolade	Ice Koolade
Hot Cocoa		

3. Chieu Hoi, also Hoi Chan, a returnee from the communists to the GVN side.

7. With the Vietnamese People in Quang Tri

1. Le Ly Hayslip, *When Heaven and Earth Changed Places* (New York: Penguin Group, 1990), 2.

2. MILPHAP stands for Military Province Health Assistance Program. The U.S. Agency for International Development initiated a program in the early 1960s to supplement the health services of the Vietnamese. Initially,

surgical teams of U.S. civilian physicians, nurses, and technicians were sent to Vietnamese provincial hospitals, commencing in 1962. With the military expansion the secretary of defense directed the services to prepare to aid the civil health effort in Vietnam, hence MILPHAP. Each team was under the supervision of the provincial chief of medicine. Quang Tri was allocated one of the teams to work in the provincial hospital. (Major General Spurgeon Neel, *Medical Support of the U.S. Army in Vietnam, 1965–1970* [Washington, D.C.: Department of the Army, 1973], 163.)

3. I had by now experienced two cases where a body had been placed on a chair in a public place.

8. Transition from District to Province

1. AMF, *Pocketbook: South Vietnam,* 39.

2. Brigadier General Harley F. Mooney, letter to the author, 21 February 2011:

> Your service as a District advisor gave you a feel for the mission and an opportunity to develop relations, both GVN and US that would give you a leg up on your position which would be a key to team success. Early on I knew we needed a solid professional to be the operations officer. The civil/military split was apparent to anyone looking. Quickly I discovered we were listed as Team 4. This was the 1st ARVN team. I took steps to change that and we became Advisory Team 19. I needed Shali' and his District Chief to stay together. This would be a key element in transforming the Province. You clearly were the guy. Early on the shape for what was to become Fisher was underway. The changeover of 3's was underway. I talked to your boss in Saigon and the deal was done. How could the civil side object, we had a real professional being underutilized.

3. Ibid. Mooney wrote: "Prior advisory team response to the Marines had not been smooth. Your actions and counsel that day were very important. It was also a beginning of a relationship with General Davis that was to pay off big for Team 19."

4. Ibid. Mooney wrote: "Mr Cross was a solid man. World War II Marine. He had encouraged me to develop a better relationship with 3rd Marine Division early on. Think he came that day undercover of the pacification program to see how we were doing with the Marine division operations. His visits always resulted in something positive for our team. When the State Department replaced him, Quang Tri was the loser."

9. Sector Staff Work

1. The Civil Irregular Defense Group (CIDG) was a program devised by the CIA in early 1961 to counter expanding Viet Cong influence in South

Vietnam's Central Highlands. Small A-Teams of the U.S. Army Special Forces assisted in the training of villagers (mainly Montagnard). The program moved from the CIA to MACV, with CIDG units moving into a border surveillance role. Most of the units converted to Vietnam Ranger units in 1970. (See Colonel Francis J. Kelly, *Vietnam Studies: U.S. Army Special Forces 1961–1971* [Washington, D.C.: CMH Publication, 1989].)

2. PRU. A covert civilian-based intelligence gathering organization. A person named Mertish was in the Cua Valley, but his role was not known to the advisors. (Davies and McKay, *The Men Who Persevered,* 385.)

3. Stanley Karnow, *Vietnam: A History* (New York: Penguin Books, 1984), 684.

10. Pacification Campaigns, Strengthening the Spine

1. A visit to Gio Linh in May 2012 reinforced this view. Monuments, memorials, cemeteries, and museums commemorate the events and sacrifices made in the Gio Linh area for the "liberation" and reunification of Vietnam.

2. Karnow, *Vietnam: A History,* 278.

3. GVN, *The Viet Cong Infrastructure, Modus Operandi of Selected Political Cadres (U),* 54.

11. Operation Fisher, Refugee Relocation at Gia Dang

1. Later in his career General John Shalikashvili served as NATO's Supreme Allied Commander Europe, 1992–1993, and as chairman of the Joint Chiefs of Staff, 1993–1997.

2. By reference to my diary, I was able to inform Ian McNeill of some of the elements of the relocation operation that are recorded in his book, *The Team.* The phased plan listed here is drawn heavily from his short description of the phased plan for Operation Fisher. (McNeill, *The Team,* 248–249.)

3. Brigadier General Harley F. Mooney, letter to the author, 21 February 2011: "From the beginning of [Operation] Fisher it was apparent Bob Brewer was content to let the military team carry the ball in moving forward. Two factors were involved: first, that was where the planning talent lay; second the ability to get the logistic support for the task."

4. Ibid. Mooney wrote: "Clearly this sale was important. We were like the bum who shows up with a rock and asks permission to make rock soup. He then proceeds to get a pot to cook in, some wood for a fire, some water, a few veggies along the way and a beef bone. If you are not an old rock soup eater, you would think it's vegetable soup. Such was life in the advisory business."

5. Ibid. Mooney wrote: "This was the beginning of getting Colonel Am back into business. He had done well at Tet but was shaken."

6. Ibid. Mooney wrote: "David, that crown [major rank] on your shoul-

ders sent a real message. This guy is something special and you better pay attention. Our Team was all the better for it."

7. Ibid. Mooney wrote: "This was a matter I brought to the Province Chief. We simply had to help the people or else. I think if the Quang Tri anti-corruption committee had been put in jail we would have been better off."

8. Ibid. Mooney wrote: "Some folks didn't realize that the train was leaving the station and they better get on board. There are three kinds of people in this world. People who make things happen, people who watch what happened, and people who want what happened. This was an opportunity to become a MACV/CORDS team, and I meant to do so."

12. Contingency Planning for Tet 1969

1. Lewis Sorley, *A Better War* (San Diego: Harcourt, 1999), 14–15.

13. Sector Staff Work

1. Vietnamization. The process of transferring responsibility for the war to the GVN started in 1969, the year the phased withdrawal of U.S. combat troops commenced.

2. I hold an after action report on this incident: Contact at Phu Le, Quang Tri, 25 January 1969 (Dong Ha, 1969).

3. GVN, *The Viet Cong Infrastructure, Modus Operandi of Selected Political Cadres (U)*, 3.

4. As it transpired, there was a big NVA assault into Quang Tri Province on 31 March 1972.The Citadel was occupied for eighty-one days. The NVA withdrew in September 1972. In 1975 South Vietnam was overrun by the NVA.

5. U.S. Marine Corps, *The Marines in Vietnam, 1954–1973: Anthology and Annotated Bibliography* (Washington, D.C.: History and Museums Division, Headquarters, U.S. Marine Corps, 1985), essays by USMC Brigadier General Edwin H. General Simmons, 134.

6. M50 Ontos. A lightly armored tracked antitank vehicle, mounted with six 106 mm recoilless rifles. A secondary role was for direct fire support against infantry.

7. Bernard Fall reported the operation under the chapter heading of "Street Without Joy."

14. Operation Kangaroo, Cam Vu Resettlement

1. Major Harry L. Bell, letter to the author, 10 December 1969.

15. Faith at Work

1. Leaflet prepared by Rev. Father John the Baptist Nguyen Van Dong, La Vang Basilica, Quang Tri, 1968. The basilica was destroyed during the invasion of the North Vietnamese in 1972.

2. AMF, *Pocketbook: South Vietnam*, 26, 27.

16. Paris Peace Talks and Ripple Effects

1. Karnow, *Vietnam: A History*, 566.

2. Nguyen and Schecter, *The Palace File*, 26.

3. Bowman, ed., *The World Almanac of the Vietnam War*, 216.

4. "Rolling Thunder" was the U.S. code name for the bombing of North Vietnam.

17. Australian Leaders in South Vietnam

1. The Australian Forces Overseas Fund was supported by the Australian public to provide some comforts to the troops.

2. Davies and McKay, *The Men Who Persevered*, 256. Nigel Gordon Fitzgibbon is now known as Gordon Grant.

3. Tom Johnstone, *The Cross of Anzac: Australian Catholic Service Chaplains* (Virginia, Qld.: Church Archivists Press, 2000), 281.

18. The Shield in a Limited War

1. U.S. Marine Corps, *The Marines in Vietnam, 1954–1973*, 121.

2. Ibid., 121. "Trouble came from enemy shelling of base areas during June. The dump at Camp Kistler, Cua Viet, had been hit and sixteen 10,000 gallon fuel bladders had gone up. Worse yet, on 20 June at Dong Ha, light shelling set off an ammunition dump fire which cost the Marines a quarter-million artillery and mortar rounds. Operation Thor was conceived with the purpose of getting at the enemy's artillery positions and also at his sanctuary, by means of a massive application of air, artillery and naval gunfire. It was begun on 1 July. The impact area was bounded by the southern edge of the DMZ, then north along the coast ten miles (16 kilometres) to Cape Mui Lay, then straight west for 16 miles [25 kilometres] then a closing leg due south to the DMZ. Marine, Navy and Air Force attack aircraft, Strategic Air Command B-52s, two cruisers and six destroyers, and some 118 pieces of Marine and Army artillery were all brought to bear in a seven day barrage."

I visited the Vinh Moc tunnel system on the coast about six kilometers north of the mouth of the Ben Hai River in late May 2012. The system was composed of eleven entry/exit points over three levels. The tunnels would have provided adequate overhead protection from the bombing.

3. Bowman, ed., *The World Almanac of the Vietnam War,* 200, 201.
4. U.S. Marine Corps, *The Marines in Vietnam, 1954–1973,* 124.
5. Bowman, ed., *The World Almanac of the Vietnam War,* 428.
6. U.S. Marine Corps, *The Marines in Vietnam, 1954–1973,* 136.

19. Colonel Harley F. Mooney Leads the Way

1. Brigadier General Harley F. Mooney, letter to the author, 24 February 2011. Mooney wrote: "We needed to shape up. We were in a war zone, but seemed to have checked our skills at the door."

2. Ibid. Mooney wrote: "No doubt I came on stronger than I would under a normal changeover. Fisher was looming and the military staff had to carry the ball. As the exercise unfolded the civil side would be forced by success to get on board. By this time I had talked to Mr. Cross and let the chips fall re the PSA job."

3. C. W. Bean, *Official History of Australia in the War of 1914–1918,* vol. 6, *The AIF in France* (Sydney: Angus and Robertson, 1942). American regiments of the Pershing army were attached to Australian brigades in the front line from 12 June 1918 onward. Companies were allocated to each battalion for a pending attack, the Hamel Plan. Platoons joined companies. The Tank Corps was integrated into the battle plan. The assault on 4 July was a success, strengthening the Allied position on the Villers-Bretonneux Ridge. Haig, the British commander in chief in France, noted: "Monash is a most capable commander, who thinks out every detail of any operation and leaves nothing to chance."

4. Brigadier General Harley F. Mooney, letter to the author, 24 February 2011. Mooney wrote: "In my service to date this was the sloppiest hand off I had experienced. Much of what was not revealed caused difficulties with the spooks and other intelligence operators in the province."

5. One role of the 525th Military Intelligence Group was to command most of the U.S. Army elements involved in intelligence throughout South Vietnam.

6. Brigadier General Harley F. Mooney, letter to the author, 24 February 2011. Mooney wrote: "After Operation Fisher and the 1968/1969 Plan, it was time to change roles, and we did. Colonel Am was a good and decent man and a solid soldier."

7. The NVA attacked, overran, and occupied South Vietnam in 1975.

8. Brigadier General Harley F. Mooney, letter to the author, 24 February 2011. Mooney wrote: "The Team 19 story illustrates a group of military and civilians coming together, sometimes reluctant, but became a real united team supportive of one another and the mission. At least for a moment we were able to provide a better and more stable life for some South Vietnamese."

9. McNeill, *The Team,* 185. When discussing the raising of a new 3rd

ARVN Division in 1971, McNeill wrote: "Units of the Territorial Forces in Quang Tri were transferred to the regular army and became part of the new force."

20. The Omega and a New Alpha

1. Karnow, *Vietnam: A History*, 640.

2. Nguyen Duy To, *Quang Tri Citadel Booklet* (Hue, 2010), 20.

3. Ibid., 36.

4. Bowman, ed., *The World Almanac of the Vietnam War*, 338.

5. Nguyen Duy To, *Quang Tri Citadel Booklet*, 40. The Ministry of Culture and Information, Vietnam, has ranked Quang Tri Citadel and other sites in the province as national relics.

6. Karnow, *Vietnam: A History*, 669.

7. Ian Macphee, Minister for Immigration and Ethnic Affairs, Canberra, letter to the author, 8 January 1982.

Bibliography

Books

Appy, Christian G. *Vietnam: The Definitive Oral History Told from All Sides.* London: Ebury Publishing, 2007.

Atkinson, Rick. *The Long Gray Line.* London: Fontana/Collins, 1990.

Bannister, C. *An Inch of Bravery, 3 RAR in the Malayan Emergency 1957–1958.* Canberra, A.C.T.: Directorate of Army Public Affairs, Canberra, 1994.

Bean, C. W. *Official History of Australia in the War of 1914–1918,* vol. 6, *The AIF in France.* Sydney: Angus and Robertson, 1942.

Blair, Anna. *There to the Bitter End: Colonel Ted Serong in the Vietnam War.* Crows Nest, NSW: Allen and Unwin, 2001.

Bond, F. R. *Vietnam: A Basis for a Right Opinion.* Blackburn: Acacia Press, 1969.

Bowman, John S., gen. ed. *The World Almanac of the Vietnam War.* New York: Pharos Books, 1985.

Burchett, Wilfred. *Grass Hoppers and Elephants.* Urizen Books, 1977. Reprint, Narrabri: Outback Press, 1977.

Cawthorne, Nigel. *Vietnam: A War Lost and Won.* London: Arcturus Publishing, 2004.

Colman, Mike. *Payne VC.* Sydney: ABC Books, 2009.

Cross, Charles T. *Born a Foreigner.* Lanham, Md.: Rowman and Littlefield, 1999.

Davies, Bruce. *The Battle at Ngok Tavak.* Sydney: Allen and Unwin, 2008.

Davies, Bruce, and Gary McKay. *The Men Who Persevered.* Sydney: Allen and Unwin, 2005.

Fall, Bernard B. *Street without Joy.* Mechanicsburg, Pa.: Stackpole, 1961.

Ham, Paul. *Vietnam: The Australian War.* New York: Harper Collins, 2008.

Harverson, Stuart. *Doctor in Vietnam.* London: Lutterworth Press, 1968.

Hendrickson, Paul. *The Living and the Dead: Robert McNamara and Five Lives of a Lost War.* New York: Vintage, 1996.

Johnstone, Tom. *The Cross of Anzac: Australian Catholic Service Chaplains.* Virginia, Qld.: Church Archivists Press, 2000.

Karnow, Stanley. *Vietnam: A History.* New York: Penguin Books, 1984.

Le Ly Hayslip, with Jay Wurts. *When Heaven and Earth Changed Places.* New York: Penguin Group, 1990.

Lunn, Hugh. *Vietnam: A Reporter's War.* St. Lucia, Qld.: Univ. of Queensland Press, 1985.

McNamara, Francis T. *Escape with Honour: My Last Hours in Vietnam.* London: Brassey's, 1997.

McNeill, Ian. *The Team: Australian Army Advisors in Vietnam 1962–1972*. St. Lucia, Qld.: Australian War Memorial, 1984.

Moyar, Mark. *Triumph Forsaken: The Vietnam War 1954–1965.* Cambridge: Cambridge Univ. Press, 2006.

Nagl, John A. *Learning to Eat Soup with a Knife.* Chicago: Univ. of Chicago Press, 2002.

Nguyen Tien Hung and Jerrold L. Schecter. *The Palace File.* New York: Harper and Row, 1986.

Ninh, Bao. *The Sorrow of War.* London: Secker and Warburg, 1996.

Nolan, Peter. *Possums and Bird Dogs.* Sydney: Allen and Unwin, 2006.

Pennington, Vic. *The Team in Vietnam: The Lighter Side.* Cambridge, Mass.: Wakefield Press, 1992.

Petersen, Barry, with J. Cribbin. *Tiger Men.* London: Macmillan, 1988.

Podhoretz, Norman. *Why We Were in Vietnam.* New York: Simon and Schuster, 1982.

Prados, J., and Stubbe, R. W. *Valley of Decision: The Seige of Khe Sanh.* Annapolis: Naval Institute Press, 1991.

Schell, J. *The Real War.* London: Corgi Book, 1988.

Sheehan, Neil. *A Bright Shining Lie.* London: Jonathan Cape, 1989.

Sorley, Lewis. *A Better War.* San Diego: Harcourt, 1999.

———. *Westmoreland: The General Who Lost Vietnam.* San Diego: Houghton Mifflin Harcourt, 2011.

Trotti, John. *Phantom over Vietnam.* New York: Berkley, 1985.

Walters, Ian. *Dasher Wheatley and Australia in Vietnam.* Darwin, N.T.: Northern Territories Univ. Press, 1998.

Woodard, G. *Asian Alternatives: Australia's Vietnam Decision and Lessons on Going to War.* Melbourne: Melbourne Univ. Press, 2004.

Published Documents

AATTV. *Unit War Diary, 1–30 June 1968.* Australian War Memorial AWM 1/2/54.

AMF (Australian Military Forces). *Pocketbook: South Vietnam.* Issued by the Military Board AHQ Canberra, 1965.

Clark, J. *The Team: Unique.* Adelaide: Gillingham Printers, 1997.

GVN. *The Viet Cong Infrastructure, Modus Operandi of Selected Political Cadres (U).* GVN, December 1968.

Kelly, Colonel Francis J. *Vietnam Studies: U.S. Army Special Forces 1961–1971.* Washington, D.C.: CMH Publication, 1989.

Leepson, Mark. *The Heart and Mind of USAID's Vietnam Mission.* Washington, D.C.: American Foreign Service Association, 2008.

MACV Office of Information. "Tet." Pamphlet Number 4–69. January 1969.

The National Executive, AATTV Association. *The Team in Pictures: A Pictorial History of AATTV 1962–1972.* Canberra: Canberra Printing Services, 1992.

Neel, Major General Spurgeon. *Medical Support of the U.S. Army in Vietnam, 1965–1970.* Washington: D.C.: Department of the Army, 1973.

Nguyen Duy To. *Quang Tri Citadel Booklet.* Hue, 2010.

U.S. Marine Corps. *The Marines in Vietnam, 1954–1973: Anthology and Annotated Bibliography.* Washington, D.C. : History and Museums Division, Headquarters, U.S. Marine Corps, 1985.

Unpublished Documents

Advisory Team 1, HQ 1CTZ. "Principles for Cordon and Search Operations." 15 November 1968.

MACV Team 19 Brochure. Quang Tri Province, 1968.

Presentation on "The Roles and Achievements of the Australian Army Training Team, Vietnam." Chief of the General Staff's Exercise. Canberra, 13 August 1970.

Reports

Bell, Major Harry L., Senior Territorial Forces Advisor. "Quang Tri Province Narrative RF/PF Evaluation-Overview." Quang Tri City, August 1969.

Contact at Phu Le, Quang Tri. 25 January 1969. Dong Ha, 1969.

MACV Team 19, Office of the Province Senior Advisor. "1969 Pacification and Development Phase 1 Reporting." Quang Tri City, 1969.

Millie, Major David R., S3 Advisor. "Quang Tri Province RF/PF." Quang Tri City, 22 March 1969.

Articles

"Address by General W. C. Westmorland (Ret)." *Pacific Defense Reporter.* February 1979.

"AFOF Hut Report." *Australian Army News.* 16 January 1969.

"Helicopter Crash." *Pacific Stars and Stripes.* 6 April 1969.

Le Thi Thuy Phuong. "Vietnam: A Matter for Conscience." *Canberra Times.* 25 April 1995.

Personal Documents and Letters

Bell, Major Harry L. Letter. 10 December 1969.

Burns, Creighton. "The Age Melbourne, Saigon." Letter. 1 October 1968.

Coviello, Bill. Letter. 18 August 2010 and 4 September 2011.

d'Arcy, Matthew B. Letter. 15 November 2011.

Do-Ba Ai, Father, Director of Catholic Action in Quang Tri. Quang Tri. Letter. 3 March 1969.

———. "Sermon: The Understanding: Gate Towards Unity." Document. February 1969.

Gurner, Colin M., Director General Medical Services, Melbourne. Letter. 22 July 1968.

Harry, Ambassador R. L., Australian Embassy, Saigon. Letter. 1 April 1969.

Long, Interpreter. Letter. 28 January 1969.

Macphee, Ian. Minister for Immigration and Ethnic Affairs, Canberra. Letter. 8 January 1982.

Millie, David R. Diary. 1968–1969.

———. Personal letters. 1968–1969.

Monkhouse, Ron, Administration Officer AFOF. Letter. 14 January 1969.

Mooney, Harley F. Letters. 21 February 2011.

Nguyen Am, Colonel, Quang Tri Province Chief. Letter. 22 December 1968.

Nguyen Van Dong, Rev. Father John the Baptist. Lavang Basilica. Letter. 23 August 1968.

———. Leaflet. Quang Tri. 1968.

Varwell, Lieutenant Colonel Peter, British Embassy, Saigon. Letter. 8 October 1968.

Index

Page numbers in *italics* refer to photographs. Page numbers followed by the letter "t" refer to tables.